RUSH

THE DAY I WAS THERE

By Richard Houghton

THIS DAY IN MUSIC BOOKS
thisdayinmusicbooks.com

A catalogue record for this book is available from the British Library.

Front cover design by Gary Bishop
Book design by Gary Bishop

THIS DAY IN MUSIC BOOKS

This Day in Music Books
Highfield
Bishopswood Road
Prestatyn
LL19 9PL

WWW.THISDAYINMUSICBOOKS.COM

'When we toured with Kiss in 1975 we couldn't believe we were playing in America and travelling around. I still have the keys to every hotel room from that tour. I kept them because I never thought I'd ever be in Luccock, Texas again. And in fact I haven't been to Lubbock, Texas again.'

Geddy Lee

INTRODUCTION

Geddy Lee once described Rush as the world's most popular cult band and it's hard to argue with that description. The statistics – over 2,400 shows played, more than 15 million tickets sold, in excess of 40 million albums sold – belie the fact that the average man or woman in the street probably hasn't heard of Rush. Maybe they'll know 'The Spirit of Radio'. It got to number 13 in the UK charts, the only Top 20 single they achieved. But they scored seven Top 10 albums in Britain. And around the world they did a whole lot better.

When I started compiling this book back in 2019, Rush had retired from playing and the band had made it clear they would not be touring. But Neil was still with us and there was some hope amongst fans that they might do the odd one off show or a residency or a festival, with endless speculation as to what and where that might be. Then news emerged of Neil's passing. There is no speculation about a Rush reunion now. As one contributor to this book put it, without Neil there is no Rush.

I have tried through the many fan memories I have collected to capture the essence of what it was that made Rush one of the biggest bands over four decades, from memories of their earliest shows through to *R40*. This is not a complete history of Rush. It does not chronicle every show. But hopefully it gives the reader a glimpse of a better, vanished time.

Confirming the actual date that shows were played from the 1960s and 1970s is notoriously difficult. Bands cancelled at the last minute or whole shows were cancelled and yet the press advertisements or foggy memories of those who were adamant they were there sometimes confirm memories of a line up that didn't actually happen. There are a couple of examples of this in this book. Using the internet and the fabulously detailed *Rush: Wandering the Face of the Earth* as reference material, I have done my best to insert the story in the right place in Rush history. Where I have not succeeded in triangulating dates, venues and support acts (or headliners), I have largely gone with the contributor's memories. After all, they were there.

Richard Houghton
Manchester
October 2020

THE GREAT FROG

1971, CARNABY STREET, LONDON, UK

I WAS THERE: PETER BROCKBANK

Peter Brockbank met Neil back in 1971 in London – photo Peter Brockbank

In 1971 I went to London with a guy called Robin Coulthard from Carlisle. The idea was that the streets were paved with gold and Robin was a musician and we'd go down there and have a bit of fun. Robin got a job. He was a typical long-haired good looking rock star, but he wasn't good enough to be one. He got a job in Carnaby Street. Neil was working in the same shop. That's where I met him. Robin got a job playing rhythm guitar and singing with a band and they didn't have a drummer. Neil was obviously already a drummer and he joined and then they didn't have a van. I was working for a water softening company and had just bought a brand new double-rear-axle Ford Transit van, which was the top group van at the time. I nicked that, had it resprayed, and drove them about. The joke was that in winter you didn't need heating in the van because it was so 'hot'.

Neil was quite amused. He wasn't making much money with the band because we weren't playing very much. He was perfectly aware of the situation. He seemed to have more good friends who were jailbirds than straight people. I used to do a little bit of thieving. He asked me if I would take him on some little job now and again. My actual words to him were, 'Listen Neil, if you ever want to come back with a band, and you get a police record, they might not let you in.' In those days you needed a permit to get in the country, America wouldn't let certain English groups into the country – so groups coming in had to get what amounted to a work permit.

English Rose only lasted a short time but I got them some leads up in Cumbria. All the time that we drove between gigs, always at night, Neil never slept. He would do a three hour show and then stay awake for a five hour drive sat up front, 'riding shotgun' as he called it. And when we got to the other end he'd get the map out and tell me where I should go. He wasn't a rock star at all.

I've been banged up (in prison) a couple of times over the years and every six or eight weeks I would get a letter – handwritten in those days - and a cheque for 200 quid from him. Neil never forgot his friends. He was a lovely, warm, caring and very funny guy.

In '88, he asked me if I would do the job of driver on their European tour. Until then Neil had always toured with the band but he hated all the hoopla. It brought him closer to the tour and he never, ever enjoyed that. He would record and play and rehearse but he never enjoyed touring. I immediately said 'yes'. I did the '88 and '92 European tours. The first time I was driving a 750 BMW, which at the time cost 55 grand. There were only eight of them in England and none available to rent so I had to be flown to Frankfurt to pick one up and bring it back. The senior members of the management team at Anthem were just horrified. Because Neil was honest: 'He's a bit of a villain and blah-blah-blah…' They had visions of me disappearing with a 55 grand car. You can imagine.

I turned up to pick him up at the airport, went to a desk to ask where to go and got sent to the wrong terminal. Neil had stopped smoking around that time. When I eventually found him about 30 minutes after he'd come through – this was before mobile phones – he'd got all his bags and everything and had started smoking again. He said, 'I'm so glad to see you. I thought I was going to have to ring up and say 'he's disappeared with the car!'.' He just took it totally on trust that I wouldn't let him down. I was so conscious when I was driving that I've only got to make a mistake, and he breaks a finger and he can't drum. It took me about three days to enjoy driving a wonderful car like that.

He wasn't a miserable bastard. He laughed and joked. But he was a very serious guy and very, very, very shy. He was panicky if fans were about. On the tour of Germany in '88, we were just going into the underground entrance to a car park underneath the stadium and there was a barrier. There was a little Hitler-type parking attendant who wouldn't let us in. We hadn't been in so we didn't have the passes and as I was explaining to the guy, 'Look, this is the drummer out of Rush, etc.', about 100 yards away three buses from Italy pulled up. Neil saw these Italian fans starting to walk towards us and one of them pointed towards the car from about 50 yards away. The barrier was slightly elevated and Neil said to me, 'Can you get through there without hitting him? Don't worry about any damage. Just fucking get me out of here now.' He was absolutely panicking he was going to be trapped in the car. I went forward and nudged the barrier with the bonnet of the car and it went up and we went straight through.

Neil used to say, when he went to see The Who, he rated the drummer. 'I want to see him on stage, but why would I want to go backstage and get his autograph or sit outside a hotel and watch Moon come in or go out?' He just did not understand that sort of adulation. It was only during the '92 tour that I found out that there was such a thing as 'meet and greets'. Alex and Geddy did them. Neil never did a meet and greet in his life.

On that second tour, I did all his interview arranging. If anybody wanted to speak to him, they were put through to me and I would take all the details and I would ring Neil or go up and see him in the room and ask - did he want to do it? I would take him in, introduce him, make sure there was coffee and biscuits delivered by room service and say, 'See you later, Neil.' And 30 minutes later I had to ring him. It was the 'get out' phone call. He'd either say, 'Oh no, you deal with that' or, 'Oh, okay, I'll come up right away.' That was his get out if he needed it. When he was working, he'd have his work head on and I'd be working for him. So I might not see him for two days.

We were in Berlin in '92, on the second tour I did with him, and were watching the Freddie Mercury tribute concert at Wembley on MTV in Berlin. He called me up and we were just smoking joints and drinking. At one point Roger Taylor was playing full-sized bongos stood up and this noise was coming out and Neil was going, 'What the fuck is he doing?' That isn't the noise you make from those!' And he got a drumstick and hit the blunt end on the side of a snare drum to get that sound. 'Why does he have to stand like that, posing?' He was hyper-critical of people, but only because they weren't doing what they were supposed to do. He didn't like any kind of trying to cheat the public. He just wanted people to go on and do what they were supposed to do, not stand there looking flash. He did not suffer fools at all.

Because Neil was my mate I didn't need to or want to get friendly with the other two. I did meet Alex and Geddy. Geddy was very suspicious early on because that's Geddy. Alex was an absolute darling, an absolute sweetheart. I had two or three decent nights with Alex and a few others in the hotel with a few drinks and a bit of weed. Alex is such a lovely, happy lad. He's a party animal. We were in a hotel in Sheffield, England at the beginning of the '92 tour. I was in the bar just having a quiet vodka and tonic. A lot of the road crew were in the other side of the bar. All of a sudden Alex came into the bar, saw me and said 'Peter!' and gave me a big hug. He said, 'Have a drink, mate, have a drink. Come on, come on, come and have a drink with the fellahs.' Geddy would have waved and said 'hello', but he wouldn't have done that.

Neil was very much a lonely figure on tour. On the '88 tour he used to have a bow and arrow and a mobile target. He'd go and practise for an hour, an hour and a half, firing arrows at this target on his own. He wasn't really close to any of the crew except his own technician. There was work Neil and there was social Neil. But when we were on tour together the two combined. Not only was Neil a warm, kind-hearted generous person, he was totally genuine.

I knew he was having his third round of chemo. I wrote to him in 2019 when I heard about the cancer. I don't know whether he got it or not. I couldn't tell anybody because I was asked not to. It was still a horrible, horrible shock. He wasn't an old man. I have incredibly fond memories of Neil. Even though I knew he was dying, I cried like baby when I heard. I still well up when I see him on television, especially when he's talking.

The eponymous studio album, *Rush*, was released on 1 March 1974. It was recorded the previous year. John Rutsey played on the album, having been Rush's drummer in the preceding years. Neil Peart was to join Rush on 29 July 1974, two weeks before the band's first US tour.

DON MILLS COLLEGIATE INSTITUTE

21 APRIL 1974, TORONTO, CANADA

I WAS THERE: CHUCK DILL

The first time I saw them was at Don Mills Collegiate. They were great so we travelled again early to see them in Port Credit at the high school with Max Webster. I was too young for any of their bar shows. I did manage to see them one more time that year, when they played Massey Hall with Nazareth. For the longest time, Massey Hall was the place to see them and Max Webster seemed to be the partner of choice, Nazareth too. Over the next few years I saw them numerous times there plus at Iroqouis Park in Whitby.

We kept waiting for them to play Maple Leaf Gardens and it seemed to take forever before they debuted there on New Year's Eve 1976. Being only 15 it took some major convincing to get my mom to allow me to go. But it's my best memory of them in concert.

I started collecting music at the age of 11, each Saturday going to Sam the Record Man on Young Street. These records and skateboarding, hockey and baseball were my existence. My room was where I could turn the lights off, place that needle on the vinyl and listen to how the trees were all kept equal by hatchet, axe and saw, or learn about driving my uncle's red Barchetta. It was a place to escape from life, from school, from sports and other pressures. To this day I still utilise this pleasure in a room dedicated to Rush, Floyd, Zep and the Stones.

Today people wait on line for tickets to go on sale. We had to camp overnight outside Maple Leaf Gardens to buy the tickets, another experience that lent itself to the music. The friendships made in line and the joy of going to school the next day with that ticket in hand, making other jealous because their dad would never let them line up!

THE ROCKPILE AT DUFFY'S TAVERN

17 – 22 JUNE 1974, HAMILTON, CANADA

I WAS THERE: MARK GEMMELL, AGE 12

My older brother took me. John Rutsey was their drummer at the time. This was in support of their self-titled first album. Fast forward to the Memorial Gardens in Guelph, Ontario where I saw them again in support of *A Farewell to Kings*. They played '2112' in its entirety for the first time ever, I think. I then saw a slew of shows in the 80s. The first one was *Grace Under Pressure*. They changed from hard rock to new wave rock. I didn't like it at first but when I saw them do it live, I got to liking it right away. You could tell that they really cared about their music because they were so tight live. They no doubt practised really hard and long, because it really showed. The biggest impression on me as a guitar player was watching Alex Lifeson during 'The Weapon' from their album *Signals*. His lead playing was very unconventional but very creative at the same time. I couldn't take my eyes off all three of them as they melded their awesome sound together while playing live. A few times during the show, Alex would go over to Neil or Geddy making faces at them. Eventually they would crack up laughing.

MINKLER AUDITORIUM, SENECA COLLEGE

1 JULY 1974, TORONTO, CANADA

I WAS THERE: BRIAN POTTS

Brian Potts saw Rush in 1974 but also in 2007

In the early 70s in Toronto, there were a myriad of local bars where you could go, slug back a few beers, look for women and listen to fine live rock bands. Hotspots included The Gasworks, The Meet Market, The Abbey Road Pub, The Piccadilly Tube and many others. Rush was the band that my friends and I used to search out each week.

They attracted lots of young women our age, and their music was the tightest and best.

Our favourite local was The Abbey Road Pub. It was on the second floor above a jazz bar called Bourbon Street and it had a stainless steel dance floor which made all the 'moves' that much easier for us. The seating was tiered with the main floor and then a riser to more seating. Between sets, Geddy would take his usual spot at a table on the upper floor, with an entourage of young ladies clamouring for a spot close. Alex and John would mix with the crowd occasionally. John would often dance in between sets.

The band played many of their own tunes, 'In the Mood' and 'Working Man' always being highlights. Another was a cover of Bowie's 'Suffragette City'. The dance floor was always full and good times were had by all. The band at that time wore clothes that bordered on Glam. Alex would sit with the friends and me to talk about how things were going. I remember the first time I mentioned that I thought that they would end up very famous. He looked at me and said, 'Do you think so?' I said, 'Of course.' I'm not sure I expected what was to come but I always wonder if Alex remembers that conversation.

Another time, my buddies and I were at the Piccadilly Tube. It was 1973. Alex bopped in and sat next to me. He asked us if we'd heard their single, 'Not Fade Away'. I was the one to tell Alex that I thought it wasn't well produced, way too trebly without enough bass. I hated to tell him but I figured if they were ever to be famous, he needed to know.

The last time I saw them live with John Rutsey on drums was when they opened for Nazareth at the Minkler Auditorium. They were amazing in the concert environment. They were very well received and 'Working Man' again was the highlight. Not long after this gig, Neil Peart would join Rush as their new drummer and their trajectory would change.

The last time I saw them live was at the Air Canada Center in Toronto in September 2007. They played for over two hours with a short intermission in the middle. There was no opening band, just them. Just how we wanted it.

B'GINNINGS

7 NOVEMBER 1974, SCHAUMBURG, ILLINOIS

I WAS THERE: SCOTT WALLENBERG

Like so many others, I became a Rush fan hearing 'Working Man' on the radio. I bought the 8-track and blasted it out of my Dodge Van while heading to race motocross throughout the Midwest. B'ginnings was a supper club west of Chicago in the suburb of Schaumburg named after the famous Chicago tune and owned partially by the band's drummer, Danny Seraphine. I went with a couple of motocross buddies. Mark had lost 90 per cent of his hearing as a child due to a misdiagnosed ear infection. My other buddy, Alex, saw a ton of shows with me.

In order to see better, Alex and I stood on huge glass beer steins that were super tall and thick to support our weight. The sound was incredibly loud and it pushed our chests in with every beat. When it was over we asked our buddy Mark with the poor hearing how he liked it. He said, 'They sounded pretty good.' My ears are still recovering - but he was right!

PARAMOUNT THEATER

19 NOVEMBER 1974, SEATTLE, WASHINGTON

I WAS THERE: CHRIS EUGENE SETTERGREN

My school buddy Steve's older brother turned both of us on to them prior to *Fly by Night*. I was just a 15 year old kid in 1974 but I got concert educated kinda fast after that show in Seattle. That night I fell in love with the drum kit. My folks hated it because I beat on anything at home. I also noticed most of us fans were all guys.

VENTURA THEATER

26 NOVEMBER 1974, VENTURA, CALIFORNIA

I WAS THERE: KEVIN CHINERY

There was no radio play for Rush in southern California. The very first time I heard Rush on the radio was on a station called KROQ and a female DJ, who was on one night a week, played 'The Trees' one night. When I was a senior at high school I got a petition up to get Rush played on the radio. I got 2,500 signatures and I mailed it to the local rock station. It didn't happen. *2112* got zero radio play but went platinum in the US. I didn't hear Rush on the radio again until 1979, when 'The Spirit of Radio' came out.

Kevin Chinery and pals

Kevin Chinery's license plate

In '74 I was 14 and discovered them via a friend's older brother. He had the first album. They played a very small theatre out here called the Ventura Theater. I hitchhiked there and snuck in because I was under age. I didn't see them again until they toured with Ted Nugent a couple of years later. And then the next tour was

A Farewell to Kings. I saw them at Santa Monica Civic with UFO, another small arena. And that's up there as one of my all time favourite concerts, along with seeing Led Zeppelin and Pink Floyd's *Animals*. It was just an amazing show and the first time they had used video. I wore out three vinyl copies of *A Farewell to Kings*.

I've probably seen about 100 shows. They'd play two shows in California and I'd try to go to both of them. I'd try and do Vegas. I've got a couple of friends who I turned onto Rush, one in Nashville and one in Jersey. For *Snakes & Arrows* they both flew out to California and we saw them at the Hollywood Bowl. I've seen them in Nashville, Madison Square Garden, Jones Beach in New York, Glendale Arena in New Jersey.... in six states and 10 or 12 different arenas.

Living in California I got to see them get their Hollywood Walk of Fame star. And I was there when they got inducted into the Hall of Fame. The ceremony just happened to be in LA that year. You can actually hear my garbled voice screaming 'Neil is God!' when he's giving his speech. You can't make it out but I know it's me!

I was there for the very last show too, when Neil came out from behind the drum kit. Little did I know that that would be the last time that we would get to see them live. I used to say to my friends, 'If I ever win the lottery I'll hire Rush for a private show.' It was devastating news when Neil passed away. It was hard to take.

SHRINE AUDITORIUM

27 NOVEMBER 1974, LOS ANGELES, CALIFORNIA

I WAS THERE: BILL HAROLD SNOWMAN

It was right after the release of their first album. Back then everyone said they sounded like munchkins on speed, but I recognised their uniqueness and followed them through the years to see some of the most finely crafted metal music ever made. I saw them five times, once in a small venue in Medford, Oregon. My last concert was on the *Clockwork Angels* tour.

The *Fly by Night* tour started in February 1975 and ran through to June of that year.

XAVIER UNIVERSITY

22 MARCH 1975, CINCINATTI, OHIO

I WAS THERE: DALE WALTON

I saw Rush, Styx and Aerosmith in a tiny gymnasium at Xavier University in Cincinnati. We were there to see Aerosmith. No one had heard of Styx and we barely knew Rush. *Fly by Night* was on the radio. They were like a garage band. They played on the floor in front of the tiny stage. They came in, set up and left - like a last minute add on. But they rocked it.

KSHE KITE FLY FESTIVAL, AVIATION FIELD

13 APRIL 1975, ST LOUIS, MISSOURI

I WAS THERE: DENNIS NAIL, AGE 17

It was a fantastic concert. 10,000 people were expected, 34,000 showed up. It was a great day. We had never heard anything like Rush. We had their first album, simply called Rush. It's still my favourite today. Don't get me wrong. I loved the transition to Neil. It was like having two bands in one. It was a sad day when he passed.

FREEDOM HALL CIVIC CENTER

24 APRIL 1975, JOHNSON CITY, TENNESSEE

I WAS THERE: LARRY WHITE

I was going to school in maybe the tenth or eleventh grade. We'd bring different tapes on the bus to listen to all the way to school on a little cassette player with one big speaker on it. A friend dubbed the first album. It was the first time I heard 'Working Man' and 'In the Mood'.

When they came to Johnson City a year later, close to where we lived, Rush were opening for Kiss, and opening for Rush were the Heavy Metal Kids, although on the ticket it just said The Kidds. It was $5.50 to get in. We'd hang out and party in the parking lot before the show, and inside of course. They played pretty much everything from the first album. They played 'By-Tor and the Snow Dog' and 'Fly by Night'. My friends and I were just blown away.

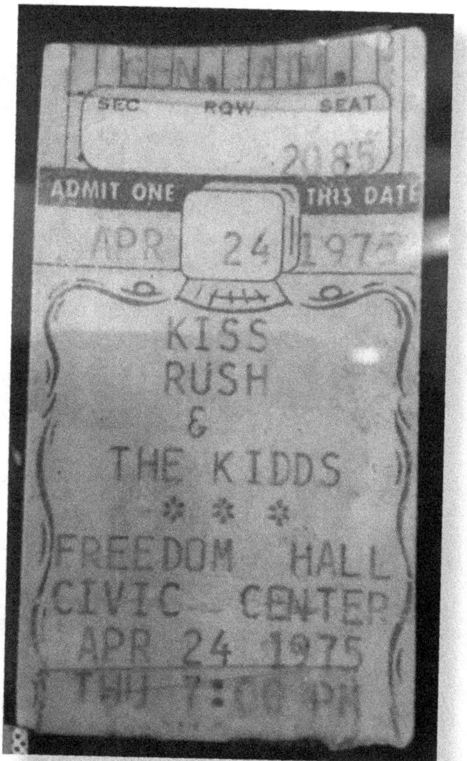

Larry Johnson's ticket for the Johnson City show

The last time I saw them was 2011 in Greensboro, when I went with my first cousin. We hadn't been to a show since right before I joined the air force, and I did 27 years in the air force! They played the entire *Moving Pictures* album, sequenced pretty much like the album. They closed with 'Working Man'. It was strange because they did a reggae version of it. They played stuff from *Snakes & Arrows*. To me that's the most impressive album they've done since *Moving Pictures*.

I missed the *R40* tour. I didn't find out about it until the last minute.

CAPITOL THEATRE

16 MAY 1975, PORT CHESTER, NEW YORK

I WAS THERE: PETER PECK

I saw these guys a couple of times. My first concert was them and Blue Öyster Cult in Port Chester, New York around the mid 70s. We sat on benches in the first couple of rows. We hung out next to their small moving van truck outside the door before the show, but didn't see them. They had Rush lettered on the doors with some town in Canada written under their name. Sadly I had no camera in my pocket in those days.

SAHARA HOTEL SPACE CENTER

29 MAY 1975, LAS VEGAS, NEVADA

I WAS THERE: ECA NOR

The first time I saw Rush was completely by surprise. They used to play clips from songs on the radio when they would announce a concert. They were playing Jefferson Airplane clips but announced it as Jefferson Starship. They said the name was changed because 'now they're more spaced'. 'And with them, the hottest Kiss you'll ever get.' The two bands battled over who would be the headliner with Jefferson Starship eventually bowing out. They announced the new band, which was Rush. I had never heard of them and expected very little but was hugely surprised as they were awesome! They were the warmup band but much better than Kiss. And the concert started at 2am.

I saw them three more times, in '81, '84 and 2008. Tickets for the first one were $8.50 and for the last one $127. I still liked them, but Geddy couldn't hit the high notes anymore on *2112* and tickets were getting pricey, so that was my last time.

The *Caress of Steel* tour began in August 1975, ending in early January 1976.

INDIANA STATE UNIVERSITY

21 NOVEMBER 1975, TERRE HAUTE, INDIANA

I WAS THERE: BILL SMITH, AGE 17

I saw them open for Kiss. I was very impressed by the way those guys had command of their respective

Bill Smith with his son Ethan on the Snakes & Arrows tour

instruments. Now you can find Neil and Geddy on almost any list for drums and bass. Alex is talented too. The Rock and Roll Hall of Fame induction video shows the respect he gets from those in the craft. I have seenthem 12 to 15 times and spent thousands of dollars on LPs, cassettes, 8-tracks, CDs, DVDs and VHS tapes, plus merch. I took my adult son to see them for the first time on the *Snakes & Arrows* tour in Kansas City, Missouri. It was an outdoors venue on a nice cool evening. We had a great time. I cried.

CIVIC ARENA

20 DECEMBER 1975, PITTSBURGH, PENNSYLVANIA

I WAS THERE: PHILIP GITZEN, AGE 15

I remember reading a short article about a trio from Toronto that 'sounded like Led Zeppelin' around Thanksgiving 1974 and saw the LP in my cousin's record collection. He played 'Working Man' for me. This was the first concert I ever attended. My best friend swiped a bottle of wine from his dad's liquor cabinet and we got high in a field before walking downtown to the arena. It was a cold night but we walked everywhere then and it didn't bother us. Rush was the opening act on a bill that featured Kiss and Mott. Our seats were behind the stage and a group of teenage girls in front of us were screaming for Kiss. Rush came out and played four songs. They were only on stage for about 25 minutes. I think they played 'Bastille Day', 'Anthem', 'Fly by Night' and 'Working Man'. 15,000 people were there to see Kiss but we were there to see Rush. Since then I've probably seen them around 14 times and they've never disappointed me.

In 2008 the *Snakes & Arrows* tour came to Pittsburgh at the Star Lake Amphitheater. I knew someone who was friends with a DJ at a local radio station and he got us backstage passes and a meet and greet. We had our picture taken with Geddy and Alex. Geddy was wearing a Pittsburgh Pirates t-shirt and I thanked them for coming to Pittsburgh every tour. The picture they took of us was on the tour website but my computer crashed. By the time I got it fixed the pictures were gone so I never downloaded them.

ARAGON BALLROOM

26 DECEMBER 1975, CHICAGO, ILLNOIS

I WAS THERE: DONNA LEVATINO

Also on the bill were Rory Gallagher and Blue Öyster Cult. I remember thinking how tight Rush sounded and the unique high voice that Geddy Lee has.

(Other sources suggest Artful Dodger opened the show, with Rush on second and Blue Öyster Cult headlining).

COBO HALL

29 DECEMBER 1975, DETROIT, MICHIGAN

I WAS THERE: KEN KAZERSKI, AGE 15

One day I went to school – I was in ninth grade – and a friend asked me if I would like to go and see them. I said yes, not knowing who they were. He said, 'We need to skip school to get tickets.' We left school and took a bus from Grosse Pointe to Cobo Hall, standing in line for hours. On the night of the show, a guy in the bathroom sold us each a hit of acid. It was my first time. When we got to our seats up in tier A, a guy came up with a broken leg and asked to trade seats due to his leg. So we ended up on the floor, sixth row centre. In the seats all around us, people were passing joints around. I have worked with the MC5, worked for a rock 'n' roll magazine and have been to thousands of concerts. But the first time I saw Rush still sticks in my head as one of the best shows I have ever seen.

The *2112* tour began in February 1976 and ran through to August of that year.

MEMORIAL AUDITORIUM

27 FEBRUARY 1976, BUFFALO, NEW YORK

I WAS THERE: PAUL A CICHON

They were in the mist of the Chinese-type clothing and heavy make up they would wear. A lot of the fans in attendance were dressed the same way and, being my first show, I thought they were a bunch of gay people. They were just emulating the band's wardrobe!

RANDHURST MALL ICE ARENA

5 MARCH 1976, PROSPECT, ILLINOIS

I WAS THERE: SCOTT BRENNER

The girl I was dating was two years older and turned me onto them. Rush were very popular in the Chicago area, where I grew up. A bunch of Canadian bands were trying to make it in America – Triumph, Three Dog Night, The Guess Who.

I was a burn out. I smoked dope since I was 12, doing drugs and stuff. Rush was pretty much a burn out group. It was also unusual to have a three guy band. I was trying to learn to play drums back then and the drummer was the pulse of the band. That was an attraction for me. They were the second band I ever saw in concert. It was Rush, Foghat and someone else I don't remember. It was a cheap ticket, like $3 or $3.25. It was general seating. It wasn't a big venue. I think it held about 5,000 people. *Fly by Night* was one of my all time favourite albums, but I stopped listening to them after *2112*. I started getting into electronic dance music.

ST PAUL CIVIC CENTER

29 MAY 1976, ST PAUL, MINNESOTA

I WAS THERE: RANDY FULLERTON

It was four bands for $4 and the running order was Steve Marriott's All Star Band, Rush *2112*, REO Speedwagon and Blue Öyster Cult. It was a general admission concert which we called 'run for your life' seats. We were the first people in line so our hands were on the stage and there were no ropes. Steve Marriott got snowed in somewhere and didn't make it so the boys tried to play but they got booed off the stage after the first or second song. The rest of the concert was one of the best I have ever seen.

(Other sources suggest Steve Marriott's band had split two weeks prior).

MUNICIPAL AUDITORIUM

7 JUNE 1976,
SAN ANTONIO, TEXAS

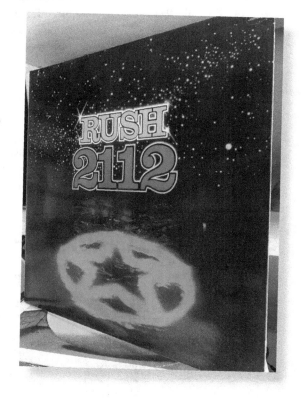

I WAS THERE: GD RANKIN

It was more than a band, more than the music, even more than the experience at one of the 30 plus live shows I enjoyed. In 1974, at least in my area, their music was new and of course they were unknown and not well received by everyone. Being a Rush freak was a vehicle to ride down a road less travelled by the average Joes, which was more than fine by me.

When I first heard Joe Anthony, a DJ from 99.5 KISS FM, talking about this new band from Canada and playing a track from the newly released *Caress of Steel*, I was in awe. 'Bastille Day' was full of intrigue and energy and yet completely different from the current popular hits.

I had recently started seriously dissecting music and picking out all the different instruments and parts of songs. Lyrics had become secondary when listening to normal bands of the era. With Rush, the vocals were often times difficult to understand. Geddy's voice was almost like a fourth instrument in the mix.

Because not all the words were easy to comprehend, having the lyrics available in the album opened the door to a deeper and more immediate understanding of their music. Being able to read along as the songs blasted at the highest volume my headphones could produce helped it all make sense. There may have even been some consumption of a few mind-expanding enhancers of the time along the way, which of course made the music feel more personal. It was like the songs were telling their stories directly to me.

I sat in the 13th row on Geddy's side of the stage at my first live show. It was the *2112* tour. The album had not been out long enough to really sink in. Thin Lizzy opened with their *Jailbreak* set and got the crowd in the mood to rock. What came next was the birth of a serious addiction for me and many others in the San Antonio area.

I was blessed to get to see Rush perform live every year for the next 15 years. Many times they'd have back-to-back performances, selling out two nights in a row. I was small enough to wiggle my way through the crowds and ended up on the front row on many occasions, often times sharing a seat or standing the entire show, and always on Geddy's side of the stage.

That first show could be the blame for my infatuation with the bass and that distinctive Rickenbacker sound. Pretty much all the neighbourhood kids played air guitar and imitated Hendrix and Page. Those guys were great as was Alex. But there was something about those high energy, punchy, mind-blowing bass lines that Geddy ever so effortlessly blasted us with. By 1978 I had my first 4001 Ric and was on my way. A couple of years later, having moved out of my parents' house, I had to have a Sunn amp to let the neighbourhood in on the fun. My roommate played lead guitar and we moved a friend's drum kit into our living room and formed a band.

Rush had a major influence on our style, and Geddy Lee was and always will be my hero. In my mind he's the best bassist of all time. Neil was, and still is, one of my all-time favourite human beings to ever grace this planet. And Alex should also be considered one of the all-time best guitarists – a guru with style. What a trio. What a band!

SHREVEPORT MUNICIPAL MEMORIAL AUDITORIUM

8 JULY 1976, SHREVEPORT, LOUISIANA

I WAS THERE: CHARLES OVERFIELD

I used to go to there on Sundays and watch Gorgeous George and the Von Erichs wrestle. I remember the Rush show being full to overflowing and the drummer wearing a kimono, and the bass and guitar players

Charles Overfield caught the 2112 tour in Shreveport – photo Richard Houghton

wearing white dusters. This was the *2112* tour. Watching a young Neil Peart on the drums showed me things I never imagined. Over the years I made every Rush concert that came within 100 miles of my home but felt they were going mainstream around the time of *Presto*, especially when Neil cut his hair. But I returned to the scene of the crime. I have many pieces of Rush memorabilia, the most prized possession being a copy of *2112* signed by all three with a certificate of authenticity.

TRIAD ARENA

23 JULY 1976, GREENSBORO, NORTH CAROLINA

I WAS THERE: STEPHANIE BATES CALDWELL

I saw the *2112* tour. I really wish I could tell you about it. I had a few chemicals and just remember the most fantastic light show and being mesmerised by the music three people could produce. I wasn't really informed about them before the show, but left a fan forever.

The *All the World's a Stage* tour began in August 1976 and concluded in Europe in June 1977. This was a mammoth tour comprising over 150 shows.

AGRICULTURAL HALL

20 SEPTEMBER 1976, ALLENTOWN, PENNSYLVANIA

I WAS THERE: STEVE O'DONNELL

I saw them 54 times in their long career, 48 from row 10 or closer. I was in college when a few friends asked me if I wanted to go on a road trip to Allentown Fairgrounds to see this fairly new band. I had heard 'Working Man' a few times and said, 'Sure - road trip? Why not?' My friends were familiar with how crowded the fairgrounds got so we got there early and right up against the stage towards the right side, where Geddy's keyboards would be. The crowd was fairly accepting of the opening act – Max Webster - but they wanted to see Rush.

Then darkness and the groaning, swirling sounds of Geddy's keyboards. The pin points of stars appear on the screen backdrop, with something red, in the centre, starting small and growing…. The Starman logo... and then - 'DUM, DUMPF' - the opening notes of *2112* and Neil's amazing high twirling stick tosses that timed when the next notes would be. They'd taken care of everything - the words we'd hear, the show we'd see, the picture that was plugged into my eyes. Their music and words were basically unknown to me but my eyes and ears were glued to the stage and this amazing performance. I knew they'd be making music for many years to come. The talent that all three of them displayed was simply amazing and by the time they pulled out the double-necks for 'Xanadu', I already knew I was a fan.

CIVIC CENTRE

10 OCTOBER 1976, OTTAWA, CANADA

I WAS THERE: MIKE PERRON, AGE 16

We all started hearing more stories about this great three piece band, including an amazing drummer. We paid five bucks for the tickets. At that time you'd do what was called 'the crash and dash' to try and get the best seats once the arena doors were open. One of my friends had a problem. His mom had done the laundry and his ticket was in his jeans pocket. He showed us the wilted and faded piece of cardboard in hopes of a plan. We scraped through our pockets and eventually rounded up five bucks for another ticket for him.

After the opening bands the lights dimmed, creating a hypnotic feeling, and Rush appeared. '2112' opened. It was as though we were in a ship. There was the burst of Neil on his drum kit, rolling into an energetic guitar and bass with Alex and Geddy. My friends and I had never seen a band of three players put out such a full, deep sound. Everything they played had so much atmosphere. It was mystical. We instantly couldn't get enough of this band. Everything they played was always fresh and interesting.

The passing of Neil Peart is a sharp sting and a painful moment in rock and roll history. Many air drummers were affected by the event. All drummers around the world hold your sticks up - for Neil!

CAPITOL THEATRE

10 DECEMBER 1976, PASSAIC, NEW JERSEY

I WAS THERE: WAYNE M UGLIONO

In 1976, I was hanging with the cool guys. They were going to a concert at the Capitol Theatre and they said 'Would you like to go?' At that time, I used to get my balls broken in high school for being a Kiss fan and an Elton John fan. My cousin turned me on to the first Kiss live album. Everybody broke my chops about it. Everybody laughed at Kiss. And people laughed at me for liking Elton John because it was Elton John. The guys were all into Zeppelin and Pink Floyd. I wanted to be a cool kid so I said I'd go. Cheap Trick were the warm up act. And then I saw Rush for the first time. I said, '*That's* the band.' I was an underdog. Rush was another underdog band, like Kiss. Rush were *my* band. It's hard to explain. It's like finding Jesus. It was that kind of moment. They never got on the radio until 'The Spirit of Radio'. The ride got even better then, because I could say, 'I told you so!'

I saw them 32 times. I did not miss a tour from '78 to *R40*. I saw them five nights in a row at Radio Music City Hall. Every time I got to see them I would shake my head because, besides the music, their shows got better and better every time they went out and toured. They had lasers, they had effects, they had planes, they had the videos on the back screen. It was well worth the money to go see them.

I WAS THERE: ED TREMBICKI-GUY

My eleven years older brother came home from college one year and put this record on. I heard this voice come out. 'Immigrant Song' by Led Zeppelin was life-changing. That was around 1972. I became a huge Zeppelin fan.

In 1976, there was a mail order outfit called Columbia House where you sent off for albums by mail. They had this promotion to get you started – seven albums for a penny, with tiny little stickers that you would peel off, stick on a form and mail in. One of them said 'Rush – *Caress of Steel*'. I'd seen Frank Marino and Mahogany Rush at California Jam and I said, 'That must be Mahogany Rush and they just didn't have enough room on the sticker.' I mailed off my order.

When my parents and I got back from a trip away from home there was this box of multi albums. I saw the cover of *Caress of Steel* and said, 'I've got to play this.' I put the record on the turntable, dropped the needle and heard the intro of the guitar and the drums and I went, 'Yeah, this is good, this is good.' Then I heard the voice and went, 'That's not Frank Marino! But it's good!' Something about that album just spoke to me. I had no idea at the time that nobody liked it and the critics panned it. I didn't know any of that. I just knew I had found this band called Rush.

I was sat in the bleachers where they were deciding who goes to which gym glass at the start of high school. I overheard another Zeppelin fan telling a kid, 'If you wanna know anything about Zeppelin you gotta talk to Eddie.' We started sizing each other up. One of us mentions Rush and the eyes bug out. As soon as I said '*Caress of Steel*' he said '*2112*'. And we're both dumbstruck. 'There's another album?' Then we find out there are two more. And somehow, maybe through reading the music magazines in that pre-internet age, we found out Rush was going to be coming to New Jersey to promote *All the World's a Stage.*

Most of the time the Capitol Theater was an old movie house. It showed X-rated movies that old men would go to see. Rush opened for Foghat. Ronnie Montrose was the special guest. Most of the people were coming to see Foghat or Ronnie Montrose and had no idea who this opening act was. But we were only there for Rush. We even knew who their stagehands were. I don't know how, and I don't remember his real name, but there was a big guy they called Lurch. As he was setting out the equipment we were these little kids shouting out, 'Lurch! Lurch!' The guy finally turns around and waves at us. He was probably thinking, 'How do they know my name?'

They only had about a 20 or 25 minute set. Everyone was going into the bathroom to get high and it was so tightly packed that I could take my feet off the ground and still move forward. There was smoke everywhere. But when you walked out of that theatre all you heard people talking about was, 'Did you get that drummer in that opening act?' Everybody was so enthralled. And we were like, 'Yeah, we know.'

They came back three more times while I was at high school. They opened for Kansas the second time. And one time Cheap Trick opened for them. I was in about the sixth row and Rick Nielsen would be flicking out his guitar picks and then raising his arms to get people to cheer. Every time he did that I yelled 'Rush!' He gave me the dirtiest look.

They finally got radio airplay with 'Spirit of Radio' and 'Freewill', which catapulted them. They never got on the radio before then. And then of course *Moving Pictures* was the one, and it seemed like their fan base grew tenfold.

After that I was at the University of Texas in Austin and went to see them at a venue where you had to stand on your chair to see them. They kind of lost it for me then. Of course, most bands lost it and went too much into synthesisers in the 80s.

AUDITORIUM THEATRE

16 DECEMBER 1976, CHICAGO, ILLINOIS

I WAS THERE: MICHAEL MOESE

I honestly don't remember much about the show (there may have been drugs involved) other than that it was at the Auditorium, the plushest, nicest music venue in Chicago at the time. I also remember Peart's drum kit – Chromey, as it's now called. It was at the time the biggest, wildest, most awesome kit my buddies and I had ever seen. Fond but foggy memories.

MAPLE LEAF GARDENS

31 DECEMBER 1976, TORONTO, CANADA

I WAS THERE: MARK JAY, AGE 18

Back then I went to a lot of concerts. It was a long time ago but what I do remember is the drug scene, with magic mushrooms, acid and marijuana. Me and three friends hung out a lot together. We heard about this Canadian band coming to Maple Leaf Gardens for New Year's Eve and figured it would be a great party! I knew someone that was able to get tickets to events there and she gave me four seats, front row centre. How great was that? From what I can remember it was loud and it was a great party… from what I can remember. Of course, almost everyone was high on something and everyone was happy!

HOUSTON MUSIC HALL

6 JANUARY 1977, HOUSTON, TEXAS

I WAS THERE: JOHN HILL

I have played drums since I was three years old. The first time I heard Rush I couldn't believe a drummer could play that much and yet it fitted the music perfectly. I practised on my drums every day after school trying to figure it all out - and actually did a good job. Neil Peart made me a better drummer and listener. It amazed me three people could make so much music.

The first show I saw was at Houston Music Hall. My friend Chris and I got a ride from my oldest sister down there around 3pm the day of the show. The band arrived and talked with us for a while. Neil was quiet even back then.

On the *Hemispheres* tour they played Houston's Sam Houston Coliseum and once again we went down to the venue and patiently waited. The band was already there so we figured they were in the venue until after the show. When they came out after, all three of them signed our LPs but they were in a hurry so not much conversation was had.

Back at the Sam Houston Coliseum in February 1980, we had fifth row tickets and were in heaven. It sounded great, but mid-show a water pipe backstage burst and the show ended after they'd played just seven songs. We were disappointed and there was no refund either. The band was upset and pretty much gone by the time we got around back.

(A cherry bomb was reportedly dropped down a toilet, a trick much played on hoteliers by The Who's Keith Moon).

KIEL AUDITORIUM

13 FEBRUARY 1977,
ST LOUIS, MISSOURI

I WAS THERE: MICHAEL PICCHIOLDI, AGE 14

Michael Picchioldi saw Rush in St Louis several times

I was in junior high school in 1975 when I heard 'Fly by Night' on KSHE radio in St Louis. I was amazed at Geddy's voice and the sound the band put out. I had no idea who they were. My friends and I got together and I was telling them about the song I heard. My friend Tony said, 'If you liked that song, wait until you hear 'Working Man'.'

I bought a copy of *Circus* magazine at my local pharmacy which had Rush's name on the cover. I was completely amazed to find out Rush was only three people. I begged and begged my parents to take me to a record store, where I purchased *All the World's a Stage* on 8-track. I played that 8-track over and over. I then picked up their first self titled album on vinyl, and eventually on 8-track. I bought *Fly by Night* and *Caress of Steel* on vinyl *and* 8-track. When *Archives* came out, that was my next purchase. I loved that 8-track.

My first Rush concert in 1977 was the second concert I was allowed to attend, and I had to go with my older aunt. This concert blew me away. From that day on, I never missed a Rush concert in St Louis. My favourites were the multiple night shows in 1980 (three shows) and 1981 (two shows). But the *R40* show was the best. It was in the back of my mind that it might be their last, but I kept pushing it from my thoughts. I had ninth row aisle on Geddy's side. I was not disappointed. I look back and it saddens me to think that was the last time I'd see them perform live.

MICHIGAN STATE UNIVERSITY

2 MARCH 1977, LANSING, MICHIGAN

I WAS THERE: RUSSELL SHINEVAR, AGE 16

I still have their first album which I bought the day it came out. I saw them live with Max Webster. Rush played their entire *2112* album. I've seen hundreds of concerts and it's still my favourite. I was a junior in high school when I went to see them. I don't remember who I went with. But I still listen to Max Webster as a result of that show.

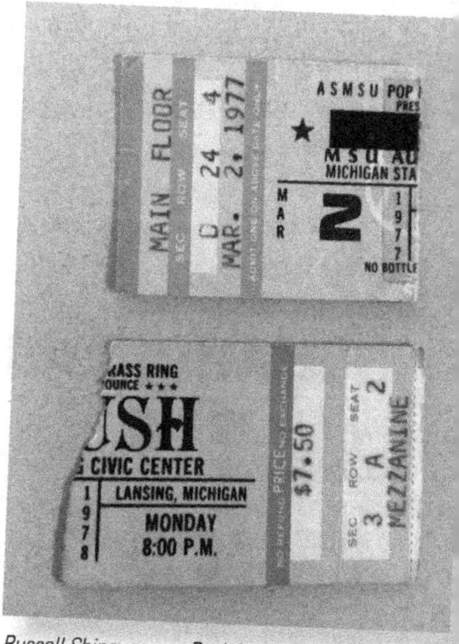

Russell Shinevar saw Rush in 1977 and 1978

THE PALLADIUM

6 MARCH 1977, NEW YORK, NEW YORK

I WAS THERE: PAUL DI SAVERIO

I only learned of them one month before I went to see them. I was living in Italy before that, and then I flew back to Italy. I was only in the States for seven months. Back in Italy in 1977, 1978, nobody knew Rush at all. There were no Rush records in Italy. But I had a rock music programme so I started playing them on the radio. I was pushing Rush every day I was there. And while I was doing that they started to import Rush records. The first one was *A Farewell to Kings* and then they started to import the older ones and then the new ones. I wasn't able to see Rush live again until 2004, the first time they ever came to Italy. I drove 600 kilometres to go and see them in Milan in 2004 and then again in 2007. They never came to Italy again after that. But I saw them in 2011 in Frankfurt and in 2013 in Cologne, Germany.

AGRICULTURAL HALL

20 APRIL 1977, ALLENTOWN, PENNSYLVANIA

I WAS THERE: JOHN FEICHTEL

Rush was the third concert that I ever saw. My friend said, 'There's this band you have to listen to.' The venue wasn't very good for concerts. It's just a big square arena. This was right after *All the World's a Stage* came out. We were drinking a bunch of beers before heading into the concert. We bought tickets on the spot right before going in. We were right at the doors. When they opened up the doors we were the first ones in. There wasn't an area between the stage and the audience. Our chests were literally up against the stage. The microphone stand was within arm's reach. That's how close we were to the band.

Geddy's bass guitar had that twang like the band Yes. The pick ups give it that little high-pitched note, the top of the bass notes. That was what got me hooked. Geddy would normally be on the right side of the stage as you looked from the audience but when I saw them he was on the other side. He was standing on a white shag rug and for 20 years or more I had just a little tag of that rug in my car. One day my friend volunteered to clean the car and he vacuumed up that piece of rug and I never saw it again.

I saw them 21 times, all over the place. I saw them a lot with my cousin, in Philadelphia and New York City. We'd try and get as close to the stage as possible, not in the pit area where everyone gets pushed around. You might get to catch some guitar picks and drumsticks also that way. I have a collection of guitar picks but none from Geddy because I could not get close enough from him. The last time I saw them was in Philadelphia. We couldn't get real close and pre sales were already sold out.

I still have all the vinyl. I have a bunch of them on 8-track. Of course they malfunction after a while.

ARAGON BALLROOM

21 MAY 1977, CHICAGO, ILLINOIS

I WAS THERE: BRETT WILLIAMS

I grew up in Southern California and surfed and rocked out, etc. I went to rural Michigan to visit family in the summer of 1974. They had the first Rush album on 8-track to play in the car. It was the first time I'd heard them. I got home and Los Angeles radio wasn't playing it and my friends had never heard of Rush. But we went to the local record store and they had the vinyl.

Brett Williams' home set up

In 1977 I was in the US Navy, going to school near Chicago. Some of us went to see them at the Aragon Ballroom. It was a small venue with a capacity of maybe 1,000 – 1,500. The most memorable thing (not to take away from the music) was the venue itself. It reminded me of a Spanish villa, with the floor seats being courtyard with one balcony level above in that motif. And the ceiling was like a night sky, with twinkling lights and wisps of cloud. It was a surreal setting.

Film of Rush performing 'Finding my Way' aired in the UK on BBC2's *The Old Grey Whistle Test* on 31 January 1975. The New Year's Eve show was traditionally a round up of the most popular items broadcast over the previous twelve months.

FREE TRADE HALL

2 JUNE 1977, MANCHESTER, UK

I WAS THERE: SIMON MUSK, AGE 19

I've been a Rush fan since New Year's Eve 1975, when I first heard them at a party. It was a special edition of *The Old Grey Whistle Test*. I think they played 'Working Man' off the first album and I was completely hooked.

Most of my mates who'd been into stuff that we were into then - like Led Zeppelin, Deep Purple, Black Sabbath and all those – had seemed to decide that punk was the new thing. I just didn't get it. I was on my own in liking Rush. After they released *All the World's a Stage* in '76, there was a PO box address to write to them for information so I wrote a long letter and a couple of weeks later got a personal letter back from Alex with a signed photograph.

Simon Musk and Alex Lifeson would exchange letters in the early days

We kept in touch with a few letters here and there, and then I found out that they were touring the UK for the first time in June 1977 so another letter followed and Alex invited me along to meet the band at the Free Trade Hall in Manchester. I lived in Leeds and was three weeks short of 20 at the time. I booked a hotel for the night and I got the train over.

Being a young lad I just wandered into the hall as they were soundchecking. I watched the soundcheck in an empty hall. They ran right through 'Xanadu' which they'd only just started to do live. I almost got thrown out of the hall by a security guard and Geddy Lee took pity on me and ushered me downstairs to the dressing room, where I met the band. I spent all day with them, just chatting. They were incredibly humble and friendly people. I could have had some amazing backstage photos as I had a cheap camera with me, but the film jammed. Alex did his best to unjam it, with a towel over his head so that it wouldn't expose the film, but it was knackered. It's a real shame because those photos would be an amazing thing to look at now.

Alex said to me, 'Where would you like to watch the show from?' I said, 'Where can I?' he said, 'Wherever you want!' I'd already bought a ticket for the show but he said, 'No, you don't need that.' He got the manager to sit me down on his side of the stage on the flight cases behind the PA and I watched the entire show from there. After the show I went backstage again and had a chat with them, had a drink, said my farewells and toddled off to my hotel for the night.

They recorded *A Farewell to Kings* at Rockfield Studios in Wales the same year and I remember getting a letter from Alex, which he'd written on Concorde on the way back to Canada. It was on Concorde-headed notepaper!

The following year, when they came back to the UK to play, I was really ill most of the year and I just couldn't make it. We said we'd keep in touch but obviously they got bigger and bigger. And time moves on and we lost contact.

I actually didn't see them again live until the *Time Machine* tour at the O2 in London. A lot of years had flown by in between. I wondered about asking one of the road crew to ask Alex if he remembered me, but he must have met hundreds of thousands of people since then and so it's unlikely.

I can't believe that it was 43 years ago that I met them and spent the day with them.

HAMMERSMITH ODEON

4 JUNE 1977, LONDON, UK

I WAS THERE: JEAN-PAUL SRIVALSAN

My 40 year plus obsession with Rush began in late 1976 in the playground of a nondescript secondary school in a West London suburb. My musical taste was heavily invested in rock and prog. Led Zep, Deep Purple, Black Sabbath, Yes and Genesis were the soundtrack to my young life. Exotic sounding American bands played a part as well with Aerosmith, Kiss, Boston and Ted Nugent gaining some traction with our small group of rockers.

One of the lads had the knack of finding new bands for us to explore and played their music on his portable cassette player. One sunny morning at break time he taps me on the shoulder and suggests I have a listen to a Canadian band and their new live album as I may well like them. He cues it up and I hear, 'We'd like to take you back to our first album and do something... this is called 'Working Man'.' Then, and to paraphrase a line from *Jerry Maguire*, Rush 'had me' at that riff! The raw power, the weird vocals, the scorching guitar solos and the segue into 'Finding My Way' leading to the stunning drum solo towards the end. I'd not heard anything like it and I knew I had to have more.

I tracked down a copy of *All the World's a Stage* in a secondhand record store and total and complete Rush addiction ensued. The first three albums soon followed and were played on non-stop rotation, which worried my parents for a while. But the best was yet to come as Rush announced dates for their first tour of the UK.

4 June 1977 at the Hammersmith Odeon was my first Rush concert. It was everything I'd hoped for and more. It was a tour supporting *All the World's a Stage* but we got snippets of 'The Necromancer' during 'By-Tor' and they previewed a 'work in progress' version of 'Xanadu' which sounded and looked so cool, with dry ice enveloping Alex during the slow burn intro on his famed double-neck guitar. I left that gig buzzing and excited about the new album, *A Farewell to Kings*, which would be released later in the year.

I WAS THERE: STEPHEN CREIGHTON

It's 1976. I am still at school. I am 15 years old. Me and five friends are well into our prog rock music, not like most people at our school. We take turns listening to records at our houses. We are into Yes, Genesis and ELP. One of my friends has a cousin who is 18 years old and is well into prog rock. We are invited to his house to listen to some music. He puts on Yes first - *Close to the Edge*. Then he excitedly brings out an LP called *Fly by Night* by a band from Canada. Before he puts it on, he says, 'There are only three in the band and the sound they make is unbelievable!'

We sit there and cannot believe the sound that's coming out - great bass, great lead guitar and singing that is very different but we love it. And the drums are incredible. It's a great start with the song 'Anthem'. But after a few plays the song that really got me was 'By-Tor and the Snow Dog'.

Stephen Creighton saw Rush on their first visit to London

The next time we were at his house was two weeks later and I could not wait. He had ordered a copy of *Caress of Steel* on import as it wasn't released in the UK. It meant paying three to four times the price of any other LP so it was out of my range. We got to listen to this LP and - my god - it knocked me for six.

As the year went by I got myself a job delivering morning papers so I saved up to buy *Fly by Night*, *Caress of Steel* and *Rush* all as imports as there were still no Rush LPs released in Britain. It was great not having to wait to go the friend's cousin's house to get my Rush fix. I had them all to myself.

In 1977 there were rumours that Rush were coming to UK. And it was true. Tickets went on sale and I got in the line to get my ticket. Four of us were buying 10 tickets. We were at the front of the line, having got there two hours before they went on sale. I got front row tickets.

On the night all 10 of us arrived at the Hammersmith Odeon with dodgy IDs so that we could join in the pre-gig excitement in the Britannia, the pub over the road. The pub was packed with Rush fans. Everyone had so much to share, and everyone was looking forward to seeing our heroes.

Finally the time had come and we headed over to take our places. After the support band, Stray, it happened, Rush were introduced over the PA and they hit us with 'Bastille Day' and then went into 'Anthem'. I was leaning on the stage and was that close I could see the surprise on Geddy and Alex's faces with the crowd and our delight at seeing Rush play live. The biggest highlight was when they played 'Xanadu', which was to appear on *A Farewell to Kings*. I get goosebumps when I hear unbelievable music, but this was goosebumps on goosebumps. And the drum solo from Neil was unbelievable. I went on to see them live so many times.

I WAS THERE: GLEN BAYFIELD, AGE 19

I was feeling sorry for myself. I had a broken arm after having a bad motorbike accident. My friend came round and said, 'Come on, we'll go and see a concert tonight. Rush.' I said, 'Rush? Never heard of them.' It was the 70s, so I thought it was going to be a punk band. I've always been a metalhead. I was a Queen fan for the first three albums, until they sold their soul to the devil with 'Bohemian Rhapsody'.

We had a few beers beforehand. They came on and it was these three guys. Then they started playing and I thought, 'Hold on, this isn't bad!' They started with 'Bastille Day', then went on to 'Anthem' and 'Lakeside Park' and then they did '2112', which was gobsmacking to watch. When they played 'Xanadu', my jaw dropped. I thought, 'I'm in love with this band.' From that moment on I went to see them at every gig possible. And of course I played them in the car all the time.

I followed that concert with *A Farewell to Kings* at Hammersmith and the *Hemispheres* tour at Hammersmith, when they did five nights. They were starting to blow my pocket but I thought, 'I'm still going.' I had a good job so I could afford to go every night. I also saw the *Exit... Stage Left* tour and that was the first time they played 'The Camera Eye', which is one of my favourite tracks. I went to the Brighton Centre first, on my own. It was hard getting friends to go with me. But my friend Danny was a drummer and he liked Neil Peart and appreciated how good he was. It was like, 'Wow, I've never seen a drummer like it.'

CITY HALL

11 JUNE 1977, NEWCASTLE, UK

I WAS THERE: FRED SMITH

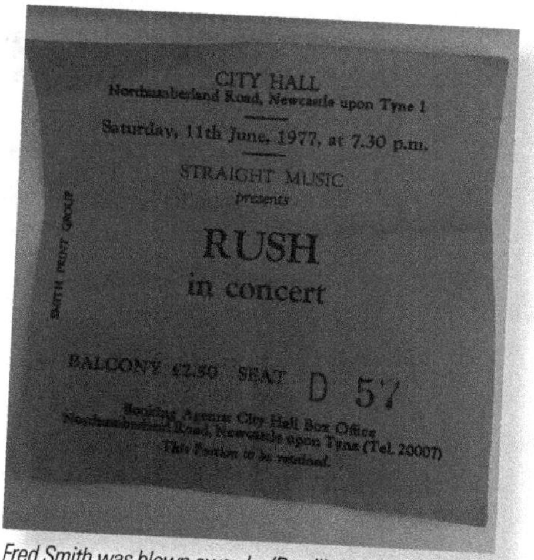

Fred Smith was blown away by 'Bastille Day'

It was just after Christmas 1976. I was 17. My best mate and I were always swapping albums in a sort of arms race to see who could discover the best band.

We sat in my bedroom and he gave me a triple gatefold, Canadian import double live album with a picture of a naked man in front of a red star above a stunning drum kit. He went home, I put in on the stereo and the first chords of 'Bastille Day' blew me away. A love affair started that would never end. Who was this bloke with a voice like a strangled cat that somehow just worked?

Fast forward to June after purchasing all five of their albums and asking my mam to decorate the back of my denim jacket with the naked guy in the red star. (My God mam, you could embroider!) Rush are playing the City Hall on the *2112* tour. Tickets purchased for £2.50 and off we went - Gary, Jacko and me - three gormless teenagers going to our first live gig.

Expecting a half empty venue we were very surprised to see that it was sold out. But Newcastle has always embraced Rush. It was a fabulous show with white carpets and yellow spotlights, blazing out from the drum kit. 'Attention all planets of the solar federation, we have assumed control.....' That they had, and I bought the obligatory sweatshirt on the way out.

34 years and 10 shows later they were back again, this time at the Metro Arena for the *Time Machine* tour and - although I didn't know it - the last time for me. What a brilliant show and, boy, could they still hack it! Rush, and Neil's lyrics, have provided the soundtrack to my life. They are still my favourite band and the albums are played constantly. Not many people other than your parents affect your life the way they have mine. 40 odd years later I still remember hearing that album and seeing them live for the first time. I've still got all the tickets and I've still got the denim jacket.

Thanks again, Mam, now 95 years old and knitting a hat for her imminent great grandson.

I WAS THERE: JAMES GIBBON, AGE 16

It was a 45 minute journey from my home town to Newcastle where I was about to attend my first rock concert. My two friends and I arrived an hour beforehand and decamped to the City Tavern. I sipped my beer slightly apprehensively in a dark corner. This was the first time I'd drunk alcohol in a pub, and I was a bit nervous about being caught, just a few weeks before my 17th birthday and more than a year before I could drink legally in a pub. But soon enough we wandered along to the venue, through the main doors and into the foyer. People were milling around there, queuing for badges and programmes – I still have mine, of course – and it all seemed very exciting.

When we entered through the big door into the hall, I could barely believe my eyes. The stage was so close and it was all a lot smaller than I'd expected. I'd somehow formed an impression of concert venues being huge, cavernous places which they usually are now. This seemed smaller than a cinema and was in fact a theatre venue with a capacity of about 2,100 seats.

I took my seat and read my concert programme. It's the one in which *Sounds* magazine's Geoff Barton writes an entertaining little story about the Priests of the Temples of Syrinx, managing to work the band themselves into the plot. But as I read the programme I kept glancing up at the stage. I couldn't believe my heroes were going to be right there, in the same room as me. They must already be in the building somewhere! It seemed unreal. Neil's drums were already on the stage, with a little Starman logo.

I'd managed to cultivate a quite unhealthy obsession with Rush by this time. I had nearly worn out my illegal cassette copy of the band's live album, *All the World's a Stage.*

Recorded for posterity exactly one year earlier I had closed my eyes and immersed myself into that concert in Toronto dozens of times.

The support band, Stray, were really good. I was impressed by the light show. And they were loud! A *lot* louder than my parents' hi-fi. Wow! By the time the lights went down, I was almost sick with excitement. My heart was pounding and the crowd was roaring.

Then suddenly, my life changed forever. The stage burst into light and Alex was there, leaning over a Gibson guitar, his blond locks tumbling forward, cranking out 'Bastille Day' louder than I'd ever imagined it. It is a moment that is burned into my mental retina for all time. The crowd was going wild around me; everyone was on their feet. Geddy was strutting along the front of the stage, grinning widely, wearing what appeared to be a bed sheet as a cape, coaxing bottom-end loudness from his Rickenbacker bass. And Neil was hitting those drums hard and already twirling his sticks, something I hadn't expected at all.

It was sensory overload. I probably went into slight shock. The show seemed to pass so quickly. A rip-roaring 'By-Tor and the Snow Dog' gave way to 'The Necromancer', a tune I'd never heard but was very intrigued by. And 'side one from our latest studio album' – '2112' of course – was astonishing; emotional, intense and powerful. There was a new song called 'Xanadu'. With double-neck guitars! Wow.

It was over all too soon, but even after a rowdy and rousing second encore of 'What You're Doing', the crowd hadn't had enough. We shouted, stomped and begged very loudly for what seemed like about half an hour, to be rewarded by Alex walking back on stage, grinning from ear to ear and looking incredulous at the reception he and the band had received. The other two joined him and after a very loud, highly energetic and frankly joyous performance of 'Best I Can', it really was all over this time. As we spilled out of the City Hall into the cool of a Newcastle summer evening, my ears were ringing and I felt oddly intoxicated and elated.

APOLLO THEATRE

12 JUNE 1977, GLASGOW, UK

I WAS THERE: MIKE BRUCE

I was in Bruce's Records shop on Rose Street in Edinburgh. It was late 1976. The sleeve of *Fly by Night* really caught my attention. This was back in the days when you could ask to hear a bit of an album before you bought it… or not. I sat down on a wee vinyl-covered bench and put on a pair of ill-fitting and ill-used headphones. The sounds playing through the shop system suitably muffled, I watched the assistant take the record out of the liner with that casual reverence that only professional platter spinners perfect and place it on the deck. I can't contemplate going back to vinyl from CD, but I do miss that gentle thump when the needle hits the groove. Thump, hiss and then – blam! - the riff to 'Anthem'. Over the next few months Rush were at the top of my

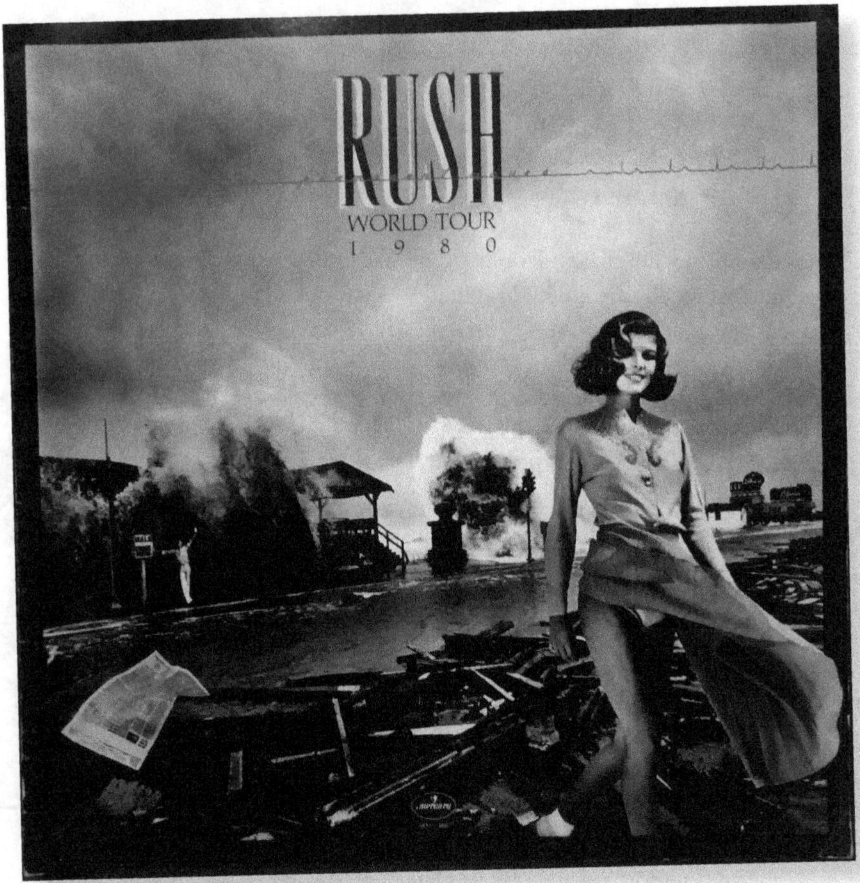

Mike Bruce saw Rush over half a dozen times & still has his programmes

playlist. It's not as though there was nothing else to listen to. *A Night at the Opera* was the current Queen album and Thin Lizzy had blown everybody away with *Jailbreak*.

In '77 word came out that Rush were going to tour the UK. A crowd of us sent away our postal orders to the Glasgow Apollo and we hired a minibus to take us from Fife through to Glasgow. 40 plus years and many, many gigs later, this gig is still in my top ten.

The set was based around the *All the World's a Stage* album but just after they played '2112', Geddy Lee introduced a new song and we heard 'Xanadu' for the first time. Keyboards, acoustic guitar, bass pedals. We didn't really appreciate it at the time, but Rush were starting the next chapter of their story. But maybe I shouldn't just say 'their' story because one of the most endearing things about the band was always the fact that they really were a *people's* band. On the bus back from Glasgow that night, one of the boys said an older bloke in the crowd was saying he'd seen Zeppelin, Sabbath and rest live but, that night, Rush had been better than any of them. None of us knew that for sure but we all kind of hoped it was true.

Zeppelin were away out in a league of their own, rock gods on their own Mount Olympus. Deep Purple's story was already told, and you got the feeling that it was the same with Sabbath. Sure, you had the home grown second division of Priest, UFO and Lizzy but Rush were just that bit different, more attractive. Their being Canadian added a touch of the exotic, or maybe it was the fact that they'd taken the trouble to cross the pond and had clearly gone back taking a bit of Scotland with them. Whatever the reason, Rush were our band.

In the British music press (Geoff Barton aside) they couldn't get arrested, but that just made us like them even more. This was just as punk was turning into new wave. Liking Rush back then was almost as much of a left field musical choice as jumping on the punk/new wave bandwagon. You didn't have the luxury of belonging to a movement. You and a small band of Rush fans with you were way out there in the boonies.

I saw them several times over coming years. I'm still chuffed to be an honorary Glaswegian in the Glaswegian Chorus on *Exit... Stage Left*. That album was recorded on the *Permanent Waves* tour. It seemed like half the audience queued up round the back of the Apollo to meet the band that night, but the band stayed and met everyone who did. Although somewhat baffled by my bizarre questions regarding the lyrics to 'The Necromancer', delivered as they were in a thick Scottish accent with a bit of a nervous shake to it, the band were unfailingly polite and friendly.

A trip to London in 1981 was memorable for the wrong reasons, involving horrendous coach travel with what felt like dysentery and Bri-Nylon sheets in a ropey B&B. The band themselves made it worthwhile though. The London gig was good, but the gig two nights later at Ingliston near Edinburgh was even better.

By the time I saw them in May of '83 things were changing. The set lists still featured a lot of their older material and they were still great live, but I wasn't so keen on their newer material. It wasn't just the band's music changing, though - my tastes were changing too. Musical virtuosity was maybe a bit less appealing to me at that point. The more keyboard heavy approach was increasingly leaving me cold. Album-wise, *Signals* was okay and *Grace Under Pressure* a bit of a return to form, but with *Power Windows* the romance was more or less over. I didn't really enjoy the gig I saw in 1988 or feel much in common with the audience any more. It was like seeing an ex you've grown apart from with a new hairdo and someone else on their arm.

I still love the Rush that were my band, and I wept buckets when Neil Peart passed. Now I think Rush and I are a bit like Rick and Ilsa in *Casablanca*. But instead of Paris, we'll always have the Apollo '77.

I WAS THERE: GRAHAM PLATT, AGE 14

Friends in school put me onto them. I paid £1.50 on the door. It was my first ever gig and I was in awe. I remember walking in and Peart's drums were covered. Being a drummer myself I couldn't wait to see his drum kit. Then the lights went out, the cover came off the kit

Graham Platt was at the Apollo

and the show kicked off with 'Bastille Day'. I just stood mesmerised, with smoke and explosions and three guys making the best loud noise. I hadn't seen or heard anything like it. It was half full and we paid for cheap seats up in the gods but moved down near the front of the circle about halfway through the show. I have an original Apollo poster from the '77 show signed by Alex.

I saw every British tour they played bar the *Roll the Bones* tour. They came back eight months later and sold out two nights. It was supposed to be one night in Glasgow and one at Edinburgh Odeon but the Odeon had a fire or something so that show was moved to Glasgow. They came back to the Apollo in '79 for the *Hemispheres* tour and '80 for the *Permanent Waves* tour, which was the last show in Glasgow for seven years. They played Ingilston in Edinburgh on the *Moving Pictures* and *Signals* tours.

I WAS THERE: IAN GILLAN, AGE 14

It was very unusual for me to pay to go and see a band I'd never heard of, never mind listened to. Money was tight as I only earned a few pounds a week stacking shelves after school. My ticket that evening cost £2.50. I still have the ticket stub and programme. A friend who was familiar with Rush persuaded me that they were worth seeing so I decided to take a gamble.

I remember the venue being half empty and the support act a bit tedious. I was beginning to wonder if I should have stayed at home but as soon as they played the opening notes of 'Bastille Day', I knew my ears were in for a treat. During the opening number a couple of pyrotechnics were detonated. I don't think these were properly calibrated as I felt the heat flash on my face - and I was sitting upstairs in the circle!

Ian Gillan recalls a half empty Glasgow Apollo

The rest of the show didn't disappoint and I remember trying to hunt down their albums in the subsequent weeks. I think they were a bit hard to find but maybe I just couldn't afford them immediately. Word soon got round about how good the show had been and only eight months later they sold out the same venue two nights in a row, as they did in '79 and '80. I saw Rush all seven times that they played the Apollo and although my musical tastes have changed over the years I still dust down my copy of *All the World's a Stage* once in a while and relive those great days.

LIVERPOOL EMPIRE THEATRE

13 JUNE 1977, LIVERPOOL, UK

I WAS THERE: STEVE EDWARDS, AGE 16

My friend, the drummer in my band, and I made the journey from Bebington on the Wirral to the Liverpool Empire to book tickets for our first ever concert by a band

Steve Edwards (right) bought Rush tickets because they were 'a bit like Led Zep'

whose name I have long since forgotten. On arrival, our disappointment was total when we were told by the girl at the box office that the concert was sold out. Not wanting a wasted journey and with newspaper round money burning a hole in my bell bottom jeans, I asked, 'Is there anyone else appearing who isn't sold out?' The response was life changing. 'Rush,' the girl replied. 'They're a Canadian rock band.' Unimpressed we asked the question, 'Who are Rush?' She replied, 'They're a bit like Led Zep.' Our response? 'Gimme the tickets!'

We paid a visit to Diddy Dave, the local muso geek whose front living room was a shrine to vinyl. 'Dave, have you a Rush album we can listen to?' knowing the answer would be yes. *All the World's a Stage* was produced and the rest is history. I saw them on the first two UK tours at the Empire, then the Deeside Ice Rink and finally the last two UK tours in Manchester. Life long fan.

The *A Farewell to Kings* tour began in August 1977, with the band having barely been off the road for two months after the *All the World's a Stage* tour. This was another gigantic tour, with over 140 shows before winding up in April 1978.

EXHIBITION STADIUM

23 AUGUST 1977, TORONTO, CANADA

I WAS THERE: CHUCK DILL

CNE Grandstand was another memorable one. It was outside under a night sky and this one stood out because I was right in front of the stage. I found myself mesmerised, and focused strictly on Neil and his drumming. I think I was likely standing there with my mouth open, looking like I was a little special. His precision was cutting. I dabbled in drums and that day realised that drumming could be taken much further than I ever imagined.

TULSA ASSEMBLY CENTER

14 OCTOBER 1977, TULSA, OKLAHOMA

I WAS THERE: MARIO VAZQUEZ IV

Max Webster and the classic UFO line up opened the show. Rush were supporting *A Farewell to Kings* and UFO were touring for *Lights Out*. I had known about Rush since their *All the World's a Stage* record and I had really wanted to see them. And I'd also read and heard great things about UFO. Needless to say, both were awesome! They sounded exactly like their records, and were a lot louder and heavier live. UFO were one of the best opening bands I'd ever seen and made Rush work extremely hard for their applause.

CIVIC CENTER MUSIC HALL

15 OCTOBER 1977, OKLAHOMA CITY, OKLAHOMA

I WAS THERE: LEE PARMAN

A friend who introduced them to me while in school wanted me to go to this concert. It was a small venue in a theatre and perfect for acoustics. I became a lifelong fan after that.

In 1980, I went to a small business school in Durango, Colorado where I met friends that were Rush fanatics. We heard about a concert in Albuquerque, New Mexico. We packed up and arrived a day before the concert, hoping to find same hotel as the band, like a bunch of groupies. They weren't at the hotel that night.

Next day we saw their bus at the Hilton. We booked rooms there. The concert that night was packed. They even stopped the music and told everyone to back up. It got pretty bad. Later that night, we went back to hotel and one of my extrovert friends located them in the lobby near their rooms. We didn't believe him but followed him back there. I've never been one to bother anyone like that but we walked down the hall, passing by Neil Peart's room. He was exhausted, of course, and crashed on his bed, the doors open. Then we went on down the hall and Geddy was standing up against wall, talking with a few people. Like an idiot I asked, 'Are we intruding?' 'Ha ha.' he said, 'Probably.' The anal retentive bass player. Broke my heart!

We walked on, feeling embarrassed, and my friend Bill said, 'Hope to see you in Chicago.' Geddy responded but nothing much was said. Geddy and his crew went back into their rooms and we saw Alex and he was very kind. My friend asked, 'Can we get an autograph?' He said, 'Okay, quickly.' Ha ha - typical Alex! Funny guy.

THE PALLADIUM

12 NOVEMBER 1977, NEW YORK, NEW YORK

I WAS THERE: ANTHONY AGNELLO

I had just started my sophomore year in high school in New Rochelle. A few kids from the Bronx told us about this great band that was playing at the Palladium. Cheap Trick and UFO were the opening acts. We purchased the tickets for less than $15. Our seats were sixth row. We drove down to the Bronx and took the subway into Manhattan. Back then it was a case of anything goes at

Anthony Agnello saw Rush at the Palladium

a concert. People were selling drugs and smoking pot, and a girl was piercing a guy's ear with a safety pin as we walked in. The Palladium is a smaller venue, so every seat was a great seat.

I was so impressed with the stack of speakers on each side of the stage. Cheap Trick came out, and the guitar player was a trip, flicking picks into the audience. I really don't remember UFO, other than them being loud. When Rush came out the place was rocking. They opened with 'Bastille Day', with the spot light on Alex, and then Geddy's thundering bass so loud you felt the whole place shake. Back then Geddy's voice really went through you. But they were a loud band and Geddy's bass sounded like the roar of a subway train coming into the station. From 'Cygnus' to '2112' to the start of the jam on 'Working Man', that Ric commanded your attention.

Neil's drumming was fantastic as was Alex's guitar playing. You felt the wind from the speaker stacks on your face. A week after that concert, I put a deposit down on a black 4001 Rickenbacker bass.

ONONDAGA COUNTY WAR MEMORIAL AUDITORIUM

18 NOVEMBER 1977, SYRACUSE, NEW YORK

I WAS THERE: MARC KINGSLEY

They were my second concert ever. They were still doing *2112* and - I think – *A Farewell to Kings*. I was 15 or 16 at the time. It was a great concert. Neil's drum solo really stood out. I believe the Crawlers opened up for AC/DC, when Bon Scott was still with then, and they opened up for Rush.

WAR MEMORIAL ARENA

24 NOVEMBER 1977, JOHNSTOWN, PENNSYLVANIA

I WAS THERE: KEITH VITOVICH, AGE 14

I couldn't believe one of my favourite bands was coming to my hometown on Thanksgiving Night 1977 when they were already selling out bigger arenas. Also on the bill were opening act Cheap Trick, who were very impressive, and Mark Farner of Grand Funk Railroad fame. It turns out that was the only night Mark played on the tour so that was a rare treat.

Concerts were a totally different atmosphere and experience then. Joints were fired up and passed around and there were frisbees and beach balls and let's not forget the firecrackers and M-80s. And there was also general admission seating, so I went early and got right up front and centre. I still can't believe that three guys had that much energy and could look so cool on stage with their double-neck guitars when they played 'Xanadu'. The album *Different Stages* has a bonus disc of them live at the Hammersmith

Odeon in 1978, the same show I'd seen a few months earlier. It's still the best of the 15 Rush shows I saw.

I missed the next three tours; they didn't come to my hometown and I wasn't old enough to go to Pittsburgh until *Signals*, when they played the Civic Arena. Second song in, Geddy stopped the show as a fight broke out. There was electricity in the air at their concerts back then you could cut with a knife. You can see it in some of the old live footage on YouTube. It was the only time I saw a fight break out at one of their concerts. *Grace Under Pressure* live was awesome too. They were on the top of their game.

Clockwork Angels turned out to be my last time seeing Rush as they didn't come to Miami on the farewell tour. I said to myself, 'It's okay, you can see them in Pittsburgh, no problem.' Then I learned that Pittsburgh wasn't a tour stop and I was scratching my head thinking, 'That's where it all started professionally for them.' So I said to myself, 'You have family in Cleveland. It's your last resort.' I hate Cleveland, being a Pittsburgh Steelers fan. Anyway, Cleveland ended up not being a tour stop either. I had three strikes and then I was out. I said to myself, 'Why be mad? Be happy you got to see them 14 times.' With the shocking death of Neil, I know there will never be Rush again. That's why we thank God for our memories.

MAPLE LEAF GARDENS

30 DECEMBER 1977, TORONTO, CANADA

I WAS THERE: STEPHEN JOHNSON

I was about tens rows back from the stage. 40 years later it's still one of my best shows. My best friend had been at the show the night before and gave me a warning before the flash bombs went off. We were that close they tend to blur the vision for some time!

MORRIS CIVIC CENTER

2 JANUARY 1978, SOUTH BEND, INDIANA

I WAS THERE: BRUCE J BENNETT

Notwithstanding all of the awkwardness that comes with being a near pubescent 13/14 year-old, music was just starting to click for me in 1977 and '78. You could buy vinyl LPs for under ten bucks. You could send a penny into Columbia House and get all kinds of cool 8-tracks. Cassettes were also a thing. But best of all, the bands coming into their own around that time were killing.

But also around that time, kids in my neighbourhood picked up instruments. At first I wanted to play keys, but this was long before the advent of the less cumbersome electronic keyboards of today. Drums were out of the question – think the episode of *I Love Lucy*, where they buy Little Ricky a snare drum. My dad greatly discouraged all things musical but sprung for a cheap Teisco Del Rey electric and a plastic amp, but that thing called a pick was too much for my sausage fingers.

Bruce Bennett saw Rush in a small venue in South Bend

A guitarist friend suggested bass. I wasn't even sure what one was. But we listened to various bands of the day. The one that caught my ear first was Paul Goddard of Atlanta Rhythm Section and I can still play the solo from 'Champagne Jam'. But being a superficial teenaged smartass, I didn't want to become a fat guy with black horn-rimmed glasses. Spitting blood and fire like Gene Simmons were closer to my tastes.

I joined a band in which I was forced to sing. I think it was because my voice hadn't quite changed yet. We did a lot of The Cars' first two albums, and Ben Orr was also someone cool to emulate. Once you start seriously getting into the instrument, however, you look for something more. That 'more' for me was Geddy. I hung with a number of older kids with cool record collections; I didn't know that it would have been uncool not to have *All the World's a Stage* or *2112*. Singing about the Solar Federation? Equating trees with union labour? Sailing into destiny? The intellect expands....

In '78, I finally had the first opportunity of many to see Geddy and Rush up close and personal, in a 2,500 seat theatre in South Bend, Indiana during their *Hemispheres* tour. It was an intimate place to see a show. I scored tickets in a balcony. They had the longer hair. The oriental robes. The Rickenbacker bass. Taurus pedals (only). It was... glorious!

Keep in mind that Rush hadn't quite got to where they were as 1980 approached. 'YYZ' blew my mind even more than the spectacles for which a Rush show eventually became known. But you could tell it was going to happen. Exactly 'what', I did not know. But the communal aspect of a Rush show was evident even back then. I saw and reminisced with many people there that night at their1980 tours and several thereafter.

Flash forward to today – while I am nowhere near famous, I have got to see a fair portion of this country because of four, sometimes five, strings. While I have done so playing things far less intricate than, say, 'La Villa Strangiato', I can easily say that the biggest influence on my instrument is one Gary Lee Weinrib. He makes a guy want washer and dryers or rotisserie chicken ovens for amps....

ARAGON BALLROOM

7 JANUARY 1978, CHICAGO, ILLINOIS

I WAS THERE: BARRY W KOLLER, AGE 12

It was the *A Farewell to Kings* tour. Older friends had purchased the ticket for me and brought me along. This particular concert and venue was exciting, dangerous and exhilarating all wrapped up in one. The hall was the Aragon Ballroom on West Lawrence Avenue in Chicago, Illinois. Its nickname was 'The Aragon brawl room'. It only seated 6,000 people and was kind of dirty and run down at the time. It was dangerous, because it was general admission and there were people jumping one and two storeys down from the next door parking garage leading into the alley next to the ballroom. Either the elevator was too busy and not working well - or they were high and intoxicated.

There were two huge plate glass windows in the front of the building on each side of the entrance and people were pushing so much that I thought surely it would smash or crack the plate glass from the pressure being applied. People were standing outside for a total of 10 hours to see the band. I finally got in about 6pm that night with the three other people with me and we got four seats right in front that were diagonal to the stage.

In my opinion *A Farewell to Kings* was a complete musical change for Rush, and for the better. But their production was quite strange. They had roadies dressed up as jesters and jokers, and magicians running across the stage during a few of the songs played from that album. They only performed seven or eight songs that night but at the end of one of the last songs, four huge flash boxes were ignited, two at each end of the stage. It practically blinded us! The acoustics were not too good at the Aragon but they made it sound pretty clear.

I saw them again on December 14th, 1978 on the *Hemispheres* tour at the International Amphitheatre on 43rd Street and Halsted Street. The sound was much better than at the Aragon Ballroom. That section of Chicago was a very violent place and two major things occurred. My friend's brother's car, a brand new 1978 Pontiac Grand Prix with silver paint and black top, was stolen from the parking lot meaning we had to find another way to get home, three miles north and then 10 miles west back to Elmwood Park. Immediately he found out our ride was stolen, one of the friends with us jumped on the 43rd Street bus. We found out the next day that he was robbed at the connecting bus waiting station.

The *Permanent Waves* and *Grace Under Pressure* tours are a complete blur and I missed the *Signals* and *Hold Your Fire* tours. The next tour I attended was *Presto* in June of 1990 in East Troy, Wisconsin. Many people say they didn't appreciate this album but I did. In my opinion it was the most enjoyable light show with at least 20 laser machines working simultaneously and two 30 foot Easter bunnies on each side of the stage, bouncing up and down to the beat of the music. This was the first time I introduced my wife-to-be to Rush. I had 30th row on the main floor and the seating was on an upward incline so the seats were perfect.

I WAS THERE: ROB WINTERCORN

Rob Wintercorn (pictured right) with his brother Joe

My mother dropped me off at a junior high school party and picked me back up at about 9pm. As my host walked back to meet her parked out front, I heard the beginning of 'Overture' blaring out of his front door. I quickly said, 'Dang, who is this?' He proudly boosted, 'Rush, dude. They are the best!' I got home and went through my siblings' record collection and – sadly, nothing. Growing up the last of seven kids, music was a big deal to me. The brother who is 15 months older than me liked Queen, The Police, Yes and UFO, and the same bands as our older siblings. He was never really a fan of any one band, but just liked music, and he was the concert goer! He never really bought albums and mostly borrowed from friends. But he was quick to do what it took to get concert tickets, be that early mornings at Sears, JC Penney or the local mall to wait in line at their Ticketmaster section for upcoming Chicago area concerts.

Finding Rush weren't in my siblings' record collections, I set out to buy various of their albums. My first purchase was *Hemispheres,* sadly on 8-track. My brothers were fine when I played Rush but not, like, into it. One brother borrowed *2112* from a friend and when I saw they had the words I was done! I was sucked into these strange arrangements of words that didn't talk of girls, sex, drugs or any of the usual rock and roll things. They talked about space, plant federations, gifts and the wonders of hard work, discovering an instrument or even trees forming unions. I credit my discovering girls later in life to Rush.

I listened to Geddy belt the lyrics out and Alex making his guitar speak and show emotion. Need I say anything about the timely beat of the drums, as if the drummer was the writer of the lyrics and knew exactly what direction to take the words belted out by Ged? Of course I was 13 years old and did not put any of that together until later in life.

My cool brother Joe said, 'Lets go see Rush.' I'm like, 'How?' 'We'll figure it out,' he said. He borrowed our parents' car and we headed to the Aragon Ballroom in Chicago, parked the car and walked up and got tickets. I was in awe and could not believe my eyes and ears. The very music I knew and loved was being performed live. We were way back in the crowd. It was still general admission tickets back then, but it didn't matter because my brother taught me to storm the stage as soon as the lights went out. That's where you run out of your seats and get front and centre the best you could. Folding chairs go flying everywhere and then you try to find each other when it settles down, advancing always closer to the stage as the crowd allows. I was so sold that this was my band. After this event I bought every album within weeks of the release date.

Now I'm a freshman in high school. The *Permanent Waves* album is about to be released right around my birthday. The radio has been playing 'Spirit of Radio' like crazy and just getting into playing 'Freewill' a bit for the night radio crowd in the Chicago area. That was WLUP and WMET, two rival rock stations that were always trying to one up the other. My siblings kept the dial on WXRT which hated Rush.

With my birthday money I walked one and a half miles in the January snow to our closest record store to get the *Permanent Waves* album. I rush home (no pun intended) hoping my siblings won't care if I use the turntable. I open the album as I'm saying in my head, 'I hope they have the lyrics, I really hope they do,' not knowing it's a Rush thing to always print the lyrics.

Permanent Waves. My album, my band. Once again there are no meaningless songs about girls, drugs or relationships gone bad. Instead there are songs describing a storm brewing until the beautiful end, with sunlight shining through the clouds. Tide pools. Cause and effect. These songs changed my thinking patterns in a profound way. I truly believe they helped make me into the man I am today.

In 1980 my family took its first real vacation, a week long stay in a beach hotel in Daytona, Florida. My sister Cris, who died five years later of Hodgkin lymphoma, didn't get or understand Rush but let her little brother play a Rush tape I'd made on our little cassette boom box as we sat on our 15th floor balcony overlooking the ocean. I played her 'Natural Science' and she agreed it was 'pretty cool'.

So the 1980 *Permanent Waves* tour is set. It's all on my brother as I have no driver's license. Make it so for me please, bro! He said, 'I got four tickets and one is yours!' But as we were walking out our front door to go see Rush, my brother stops me and says, 'You're not going. I'm taking Matt Mineco - he has weed.' I stood there dumbfounded, thinking it was a joke. Matt didn't care about music. No way. I walked out to the car as it backed away, leaving the biggest Rush fan in the world to run up to his room and cry.

I fell away from Rush through Neil's family tragedies, thinking they were finished. When I found out they were back, I didn't purchase the new albums right away. I sensed a slightly different approach lyrically.

I moved to Arkansas. I'd see my family in Chicago once a year at a family reunion in late summer. Even with today's technology I don't really talk or randomly text my siblings very much, so when my brother Joe rang my phone I answered thinking it was bad news. It wasn't. It was 'mark your calendar for May 14th, 2015 and meet me in St Louis.' Yes - the *R40* tour! Without a spoken word of apology for what happened in 1980, he came out strong like a big brother would. The hotel was walking distance from the show. I could barely get the check for food or beers before him.

We knew this was it for Rush. They were just that professional. I remember having conversations with fellow long time Rush fans, setting some of them straight. These were three best friends who married young and stayed married. That says a lot about their character in a scene where rock bands hate one another and tour for the money, or walk in drunk to a venue 10 minutes after show time. My band was never even late to a sound check!

They went out big, with no plans to milk fans later by giving less than 100 per cent of themselves. Yes I knew this was it. I was blessed to see 'Jacob's Ladder' live three times, and so many other great songs, many seeing live for the first time. There were tears of excitement and occasional sadness, but they were all good times.

I considered Geddy, Alex and Neil my best friends I never met. They were just too much a part of my life, and helped make me the man - the hard worker, the father, the husband for 34 years - I am today. I was devastated when the news of Neil was announced. I cried and mourned for months on and off. I still do on occasions. I had to explain to so many something they could not grasp or understand. Being the only Rush fan in Arkansas doesn't help.

I just finished listening to 'Necromancer' with tears still in my eyes from the 'Fountain of Lammeth'. Singing along to 'Time Stand Still' or 'Losing It' wrecks me in a good way, making me want to hug my kids or just push them on a swing one more time!

NASSAU COLISEUM

13 JANUARY 1978, LONG ISLAND, NEW YORK

I WAS THERE: TONY FERRARI

My very first Rush show was on the *A Farewell to Kings* tour. I believe a light fell during soundcheck and damaged Alex's cherry coloured double-neck guitar. They opened for Blue Öyster Cult. The crowd was nuts over them and wouldn't let them leave. They came out for extra encores - unpaid I was told by a Coliseum employee. It was like seeing and hearing the *All the World's a Stage* and *A Farewell to Kings* albums. Neil now had his black Slingerland drum kit, Geddy and Alex their Taurus pedals. I believe Geddy's double neck was custom made for him by Rickenbacker because he needed a bass and guitar in one for certain songs and I don't think that such an instrument existed. Or at least not a Rickenbacker. And they had the dry ice and an excellent light show. And of course the great musicianship, music, production, etc., by band and crew.

It was September 1976 and I was 15 years old when I discovered them. I was 'In the Mood' for a new album but especially for some new music, a new band. It was just one of those things. I rode my bicycle to the Bayshore Mall and went into Record World, the one album-selling outlet we had back then. I looked at the display of albums along the wall and there it was. This live album with a drum set and concert stage on the cover. It was by a band named Rush and the album was entitled *All the World's a Stage*. And that was it. I just felt it. I thought to myself that I had heard of them, but to tell you the truth, I probably had not. I went home to listen to it and that was that. I loved it immediately; the music, the three piece album gatefold of photos, the drumming! Even Geddy's voice.

SPASH FIELD HOUSE

28 JANUARY 1978, STEVENS POINT, WISCONSIN

I WAS THERE: RUSS VANDER MEULEN

It was their *Farewell to Kings* tour. I was two months shy of my 18th birthday and it was my very first concert. Thousands of people were gathered outside in the cold waiting for the doors to open. My friend and I had each brought along a date. The four of us were stuck in the centre of the enormous crowd waiting for several hours to get in. Suddenly, a wave started from the front of the crowd and rippled its way towards the rear. Of course, with us being in the centre of it all, we were caught off guard and were nearly crushed.

Russ Vander Meulen saw Rush on the A Farewell to Kings tour

After the first wave had passed, we anticipated another one to follow. My friend and I were able to get our arms free and positioned our girlfriends in front of our bodies and placed our hands firmly on the backs of those directly in front of us in hopes of preventing our dates from being injured. Sure enough another wave hit us, but this time it came from the rear. It was more intense than the first one. I had to use all of my strength to prevent my body from crushing up against my date. She was safe as long as I could hold my arms fully extended outwards. That wave too had passed without any of us being injured.

But wait! Here comes a third one. This time from the front. Once again, our girls were protected and that one soon passed. The waves continued until three glass entry doors finally gave in and shattered. Several people were injured.

After the mishap, the crowd started to migrate slowly towards the field house entrances. The four of us were very relieved that we were finally moving. As we got closer, I could see the damage that was done. Several doors were broken loose from their hinges and glass was being swept up by custodians. I was briefly saddened about the individuals who were injured, but soon refocused my attention towards the upcoming show.

As we were walking through the doors into the building, I could see armed security personnel searching individuals for contraband. Well, it turns out that I just happened to be a minor who was bootlegging a small bottle of brandy on my person. Without thinking twice, I reached down and pulled the bottle from my boot, laid it on its side on the floor, said a quick 'good-bye' and slid the bottle with the side of my foot into the unsuspecting crowd. I really didn't want to be going to jail on my first concert.

Once we got past security, the crowd slowly ventured deeper into the venue. I could see a second set of open doorways ahead of me. This, of course, is where all of the much anticipated action was about to go down. My heart was racing. When we finally reached the second set of doors I could see the tell-tale bluish hue of smoke that lingered in the air throughout the entire arena. Yup! Just as I figured, I could smell pot, and lots of it. Rush fans were getting stoned.

As the four of us stepped into the arena it became clear that this was the real deal. Now all we had to do was find our seats. As we were slowly navigating our way through the crowd to our nosebleed seats, I'm thinking to myself, 'This is going to be a great concert!' Our view of the show was perfect. We were sitting up high and centred on the stage with no obstructions.

All we had to do was wait for the show to start. It seemed like an eternity until the emcee finally walked onto the stage only to announce that Jay Ferguson (the opening show) was cancelled because of a flight delay due to snowy weather conditions. That was just fine with me because I really didn't feel like making love on Thunder Island anyways. I was there to rock!

After another long wait, the emcee finally returned to the stage and announced Rush. The crowd went wild. I was overwhelmed with excitement. The lights went out and the trio of rock 'n' roll got smack dab in our face with some serious chords and percussion. I was at a loss for words as to what I was experiencing. It was the most magnificent (yet somewhat intimidating) feeling I've ever experienced. After several songs into the set, I was starting to get accustomed to all of the energy that was on display that night in the arena.

Watching Rush from high up in the bleachers through a thick blue hue of smoke is a sight that I'll never forget. The cops lining the gymnasium floor with their arms crossed were either oblivious to the illicit drug use going on behind their backs or they just didn't care. It was obvious they were enjoying the show too.

As the show played on into the evening it became apparent to me that something else was fast becoming of great concern. Can anybody guess what that would be? Anybody? Well, I'll give you a hint - my teeth were starting to float. Yup! You guessed it, nature was calling me and it wasn't gonna hang up the phone until I answered. Ugh!

Just the thought of having to make the long descent down the bleachers and then navigate my way through a bunch of stoners packed like sardines on the main floor while trying to walk normal was a bit unnerving, but I had no choice. I told my friends that I'd be back as soon as I could and bravely set out on a course to liberate my bladder from almost certain doom. Faced with the uncertainty of where the restrooms where located within the venue, I stood up from my seat and half-hesitantly started the long trek down the bleachers towards the massive crowd of Rush fans.

Once I was on the main floor, I had no idea where to go. At this point and time, the urge to 'hit the can' was at an all time high. Luckily for me I saw a guy wearing a 'staff' shirt and I asked him if he could point me towards the restrooms, which he did. I thanked him and hurried off in the direction he pointed. While trying to stay centred on my thoughts, I did eventually manage to make it through the dense crowd to an entrance of a corridor that ran alongside the stage.

Once I was there, I could see the restroom sign way down at the end of the hallway on the left. I was somewhat relieved that I was almost to my destination and was focusing on finally being able to put an end to this lengthy nightmare. As I was entering the corridor, I noticed ahead of me that there was a small stairwell on my left that lead up to the stage. Two big bouncer-like staff members were standing guard on each side of the stairs. It was obvious they didn't want unauthorised personnel on the stage.

As I slowly pushed on towards to my destination, I happened to notice another staff member coming down the steps from the stage. Immediately following behind him was another fellow with long hair and a moustache. He was wearing a white tank top with a small white towel draped over his shoulders. Could this possibly be who I thought it was? Why yes! Yes it was! It was none other than the man himself, the 'Professor of Drums', Neil Peart!

I couldn't believe my eyes. I was within three feet of him. I felt the urge to say something to him so I had to think fast. The only thing that came to my mind was to say: 'Awesome drums!' He gave me a quick smile and thanked me for the compliment and was whisked away to safety by security.

I finally made it to the restroom without incident. I am forever grateful for the brief encounter I had with the best drummer in rock 'n' roll history, and it's all thanks to over-hydration.

ODEON THEATRE

12 FEBRUARY 1978, BIRMINGHAM, UK

I WAS THERE: MARC BROUGHTON

1977 was a year that was memorable for the Queen's Silver Jubilee, street parties, a Brit winning at Wimbledon - and Rush first gracing my ears. I was 13 years old, my musical tastes moving away from the friend-influenced disco pop people were buying and leaning more towards rock. Black Sabbath, Thin Lizzy and Deep Purple were already on my radar.

It was the school summer break, that wonderful long six-week drag of no classrooms, teachers, homework or books. 'School's out for summer!' as Alice Cooper screamed. I'd often cycle over to see my cousins during this holiday, particularly my older cousin. John was 17 and had just got his first motorbike, so he was kinda cool. He was also a big rock fan and had far more vinyl than me. He'd always be playing something on his turntable when I went over.

This particular day he was playing Rush, a band I'd never heard of. A couple of months later, he turned up at my house with a tape he'd made of their brand new album, *A Farewell to Kings*. He said that what I'd heard previously was *2112*, apparently far too intricate for me to absorb as a first encounter, hence the *Farewell to Kings* tape. I played it to the point of being worn out every day on the walk to and from school and learned every word and note in a week.

My weekend job funded its purchase on vinyl, followed swiftly by *2112*. I had to go to specialist shops in the city centre to get the earlier albums, as they still weren't a well known band and local record shops didn't stock them. Later that year that John told me Rush were touring the UK in the New Year and did I fancy going? Hell yes! The venue was packed, the atmosphere electric, the show beyond amazing. I was now well and truly in a world that would see me through all of the ups and downs of life for the best part of the next 40 years.

I attended every tour and UK show after that; the multi-nighters at the NEC on the *Signals* tour, with different view points each night. If the Odeon had been packed, Stafford Bingley Hall in 1979 was beyond packed, dangerously so as it turned out. Apparently the show was oversold – 100 per cent oversold as people reported. A venue that had maybe a 5,000 to 6,000 capacity had twice that rammed inside! It was literally a sardine-can experience. But it was still a great night and remains the only show where I failed to buy either a tour shirt or a programme. The merchandise stand was closed for 'safety reasons' by all accounts.

APOLLO THEATRE

17 FEBRUARY 1978, GLASGOW, UK

I WAS THERE: BRIAN PETERS, AGE 17

My first big proper gig was on the suggestion of a friend. I was still sweet 17 and in my final year of school. Living in Glasgow, the Apollo was legendary far beyond our area. AC/DC, Status Quo, Roxy Music, Alice Cooper and others have recorded live albums there and it was probably the top live venue in the UK for atmosphere and crowd reaction. Paul McCartney described how freaked out he was by seeing the balconies visibly move during a Wings show, and that was

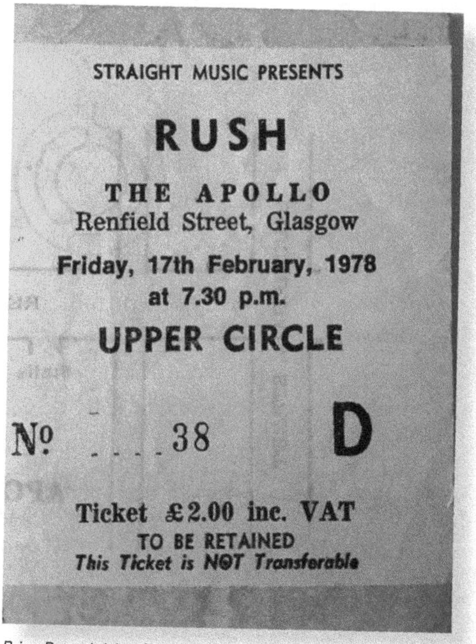

Brian Peters' ticket for the 1978 Glasgow show

nothing unusual. It's slightly less scary than it sounds as the balconies were designed to move a bit, if need be, but to do so that much, visibly from the stage, with chunks of plaster flaking off and onto the heads of those in the stalls below, was probably far beyond what the original design allowed for. That was many years before hordes of long-haired rock fans would descend, as if from Babylon, bouncing on the seats, playing air guitar and singing along at volume, with a hard time guaranteed for any acts that didn't cut it live.

Not knowing Rush from Roger Whittaker at the time, I decided to go give them a listen in the local record shop near school, handily called Listen, where the staff would kindly put albums on so you could listen on headphones if they judged the band worthy of attention. One side of *2112* and a bit of *A Farewell to Kings* was enough to persuade me.

We got decent seats near the front of the circle, the lower of the two balconies. We turned up early enough to see the support. The Tyla Gang were described as 'journeyman rock' in the programme. When they went off, gig virgins as we were and with good seats to observe the rituals, we watched their amps and other gear be quickly cleared away and…what's this? A carpet? I can't remember now whether it was already there or rolled back somehow, but once in full view it looked like power trio Rush were going for a homely living room feel, perhaps with flasks of tea rather than the Jack Daniels. Either that or they were trying to create a rather well furnished garage. It looked a bit like an Afghan rug, with tassles at the edges.

Soon enough, after the roadies were done their prep, plunking guitar strings - 'one choo! choo! choo! one choo!' mic tests and so on - the lights dimmed and the dry ice started to creep across the stage. We saw torch lights and shadowy figures come on stage in what were probably flowing robes. It might have been 1978, but it looked like Geddy and Alex had not paid much attention to the punk wave that had swept across the UK only the year before. Seconds later, perhaps after a polite 'hello Glasgow!' it all kicked off. Bang!

Lights, music, more dry ice. I recognised all the songs from *2112* and *A Farewell to Kings*, which I'd had a proper listen to by then, and remember really enjoying the show. What's more, what's this - a genuinely interesting drum solo that wasn't just an opportunity for the rest of the band - and a large proportion of the audience - to go to the toilet?

Rush played long songs - some really long songs - and Geddy Lee sang in a distinctively high pitched falsetto, but this was live music and I was loving it. The songs tended to build, move through phases, with crescendos at some point. I had bought into punk alright, which was all about power and attitude and simplicity, but I started off on Pink Floyd so liked my long ambitious songs too. Why not love the best of both?

I saw Rush again in 1979. With me now at college, a crowd of us met up in the Strathclyde University beer bar that afternoon so we were in high spirits by the time we left, on a lovely warm and sunny late April evening which is still clear in my memory. Lovely and warm and blue-skied by Glasgow standards, at least, and not so busy either at that time of day.

We walked across the bridge near Queen Street and were stopped by two policemen for what they took to be our loud rendition of controversial, possibly sectarian, lyrics, which remain a touchy subject in Glasgow. They took some convincing that our shouting, as you could hardly call it singing, 'We are the priests of the temples of Syrinx' at our fullest lung power, with little sense of tune or melody, was not offensive to local sensitivities, and didn't warrant at least a night in the cells.

The police didn't look like rock fans but they eventually let us go with a warning, and I bet they still are none the wiser about 'Cygnus-X1: Book II' or anything else by Rush. Yes, *Hemispheres* was in the shops by then. We had tickets for the stalls that night, so I didn't get to see whether there was a carpet again, but I do remember it being rather loud, but as dynamic and powerful as any punk band.

We caught the end of Max Webster but were too late to get the flexidisc single being given away for free before the gig, but it was another heady night. I remember punching the air in time to the dynamics on stage and managed to avoid dislocating my wrist or neck somehow. But I felt rather dislocated the next day.

I wish I could download these little bits of videotape still in my head from that night for upload to YouTube to show you what I'm on about. What a night. What a Rush. RIP Neil.

I WAS THERE: IAN MACLAREN, AGE 17

Ian MacLaren was at the Apollo in Glasgow

I was listening to Emerson Lake & Palmer and a bit of Yes. But I also loved Uriah Heep. I had a friend in Ayr with a lot of musical connections; other friends at school with big brothers. He borrowed this album in early 1977 called *2112* and played it to me one day. I thought it was amazing. It was in the days when we couldn't always afford to buy albums so I got a C90 cassette and put it on one side of the C90 and he did the same. Later that year he got *All the World's a Stage*. I got a Saturday job and used my money to buy albums. Having to decide between *2112* and *All the World's a Stage*, I went for the latter because it was a double album live and had side one of *2112* on it. I thought that was an absolutely amazing album, and I still do. A few weeks later, I had saved up a bit more money and *A Farewell to Kings* came out so I bought that. I loved it – 'Xanadu', 'Madrigal' and 'Closer to the Heart'.

The first time they played Glasgow was June 1977. I was too young to go. They played Glasgow again in February '78 with *A Farewell to Kings* and again I was a bit too young. But my mate who got me into them went to that gig and said it was amazing. After that I vowed I would go and see them the following year.

So 1979 and the *Hemispheres* tour was the first time I saw them and I was blown away. I took the train in. It was only 50 minutes. But I'd heard that it was going to be a long gig. A friend's mum or dad picked us up and took us all back afterwards.

I was four rows from the front, in the circle, so had a really good view right down onto the top of the stage. They opened up with 'Anthem' and then went into 'A Passage to Bangkok' and then 'Xanadu' and then a whole load of stuff from *Hemispheres*. They played for about two and a half hours. I was just in awe of Neil Peart's drum kit and the twin-necked guitar and bass of Alex and Geddy. It was Glasgow and the crowd were as loud as the band. My favourites that night were 'A Passage to Bangkok', 'The Trees' and 'Cygnus'.

A few weeks after the *Hemispheres* gig I'd heard the Pinkpop show on *The Friday Rock Show* and recorded it on my tape recorder. It was a pretty ropey recording but it did me at the time. They remastered *Hemispheres* a couple of years ago and put the cleaned up version of the Pinkpop gig out with it. It brought back so many memories.

I WAS THERE: IAN ROULSTON

As a teenager, I played a lot of sport. I was as fit as a fiddle without being a fitness fanatic. But in 1977 I sustained an ankle injury which stopped me from playing. One October Saturday morning, I decided to go and watch my team play. But before the game started, I walked up to the small music shop to purchase *News of the World* by Queen, which had only just been released. But with this being a small music outlet, new releases weren't always 'new' by the time they arrived in this particular shop, and *News of the World* wasn't in stock. I was determined not to leave the shop without a purchase. I stumbled across *A Farewell to Kings*. I bought it. It was a purchase that would change my reading habits. Change my intellectual outlook. Change how I looked and approached things in general. It changed my life.

I'd heard *2112* and *All the World's a Stage* and been relatively impressed but not bought them. I remembered Geoff Barton in *Sounds* magazine giving *A Farewell to Kings* five stars. 'OK,' I thought. 'What's to lose? Just £3.99 of my hard earned paper round money.' Once it was on my turntable I was transfixed. I'd just bought an album by the world's smallest symphony orchestra; classical guitars, tubular bells, glockenspiels and xylophones. Compositions like I had never heard before. I was 15 and I had grown musically in 11 minutes and two seconds of 'Xanadu'. And my mates hadn't heard of Rush. This was my band now. And you're not getting near them!

The back catalogue was purchased within two months. I scanned the music press to find out when this trio were touring. I had to see them. Then, finally – yes - the tour was to take place in the winter of 1978.

It was a particularly hard winter in 1978. Snow seemed to be on the ground for months. Where I lived was on the top of a hill that dropped down to a small valley river bed to a field that sat opposite my house. The field rose at a 45 degree angle up the other side of the hill. It was as big as a football park. It took ages but I entered the field and used my feet to scrape away the snow down to the grass and emblazon in bold capitals, 'RUSH'. This logo took up the whole field and was unmissable. And because of a thick overnight freeze, it was there for around six weeks. Not only could I see it from my bedroom window, everyone who walked down the path saw it. It was the talk of the area for weeks.

The Friday of the gig, I was beside myself with excitement. Glasgow Apollo was an atmospheric place at the best of times. But it was then I realised the Rush philosophy of 'more being more'. The souvenir programmes were of a better quality.

The t-shirts were of a better quality. Even the fans appeared to be a cut above your average gig-goer. I remember sitting there for an hour, staring at the cover of Neil's kit, just desperate for it to get pulled away so I could see the magnificent, almost pornographic quality that was the Slingerlands. Even when the white shag pile was rolled out on the stage before the opening bars of 'Bastille Day', you just knew these three were different.

The two and a half hours on stage passed in a microsecond. I just never wanted them to stop. The sound was magnificent. The white Gibson 355 and Ricky 4002 looked resplendent. As for the double-necks... well, more is more, isn't it? And don't get me started on the Prof's kit. It looked as big as the Great Wall of China!

I was gone, changed forever, and in tears most of the time, just with emotion. How can three guys do this? I wanted to see them every day for the rest of my life. Unfortunately I then had to wait until June of 1979 when I saw them three nights running on the *Hemispheres* tour. Between 1978 and 1982 I saw my heroes 13 times. But nothing will ever be as magnificent as that freezing cold Friday in February.

So back to the start. That injury? The most pleasurable pain ever. Geddy, Neil and Alex. Thank you for making me be me.

HAMMERSMITH ODEON

19 & 20 FEBRUARY 1978, LONDON, UK

I WAS THERE: STEVE GRIFFITHS, AGE 16

My friends at the time and I went down on the train. We had some pictures of Rush from *Sounds* magazine. They were never good with the fashion but we tried to imitate the look. And we got some looks!

My most memorable show was probably *Hold Your Fire* at the NEC because they recorded some of *A Show of Hands* there. I think they played Thursday night, had Friday off and then did Saturday and Sunday. We saw them Thursday and Saturday. Five of us drove down to Birmingham in a rented Fiesta and slept – or tried to - in the car Friday night. I got to meet Geddy and Alex on the Thursday. We knew where they were staying. We were hanging by the hotel and we saw Geddy just hanging around in the foyer. Then Alex turned up and they came out to meet the eight or nine of us that were waiting outside. I never met Neil. It was always Geddy and Alex. I did see Neil once. It was the *Time Machine* tour at Manchester Arena. That was pretty cool. He was never the one for meeting people.

Neil's lyrics seemed to mean something to everybody who listened to them. Whatever song it was meant something. As the years have gone by - I know it's a cliché but - they've helped me with my life. I cried like a baby when Neil passed away, because I knew that was it. I think some of the fans thought that they were going to do more. With the sad passing of Neil, everybody knew that was it.

I took the wife to see them at Birmingham on the *Clockwork Angels* tour. I got to meet Howard, the lighting director, and had my photograph taken with him. I said to him, 'Any chance of you getting me Rush's signatures on the *Clockwork Angels* ticket?' He said, 'No, not right now. But if you're going to Manchester, catch up with me and I'll get it done for you.' And he did. I caught him before the show and he got the ticket signed for me. He kept his promise. I was pretty chuffed.

EMPIRE THEATRE

25 FEBRUARY 1978, LIVERPOOL, UK

I WAS THERE: NICK BELLIS, AGE 15

I've been a sound engineer for 25 years and toured all over Europe with major bands and Rush definitely started it!

The first time I heard them was on *The Old Grey Whistle Test*, when they played about two and a half minutes of the video of 'Xanadu'. Being a drummer, Neil Peart's kit caught my eye and I bought *A Farewell to Kings*. I was a metal fan but a bit too young for Led Zeppelin. I wanted something more current and that was where AC/DC and Rush came in. I was lucky to see AC/DC with Bon Scott the same year I saw Rush and *A Farewell to Kings*. I went with a mate called Alan Kelly, another drummer. We saw a load of gigs in them days. I've got no pictures from that gig. No mobile phones. No cameras. The pictures from that gig are in my head.

My dad was a drummer so he got me into drums. I was playing drums from the age of 13 and Neil was definitely the influence for me. My dad appreciated Neil Peart. I loved Neil but every time I saw him I wanted to set fire to my drum kit because I was never going to be as good as him! He encouraged me and discouraged me all on the same album.

At the Empire I remember they played 'Xanadu'. It was all in the days before proper rock 'n' roll lighting and moving lights and stuff. They had dry ice and I remember it poured over the stage. We were in row three from the front, which was brilliant, but the two rows in front of me were literally covered in dry ice and the audience sat there wouldn't have been able to see the stage!

For the *Time Machine* tour I'd already seen them in Manchester but they played the O2 and I was in London with work. I worked for a company that had put the rear-hang system in the O2. When big bands come in they bring their own PA but sometimes they don't fly speakers at the back because it's a pain in the arse so they just tie into the existing system at the back of the venue. I knew who babysat the PA. He said, 'Rush are playing London tonight' and I said, 'Are you working today? Can you get us in?'

Although he was my age, he'd never heard of Rush. He got me in for the soundcheck. Neil doesn't soundcheck, but it was great seeing Alex. When I went backstage, Alex was literally five feet in front of me. I was walking behind him as he went to check his guitar. Half of me wanted to grab hold of him and say, 'Alex I love you, you're amazing.' And the other half was obviously being very professional, because when you work with a million bands it's the unwritten rule that you don't mither them. To this day I regret that. Alex is dead sound. I'm sure he would have been fine.

I had AC/DC, Kiss and Rush patches which I asked my mum to sew onto my jeans, which is not the most rock'n'roll thing to do. But we all did it, didn't we? I've still got the programmes from the *Farewell to Kings* and *Hemispheres* tours. I had them framed. It's mad that you can go to a rock gig and do all that headbanging and still come home with a programme all in one piece, not covered in ale or something.

If you're a teenage girl who's heartbroken, there's lots of pop bands for you. AC/DC was about how many birds can you shag? It was totally rock 'n' roll. Bon Scott's lyrics were fun but totally over the top and we all had a laugh but we knew it wasn't real. But Rush always have a song for you. Neil came along and started writing lyrics that meant a bit more. They were heartfelt lyrics that stuck with you, reminding you of when you were happy or when you were sad. But they were still a rock band – the guitar's on 20, they've still got 500 toms.

When I heard 'Tom Sawyer' I was like, 'Oh my god, they've gone poppy - but in a brilliant way!' They said that most of their fans are the guy who doesn't jump in the car and drive off with the girl. We're the guys who are watching that guy and thinking 'jammy bastard'. And they played to that. 90 per cent of the audience were fellahs.

I remember hearing 'La Villa Strangiato' on the radio before it was released and thinking 'what the fuck was that?' And 'Cygnus'? That was mad. I didn't do drugs then and I don't do them now but even totally sober that was brilliant. They always were and always will be my favourite band. I bought three copies of *A Farewell to Kings* because I literally wore them out.

It does become cold when bands play arenas. To see them at Liverpool Empire with two and a half thousand capacity was just brilliant.

COLSTON HALL

26 FEBRUARY 1978, BRISTOL, UK

I WAS THERE: DAVID EDDOLLS, AGE 16

A friend brought over *A Farewell to Kings* and we listened on our stereo. I had never heard anything like 'Xanadu'. I bought the album. At the Colston Hall, they were supported by a band called Stray but the fans only wanted to hear the headliners. This was my first ever Rush gig so I wasn't familiar with some of the music. I remember lots of dry ice and fans on their feet, come to witness this talented band from Canada. Rush came back to Bristol in May 1979 for the *Tour of the Hemispheres* and did two more nights at the Colston Hall. I attended both; it was the last time they ever played Bristol.

We saw that Rush were becoming more and more popular. Two shows were added to the *Permanent Waves* tour at the New Bingley Hall that autumn and although it was a long drive I had to be there. They showcased two songs from the forthcoming album, 'The Spirit of Radio' and 'Freewill'. I went on to see many other shows including the five-nighter at London's Hammersmith Odeon and the Brighton Centre. The last time I got to see them live was on the *Clockwork Angels* tour at the O2 in London in 2013. They never came back to the UK again after that.

APOLLO THEATRE

23 & 24 FEBRUARY 1978, MANCHESTER, UK

I WAS THERE: MARK APPLETON, AGE 15

I heard 'Bastille Day' on the radio and was immediately hooked. The most striking aspect was Geddy's vocals. Soon after I bought the double live album *All the World's a Stage* along with *2112* and then I was waiting like so many with bated breath for the release of the *A Farewell to Kings* album and the accompanying tour. It was one of my first ever concerts, and I always managed at least one date on all their subsequent UK tours. That first one was a life changing experience. I was absolutely captivated by everything about the show and the band.

Rush just didn't disappoint. I'm a guitarist myself and after this show I spent many years trying to emulate my heroes, especially Alex Lifeson, and unashamedly writing thinly veiled 'imitation' songs using sci-fi themes or mythological warrior tales.

I WAS THERE: ANDREW FETHERS, AGE 16

I already had a number of Rush albums and *All the World's a Stage* was on my turntable constantly. Half a dozen of us got the train from Macclesfield and then walked down to the Apollo, excitement growing with every step. I bought a programme as we entered and still have it to this day. How I managed to keep it in good condition that night I'll never know, but it is near perfect to this day.

We were in the stalls and towards the back but not long after the gig started – with 'Bastille Day' –

Andrew Fethers caught Neil's drum stick at Manchester Apollo

there was a mad rush down to the front and we all got pretty close. As it was my first big venue gig I was just completely taken in by the whole thing. The set list was amazing, mostly taken from *All the World's a Stage*. Neil's drum solo and the light show - the whole thing - was just phenomenal. At the end of the gig, the lights went up and as the band walked towards the front of the stage to acknowledge the applause, Neil threw one of his sticks and it just came straight to me and I caught it first time! No scrabbling around fighting with others. I couldn't believe it and nor could any of my mates. We travelled back to Macc on the train later that night still buzzing – the programme, the drum stick and a heap of memories.

I still have the drum stick. It is battered at the thick end as Neil always used to play holding the thinner end to get more power and volume. In the last line of his programme notes, Neil said, 'I use Promark 747 drumsticks with the varnish sanded off the gripping area', which is exactly how the drumstick looks. I never knew what to do with it. It has hardly come out of safe keeping but I do wonder if anyone would be interested in buying it. It is absolutely 100% genuine. But there's only one, so no good for playing!

GREENSBORO COLISEUM

18 MARCH 1978, GREENSBORO, NORTH CAROLINA

I WAS THERE: KEITH FULP

I remember me and my bud Pete trying to win Rush tickets on the radio in 1977. Rush had a live album out which was becoming quite popular. I owned Kiss *Alive*, *Yessongs* and of course *Frampton Comes Alive*. I was 15, Pete 14. We would smoke pot and listen to Rush and then go to Mayberrys Ice Cream to get the munching on. Well we weren't able to come up with the tickets. $7.00? Really? Then *A Farewell to Kings* came out. We were on a mission. A mission from God. We both were able find the scratch and were determined to see the By-tor/ Snow Dog battle in person. We bought our tickets at the Record Bar, 'cause that's where all the records are!

Keith Fulp was at Greensboro Coliseum

Dilemma number two. How were we going to get to Greensboro Coliseum, 85 miles away? The clock was ticking. We were young and our older friends weren't interested in Geddy's voice. Mmm, what to do? My pops had an old machine. It was a shiny car, a 1964 and a half Mustang .I begged. My dad was – is – a huge science fiction geek to the point that he didn't care for *Star Wars*, Isaac Asimov and Ray Bradbury. He had a couple of books by Rand. Anyway, he thought about it and decided he would go to the Greensboro Library and drop us off at the venue. We were ecstatic.

The seats weren't crazy good but Pete and I were there! The show was wonderful, every note. The Professor was the best. I started playing pots and pans the next day and 42 years later I still play my drums. We were able to get stoned with new found friends and had a blast with the Alex/Geddy Snowdon battle. The *Farewell to Kings* material changed my young Hemisphere mind. After the show we met up with my dad, who had been kicked out of the library due to closing. He was able to come in and watch the encores – 'Working Man', 'Fly by Night' and 'In the Mood'. He said he loved it. Good stuff said by the opera-loving guy. That night changed my perspective on music. FM radio would not be my go to anymore. Long live the music. God bless Rush and their awesome fans. RIP Neil Peart. I love y'all, kanooks.

METRO CENTRE

8 APRIL 1978, HALIFAX, CANADA

I WAS THERE: BRIAN IVANY

I saw them 27 times. The first time was in Halifax, Nova Scotia with Ian Thomas, Max Webster and then the boys. It was 7.50 Canadian dollars a ticket. It was amazing.

The *Archives* tour ran through May 1978 and consisted of 12 shows.

ALPINE VALLEY MUSIC THEATRE

28 MAY 1978, EAST TROY, WISCONSIN

I WAS THERE: JENNIFER DANIELS-LABONTE

I saw them multiple times. They were most impressive, especially Neil Peart. I loved his drum kit and I love their writing. *A Farewell to Kings* kind of opened the door for me and then I went back and became a fan of their earlier work.

I WAS THERE: DAVE JOSEPH

My first Rush album was *Fly by Night*. *2112* was a game changer and Alex became my guitar hero. I went to my first show with my eventual wife, Jan. My mother-in-law Judy also became a Rush fan and went with us to several concerts. She continued to do so after we moved to Pennsylvania. Alpine Valley in Wisconsin was my favourite venue to see them. I remember hearing 'Xanadu' live for the first time there on the *Farewell to*

Kings tour. As a guitarist, being able to figure out the guitar 'by ear' along with Geddy's bass was one of my greatest accomplishments. Overall, I was able to see them live 14 times. A true blessing!

The *Tour of the Hemispheres* started on 14 October 1978 in Kingston, Ontario in Canada and concluded eight months later on 4 June 1979 in Geleen, The Netherlands. The tour took in 110 North American dates before shifting to the UK (19 shows) and Continental Europe (12 shows).

NORTH BAY MEMORIAL GARDENS

17 OCTOBER 1978, ONTARIO, CANADA

I WAS THERE: JAMIE TOEPPNER

Jamie named his dog Geddy after a certain bass player

Back in the 70s kids in their early teens sometimes liked to get together with their friends and smoke a little of that wacky tabaky, contemplating life and existence and trying to figure out the meaning of songs. I had listened to Rush's first album, *Caress of Steel*, and when *2112* came out I got totally caught up in its complexity and spent many hours reading the lyrics and listening with headphones... there was something there I couldn't explain. It was like there was a missing track.

When the *Tour of the Hemispheres* was announced I couldn't believe they were coming to North Bay, near my hometown of Powassan. When they played parts of '2112' at the end, they were flashing these super bright lights as 'Attention all planets of the solar federation' blared. It was almost like they had come to take us away. It might have been that good weed though.

For all these years I am still a fan, although they kind of left me behind after *Permanent Waves*. In 2009 my wife and I bought an English Springer Spaniel. Picking a name is never easy, unless of course you are a Rush fan! We called him Geddy Lee, but just Geddy for short. My dream was that one day Geddy might drop over to meet my Geddy, and bring along his bass! Sadly my Geddy passed away in March 2019.

TOLEDO SPORTS ARENA

3 DECEMBER 1978, TOLEDO, OHIO

I WAS THERE: SEAN NORMAN, AGE 15

They were just starting to hit the big time. They didn't do very well with the *Caress of Steel* album but *2112* resonated with so many fans. People could relate to the story that Neil had written. It was their breakthrough success.

The sports arena was a smaller venue, a hockey rink and quite the dump, but all the bands you could ever want to see stopped there. Rush were touring in support of the *Hemispheres* album. I remember I only paid $6.50 to get in, quite a deal compared to the prices you would have to pay nowadays. Golden Earring played for about 45 minutes to an hour and then Rush played for two hours and 20 minutes. It blew me away. For just three guys it sounded unbelievable. One of the highlights of the show was when they played 'The Trees'. They also played a lot of stuff from their earlier albums.

I remember the sound of Geddy's bass playing coming through the speakers. It was the most intense bass guitar sound I'd ever heard except for John Entwistle of The Who, who Geddy considered one of his biggest influences on bass guitar. Neil had a massive drum set. Not as big as it became later on some of their tours, but he had a lot of bells and chimes, a big gong, wood blocks and all kinds of percussion. His drum solo was super, like nothing I've ever seen before. I left that show an even bigger fan of Rush and saw them probably five or six more times over the years.

PALLADIUM

13 JANUARY 1979, NEW YORK, NEW YORK

I WAS THERE: PAUL ENEA

In 1977 I was a long-haired rocker kid playing drums, wearing jean jackets and Capezios and listening to Kiss. At school, my friend's older brother Nicky turned on his brother Laurence to *2112*. He brought the album to school one afternoon in eighth grade, where Mr Nichols and three of my friends listened to side one, and some songs on *All the World's a Stage*. It started a snowball effect that even By-Tor could never challenge!

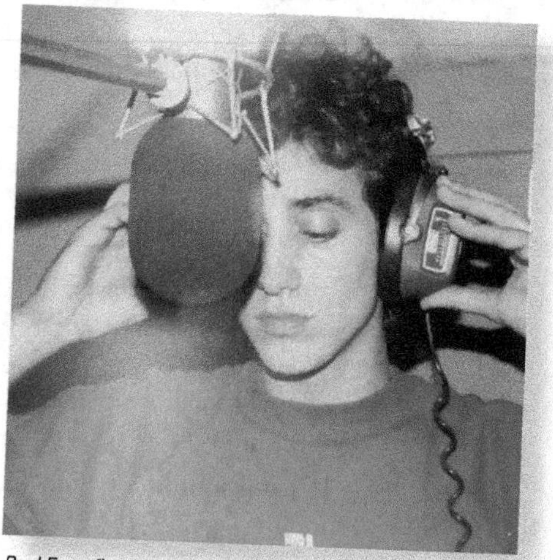

Paul Enea first saw Rush in 1979

All my closest school buddies got turned on to Rush just in time for the release of *A Farewell to Kings*. But for some reason what I heard at school and what I heard on that album was audibly different. The instrumentation sounded tight, kingly and royal, as the album art would suggested, but Geddy's voice was so high I thought my record was pressed at the wrong speed. I tried returning it to the record store. The store owner said,

'Nope, that's just his voice!' So I got stuck giving it another chance and, after three more spins, Rush would become a lifelong obsession.

Shortly thereafter, my brother Frank and I would find a bass player and we formed Triad, probably one of the very earliest Rush tribute bands around. We later performed music by other bands, but the bulk of our set was taken up by epics like 'La Villa Strangiato' and '2112' - in their entirety! When I met Geddy and Alex at the premiere of *Beyond the Lighted Stage* I told Geddy I was in a Rush cover band back in 1978 he was visibly impressed. Meeting Alex and Geddy that night was also a highlight I'll never forget.

Through the years, as a kid struggling with my sexuality, very few rock bands gave me the feeling Rush did. I loved the delicate and educational approach to the lyrics, and mostly the fantasy and escape that was necessary for me to survive during very trying times in my life. Later, Neil wrote a song, 'Nobody's Hero', which made me feel confident I had loved a band that was not only talented, but understood about life and diversity. Because of Rush, I was able to get through my teen years with just the right amount of angst and rebellion, always tempered by thoughtfulness and freewill.

As far as regrets, I have a few: I had seen every tour with the exception of *Test for Echo*, and the very last tour, thinking I would get another chance to see them, but that was not to be. But, having seen them during the *Hemispheres* tour in 1979, I can say that it set me up for my life's greatest musical journey - a journey that informed every part of my life.

Neil made me want to be better at everything I did, and I think it worked. I realise, now that I've worked for Paul McCartney for the last 18 years as a graphic designer, that it was due to the standard of perfection and pursuit of excellence that Neil and Rush instilled in me.

MEMORIAL AUDITORIUM

24 JANUARY 1979, BUFFALO, NEW YORK

I WAS THERE: DAVID CHAPMAN

David Chapman meets Geddy

As a young teenager I was really into music. I lived outside of Buffalo, New York, and I could pick up radio stations out of Toronto. Every once in a while, they'd play this group and I'd like their music. I would sit with my tape player and as soon as one of those songs came on, I'd record it. It took me a while to figure out who the band was but I found out it was Rush. I'd listen to those radio stations coming out of

Toronto and try to hear as much as I could. I kept bugging my mom: 'I like this group and I'd like to get some of their music.' She bought me *Hemispheres* and *2112* and that just had me glued.

A year or so later, and without letting me know, she bought my older brother and me concert tickets. On the day of the show he said, 'Come on, I'm taking you to a concert.' Rush at the Memorial Auditorium. I sat through the whole concert just mesmerised. These guys were spot on and it sounded like I was listening to the recordings. The music itself just touched me. So for the rest of my life I'm a Rush fan. My brother hated the concert. He wishes he had never gone.

Every time they came on tour, I'd take friends and say, 'You've got to see these guys. Their light show is incredible. Their sound and the music are awesome. Here, check out some of the lyrics.' I got to see them in Toronto a few times. It was spectacular to see them in their home town. My friends know me as a Rush fan. And it's been said before about them being the soundtrack to your life, but it's absolutely true. Everything I've been through in my life, Rush has been right there. They've been able to lift me up when I'm down. They're with me when I'm happy. It's just incredible.

I bought into Neil's philosophy. 'You don't know me and I don't know you and I appreciate your music but I'm not going to go find you somewhere or stalk you.'

But when Geddy had a book signing in Denver I had to go, because I live in Colorado. Geddy was spectacular. We talked about baseball. He was so friendly and so nice. That was a bucket list item, just to meet him in person and say, 'Thank you for all these years of music.'

Their music is so intricate in how it's put together. There's a lot of technical skill. It keeps me going from song to song. 'La Villa Strangiato' is so complex and I never get bored with it.

I missed the Buffalo *R40* show but I took a bus to Kansas City and saw it there. And then I was flying back to Buffalo but I ran into a couple of people at the concert and one lady that I met had never seen them before and after that show she said, 'Let's go to Denver to see them!' so I went to Denver to see them again. Because I knew in my kind this would be the final tour. They did the right thing going out on top. They were spectacular shows. I'm glad I went. I saw them 30 times altogether.

I was at a party for a friend of mine when I saw a Facebook post about Neil's passing. I thought, 'This can't be true.' But I checked 'real' sources and they said the same thing. I was just devastated. I came home. I cried. I put on Rush music. I put on Rush videos. I watched concerts. And I'm still doing it. But it is final. There is no more Rush.

SAM HOUSTON COLISEUM

1 MARCH 1979, HOUSTON, TEXAS

I WAS THERE: LELAND CARR, AGE 15

I saw them on *Don Kirshner's Rock Concert* in 1975. My neighbour played *2112*, *All the World's a Stage* and *A Farewell to Kings* and I became a lifelong fan. I saw them a total of 25 times starting with the *Hemispheres* tour. I only missed three tours after that, due to military obligations. I have fond memories of driving long distances to some concerts. All Rush concerts were unreal. They put on the greatest show on Earth, period. *Hemispheres* had a great impact on me and my psyche and I have so many great memories of my life with the greatest band ever. I saw them first row centre on the *R30* tour and made eye contact with Neil. I sat on the first few rows on several occasions. I really do miss my boys!

NASSAU COLISEUM

6 APRIL 1979, UNIONDALE, NEW YORK

Rush at Nassau Coliseum – photo Tony Ferrari

I WAS THERE: TONY FERRARI

When I purchased tickets for their *Hemispheres* show I magically scored third centre row. Next day at school I definitely had some bragging rights and the news spread like wildfire. So there I am, dead centre and a few feet from the stage, and Neil goes into his drum solo. When he finished he threw one of his drum sticks towards the audience. I was definitely up on my seat then. As I watched the stick twirling in the air it seemed to be moving in slow motion. It was coming right for me as I reached up to grab it but there were a few problems. I was standing on my seat, up on my toes and holding a camera, not to mention getting bumped a bit from other people. The stick lands into my right hand while I'm a bit off balance and then bounces out. By the time I jump down from my seat and turn around to find the stick, thousands of people are crammed in around me. This one guy proudly stands up with the drum stick and I swing my arm with all my might, trying to grab it whilst declaring loudly that 'it was mine'. It wasn't meant to be.

I saw the *Permanent Waves* tour multiple times too. The band was starting to get radio airplay and I remember being happy at that. I had probably turned on half of my high school and all of my friends and their brothers, sisters and friends to Rush. It was amazing being at a concert with an audience of 16,000 people and when a certain drum fill was about to come up, you could hear and feel the entire audience (myself included) hold their breath, watch and listen to it being performed, and then exhale and yell, scream and applaud in utter joy. One night on the tour, as we once again held our breaths as Neil was about to execute one of his tremendous drum fills, one of the drum sticks broke in half and he performed the exact same and very difficult fill single handedly.

On another show on this tour, I was at a smaller venue in NYC and had fourth row seats in front of Alex, stage right. During one of the solos in '2112' Alex broke a string. By the time I was grabbing a friend and telling him, two of Alex's techs ran out, one on his knees, as they swapped out one guitar for another while Alex stood there and I swear he didn't miss a note of his solo.

APOLLO THEATRE

25 APRIL 1979, GLASGOW, UK

I WAS THERE: ANDY MURDOCH, AGE 17

I could not persuade any friends to come with but no problem. Maybe because I was on my own, I snagged a great seat about six rows from the front, as near the front as you'd want with the Apollo's notorious 12 foot high stage. Every seat had a flexidisc on it with excerpts from Max Webster's new LP, *A Million Vacations*. They were excellent. I remember the anticipation as they unveiled Neil's massive drum kit. Then they hit the stage in all their 70s pomp - kimonos, double-neck guitars, etc. The show was everything I'd hoped it would be. I swear to this day that Geddy hit me with his pick as he did the 12-string to bass switcheroo, but look as I might I could not find the little bugger. But I felt it! I saw them on *Permanent Waves* at Glasgow and then *Moving Pictures* at the cavernous Ingliston Showground just outside Edinburgh. Great shows both, but my first was incredible!

I WAS THERE: WILLIAM CAVIN, AGE 15

My brother was not a massive fan in terms of rock music, but did seem to buy the odd 'good' record. I think he probably bought them because some girl had mentioned it was good and he was smart that way. Heart's *Dreamboat Annie* is one that springs to mind, and then this strange-looking album with a derelict building site and what looked like a court jester or puppet without strings, perched on his throne. Who the hell are Rush and what is *A Farewell to Kings*?

So, it's 1977 and I am a 14-year-old kid who has not long been given his first guitar and wondering how it works. My parents were big into music. My father was a world class bagpipe player who had played the Green's Playhouse (soon to become the Glasgow Apollo) with the Joe Loss Orchestra. 'Modern' music had to be listened to with the headphones on. We only had one record player and that was in the family room so there was no escaping to your bedroom to play air guitar in those days. During the middle of the evening news, I switch on this record. Headphones on, volume as high as I dare, nice classical guitar start, what is this nice music, it's okay, then – boom!

By the time of the concert I had all the up-to-date albums, some borrowed on a long term basis from mates or copied onto cassette, but I still had no idea of what this would be like. We had to stand in the cold to queue for tickets and dodge the beggars who menacingly came up and down the gig queue, even though we all knew they earned more money than us from their day jobs. Don't even look at them: 'Keep yer heed doon.' Shuffle, shuffle and past the well renowned not-so-nice bouncers who were just looking to give someone a clout. Into the stalls and I am about halfway down, slightly to the left of stage.

Your feet stick to the carpeted floor just a little bit. I'm not sure what the world of health and safety would think today. It must have been a grand venue in its heyday, but this is now a really run down place. Of course, that makes it even better. It is ours, this is where the real people go, not the Saturday Night Fever dancing bars or nightclubs. I'm not sure I even want to sit on the seat that's been allotted to me but I know it won't be for long. The audience is full of people with combat jackets they were told came from Vietnam vets and adorned with metal badges and sewn-on patches of all the bands of the time. This is my kind of people. The smell of patchouli oil is heavy in the air.

So, I am through Max Webster without getting kicked into touch by the bouncers and then there is that bloody rubbish wait while they set up for the main act and all the 'one-two' from the road crew testing the mics. The lights go down now and we're full of excitement.

From the minute this started I was totally blown away to watch one of the greatest live bands of all time. I have seen many a concert at the Apollo and elsewhere and watched most of the considered 'greats' live. But this was it. This was new and fresh and powerful. As a budding guitarist, it was not only important that Alex Lifeson was just one of the most impressive guitarist ever to grace a stage but when that white EDS1275 twin neck came out with his almost matching coloured hair, he really did just look like the personification of the Rock God that the 80s rockers would try to emulate. Geddy Lee, an acquired taste as a singer to many, was just note perfect with bass notes to match and Neil Peart was just the greatest drummer ever. Here was a guy taking the drums to new heights. This instrument was not meant to be at the back keeping time, this was at the front driving the pace and feel.

By the time they hit 'La Villa Strangiato', I was absolutely shattered with the utter excitement of what I was watching. And this was only about halfway through. At the end, I remember heading round to the dingy lane at the side of the rundown old building and waiting to get in to have my *Hemispheres* programme signed. I went home with my ears almost bleeding with the ringing noise. Is it me going deaf from all that or do they just not play very loud these days? It would take until halfway through tomorrow before my hearing would fully return.

I watched so many gigs at the Apollo. I was lucky to take my son to see Rush again in Glasgow in their last show and hopefully his son will one day listen intently to this virtuoso experience. It always gave me a buzz to think that my father stood on the same stage as Zeppelin, Bowie, Genesis and Rush. And maybe, just maybe, he stood on the same spot as Lifeson did that day. But out of them all I doubt if any made more of an impact on the world of the total perfect musicians and Rock Gods. With the sad news of Neil Peart passing, we now have to say a fond Farewell to Kings. There are no rulers left to take over the Kingdom once commanded by Rush.

I WAS THERE: ALISTAIR BLACK, AGE 16

I saw Rush both nights at the Apollo on the 1979 *Hemispheres* and 1980 *Permanent Waves* tours. Rush had a magical element that set them apart from the other gigs I went to around that time - AC/DC, UFO, Motörhead, etc. One of the '79 gigs was the night before my arithmetic O grade exam and I had to lie to my parents about the exam date to get out.

Alistair Black parted company with Rush after 'musical differences'

Sadly, after *Moving Pictures* Rush and I suffered from musical differences and I never saw them again.

I WAS THERE: JAMES FORDYCE

One of my friends let me borrow his copy of *A Farewell to Kings*. I played the first track and hated it. Geddy Lee's voice was too high pitch for me so I turned it off, not liking it. Next day my friend said 'try it again' so I did. I loved it, so much so I went out and bought *All the World's a Stage*. The *Hemispheres* tour was coming to Glasgow so we got tickets and off we went. It was mesmerising. This was the Rush with the Japanese-type silk tops and the double-neck guitars. One year later the *Permanent Waves* tour came to town. As the roadies unveiled the drum kit, it is the only time I've seen a drum kit get a standing ovation. Due to work commitments I didn't get to see Rush again until the *R30* tour at the SECC. They didn't disappoint. It was Rush at the top of their game.

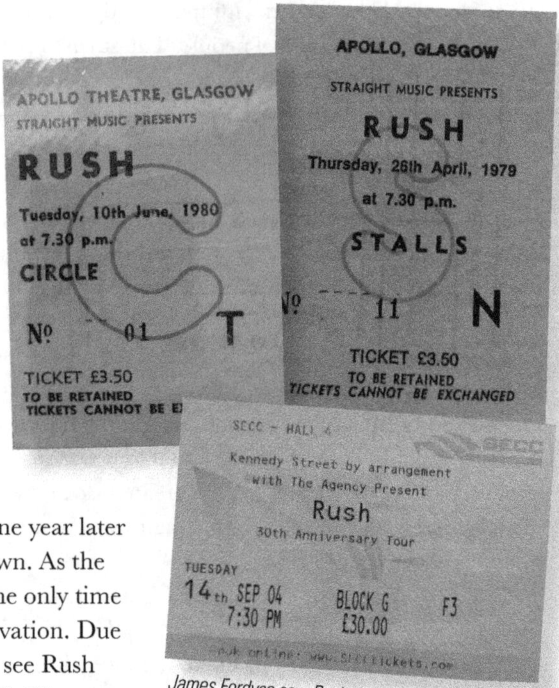

James Fordyce saw Rush three times in Scotland

ODEON THEATRE

28 APRIL 1979, EDINBURGH, UK

I WAS THERE: NIGEL FINLAY

I had only just got into Rush on the back of seeing them on *The Old Grey Whistle Test* doing 'Xanadu' back in '76. As for the concert, I think it was my first. The Odeon was a cinema and a fairy small venue but, as I recall, hot, loud and - as it was Rush - fantastic. They played plenty of back catalogue and, of course, the wonderful *Hemispheres*. I still have the programme somewhere.

Nigel Finlay remembers the Odeon show being 'hot, loud and fantastic'

APOLLO THEATRE

29 & 30 APRIL 1979, MANCHESTER, UK

I WAS THERE: MARK WELCH

I have seen Rush six times in the UK. My first show was the *Hemispheres* tour. The main thing I remember about this is the clarity of the sound, with no distortion. My next show wasn't until the *Roll the Bones* tour at the NEC. They started with 'Force Ten', another great show. The best ever was on the *R30* tour at Manchester Arena. It was the best ever instrumental intro and a three hour set list. I saw their next three visits to Manchester Arena. What can one say? They were always professional, always entertaining, and it was always a varied set list compared to the previous tour. Neil Peart... the one drum solo I always looked forward to.

I WAS THERE: MARK APPLETON

I went on to buy the *Archives* anthology of the first three albums and then it was the *Hemispheres* album and tour. Having listened to the Rocinante disappearing into a black hole, I was eager to hear the conclusion to the story. On the tour I went to both Manchester shows. Sober as a judge on the first night, watching and listening carefully, then a few beers on the second night and really rocking out – good plan! Not that there was any doubt, but those two shows cemented the band as my all time favourites. I met my future wife in the queue to buy the tickets. I met Geddy Lee on his 2019 book tour in 2019 and told him about meeting my wife. I said we weren't sure whether to thank him or blame him. He laughed so I think he knew I was joking!

I WAS THERE: GARY LUCAS

One of my mates came into school with *2112* and *A Farewell to Kings*. From that moment I was hooked. After going to a number of rock gigs with the likes of UFO and the Scorpions, tickets came along for the Rush *Hemispheres* tour. Tickets bought, we caught the bus into Manchester and went along to the Apollo in Ardwick. What can I say? From the opening bars of 'Anthem' we knew this was going to be some night.

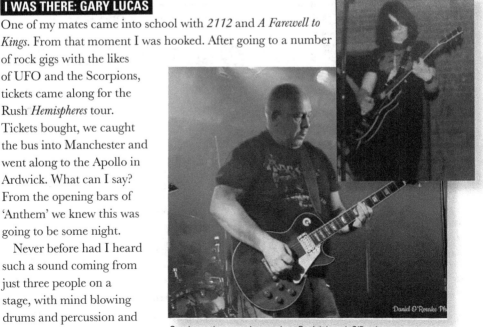

Never before had I heard such a sound coming from just three people on a stage, with mind blowing drums and percussion and

Gary Lucas then... and now - photo Daniel Joseph O'Rourke

with thunderous bass guitar licks that stood out on their own. Bass pedals and synths triggered by the feet of Geddy and the guitar mastery and complex chords and riffs of Lifeson. More tours followed, including the Bingley Hall gig later that year with the first drafts of 'Spirit of Radio' and 'Freewill' performed live for the very first time. They were in UK doing recordings for the *Permanent Waves* album.

The last time I saw them was on the *Time Machine* tour at Manchester Arena. I got very close to the stage that night and will never forget the set from all the decades. RIP Mr Peart. You were a man amongst boys in the drumming game and are sorely missed. I feel privileged to have witnessed their prowess throughout the years.

I WAS THERE: NIGEL R TAYLOR

I've seen Rush on every UK tour from '79 to their last in 2013, although I missed '88. Often I went multiple times per tour. I was into a lot of bands like Zep and Yes at the age of 11 due to having a brother five years older. Rush was on the recommendation of a school friend and then on seeing the cover of *All the World's a Stage*. Then a mutual friend, who was well into them and had seen the *Kings* tour, suggested we all go to see them in Manchester for their *Hemispheres* tour.

I managed front row tickets for Manchester 2004, bang in front of Geddy. I nearly caught a shirt he threw out but my cousin's husband grabbed it from my hand. He's about 30 stone so it would never fit him. I keep thinking of asking for it back.

John Reeves and friend Kurt then... and now

HAMMERSMITH ODEON

6 MAY 1979, LONDON, UK

I WAS THERE: JOHN REEVES, AGE 14

I saw countless bands years ago, and still do. But Rush is the one that sticks in my mind because it's pretty much the first one I went to outside of seeing Iron Maiden in my local pub, the Ruskin Arms in East Ham, where they started out.

My friend and I grew up in Purfleet in Essex, right on the Dartford tunnel. We couldn't really afford music then. But one of us would scrape up enough money to buy an album and we were into the heavy rock kind of things. The *Hemispheres* album was purchased on the strength of the cover, with the brain and the guy standing on it. We got that home and pretty much fell in love with it straight away. It was a bit different from your British heavy metal. There was something more going on there that was a lot more technical.

At the age of 14 I'd never really ventured too far into London, even though it was 20 miles down the road. A geography teacher at my comprehensive school in Essex overheard me talking about Rush. I didn't really get on with this guy. I was always tapping on the desk, like a drummer without a drum kit, and always getting told off for it. That's probably the one thing people remember me for from school. But - bless him - he came up to me and said, 'I've got a friend who owns a ticket agency. Would you like me to make some enquiries into whether I can get a couple of tickets for you?' A few days later he dropped a couple of tickets in my hand. It was quite a nice thing really because we were a bit afraid to go up to London and I had no idea how to get tickets. There were no computers then or anything. I seem to remember they were £2.50.

The punk thing was going on. It was the middle of London, and right across London as well. But we decided we were going to make a day of it, to get there and get our bearings. So we were up there for ten o'clock in the morning. We met the band at about two o'clock. We were just hanging around at the back of the stage door. The tour bus was outside and we got taken on that. We got scarves and all kinds of stuff. I got a pair of Neil Peart's drumsticks. He used a drumstick called a Promark 747. I haven't got them any more.

My friend Kurt clearly remembers Neil Peart getting a little frustrated with me and several other kids – there were probably 20 or 30 of us out there – and him picking me up and moving me to one side, I was that excited to see him.

My overriding memory, not knowing what other bands were like apart from pub bands, is that they were absolutely note perfect. In my wildest dreams, I didn't think Alex Lifeson could play 'La Villa Strangiato' and all that kind of stuff from *A Farewell to Kings* and *Hemispheres*. They all had the long hair.I saw them many times afterwards. But that's the one I remember more than anything.

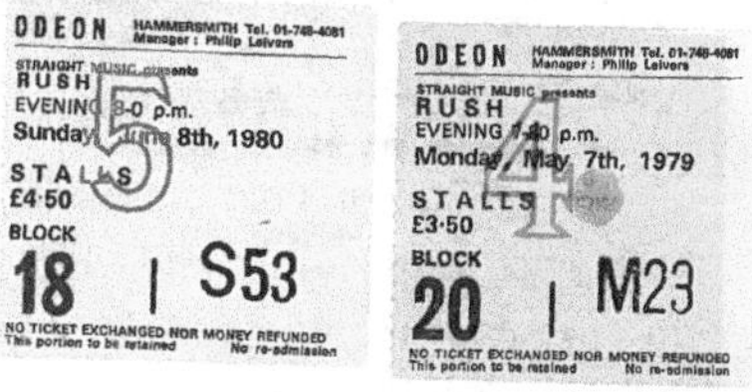

I WAS THERE: ANDREW SMYTH

Our group of friends were always bonkers about music, and it was a case in 1977 of someone saying, 'Have a listen to this.' It was the album *A Farewell to Kings* that turned my head. What I really liked was the lyrics of Neil Peart. As a lyricist he was sublime, and you wanted to read the lyrics within the lavish album cover while the album played on your turntable. Sometimes I want throwaway lyrics in a song, but these lyrics demanded your attention. The album also contained the two outstanding tracks, 'Xanadu' and 'Cygnus X-1' and any self respecting Rush fan will wonder at both songs' sheer brilliance.

Andrew Smyth was at Hammersmith Odeon

Hemispheres followed in 1978. It's all well and good you sitting in your bedroom, while your parents are shouting up the stairs to turn that racket down but what I wanted was a tour so that I could hear these songs live. Finally Rush announced they would be touring in 1979, and we got tickets for Hammersmith Odeon. I was finally going to see the band inside my most treasured venue.

After the anticipation and the wait for the gig - in the blink of an eye, it's over. But what a gig! When you go see a band you really like, you need to buy the merchandise on sale inside, everything from the tour programme to the badges, posters, patches and - most important of all - the t-shirt. You needed to make sure that people knew who you were into, and I made that very obvious by wearing them to work. 'Rush....who are they? Never heard of them.' You get the picture.

I had to wait until June 1980 before Rush would play Hammersmith again. I went on my own as nobody else wanted to come along. I was so pleased that Rush were in the singles charts with 'The Spirit of Radio'. Now I could say to those people, 'This is Rush, now listen.'

By 1981 and 1983, they were an arena band and more people wanted to see them. The gigs were superb as always, and more merchandise was purchased, but Wembley Arena is a venue devoid of any atmosphere. But the dates were packed out, which as a fan was brilliant to see.

I would not see Rush live again until 2004 and 2013, by which time they were playing the O2 in London to sell out audiences, with a wealth of material to play. You also got to see the humorous side with Rush on these tours with the stage shows, and the washing machines on stage, etc.

Sadly, with the untimely passing of Neil Peart, I'll never get to see Rush live again, but those records will always be played and will be enjoyed by generations of fans to come.

I WAS THERE: JEFF WALKER

There were all sorts of albums doing the rounds at school and factions. I fell for it big time being young and dumb. Prog vs heavy metal vs punk vs soul. Being a prog head my 'go to' album at age 13 was *Yessongs*. Then somehow I got to hear *All the World's a Stage* and it was goodbye Bill Bruford and Alan White and welcome Neil Peart. But I still love both bands.

I recall being really impressed by the song 'A Farewell to Kings' even though I was more familiar with *Hemispheres* and really loved Geddy for his other worldliness. I'm a drummer but Geddy owned that gig and forced me to take bass players more seriously. I felt left out during 'Closer to the Heart', not really knowing it when the rest of Hammersmith did. My friend and I were in the balcony and I could swear that shit was going to collapse! Everyone was going nuts.

Mil Garofalo saw Rush on the strength of a Melody Maker ad

I WAS THERE: MIL GAROFALO

In 1979 I quit my well paid day job at the Bank of America, Luxembourg and left with a friend for London in search of a professional music career. Shortly after our arrival, we decided to go to a concert. I came from a village with 200 inhabitants and neither me nor my friend knew many bands, so we bought a copy of *Melody Maker* and looked for a venue not too far away. Finally we stumbled upon an ad for the band Rush with support by Max Webster.

Both bands were unknown to us but it said Max Webster would be playing some intricate music with emphasis on the guitar player. I said to my friend, 'Let us go to the concert for Max Webster and we'll stay for one song of this Rush band. If it's rubbish we'll leave and go for the local pub.' Max Webster came on and we really liked what they played.

Reluctantly we stayed and waited for Rush to start. I will never ever forget what happened next. I do not remember the exact stage entrance of the guys but I do remember their first chord of 'Hemispheres'. (F# 7/4 for the musicians). It took me an evening to figure it out, not being blessed with perfect pitch, and it still rings in my ears after 40 years.

We were in for a treat during the whole concert because, after a rather long intro, Geddy Lee started to sing and that was the second mind blowing experience. Not to speak of the drummer, the overall sound and lights. The whole concert, as every other Rush concert I saw in my life, was nothing short of phenomenal for these two lads from a small Luxembourg village, trying to find fame and money in London.

COVENTRY THEATRE

9 MAY 1979, COVENTRY, UK

I WAS THERE: JOHN STRISINO, AGE 16

I discovered Rush after hearing *All the World's a Stage*. There was a great rock/metal pub in Coventry called The Lady Godiva ('the Dive' to the regulars, which was naughty as we were underage). There was also a Friday night rock/metal disco at the Lanchester

John Strisino got the band's autographs

Polytechnic (the 'Lanch', now Coventry University) where we would go to socialise, listen to our favourite bands and plan our next gigs.

In the late 70s Coventry attracted some great bands to the now defunct Coventry Theatre - Black Sabbath (with Van Halen opening), UFO (twice) and Whitesnake. And Rush. I'd missed them the previous year at Birmingham Odeon, but not this time. Myself and several close rock/metal friends had our tickets.

Max Webster were pretty good as support bands went but when Rush hit the stage it was something different. It was the *Hemispheres* tour and the album remains my favourite. To see it live was fantastic. The band and the musicianship sounded superb. Being into drummers, I was transfixed by Peart. Rush had become one of my favourite bands. As always, we exited with elation!

In June of 1980, Rush returned to the Midlands but this time we saw them at Leicester's De Montfort Hall. When they hit the stage, memories from Coventry the previous year flooded in. Rush as a live band do not disappoint. They were so good we missed the train back to Coventry as we had the chance to meet the band after the show. I got my programme and my merchandise flyer signed.

Rush were back in 1981 for the *Moving Pictures* tour. The all standing New Bingley Hall was a large cowshed. I'd seen The Who there in 1979 and hoped the crush wouldn't be as bad. It wasn't the best of venues but being six foot one I was able to see above people's heads. It was a great show, but hampered by the venue and its hustle and bustle. They gave us a taste of 'Subdivisions', which was yet to be released.

I saw Rush again on the *Signals* and *Hold Your Fire* tours at the much larger NEC. The shows were much bigger in terms of lighting and stage presence, and were amazing. I was always captivated by the quality of their playing, my eyes flitting from Geddy to Alex and mostly Neil. *A Show of Hands* serves as a great memory of the 1988 show. I saw them at the LG Arena in Birmingham in 2004. What struck me then was Geddy's washing machines in front of his amps. It was another marvellous show and they played some great covers, including The Who's 'The Seeker'. Perched higher up in the auditorium, I had a great view and Neil's drum solo was immense. Rush are up there with some of the best shows I've attended in the 40 plus years.

COLSTON HALL

14 & 15 MAY 1979, BRISTOL, UK

I WASTHERE: ALEX MENADUE

Alex Menadue went to see Rush with his dad's workmates

A workmate of my father gave me a tape of the recently released *A Farewell to Kings*. I was 14 and blown away by its creativeness, skilled musicianship and power. I bought all the back catalogue and was thrilled when my fathers' workmates invited me along to see Rush play Bristol as part of their *Hemispheres* tour. It would be my first gig.

We caught the train from Bridgend to Bristol one sunny evening and had a quick drink in a pub around the corner from the Colston Hall. Some of Rush's roadies were in there. Our seats were on the balcony level but there was a great view. Max Webster were support. They weren't bad but I didn't know any of their songs.

Then Rush came on. It was the loudest thing I had ever heard. Peart's drums sounded like they were in my head, Alex's guitar shredded my ear drums and Geddy's bass pounded my chest. It was unbelievable. They looked and were dressed much as they were on the cover of *2112* and their PA system was as high as a house either side of the stage. There were explosions as they performed '2112' which blinded me on top of being deafened. I was almost stone deaf for three days afterwards but it was worth it. It set the standard for every gig since.

PINKPOP FESTIVAL

4 JUNE 1979, BURGEMEESTER DAMEN SPORTPARK, GELEEN, THE NETHERLANDS

I WAS THERE: MARC MAEGH

A friend played me the just released *Hemispheres*. Just a few months later, Rush were playing their first ever festival gig at the Pinkpop Festival. I attended only knowing the songs from *Hemispheres*. After that gig I became a huge fan and saw a couple more gigs in Belgium and Holland in the later years. In total I saw Rush four times. There really is no other band like them.

The *Permanent Waves* tour kicked off in Iowa in August 1979 and finished in the UK in June 1980 with an 18 show British leg, 121 dates in total.

COBO HALL

28 AUGUST 1979,
DETROIT, MICHIGAN

I WAS THERE: JOHNNY ACKLEY

Johnny Ackley met Geddy at his 2019 book signing

Johnny's favourite photo of Rush at Red Rocks was signed by the band

I had this great record store and head shop owner who'd guide me to my next record each week. I simply walked in with my $6 ($5.99 was a typical record price) and asked, 'What am I buying today?' That's how I got exposed to some of my favourite music. I bought *All the World's a Stage* and *2112* within days of one another.

I had a ticket for a January 1978 show in Milwaukee, Wisconsin but on the day of the show, it snowed 24 inches and I was unable to convince my mother to drive us the 20 miles into the city. The first show I attended was in 1979 at Cobo Hall. We were about as far away from the stage as you could be in that venue; tier C at Cobo was *way* up there. The next show was at The Joe Louis Arena, the first concert ever held at The Joe. Max Webster opened.

I attended one show on each of the *Signals*, *Grace Under Pressure* and *Power Windows* tours, all in Milwaukee. I did manage to catch a show on the *Presto* tour at Alpine Valley, near Milwaukee, a few months before I moved west but didn't see them again until the *Test for Echo* tour in 1997.

I was excited when *Vapor Trails* was released but had no idea how significant its arrival really was until many years later. I saw that tour in Milwaukee. When *Feedback* was released and the *R30* tour started taking shape, I decided to pull out the stops and managed to see eight shows. On all the subsequent tours, I attended at least two or three shows, six on *Snakes & Arrows* tour. I have bought tickets from other fans, scalpers (I got front row in Seattle), fan club pre-sales/ VIP packages and TicketMaster's 'Official Platinum' offerings. As best as I can count, I've been to 37 shows in 15 or 16 different cities in eight US states, plus Ontario, Canada. I've attended RushCon at least three different times and continue to display my Rush obsession at every opportunity. My vehicle license plate is Rush inspired and the tailgate of my van looks like a Rush shrine.... in a good way.

My favourite shows include a second row experience at the Concord Pavilion, in California, where I was right at Ged's feet all night and the final show at The Forum in Los Angeles. I had a very brief encounter with Neil's daughter and wife in the pre-show VIP lounge at The Forum, and was very fortunate to have a quick meet and greet with Geddy at a *Big Beautiful Book of Bass* signing session in Chicago in 2019. I also met both Ged's and Alex's mothers at one of the RushCon events in Toronto.

My very favourite photo is from the *Time Machine* tour at Red Rocks. I had a poster of it made and sent it off to the band. They signed it for me and I had it framed.

CIVIC CENTER

29 AUGUST 1979, LANSING, MICHIGAN

I WAS THERE: JAMES PRATT, AGE 13

I was there with friends. I learned about the show from a radio station, 101.7 WILS. I bought tickets for perhaps $6 at Sounds and Diversions in downtown Lansing. The Civic Center maybe held 1,000 people. I remember the opening act was New England and the drummer had a big ass afro.

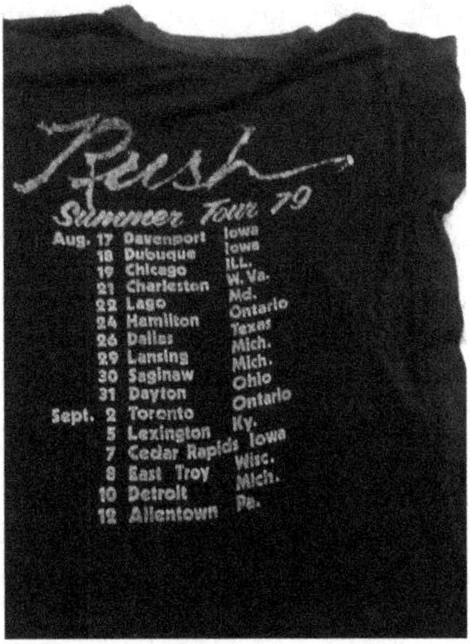

James Pratt still has his Hemispheres t-shirt

HARA ARENA, UNIVERSITY OF DAYTON

31 AUGUST 1979, DAYTON, OHIO

I WAS THERE: STEVE CRANE

I've seen them live since December 30, 1975. The best seats I had was third row at University of Dayton Hara Arena on August 31, 1979. I was never disappointed by any show I went to. I was never a stoner but as the music played I was always in a euphoric state because these three men gave me something to hang onto during some very difficult times. The lyrics were special to me because they consoled me during those difficult times. Their entire catalogue was the soundtrack to my life. Every song, spanning those 45 years, gave me a sense of awareness and reason to keep going.

VARSITY STADIUM

2 SEPTEMBER 1979, TORONTO, CANADA

I WAS THERE: TIM SCAMMELL

As I was walking home I noticed an old record player in someone's garbage. I had a hunch that this record player may still work and, being only 12 years old, I brought it home with me. My family had an 8-track player and I had a cassette recorder/player but we didn't have a record player. I had won a Bobby Sherman vinyl album at a school safety patrol Christmas party. It had never been played and wasn't my choice of music to listen to, but it suited the purpose of seeing if my new/old record player worked. It worked perfectly. But when I touched the centre post or any metal part of the player I got an electric shock. That's why it was in the garbage.

Soon afterwards I took a trip down to the local public library and checked out the assortment of LPs available to borrow. I went through the records and stopped at *Fly by Night*. The cover was so cool, with a big snowy owl coming right out at me. I made my way home with *Fly by Night* under my arm, went upstairs to my bedroom, took the record out of its sleeve, zapped myself as I put the record onto the post and sat back to hear what this stuff was. At that moment a lifelong fan of Rush was born.

I'm not positive when I first saw them. But I was at Varsity Stadium. My family had to speed back to Toronto from a cottage we were using on Lake Simcoe just so that I could get to see this concert. I still have the ticket stub somewhere. After that it became a tradition to see them every time they played in Toronto or somewhere within a few hours driving distance such as Hamilton or even Buffalo. I'd change any plans to fit. A couple of times I went to the shows by myself but I always ran into friends and would spend the rest of the show hanging out with them.

When *Beyond the Lighted Stage* was released, I went to a midnight show in Moncton, New Brunswick. The family packed up and made an overnight mini-vacation out of it. This was the closest thing we had to seeing Rush in these parts. It was surreal seeing my old high school named in the movie. Even more astounding was when it showed Geddy and Alex walking around outside a church where they first performed shows in the basement. That was where I went to nursery school. And Alex attended the same high school as me, albeit several years before. It was at high school that I learned his real last name is Zivojinovich. One of the walls in the band room bore a mural he painted, and which he'd signed 'A. Zivojinovich'.

From the time my sons were babies they listened to Rush. Many times we were in the car I would have a Rush CD or cassette playing and they would rock along. In 2010, I learned that tickets were about to go on sale for a Montreal show in April 2011, the first time Rush had played east of Ontario since we had moved to New Brunswick in 2003. We were going. It was time the boys went to see their first big rock show, just a couple of days after their 13th birthdays.

This show was the best I ever saw, three hours with a short intermission. To commemorate its 30th anniversary they played *Moving Pictures* in its entirety in the second half and ended on 'Working Man'. We watched in amazement as Neil crashed away, Geddy slapped the bass like a maniac and Alex played his guitar so fast we couldn't keep up with his fingers. After playing for three hours they looked like they were ready to go for three more. The boys had their best birthday trip ever and I got to see Rush in concert again.

ALLENTOWN FAIRGROUNDS

12 SEPTEMBER 1979, ALLENTOWN, PENNSYLVANIA

I WAS THERE: DARYL OGDEN

I went out with this girl named Sharon for two years. Everything was going great. I would drive up to northern Pennsylvania and visit her at her parent's house near Allentown. I had gotten two tickets to see Rush at the Allentown Fairgrounds. Pat Travers with Tommy Aldridge was the warm-up band. Well Pat exploded onto the stage and really kicked ass. Then the moment I was waiting for - Rush come out and go right into the beginning of '2112'. We were rocking our asses off and I thought everyone was having a great time. The show was about three-quarters over when my girlfriend (knowing how much I love Rush) said, 'Let's go!'

Daryl Ogden and wife Gertrud with the shirt Daryl bought on the night his date wanted to leave before Neil's solo

I said, 'Neil hasn't even done his solo yet! Are you kidding me?' I was so offended I told her if she wanted a ride home to meet me at my car. I never saw her again and it was the best day of my life! I soon after found my now wife of 40 years, Gertrud. And she loves Rush!

NEW BINGLEY HALL

21 & 22 SEPTEMBER 1979, STAFFORD, UK

Neil Hunt was a guest of Howard Ungerleider on the Clockwork Angels tour

I WAS THERE: NEIL HUNT, AGE 17

The first time I saw them was April 1979 at the Manchester Apollo on the *Hemispheres* tour. The time after that when I saw them, and which had much more of an impact as far as I was concerned, was in September 1979. I was not quite 18. I remember it being called 'The Mini Tour of Some of the Hemispheres'. I've also heard people call it 'the Semi-Tour of Some of the Hemispheres'. But it was pre *Permanent Waves* and post *Hemispheres* and it was on a bigger scale than what they'd done before, certainly in the UK.

New Bingley Hall was a cattle shed. It's what they're talking about on 'The Spirit of Radio'. As a cattle auction shed it would certainly echo with the sound of salesmen. It echoed with the sound of Rush on that particular night.

As a 17-year-old I generally got down the front, got hot and sweaty and had a good time. But I lived in Southport and we arrived late, as getting there involved driving in a friend's father's Triumph Herald at no more than 50 miles an hour.

There had been an issue with a stage extension. I heard part of it had collapsed, dumping the support band - Brian Robertson's Wild Horses - in the pit. Whatever the reason, there were minor delays in getting in and I watched the gig from much nearer the back than usual.

It was the first concert I'd seen outside of a theatre and the first time I'd watched any concert from the back, where you could see the whole thing. And I saw what I considered to be an absolutely breathtaking live show. They used a back projection screen which was the first time I'd seen anybody do that. They'd got bespoke film on the backdrop and I particularly remember the film for 'Cygnus X-1' when an arena-sized Rocinante flew across the back of the stage. They played 'Spirit of Radio' and 'Freewill' for the first time as a teaser of what was to come on *Permanent Waves.*

Over the years I probably saw them about a dozen times, but with a massive gap from the 80s through to *Clockwork Angels*. I saw them on the *Permanent Waves* tour at Queen's Hall in Leeds, which was an old tram shed, and then went on a mate's motorbike the following night at Deeside Leisure Centre, which thanks to Geddy Lee I now have to pronounce as Deeside 'Leezure' Centre.

Inspired by that 1979 New Bingley Hall show I took up stage lighting for a living and have toured with everyone from Joe Strummer to Nirvana to The Pixies. Never Rush though. The most recent time I saw Rush was as Howard Ungerleider's guest at the Manchester Arena on the *Clockwork Angels* tour. Howard is an icon. The band have worked with Howard for over 40 years and Howard has his own little guest area at front of house. So we sat there with a load of industry professionals - Iron Maiden's lighting crew, Moody Blues' lighting designer and various others - all there as guests of the lighting designer and there to watch the light show.

For me that is always part of a Rush show, and I think it must be for Rush, because the shows are very elaborate. You don't get to do very elaborate light shows like that unless the band are into it. The light show has always got to offer something. It's got to surprise in a good way, and it always does with a Rush show. The only thing that's not surprising is that the lighting at a Rush show is always brilliant.

If I could go back in time I'd like to see that Bingley Hall show again. By modern standards it might have sounded like a bag of spanners, but Rush were a cut above the rest when it came to sound. And if there's one show I didn't see that I'd like to have seen it's *All the World's a Stage*. That's one of the best live albums by any band ever. I always got the impression that they were enjoying themselves on the stage and gave it everything. There was nothing left in the tank by the time they walked off.

I WAS THERE: JIM SCOTT

I first saw them in February 1978 in Glasgow. I have seen them 26 times in total, including in Toronto. I have them tattooed on my arm and my house is named after their song 'The Garden'. My wife and son are also massive fans. I remember travelling to Stafford Bingley Hall in September 1979 to see the band play two nights as part of their *Permanent Waves* warm up tour. Stafford was full of Mods as *Quadrophenia* was on at the local cinema. I recall walking up this road in the middle of nowhere. We eventually got to what was a giant shed, where we stood in a never ending queue to get in. Rush were on fire and blasted their way through their *Hemispheres* set and also played new material from their soon to be released new album, 'The Spirit of Radio' and 'Freewill'. The night was marred when Geddy told us a guy had died en route to the gig. Rush went onto play a blistering version of 'La Villa Strangiato' and dedicated it to him. The Mods were waiting for us outside and it got a bit messy. People slept in railway stations, anywhere, just to do it all again the next day.

Jim Scott's house is named after the Rush song 'The Garden'

I am also a member of the Glaswegian Chorus who provided backing vocals on the live album, *Exit... Stage Left*.

I went to Toronto to see them on their *Clockwork Angels* tour. I booked into a room-only hotel. Once the guy knew I had come from Glasgow to see Rush he put me into the best room in the hotel, overlooking the CN Tower, and upgraded me to all inclusive. He was obviously a fan.

I WAS THERE: MARK APPLETON

I attended one of those shows. Despite an appalling sound in what appeared to be a huge former cattle shed, the show was wonderful.

I WAS THERE: JOHN MOSELEY

'A Passage to Bangkok' did it for me. I had to have the album on vinyl. When Steve said, 'They're playing Bingley Hall', I said 'book that coach - we are going'. We were too young to drive. I just remember looking at my friend when they struck up with the most amazing wall of sound and said, 'They're only a three piece.' He just smiled and nodded his head in approval. What a night.

I WAS THERE: GARETH NOON

I was picked up mid afternoon for a 50 mile trip to the venue, a former cattle market which now played host to touring bands of the time. It was a hot day for the time of year. We duly arrived around 5pm and joined the queue. Once inside the venue it was hot and sticky. I was patiently waiting at the merchandise stall. My friend Phil didn't have as much patience as me and decided to crawl to the front, bobbed up and put his hand in a bag and came back with a collection of badges and a couple of t-shirts. Luckily, the t-shirt fitted like a glove (not that I condone this behaviour).

We took our place towards the front of the stage. Roughly 10 minutes before stage time there was a big crush and the stage manager duly made an announcement that if we didn't move back the stage was in

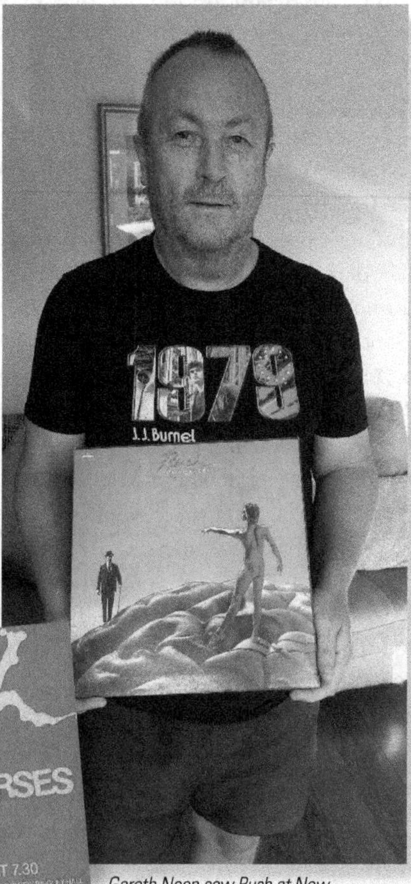

Gareth Noon saw Rush at New Bingley Hall

danger of collapse. Hence most people ignored this request and pushed further forward. Thankfully the stage survived.

Behind the stage was a backdrop of the *2112* cover with the red star being a red dot. As the band entered the arena, the red dot became larger and was in fact the red star and they went straight into '2112'. The place was bouncing with 5,000 people having the time of their lives.

During the set Rush played 'Spirit of Radio' and 'Freewill' for the first time in front of an audience (they had just recorded *Permanent Waves* in Wales). I was spilt up from the guys I went with but luckily I have good memory as it was the days before I could legally drink beer and so I found where our car was parked. Of the half dozen Rush gigs I witnessed this was the most memorable.

I WAS THERE: JEAN-PAUL SRIVALSAN

After seeing them at Hammersmith Odeon on their first British visit I saw every UK tour, watching their popularity and stage show grow as they graduated from multiple nights at Hammersmith to multiple nights at Wembley and other larger arenas. At New Bingley Hall we were promised their full American stage show, which they'd had to cut down in size to fit into the smaller halls on the *Hemispheres* tour. It didn't disappoint, with stunning videos of spaceships and black holes played on the screen behind the band adding to the spectacle of the 'Cygnus X-1'/'Hemispheres' suite . They also played early versions of 'The Spirit of Radio' and 'Freewill' as they refined them ahead of recording them for *Permanent Waves.*

INTERNATIONAL AMPHITHEATRE

3 - 6 APRIL 1980, CHICAGO, ILLINOIS

I WAS THERE: RALPH KINSCHECK

I saw Rush three times and each time the seats were very close to the stage. A great friend who was a ticket scalper was able to get me box seats at the old Chicago Stadium at face value, around $25 each. The seats were at worst 10 feet away from the stage. The show began with the full version of '2112'. The lights were amazing with a spotlight that focused on Neil Peart spinning his sticks between each of the introductory staccato guitar/bass kicks. We were all in shock and awe at the tightness of the band and the amazing light show. Rush were in prime prog mode doing extended versions of every song we knew and loved. I still refer to this as the golden age of Rush; 'By-Tor and the Snow Dog', 'Bastille Day', 'Something for Nothing' plus all the classics like 'Closer to the Heart' and 'Fly by Night', which was in a medley of the older stuff. But the apex of the show was 'Cygnus-X1' Books 1 and 2 in their entirety, complete with video screen visuals of the Rocinante sailing in space and visuals representing the people of the heart and those of the mind. It was quite the visual and musical feast.

We ended up standing on the backs of our chairs with one foot and the railing of the box seats with the other foot for the entire show. Even so, I don't remember being over tired from that. The highlight of the show was when my friend caught one of Neil Peart's drum sticks.

I only saw Rush twice more despite being a rabid fan ever since. The *Moving Pictures* tour saw the band move toward shorter songs and the long ones truncated or made into medleys. *Moving Pictures* remains one of my all-time favourite Rush albums, and the tour was still pretty good with full visuals and lights, but it was seriously shortened to under two hours.

The *Signals* tour was a huge disappointment. I think it was 90 minutes. Many long songs were eliminated – '2112', 'By-Tor', etc. – and there was not much going on with the visuals, with the lights seriously subdued. Then I was at college and did not have any opportunities to see the band. I gave up on them for about a decade until I was reunited with them on *Vapor Trails*. I regret I was not able to see them in the 2010s, but I can watch the videos.

TARRANT COUNTY CONVENTION CENTER

2 FEBRUARY 1980, FORT WORTH, TEXAS

I WAS THERE: HARRY STORM

It was February and 80 degrees Fahrenheit when we walked in and 22 degrees Fahrenheit leaving, but, it was a smoking hot concert. My lady and I had floor seats 15 or 20 rows back, stage right. The concert was about three hours but I was fairly stoned on something I later found out was called 'Sherman', liquid PCP sprayed on a two foot long joint of good weed. Geddy Lee was in fine form. The acoustics were great and Neil Peart's drum set up was massive, including the giant gong, which was at least eight feet tall sitting directly behind him. Despite being fairly toasted it was one of the best concerts I've ever attended!

SWING AUDITORIUM

7 MARCH 1980, SAN BERRNADINO, CALIFORNIA

I WAS THERE: MARK FARMER, AGE 19

My first Rush concert was at the Swing Auditorium and my last was on the *R40* tour in Phoenix, Arizona, the third to last show they performed. I saw every tour in between. My seats ranged from the back of the hall to front row. I saw Rush in Los Angeles, San Diego, Las Vegas, Anaheim, Denver, and Phoenix. I have experienced Rush concerts with friends, family members, my wife, my daughter - and by myself! Each concert was an event I couldn't wait for. I attended a show at Red Rocks, Colorado, where my brother and I had tickets for third row centre. The woman who took our tickets looked at them and said, 'You're going to love those seats!' She was right.

Mark Farmer with wife Becci and daughters Kristen (left) and Kimberly

In San Diego at the Coors Amphitheater, I sat second row with my wife and two other couples. I think Geddy, Alex and Neil were stunned to see attractive females so close who actually knew the words, as they kept pointing and playing to them. Another monster achievement was taking my daughter Kristen to see her first Rush concert in Phoenix, Arizona. She grew up listening to them from me, and has a tattoo - which I was not a fan of her getting but changed my mind when I saw it - which reads, 'I will choose FREEWILL.' She made me so proud!

The day I heard Neil died, I actually wept. I had never met the man, but because I read all of his books and lyrics over the years, I felt like a good friend was lost. I can't comprehend that I will never get to see Alex, Geddy and Neil on the same stage again. I have seen hundreds of concerts over the years and Rush tops them all live. Thanks guys.

LA FORUM

10 MARCH 1980, LOS ANGELES, CALIFORNIA

I WAS THERE: JOHN RIVERA

My family moved to Orange County, California from Latin America in 1976. My musical experience in rock and roll didn't really begin until 1977. My first 8-track was Alice Cooper's *Greatest Hits* and my first vinyl Led Zeppelin's *The Song Remains the Same*. My exposure to rock music was in its infancy. In my third year of high school a friend said he had a spare ticket to this rock group called Rush. I accepted this opportunity to watch a free concert.

Once the warm up band, .38 Special, left the stage the crew got it ready for Rush. I noticed the drums were covered with a black cloth and thought it a little weird. Rush took the stage and the cloth was removed. I was blown away. That wasn't a drum set, it was a percussion centre. Rush played and that drummer used every piece in his percussion centre. Did I mention I was blown away? They played their now signature song, 'Spirit of Radio' and many other tunes I had never heard, but have since memorised. That night a Rush fan was born.

By 1981 and *Moving Pictures* I was the Rush fan who had intently listened and air drummed to their earlier albums. One stop on the *Moving Pictures* tour was the Anaheim Convention Center. I bought a ticket for my girlfriend, now wife, who I'd met while in high school, and my brother. We walked to the venue. The warm up band was a group called FM. They were really good, and a three piece just like Rush. One member played an electric violin with a light on the bow. Once they were done, I pointed out to my girlfriend and brother the black cloth over the area the drums would be. Once Rush took the stage the cloth was removed and we noticed how the percussion centre gleamed under the lights. I was again blown away. They played 'Spirit of Radio', '2112', the radio hit 'Tom Sawyer', 'Xanadu' and many other hits.

COW PALACE

14 & 15 MARCH 1980, DALY CITY, CALIFORNIA

I WAS THERE: MITCHELL COURTOIS

I've seen them live on every tour but *Vapor Trails*. For the final tour I was on Alex Lifeson's guest list. My first live Rush concert was in 1975. I was 12. They opened up for Kiss which was why I was there as I was a big Kiss fan. At that point I went out and bought a Rush album and then there was no way I was going to miss them live. I was a die hard fan and kicked a few people's asses when they talked shit about Rush.

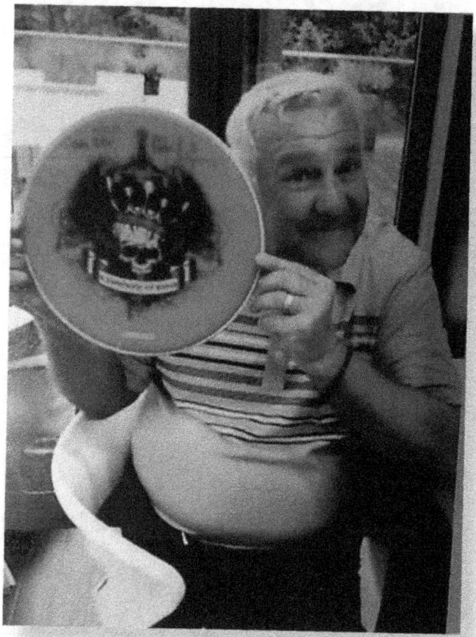

Mitchell Courtois got an ace piece of memorabilia signed by Alex and the rest of the band thanks to his brother

For the *Presto* tour I had a 1981 Honda CB500 and nobody to go to the show with so I rode that piece of crap to the show, not knowing if it would make it. It's raining and I arrive at the venue about one hour from my house. I pull into the parking lot and see what I perceive to be a security guard riding a motorcycle around the lot. As I pull in closer he signals me with his finger in a circular motion to take a lap around the arena so here's two people who don't know one another riding in the rain. As we complete the lap I turn towards an empty space and he heads to the staging area back stage and that's when I noticed he was on a BMW. I tell myself, 'Damn, that was Neil Peart! I should have followed him.' It's really raining now and I pull out a plastic drop cloth and tie it to a parking pillar and to my bike to have some shelter. Just as I sit down under this tarp this couple pulls in and ask me if I'm riding a BMW? My response was, 'Why would Neil be sitting under a tarp in the rain? No, I'm not Neil.'

While I was into rock in the 70s my older brother was listening to the Commodores, Earth Wind & Fire, etc. He actually said that the music I was listening to would not be around too long. He was never into Rush. Jump 30 years forward and I get a call from him. He asks me to guess what he's listening to. I say, 'Some R&B band.' He shocks me by saying that, no, he's listening to the new Rush album and not only is he into it but he actually knows Alex Lifeson personally. I'm in awe. My brother is a professional caddy on the PGA tour for Rocco Mediate who is a huge Rush fan and best friends with Alex Lifeson. He actually hands the guitars to Alex when he attends shows. This is how I was able to be on his guest list for the last four tours.

INTERNATIONAL AMPHITHEATER

4 APRIL 1980, CHICAGO, ILLINOIS

I WAS THERE: GREG MORALES

Back in high school, some of the other guys were playing this unique-sounding band called Rush on the boomboxes they brought to school. We had open campus during lunch hour so would fan out to the various fast food restaurants in the area, play music and enjoy our McDonalds cheeseburgers! 'Cinderella Man' was a song title I heard mentioned, along with '2112', whatever that was. In 1978 I began seeing TV commercials on my local station of Rush on stage, playing 'Circumstances'. These were adverts for their upcoming tour, which was coming to the Chicago area.

Greg Morales first heard Rush on his friends' boomboxes during school break

Aged 15 and while on a trip to California I finally took the plunge and visited a record store. I decided to buy not one but two Rush albums; *Hemispheres* was their current release but I had been hearing 'Fly by Night' on the radio. With my meagre funds I bought *Hemispheres* and *Fly by Night*.

I saw the *Permanent Waves* tour. It was amazing to see the boys up on the lighted stage. I've attended 10 Rush concerts since, only missing *Test for Echo* and *Vapor Trails*. I took my girlfriend to see saw the band on their final *R40* tour in San Jose, California. I'm grateful that the band was so diligent in recording their live tours, especially in the later years. At least we can throw on a Blu-ray or DVD and get to relive those magical shows.

MADISON SQUARE GARDEN

8 – 11 MAY 1980, NEW YORK, NEW YORK

I WAS THERE: CHRISTOPHER BOLLOTTA

I was very heavily influenced in music by my older cousin and his friends. They were five or six years older than I was. They were listening to Pink Floyd, Led Zeppelin, the Rolling Stones and Black Sabbath. I was 7 when *2112* came out, and when they played it I wasn't sure what to think. But it started to grow on me. Everything sounded awesome and they looked cool on the back cover of the LP. For Christmas the next year my parents got me *A Farewell to Kings* and Pink Floyd's *Animals*. They weren't the type to limit or censor what I listened to. After that, I'd visit the record stores and wait for the new Rush album to come - not realising at a young age that they didn't just release a new album every couple of weeks!

My cousin and his friends took me to the *Permanent Waves* tour. I really thought they were playing the album. I couldn't believe that they were that tight on stage. I'd seen Kiss and Styx and a few others live, but Rush were something else. I only ever saw them live 12 times but all 12 were like the very first time. They never disappointed the fans or played a bad show.

Knowing the *R40* tour really might be their last, my wife got tickets for my birthday. As with all other shows, I never sat down. I was Neil on drums. Geddy on bass. Alex on guitar. So was everyone else! I left that concert feeling that that was it, knowing they would be retiring. A chapter in my life was ending. I'm fortunate that they were around my entire life. I'm glad they were a part of my life. With Neil gone, life now seems a little less interesting. All those words unspoken will never be heard. But we will be forever grateful to Lerxst, Dirk and The Professor.

NEW HAVEN COLISEUM

20 MAY 1980, NEW HAVEN, CONNECTICUT

I WAS THERE: DANA FOREMAN

I was a sophomore in a prep school in Montville, Connecticut called St Thomas More. It was an all-boys school filled with all kinds of kids with all kinds of musical taste. I was just getting into more progressive rock such as ELO, Pink Floyd and the Alan Parsons Project. I resided in a second floor dorm called Kennedy, a floor which was full of guys each with his own stereo playing various rock groups whenever there was downtime.

Dana Foreman discovered Rush while at prep school

Saturday afternoons were useless, with nothing to do and nowhere to go. The campus was located in the heart of Connecticut farmland on a big lake. The only TV was in the school canteen and there was no cable - and no internet. The only phone was a payphone in the canteen. The options were play basketball all day, read a good book or simply hang out. I started hanging around this guy named Brian. We talked about music and I told him what I liked. Brian didn't seem too interested, and less so after I laid a couple of tracks on him.

'Hey, have you ever heard of a group called Rush?' he enquired. I had heard 'Working Man' when passing the dorm rooms. I always thought the lead singer had a woman's voice. 'Oh, you gotta hear this album, man - *2112*. It will blow you away,' he exclaimed, passing me the cover. He placed the record on the turntable and told me to read along with the narrative inside the cover. I was hooked by the end of the first side.

By the end of the day, we had listened to everything from the first seven Rush LPs. Brian loaned me his Rush LPs over the next few days and I listened to them, and we continued to hang. One day after classes Brian came tearing into my room. 'Did you hear, did you get the news? Rush is playing in New Haven Coliseum on May 20th and the coach is getting tickets!' (From time to time the school would actually plan trips to concerts. Molly Hatchet was another). The coach, Lou Allen, took up a collection of money from the students and bought the tickets and arranged a bus to take us down to New Haven.

I told Brian, 'Yeah, I got the funds, don't worry. I'm not missing this.' Problem was, I didn't have the 20 bucks. By the late spring my funds were depleted from the allowance account my mom had set up for me. I told another pal, Bud, of my dilemma. Bud was the assistant cook at the school cafeteria. I'd hang out with him and help out from time to time. This had its advantages - I could eat as much as I wanted in CoCo Krispies. He told me the evening dishwasher had quit and it would be a few days until the new one started. He offered me $40 for the three days work. It was sloppy, funky, stinky ass work that started at 5pm and kept you busy right up until evening study hall at 7.30pm, the mandated hours where you were in your dorm room, all the doors were open and you did your homework under three careful guise of a patrolling teacher. So there I was, busting my ass doing dishes for about 150 students and faculty, all for the chance to see Rush as my very first concert. I was so excited the work didn't bother me.

Brian thought I was nuts. I told him my money problem. The last night of kitchen duty, Brian brought down his portable tape recorder and I listened to *Caress of Steel* as I scrubbed down my last night of gross work. I had my $40 and bought my ticket.

The night of the concert, we arrived and got our seats. I was off my seat with excitement. The crowds were waving signs and throwing a beach ball about the stadium that just kept on floating over the audience. Brian and I wanted to go down and get a better look at the stage and managed to get all the way to the area above the stage, getting a great view of the set up. We watched as the roadies made adjustments and dressed the stage. I was looking down along and just behind the stage and what do I see. It's Neil Peart, in a sky blue t-shirt, walking out twirling a drum stick. Brian saw it too. 'Neil… hey Neil – up here!' he yelled and waved. Neil didn't look up. He was walking too far out along the stage and had missed the stage entrance. The roadie held back the drape and motioned for him to come back that way. 'Wow, Neil Peart!', I thought. How lucky we caught him like that.

They opened with '2112'. It was so great watching this group who were still fairly new to me play an album I already knew back to back. The rest of the night was pure magic, and always an amazing memory.

The school year ended a few weeks after that. I never saw Brian again, but am grateful that he turned me onto Rush. The following year I did not return to STM but stayed local in New Jersey for my junior year. In 1981 Rush released *Moving Pictures*. It was perfection from beginning to end and was being played everywhere. People who really didn't know Rush now knew Rush. I saw them on that tour as well, turning all my friends onto their iconic music. Friends would come over that summer and say, 'Put on some *Moving Pictures*, man.' In the 1981, there were tons of great bands putting out great music, but Rush really was in the spotlight. I felt proud that I was already a fan.

I shed a few tears at Neil's passing. I am forever grateful for that music and for the memories I have with them, and because of them.

GAUMONT THEATRE

1 & 2 JUNE 1980, SOUTHAMPTON, UK

I WAS THERE: NICK POMPEY

I was 14 and lived in Portsmouth. My friend and I were both drummers. His brother was a little bit older and they had all their music equipment set up in the house. He was a massive Rush, Yes and Police fan – all that sort of vibe. They had started a Rush tribute act. I wasn't quite as good as them at the time but they had a gig at one of the local town halls and my mate asked me to do 'Cygnus-X1' with him because there was so much to do! There were two of us behind the kit. I was doing all the percussion, bells and things like that and he was playing the main beat.

I went to see them on that tour and I remember being right at the front and just staring at Neil. I don't think I looked at anybody else during the whole performance. We'd been going to a lot of gigs and found out that you could go behind the stage and wait to see the band. I had bought the big album-sized programme. We queued up and I got to speak to Neil. I said to him, 'I was watching you, and how could I ever get to that sort of standard?' He went and got a drumstick, signed it and said, 'You stick at it, son. You'll be all right.'

HAMMERSMITH ODEON

4 – 8 JUNE 1980, LONDON, UK

I WAS THERE: RICH JOHN

Rush came into my life on the *Permanent Waves* album and it coincided with one of the first multi-nights at one venue. This was before the big arenas. Hammersmith Odeon held around 3,000 people and was a monster venue for sound and atmosphere. You can stand in the bar area and feel the entire

Rich John saw Rush on the Permanent Waves tour

building move when bands play. In those days it was a cluster of denim jackets, patches and a 'who's who' of t-shirts. Great days!

My next few experiences were never the same once they moved to the arenas. *Moving Pictures* was at Wembley Arena. The graphics were good and the set as ever was outstanding, but there was an echo on the sound and the band were dwarfed by the size. They did have one of the first large video screens in the background, and for the UK this was great and new. The set was solid, with a melody of old favourites towards the end and the new material at the start. This was start of the synth which for us, seemed odd, but we went with this.

The *Snakes & Arrows* tour at the O2 Arena was a great show. They had the washing machines in the background and the graphics were outstanding. My friend Jimbo had my tickets. He somehow got very drunk and forgot he was going. I found him and reminded him. We missed half of this show and he slept throughout the remainder, including Neil's drum solo.

The sound at Hammersmith was so good. It's that which stays in the memory.

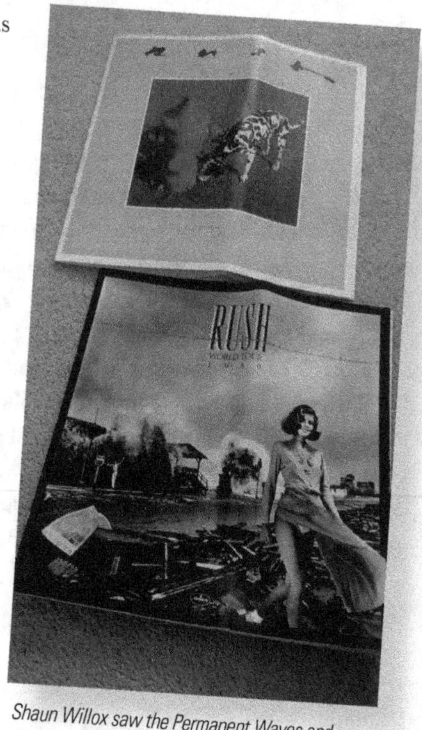

Shaun Willox saw the Permanent Waves and Signals tours – photo Shaun Willox

I WAS THERE: SHAUN WILLOX

A couple of schoolmates introduced me to them in 1977. I was studying for my 'A' levels and had a chance to get tickets for the *Hemispheres* tour but missed out. But I saw the *Permanent Waves* tour at Hammersmith Odeon. I just looked up the set list and - damn, it looks amazing. I saw them a few times from then until their last tour, at Newcastle Arena. I was lucky enough to catch a t-shirt at that show that Alex threw into the crowd.

Lee Irving was at Hammersmith for the Permanent Waves tour

I WAS THERE: LEE IRVING

I was at school. A friend gave me an album to listen to. 'What's this – two one one two?' I said. He just told me to take it home and listen. I was blown away, epic songs. I then got all the albums, one a month until I'd caught up. Me and my mate Steve got tickets for the *Permanent Waves* tour, the best show I'd ever seen. The highlight for me was 'Closer to the Heart' when

Rush played London's Hammersmith Odeon - photo Mark Sandom

Geddy didn't really sing much and just let us do it! Hammersmith was a good venue but a bit on the small side, so in 1981 we were off to Wembley Arena for the *Moving Pictures* tour, again a great show with the standout being 'Red Barchetta'. They had a 3D backdrop on a screen which made you feel as if you were speeding along in a car. I got married soon after and didn't go to a gig in years but was lucky enough to go to the 02 the last time they were in the UK. The stand out that night was 'The Trees'. Now Neil's gone I wished I'd gone more in the 80s and 90s but at least I saw them at their peak - Hammersmith 1980. I think that ticket cost me £3.50!

GLASGOW APOLLO

11 JUNE 1980, GLASGOW, UK

I WAS THERE: KEITH MACKENZIE, AGE 15

I was at the Apollo for *Permanent Waves* and the Royal Highland Exhibition Centre, Ingliston for *Moving Pictures*. Ingliston was not a good concert venue and not used as such for very long. It was a big barn type place. I remember the Apollo far more. It was an iconic building, old and falling apart with sticky carpets and red tinselled pillars. I remember the distinctive voice of Geddy Lee and the cheer when they played 'Spirit of Radio'. It was the major recognisable song and the single release at the time from their newly released album. I was in the circle and it was bouncing. I also remember all the paraphernalia around Neil's drum kit – the cymbals, tubes, etc. The Apollo show was recorded and used for Side 2 of *Exit... Stage Left*. I have boasted for years about being on a Rush album.

I WAS THERE: IAN MACLAREN, AGE 17

I bought *Permanent Waves* on the day of release. I was at college in Glasgow and was passing the record shop. I ran home like a kid at Christmas and put it on the turntable. A few months later they announced the tour dates for 1980 and I sent a cheque to the Glasgow Apollo for tickets and ended up getting a box! So I'm at the side of the stage and looking right down on the stage again. There were three or four of us in this box.

I elected not to go to the *Moving Pictures* tour. They were playing bigger venues, an agricultural showground in Edinburgh. It was a Sunday night and it was going to be a pain to get to, and as a student I couldn't afford to go to every gig. I don't regret it. I'd been to see Rainbow there earlier that year and wasn't impressed with the sound.

They didn't tour Scotland with *Grace Under Pressure* but they did with *Signals*. I was away on holiday. I saw them in '87 on the *Hold Your Fire* tour, another indoor arena, but it was Glasgow and a bit easier to get to.

The next time I managed to see them was on the *Roll the Bones* tour. I was working in Phoenix, Arizona and they played an outdoor amphitheatre. The atmosphere was a bit quieter than you've get at a British gig and not as frantic. It was all very family-oriented, with lots of families with kids with picnic rugs in the middle of the arena having a family day out. And there was me and a colleague from the UK, both really into it and headbanging away up the front! I saw *R30* at Wembley and *Snakes & Arrows* too, which was the last time I saw them.

I was very surprised when I heard the news about Neil. I didn't know he was so ill. I'd heard that he had muscular problems in his arms. I was really upset when I heard. There were rumours they were going to get together with Mike Portnoy and do a Rush gig, but it wouldn't be the same. I'm glad they drew stumps when they did. I have the *R40* DVD and Geddy's voice was struggling a bit. It was time to knock it on the head and get out while the going was good.

I WAS THERE: RODDY FERGUSON, AGE 16

A cool bunch in Glenrothes used to hang about the shops. One of them had the Starman logo on an army jacket. I thought it was cool as fuck. I've seen them quite few times. The first time was the *Permanent Waves* tour in 1980 at the Glasgow Apollo, an absolutely outstanding gig. I was 16 and went with school friends. I eventually took my daughter to the *Snakes & Arrows* tour. That was a nice memory. The last time I saw them was their last appearance in Scotland on the *Clockwork Angels* tour. In my opinion they got better musically as they got older. Geddy's voice suffered slightly but overall they are the best live band ever. I was in the Glasgow chorus singing 'Closer to the Heart' on *Exit... Stage Left*!

QUEENS HALL

15 JUNE 1980, LEEDS, UK

I WAS THERE: MARK WINTER

I was at a schoolmate's flat one afternoon. We should have been at school. He put *A Farewell to Kings* on and – well, that was it. Was it a woman on lead vocals? Why had I not heard of them before? I was brought up, via my older brothers, on Pink Floyd, Yes, Led Zeppelin, etc. This was a game changer.

Along came the *Permanent Waves* world tour. I was not going to miss out. The nearest venue turned out to be the Queens Hall in Leeds. My best mate Roy, my older brother Denis and my Rush-hating sister-in-law Carol wanted to go so - tickets sent off for - we were ready for the off. I finished work at six o'clock and needed an excuse to bunk off work early so got my girlfriend to phone work up with some convoluted excuse as to why I needed to finish at four – and it worked! My elder brother picked me up and we were on our way.

It was an intimate gig and we were close to the band. I was mesmerised by what I was seeing and hearing. As Neil was soloing we noticed people were watching from behind his drum kit, and me and my mate stood there for his solo. What a privilege, although knowing later how Neil felt about fans being in close proximity I bet he felt a little uneasy. My sister-in-law's mind about them was not changed!

After *Moving Pictures* I lost interest, not liking the direction they were going and having other priorities (marriage, kids, work, mortgage). But I later came back and rediscovered those mid 80s and 90s albums. *Power Windows* is a favourite to this day. Not in the *Farewell to King*s kind of way, but they could not go on doing that and *Hemispheres* for the rest of their careers.

DEESIDE LEISURE CENTRE

16 JUNE 1980, QUEENSFERRY, UK

I WAS THERE: LIZ STAPLEY

I was dropped off by my sister and her boyfriend. I was alone and very nervous. The queue was right round the side of the building. But the sun was shining and everyone was sitting on the floor. I soon got chatting to other fans and the waiting just flew by. Once in, everyone ran to the front. I managed to get near the front but to the right side of the stage. After standing for a while listening to the support act I started to feel unwell. I asked an attendant if I could get some fresh air but she took me to a sick bay where I sat on a bed and was asked lots of medical questions. Once I was given some water and a bit of quiet time, I started to feel better. Then all of a sudden Geddy Lee walked in, asking how everyone was. As I wasn't the only one in the sick bay, I was speechless when he came over and asked if I was ok. I just nodded my head. I was so overwhelmed on seeing him. He was truly concerned for us all. I returned to the concert about 10 minutes later and was totally blown away by the whole set. This is one of the best concerts I have ever been to.

The *Moving Pictures* tour began in Hampton, Virginia on 11 September 1980 and wound up in East Troy, Wisconsin on 5 July 1981, 98 shows later.

LAKELAND CIVIC CENTER

20 SEPTEMBER 1980, LAKELAND, FLORIDA

I WAS THERE: RICK SILVIA

I saw them six times, from *Permanent Waves* to *Snakes & Arrows*. As a young lad I ran away from home, spending the night on a friend's porch. He had a record player he had borrowed from the school. I listened to '2112' from *All the World's a Stage* and was hooked. Being a novice guitar player I would try to play that album. To this day I will throw on 'The Necromancer' off of *Caress of Steel* and am still impressed.

My first Rush concert was on the *Permanent Waves* tour in with an old friend. It was bad to the bone. I saw them again on the *Moving Pictures* tour, which was epic, and the *Exit... Stage Left* and twice on the *Signals* tour, the absolute epitome of the band. They were *so* good words cannot describe a Rush concert. It is like trying to describe a beautiful mountain to a person. You just had to be there to see it.

SPECTRUM

25 SEPTEMBER 1980, PHILADELPHIA, PENNSYLVANIA

I WAS THERE: ANDY GLABERSON, AGE 14

From the second I heard *Permanent Waves* on its release I was hooked. I then travelled backwards in Rush's discography and was a forever fan. I never missed a single tour in the Philadelphia and New Jersey areas. Being a drummer I was sure I was the best air drummer at every concert. Neil influenced me as a drummer, and as a human being. He was my modern day warrior.

LE STUDIO

DECEMBER 1980, QUEBEC, CANADA

I WASN'T THERE: DOUG MARRAPODI

Back in 1980 I was totally consuming as much Rush as I could get my hands on and was awaiting the new album, *Moving Pictures*. I decided I couldn't wait any longer and

Doug had the skinny on Moving Pictures

called Le Studio up in Quebec. At that time with no internet, etc., there was very little information available, so if you wanted it you had to dig! I first looked up the engineer from *Permanent Waves* and figured he'd be the guy again, and the person to ask for. I called directory assistance (remember that?) and ask for 'Le Studio'. No problem, I got the number. I called and asked for Paul Northfield, again no problem. 'Please hold, I'll get him.' I basically said, 'Hey Paul, I'm a huge Rush fan and was wondering if you could give me any info on the upcoming album?' 'Sure!' He was totally cool. I asked the title, and some of the song titles. He told me it was called *Moving Pictures* and then started rattling off 'Red Barchetta', 'YYZ', 'Witch Hunt', 'Tom Sawyer', etc. I'm scribbling this down as fast as I can! I also asked what the album was going to be like and he described some of it but I honestly don't remember what he said because I was sweating at that point!. We wrapped it up and I thanked him and he said it should be released in a couple months. I couldn't believe it! For a small moment in time I was probably one of maybe a dozen people in the world who had the lowdown on *Moving Pictures*!

INTERNATIONAL AMPHITHEATER

26 – 28 FEBRUARY & 1 MARCH 1981, CHICAGO, ILLINOIS

I WAS THERE: JIM MULLINS

It was my first concert. I was a senior in high school. I went with two friends who were big Rush fans. I wasn't, but after seeing them live I was! What I remember most was our seats. We were in the last row of the upper deck. We almost had to look under the rafters in see them.

MECCA ARENA

2 MARCH 1981, MILWAUKEE, WISCONSIN

I WAS THERE: JOE KACHELSKI, AGE 18

As a high-school freshman I got a job in a shoe store. The guy I was succeeding was going to go to college and he lent me his *A Farewell to Kings* cassette and ordered me to listen with headphones on. This was the summer of 1978 and I had just turned 15. I was a senior in high school when I first saw them, and it was the first time I had ever attended an arena-type rock concert. Max Webster was the opening act. I actually came to like some of their stuff, but I remember being annoyed that I had to listen to this other band instead of Rush. I was very impressed that Rush's live songs were so true to the studio versions. I knew from buying

Joe Kachelski was introduced to Rush via A Farewell to Kings on cassette

live albums from other acts that sometimes their songs lost something in translation.

I've seen them on every tour since then, sometimes more than once, with the exception of a brief period in the mid-80s. Rush is without question my favourite band, and I'm not one who normally ranks things I like. The last show was on the *R40* tour, in Chicago. I wasn't terribly surprised about their retirement. I feel fortunate that they lasted long enough for me to take my sons to several shows. They are huge fans too.

HARA ARENA

8 MARCH 1981, DAYTON, OHIO

I WAS THERE: MARC NICEWANDER

Me and my band mates were at band practice in the basement at Hauer Music in Dayton, Ohio. The store was owned by our drummer Billy's father. We were taking a break when Billy had to go take a phone call. When he came back downstairs he looked like he just found out he hit the Lotto. Billy said, 'You are not going to believe this. I just got off the phone with Rush drummer's tech. Neil needs a 13 inch hi-hat Zildjian. We have back stage passes. We are going to the show!'

I was overwhelmed with excitement. I was 21 and full of zeal, piss and vinegar. 'Holy crap, I'm meeting Rush!' So we get the hi-hats for Neil, jump in to the Hauer Music van (playing 'Tom Sawyer at full blast!) and pull up at Hara Arena. It wasn't too far from the store.

It was like a dream that went sour. I was full of zeal and young and eager and definitely not cool. I walked up to Geddy (no, no!), extended my hand out and said, 'Sir, I'm Mark with the band Nydare.' The look on his face was not good. I was just a kid. Anyways, the tech put his arm around me and guided me away, saying, 'You're OK. It's just this band. These guys are here to work, man. It was all business.'

I took a gander on the bus and saw Neil reading what looked like a thick, mythical-type book and Alex playing a 12-string. My heroes! I said hello and I got a smile from both. Not a 'hey, how are you, what's your name?' but a friendly warm smile, like 'hey'. I didn't get that from Geddy - he actually scared me and I thought he was going to kick my butt! He wasn't happy.

We had to walk across stage to get to our seats and the crowd of course thought we were the band and went crazy and started yelling! It was surreal. We took our seats and Max Webster played, and then of course Rush. I could swear Geddy was looking at me with this mean glare. I'm not joking. What I did was definitely not cool. Having read more about Rush I now know it wasn't all me, thank god. They were very, very serious and private. It's all in 'Limelight'. I should pay more attention to lyrics!

It was a great show. I learned so much about what being serious about your band and music meant. *Moving Pictures* had just been released and they nailed it hard, note for note. It was all so fresh and exciting. The guys were spot on, from Neil tossing his stick into the damn rafters and not missing a beat to Alex nailing every lick. Geddy was like Bruce Lee. He just made a statement, like, 'This is how you make it in music if you're serious.'

I have such great respect for Rush as musicians and humans. They did it their way, worked their ass off and made it happen. I saw Led Zep in Cincinnati in 1975 and I was a huge Zep fan. Rush blew them away.

LONDON GARDENS

21 MARCH 1981, LONDON, ONTARIO, CANADA

I WAS THERE: JEFF SCHAMAHORN, AGE 16

Jeff Schamahorn saw Rush at London Gardens

I had that quintessential Rush moment during eighth grade. It was the spring of 1976 and I had been playing the drums for a handful of months and was eagerly seeking the music that would help me identify with my youth; a typical pre-adolescent conundrum for a young Canadian kid who didn't excel at sports. In an effort to expand my seemingly narrow horizons, I also studied trumpet in grade eight music class. Once a week, we were allowed to sign out our instruments and take them home to practise. My friend Rob Jackson also played trumpet. He was much, much better than I could ever dream. One afternoon I went to his house to practise with him. When we took a break, and knowing I was more interested in drumming than trumpet, he asked if I had heard of the band Rush. I was familiar with the heavily played 'Closer to the Heart' and 'Working Man'. He asked me if I had heard their latest; *2112*. I had no idea what he was talking about. He disappeared into his brother's bedroom. Barry was the stereotypical 70s older brother with the black light, velvet poster and lava lamp bedroom complete with that funny odour with which a 12-year old was soon to be acquainted.

Rob came back bearing *2112*. 'You're a drummer, check this guy out!' He dropped the needle on side one while I gawked at the back cover of this most life-changing LP - three guys in kimonos, one with a handlebar moustache. Like many youths in the 70s, I became a Rush fan for life at that very moment. *2112* was my music and Rush was my band. And as my teenage years went on, Neil Peart just simply became, as my wife said when we learned of him passing away, 'my guy'. No drummer and no band would ever stand higher in my mind. This was the pinnacle.

Fast forward to 1981. 16 years of age and in high school, I was in a band. The biggest perk to being in a band was having access to a van. And not just any van, but a powder blue full-size panel van with tinted bubbled windows. The lead guitarist and bass player were brothers and had the ultimate road trip machine. It seated seven comfortably, which meant it held 12 or more. Lead guitarist Scott usually drove, bass player Mike rode shotgun and, like most drummers, I sat behind them. Mind you, I had a swivel captain's seat with a view like no other. The largest tinted window in this dream-machine was next to me. It was complete with blue shag carpet from floor to ceiling and an 8-track player. My job, while we were on a road trip, was to retrieve 8-tracks from the built-in cabinet at the rear and feed them to Mike.

Rush was playing the London Gardens in London, Ontario. It was a sold out show of 6,000 and tickets were a whopping $9.50 general admission. We needed to be there considerably early to take advantage of getting to the front of the line. Doors opened at 7 pm so of course we headed out on our one-hour journey by noon. We sat in the parking lot until the first sign of another concert goer arrived, around 4pm. I remember darting from the van, the obvious odour of Northern Lights No 4 trailing behind me, and stood guard at the main door. Mike joined me and we held a vigil post until the doors opened three hours later.

When the doors finally opened, so did my new concert-going life. I handed some carny-looking guy my ticket. He tore it in half and was about to give me directions, but I sped past him, as well as past the long-haired, Nazareth t-shirt-wearing dude selling the large oversized concert programmes, and headed for the front of the stage. I really didn't care if I wet my pants later that evening from all of the beer consumption in the van. I was not moving. Not an inch. Mike joined me and we waited in heavy anticipation. A Toronto band, FM, who I had seen once before, opened and my prog-rock-testosterone spiked. I was at a heightened level I had never experienced before. The audience was calm, and as Neil Peart wrote later in 'Countdown', the excitement was so thick you could cut it with a knife.

The lights lowered, the wafting aroma that was all too common in the 70s and 80s swelled in the air, and the curtain dropped. The three men from Willowdale kicked the evening off with '2112', the song and album that brought me to this very point in my life. As a young teenager standing mere feet from centre stage, I couldn't imagine anything in my life being more incredible than this. Rush's performance that evening was so raw, yet so refined. The edginess of their earlier catalogue and the wide breadth of prog and rock made for one of my favourite set lists ever.

After '2112', Rush hit all the highlights from *Caress of Steel*, *A Farewell to Kings*, *Hemispheres* and of course *Moving Pictures*. They wrapped up the evening by playing the second half of '2112' (side one) and encored with 'La Villa Strangiato'. 'How could one evening in 1981 be any better?' I asked myself, Alex donning his red sport coat and double neck Gibson, Geddy with his massive synth set up and of course Neil, still in his double bass drum days with orchestra bells, crotales, triangles and wind chimes. The *Moving Pictures* tour was absolute magic.

When the show was over, I found that Nazareth t-shirt-wearing concert programme selling dude packing up. I needed a programme. I convinced him in to unpack the box and sell me one. It was all I looked at during the trip home. To say that this was the most euphoric experience of my life would be an understatement.

Through the years, I was able to see Rush eight more times. I introduced my youngest daughter to them in Detroit on Neil's 55th birthday and watched her eyes light up as mine did years and years before.

My final tour was the *Clockwork Angels* tour. I was divorced, newly engaged, kids all grown up and still a fanatic. My fiancée, luckily, was and is still a Rush fan. She wanted to see them when she was younger but her then-boyfriend quashed the idea. I knew she was meant for me when I climbed into her car for the very first time and looked around and saw a Rush CD in the glove box.

So in 2012 I had a chance to get seats for their *Clockwork Angels* tour in Buffalo, New York. Through an American Express promotion I was guaranteed seats in the first ten rows. My fiancée was probably more excited about this concert than I. She could finally put to rest that boyfriend from many years prior. I bought three tickets, two for us and one for her cousin Vito. She's Italian so Cousin Vitos are standard issue. I had no idea where exactly our seats would be until we arrived and picked them up from 'will call' and to my pleasant surprise we ended up in the second row immediately in front of Geddy Lee. Their final encore that night? '2112'.

To be introduced to a band by one song, have that song kick off your concert experiences and end on that same note years later, makes the whole Rush experience personal. That's the thing about this band; everyone has their own story, yet we all share a similar experience. Thank you Alex, Geddy and Neil for decades of my life I wouldn't have any other way.

SAM HOUSTON COLISEUM

7 & 8 APRIL 1981, HOUSTON, TEXAS

I WAS THERE: JOHN HILL

They played two nights in Houston on the *Moving Pictures* tour and I went both nights. Geddy started to remember me, as did Neil. I had always begged for photo ops and Neil would never do it, but I managed to get my programmes and LPs signed once again. Geddy and Alex were extra cool to us. It was then pretty much the same story on every tour until *Counterparts*. They started playing at The Summit after the *Moving Pictures* tour. I'd go to hotel to see them if I didn't have after show passes. Neil never came out.

I WAS THERE: ANDREW ALEXANDER

I was 14. I played guitar in a crappy high school garage band. I was a total Kiss freak and the drummer a Rush fanatic. He was older and could drive. Every time we got in the car together he would pop in the 8-track tape of *Hemispheres*. The all too familiar F#7add11 guitar chord would begin to rattle the car windows and the inside of my skull. I knew that for the next 20 minutes Rush would dominate the airwaves and any conversation. I was not a fan. Kiss was so much easier! But Kiss would

Andrew Alexander was a total Kiss freak until he discovered Rush

soon release *Dynasty* and the winds of change were beginning to blow. I needed better music in my life.

Circa December 1979 'The Spirit of Radio' began to play regularly on Houston stations and I kept thinking to myself, 'I do not hate this song!' I bought *Permanent Waves* when it came out and the journey began. The first time I saw Rush, I vividly remember the show beginning with the first parts of '2112', the interlude between 'The Trees' and 'Xanadu' and the dry ice fog flowing a foot deep over the stage. It moved over a row of multi-coloured lights at the front edge and spilled down behind the barricade, a multi-coloured waterfall in the mystic caves of ice.

A huge neon green spiral endlessly turned on the rear screen as they played 'Tom Sawyer'. My mind warped. This might also have something to do with the fact that this was the first time I had ever smoked weed. It seemed like the right place and time. I remember the gleaming alloy air cars racing towards the audience during 'Red Barchetta'. And Alex wore a HPD uniform shirt for part of the show. I'm sure the Houston Police Department was thrilled! The show ended with the '2112' finale. What a show!

I remember telling my mom how much I liked this band and how crazy it was that they have a song about trees. My mother asked to read the lyrics. She looked at me and said, 'This is not about trees, silly.' 'But mom the song is called 'The Trees'!' 'No, it's symbolism. It represents anyone's struggle over oppression. It's probably about communism or something.' My mom asked then to read all of their lyrics. She loved them. Every time a new Rush album came into the house she would grab the liner notes and study them. As she read the *2112* lyrics she immediately recognised the Ayn Rand book, *Anthem*. Within the hour she was taking me to the bookstore to purchase my first books of philosophy, *Anthem* and *The Fountainhead*. She was probably thrilled a 15 year old was studying literature instead of comic books or female anatomy. My mother passed away in the summer of 1987. The album *Hold Your Fire* came out shortly thereafter. To this day, every time I hear 'Time Stand Still' I think of her.

REUNION ARENA

10 APRIL 1981, DALLAS, TEXAS

I WAS THERE: GENE WILSON

I saw them 26 times. I saw them twice on the *Moving Pictures* tour, Friday night in Dallas and Sunday night in Fort Worth. I was in ninth grade and at the Dallas show I took a break for the restroom and a soda at the beginning of 'Red Barchetta' and got back to my seat right at the end of the song. This was when the on stage screen video had the car racing in what looked like an arcade game which was full state of the art then. At the Fort Worth Sunday show I didn't get up during 'Red Barchetta'. I was blown away by the video and initially thought, 'Hey, they didn't play this the other night?' It wasn't too long before I realised.

BUFFALO MEMORIAL AUDITORIUM

9 MAY 1981, BUFFALO, NEW YORK

I WAS THERE: JOSEPH BARBERA

I saw them live numerous times, once from the front row at the Aud in Buffalo, New York. They took a photo of the crowd from that concert and put it on the front cover of *Exit... Stage Left*. You can't see me because I'm behind the curtain but my friend is standing up in the white shirt, clapping in the front row. I got him those tickets after starting a ticket line outside, 17 days before they went on sale.

BROOME COUNTY VETERANS MEMORIAL ARENA

11 MAY 1981, BINGHAMTON, NEW YORK

I WAS THERE: BOB KALKA

I was around 12 years old. My older brother had convinced me that selling my dad's old 78rpm vinyl collection was totally legitimate (it wasn't), but doing so at the West Lestershire used record store in Johnson City, New York afforded me the choice of a couple of used rock records. The first album that my eyes gravitated towards was Rush's *Caress of Steel*. All it took was for that first play of 'Bastille Day' to completely fascinate me with this band that made these beautiful sounds, somehow with only three dudes. Shortly thereafter I picked up the live *All the World's a Stage* double LP from the same used record store (sorry, Dad!) and the combination of the cover photo and hearing the complete *2112* for the first time made me a fan for life.

A few years later I was able to finally see them live on the *Moving Pictures* tour in Binghamton, New York, and the spectacle of just three guys making those glorious sounds, with those awesome lights and videos during the show ('Red Barchetta!) set the standard by which I still evaluate bands.

As a mid-teens metalhead my interest started to wane a bit given all of the synths on *Signals* and *Power Windows*. The only reason I went to their Binghamton show on the latter tour was because I really didn't have anything else to do that evening. They opened with 'Big Money'. One second after the guitar break in the middle of the song, I was in love again.

I've seen Rush perform live 30 times, including a dozen times on the *R30* tour. As a cybersecurity executive for IBM, I've spent over 100 days on the road each of the past 25 years and caught them everywhere, from Glasgow to South America. Standing in the open-air national soccer stadium in Santiago with tens of thousands of Chileans was something I'll never forget.

What was it like to see Rush live? The best description I've ever heard was in a long-forgotten magazine which said that going to a Rush show is to see a stadium full of individuals playing air-guitar, air-bass and air-drumming - usually all at the same time. Exactly!

ONONDAGA WAR MEMORIAL AUDITORIUM

13 MAY 1981, SYRACUSE, NEW YORK

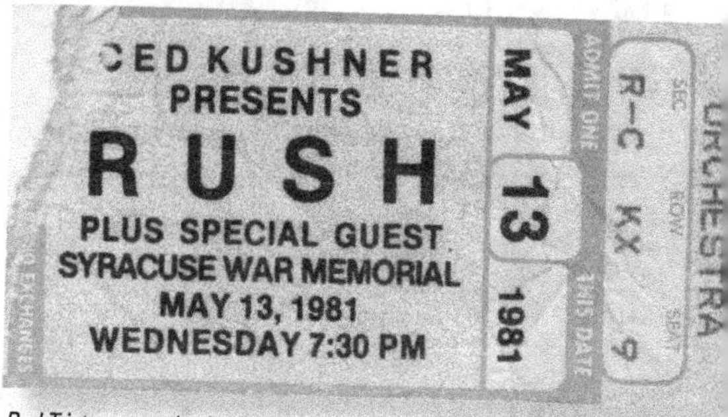

Bud Tristano caught the Syracuse show

I WAS THERE: BUD TRISTANO

I saw them three times – the *Moving Pictures* tour in Syracuse, New York, the *Grace Under Pressure* tour in Pittsburgh and *Snakes & Arrows* south of Pittsburgh. I grew up near a small town that was mostly tuned into kHz instead of MHz. I went into the military right after high school and was stationed in the Panama Canal Zone. All my fellow GIs were listening to the heavier rock and so I was hipped to the better bands like Rush. The first album I heard was *A Farewell to Kings* and I was hooked. I discovered *2112* later and then all the rest. When I rotated back to the States I was then able to see these bands live and hence the Syracuse show.

We were on the floor fairly close to the stage. I was watching Geddy, who was at the keyboards at the time, and some idiot threw a firecracker at the stage. I could see the fuse go right past his eyes. I would have never seen it had I not looked at that right instant. I could hear the firecracker go off behind him at the back of the stage only because I saw it. The music drowned it out. Geddy's eyes registered fear and anger at the same time. After the song he stopped and said to the audience something along the lines of, 'If you see anyone with fireworks, turn him in. Only an asshole would do something like this.' Of course most of the crowd did not know what he was angry about. I did not see whoever threw it in the first place or I would have reported it. Thank God no one was hurt.

CAPITAL CENTER

16 & 17 MAY 1981, LANDOVER, MARYLAND

I WAS THERE: CHRIS SUMMERS

I was 14 years old. We used to go after school and listen to records at a schoolmate's house. My parents didn't even own a turntable. My father's appreciation for music, God bless him, never extended that far. Back then, I was listening to a steady diet of Yes, Van Halen, AC/DC, and Peter Gabriel's Genesis. And then *2112* happened to me. 'Blown away' is an understatement.

When I heard that Rush was coming to my town on their *Moving Pictures* tour, I immediately begged my father to go. After some skilful negotiating on my part, he agreed that if my semester grades were all As, he would take me. The concert itself was on a weekday. My friends and I were abuzz all day at school. My father, who had worked all day, came home around 5pm. The show was scheduled to start at 7pm. He had no time to even change out of his suit and tie. We drove to the arena, picking up two of my buddies along the way, as their parents were delighted they were able to dodge that bullet. Me, Danny, Timmy, and my then 43-year-old old dad. In his suit and tie. At the Rush concert. As I think about it now, it was quite the comical entourage. As we settled into our seats, about 20 rows back and to the left of stage, I remember people in our section spotting my father and immediately extinguishing their joints, mistaking him for law enforcement.

MADISON SQUARE GARDEN

18 MAY 1981, NEW YORK, NEW YORK

I WAS THERE: WILLIAM SADOUSKY, AGE 11

I have two very cool older brothers. I remember in 1977 one brother playing an album that just blew me away. I was only seven. I said, 'Who is this?' He said, 'Rush.' It was *2112*. I was absolutely floored by what I heard and the complexities of the music. I became obsessed with them and I even learned how to play drums because of Neil Peart's amazing chops. They're the greatest band in Earth's five billion year history. And I'm honoured to have been alive for their conception. Seeing them live for the first time was like a religious experience with the sounds and the amazing light show. How three guys could make a sound like that still blows me away.

I saw them six times, the first time on the *Moving Pictures* tour. It was the most amazing show I have ever seen besides Pink Floyd's *The Wall* tour in 1979. The final Rush tour was the hardest because an end of an era was happening. Rush has gotten me through some very rough patches of my life. After my mom passed in 2019 I turned to the song 'The Garden'. It was very healing and spiritual. I played Mom 'La Villa Strangiato' and she said that Alex Lifeson was absolutely brilliant. I can't argue with her logic.

PROVIDENCE CIVIC CENTER

24 MAY, 1981, PROVIDENCE, RHODE ISLAND

I WAS THERE: RON PACHEICO, AGE 16

It was my first concert. I remember it being a great show. I was so impressed watching Geddy Lee playing bass and keyboards. I was just starting to get into Rush at that time. I'm still a fan. And the Civic Center? It's now called the Dunkin' Donuts Center.

OAKLAND-ALAMEDA COUNTY COLISEUM

5 & 6 JUNE 1981, OAKLAND, CALIFORNIA

Steve Russey has a very cool guitar

I WAS THERE: STEVE RUSSEY

I was a huge fan of progressive rock. The British triumvirate of Yes, Gabriel's Genesis and ELP were my absolute favourites, and still are. Friends suggested Rush and one loaned me *A Farewell to Kings*, their then current album. Friends assumed I would take right to Rush. I didn't. They were just too unusual, especially Geddy's voice. I listened to *Kings*, thought 'what am I supposed to do with this?' and returned it to the friend with the simple review of 'two thumbs down… way down'. He could not believe his ears!

A year passed and a different friend tried but this time suggested *2112*. My bandmates echoed this, suggesting that this could have been their strongest release to date. I acquiesced and acquired *2112*. Something clicked this time, although I still wasn't overly enamoured with the singing. I really liked the music, and the programmatic concept of the titular track (I am a huge sci-fi fan) as well as their jab at the record industry with Rush in the role of our protagonist, and the 'Priests' being the evil, corrupt, narrow-minded, rigid, egocentric record execs who want everyone to emulate The Bee Gees and Barry Manilow. And eventually defeating them as the prophecy comes to fruition and the Solar Federation overthrows the Priests, just as Rush won over an audience by not bowing down... I was fully proselytized.

I also liked the side B tracks: 'Something for Nothing' and 'The Twilight Zone' (it was nice how they dedicated *Caress of Steel* to Rod Serling when he passed in '75). Rush's affection for sci-fi interwoven with the music would always resonate with me: *Hemispheres*, 'Red Barchetta'... It gained momentum from there. I acquired all the recordings, and eventually Geddy's voice triumphed. ! Being a musician myself I could not help but be impressed by their virtuosity and prowess.

Moving Pictures came along in '81 and I finally saw them live. FM opened, but we were late and arrived during FM's final song. I had a huge circle of friends at the time, and 18 of us went. There were lots of people to pick up, three cars' worth, so I don't blame anyone. We should have left earlier. It was a fantastic show, with the best of their canon from the eponymous debut through to *Moving Pictures*.

I was looking forward to seeing them on the *Signals* tour and thought they would come back through the San Francisco Bay Area but much to my disappointment the closest they came was Southern California. Why, guys, why? I don't travel to see a band. I tip my hat to those Deadheads that would follow the Grateful Dead around the globe. Not I.

Forward to '95 and I saw them a second time at the Cow Palace on the *Counterparts* tour with The Melvins opening, a complete mismatch, like Hendrix opening for The Monkees. The pinnacle came when three songs into the set Rush performed 'Analog Kid'. Right then I knew my Rush experience was complete. I had got to see the boys play my favourite track live. Then I waited for a live version to be released. People told me, 'It's too obscure a song to be released commercially.' But with *Different Stages* my wish came true. Now I await a live version of 'Afterimage'. Since they're releasing all of this archival live material I may get that with the deluxe *Grace Under Pressure*. Cross your drumsticks!

LA FORUM

10 & 11 JUNE 1981, LOS ANGELES, CALIFORNIA

I WAS THERE: ANNE STEVENS

I am from Los Angeles and saw Rush at the LA Forum numerous times. I also saw them in Salt Lake City when I was travelling. They were always outstanding, and worthy of their legendary reputation. My memories of seeing them include just being so impressed with how skilled they were. I was blown away by Neil's drum solos. Watching such skilled musicians at work has always inspired me to become a better musician myself. I took mental notes on what makes a live show fun and memorable. Geddy was always very friendly with the crowds. And Alex's antics and charm was an added bonus on top of his skill, which he made look effortless. It was amazing to watch Geddy perform intricate bass lines while pouring out the involved lyrics put out by Neil. Their influence is vast and eternal.

My first tour was *Moving Pictures* in Los Angeles and it was phenomenal. My last tour was *Clockwork Angels* and I'm still kicking myself that I didn't see them for *R40*. I thought I'd see them on their next tour, which sadly never happened. I was very sad to see the great Neil Peart pass away.

ALPINE VALLEY MUSIC THEATRE

4 JULY 1981, EAST TROY, WISCONSIN

Meridien Skye first saw Rush on 4th of July weekend

I WAS THERE: MERIDIAN SKYE

My first Rush show was 4th of July weekend at Alpine Valley. The first show sold out so they added a second show. I couldn't get any one to go with me. Most of my friends were spending the holiday with family. I caught a ride down with a friend whose mom owned a bar in Milwaukee. He and his friends tailgated with me before the show. Joe Perry Project opened and had a great set, but as Perry left the stage he took his Les Paul and put it through one of the PA speaker cabinets. The guitar hung there and fed back for quite a long time until a roadie came and pulled it out of the cabinet.

Most of the songs they played are on *Exit... Stage Left*. My seat was section 2 row GG seat 1. So I had a decent seat for $13.25. Then I had to hitch hike back to Milwaukee. I was picked up by this drunk couple who were still drinking in the car. I remember praying most of the way back under my breath that we wouldn't die in a drink driving accident. They were wasted.

I saw every tour after that one from '86 to *R40* and some tours multiple times, including another 4th of July show in 2013 at Summerfest. Rush is still my all time favourite band!

The *Exit... Stage Left* tour began in October 1981 with 18 British and European shows followed by 17 US shows, concluding in December 1981.

NEW BINGLEY HALL

30 OCTOBER 1981, STAFFORD, UK

I WAS THERE: MARK APPLETON

They played two nights at New Bingley Hall and I went to the second of those on 30th October and immediately after the show drove to Deeside Leisure Centre in North Wales for the show the following night, where a friend and I slept in the leisure centre car park in my Ford Cortina, watching the trucks arrive in the early hours for the crew to begin setting up for the show. We were wrecked and smelly - but very happy.

I WAS THERE: STEVE POTTER, AGE 16

In my last two years at school I started to get into rock music but I'd never really heard Rush except maybe on (BBC Radio 1's) *The Friday Rock Show*. In the summer of 1981, I went round to this chap's house. There was some music on and I thought, 'Who's this woman singing?' He was playing *2112*. I really didn't pay too much attention. Someone said, 'We're going to get tickets to see them in October – do you want to go?' I started at college in the September and a chap there played me a couple of their records and I just fell in love with the band. I saw them 25 times in total.

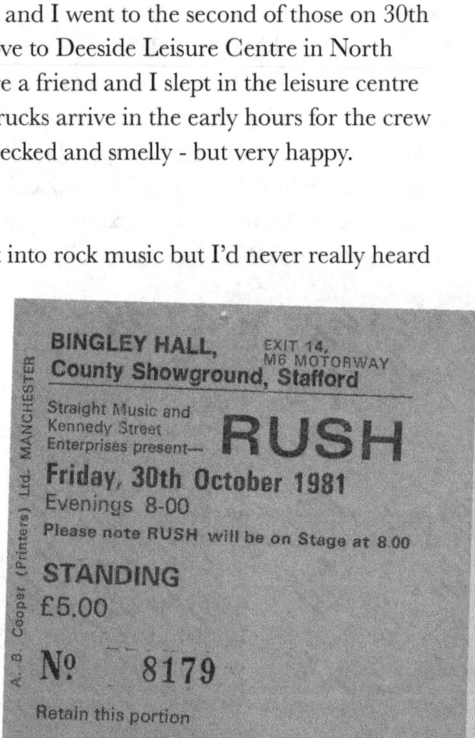

Steve Potter's ticket for the first of 25 shows he saw

Neil gets praised as the greatest rock drummer of all time and Geddy's an amazing bass player but Alex gets overlooked a little bit. He's such as tremendous guitar player. They were a band that nobody else seemed to bother about. Out of my circle of friends, a few others liked bits and pieces, but I was pretty much 'the' Rush fan. I thought I was a big Rush fan until the first time I went to a Rush convention and it was like, 'Okay, I know nothing!'

My first show was at New Bingley Hall in 1981. It rained during the afternoon and they opened the doors to let us in because we were all soaking wet. It was such a crush inside. For a first gig, it was exciting and scary and everything all at once. I lent one of the two guys I went with the money to buy a programme and all I had the money for afterwards was a scarf that I bought off a bootlegger outside. Since then, if there's a programme on sale at any concert I've ever been to, I've always made a point of buying one.

WEMBLEY ARENA

4 – 6 NOVEMBER 1981, LONDON, UK

I WAS THERE: DAWN HARRISON

I used to go to two gigs every time they toured in the UK to make the most of them being here. The first album I bought was *Fly by Night* when I was 13. A friend's brother thought I might like them and I saw the album in a record shop and bought it as I liked the cover! I queued outside Wembley Arena for their autographs after the *Moving Pictures* tour. They signed my programme. I have a set of golf club head covers commemorating their *R30* tour. I've used two of them ever since I've had them so they're a bit tatty now, but the driver cover has never been used.

My favourite track is 'Entre Nous'. I have asked for it to be played at my funeral.

ROYAL HIGHLAND EXHIBITION HALL

8 NOVEMBER 1981, EDINBURGH, UK

I WAS THERE: ERIC MARSHALL

As a poor young Irish lad brought up on the mean streets of Belfast, and all that it entailed for a catholic kid from the Falls, I had two escapes from my world - Anne McCaffery and music. More specifically, Rush. I pulled every trick, called in

Eric Marshall was second row centre at the Royal Highland Exhibition Hall

every favour, begged, borrowed, and stole just to get my second row centre ticket at the Royal Highlands Hall. Not to mention what I went through to make it to the show. It was a moment that helped define my music career and my life, and was one of those epic 'larger than life' moments that compelled me to do my utmost to sear every nuance directly into my memory. I was there to learn, study, and take in this experience with every fibre of my being.

As a young musician who had recently switched from guitar to bass, and as a new Rush fan, I was completely obsessed with this new, intricate, challenging music. I had started listening to Rush early in 1979 after seeking something beyond the usual run of the mill rock. The bass work in most rock/hard rock was quickly becoming rather boring. From the moment Rush began playing 'Overture' from *2112*, I experienced a complete euphoria, being drawn ever deeper into the performance. I couldn't stop smiling, and periodically giggled as they continued through their set.

They played some more from *2112* but then went onto 'Freewill' and then 'Limelight' from their most recent album. I recall hearing 'Subdivisions' which would appear later on the *Signals* album. The highest points for me were 'YYZ', singing along with the intro of 'Closer to the Heart' and the encore, when they played 'La Villa Strangiato'. During the entire show I was keenly aware that I was actually in the same room as these great artists who had inspired me to such greater things for my music, and for myself. To see beyond the world I came from, and strive for greatness. I spent days afterward labouring to remember and apply every single thing I had gathered from that one life-changing night. I owe so very much to Geddy, Neil, and Alex for my music, as well as my journey from war and strife to America and new dreams, and hope that somehow they knew how profoundly they touched people's lives.

AHOY SPORTSPALEIS

14 NOVEMBER 1981, ROTTERDAM, THE NETHERLANDS

I WAS THERE: JEAN-PAUL SRIVALSAN

In 1981 I ventured abroad to see them via a coach trip to Rotterdam. A couple of journos were on the trip with us and, before the show, they interviewed Geddy who was apparently surprised we had made such an effort to go see them in Holland so soon after they had extensively toured the UK. On the bootleg of the show, *Exit Ahoy... Left?*, you can hear us Brits cheering when Geddy gives us a shout out as he introduces 'La Villa Strangiato' at the end of the show.

I met them once, very briefly after a show at Wembley on the *Signals* tour in 1983, when they graciously did an autograph session backstage. It was a fairly sedate affair, with the few of us who had waited over an hour lining up quietly and politely to have our tour books signed. All three were sat behind trestle tables with the tour books simply signed and passed down the line.

HARTFORD CIVIC CENTER

20 DECEMBER 1981, HARTFORD, CONNECTICUT

I WAS THERE: BARRY JOHNSON

I was in high school when I attended my first Rush concert. I went with my friends Wade and Jeff. We took a Greyhound bus and had to hitchhike home. I remember the big screen with the moving pictures. It was a cold night. We got tenth row on the floor on Geddy's side. 'Tom Sawyer' was amazing. We were all on LSD and drinking Budweiser. You could feel the Civic Center moving with the sounds.

Laura Colon was enraptured by the video for 'Tom Sawyer'

BRENDAN BYRNE ARENA

21 DECEMBER 1981, EAST RUTHERFORD, NEW JERSEY

I WAS THERE: LAURA COLON, AGE 13

I turned 13 in the summer of 1981. I used to look forward staying up late on the weekends to watch *Don Kirshner's Rock Concert*. The show must have been a little dull on this particular night, as I fell asleep on the couch. When I woke up, a music video of a rock band consisting of only three members was on the screen. The singer had a most unusual yet intriguing voice. I watched intensely, waiting for the video to end to find out that the band I had just witnessed for the first time in my life was named Rush and the song 'Tom Sawyer', which the band was filmed performing live at Le Studio in Quebec. From that first time I knew that they were something really special. I vowed to find out everything I could about them. I purchased *Moving Pictures* on cassette tape and started building my collection of Rush titles.

I probably drove my parents crazy, droning on and on about the band and constantly playing their music in the house and in the car on weekly trips to my grandparents' house. They were playing at the Brendan Byrne Arena that December and I asked if we could get tickets to see them. As an early Christmas present my aunt, who at the time worked with concert promoter John Scher's daughter, agreed to take my younger brother and I to our first Rush concert. I couldn't have been any more excited!

About a week before the concert, there was plenty of fresh snow on the ground and my brother and I decided to go skiing. My parents dropped us off at the local ski area near our home in Vernon, New Jersey. Unfortunately, they ended up having to come pick us up a few short hours later for me to be transported to the emergency room with a broken collarbone. I recall my mom calling my aunt to tell her that we weren't going to be able to go to the concert, and suggesting she should sell the tickets, as I was in a sling and on pain meds. I was crushed.

I was in a lot of pain but somehow convinced my parents I was okay and that it was no big deal. I can remember my aunt holding her hands up, trying to protect me as we pushed through the crowd to our floor seats. A pretty intoxicated guy attempted to stumble past us to get to his own seat and she shouted, 'Watch it, my niece has a broken collarbone!' That was a close one, but after that, we settled in for the show. I noticed the crowd was mostly 20-something year old males, which I thought odd. After all these years, I'm still one of the few women I know who likes Rush, so maybe I shouldn't have been so surprised.

When Rush began playing, they sounded every bit as great live as on tape. My brother and I walked out of the concert with raglan *Moving Pictures* shirts my aunt bought us, which we still have to this day. And so began my love for what was and will always be my all-time favourite rock band.

I WAS THERE: TONY FERRARI

I was sitting third row on the aisle in front of Geddy. For some reason the security guards were strictly trying to keep everyone seated. That was impossible for me and I guess Alex had noticed and during 'Freewill' he came running to centre stage, having my attention, and tossed a guitar pick to me, along with a big smile and recognition of our eye contact. I was the only person with floor seats who was standing, personally defying security. That night they also played 'Subdivisions', which would be included on *Signals*. I had never heard them perform a song before that was yet to be released and I remember Geddy announcing this new song.

After 10 dates in April 1982 entitled the Deep South Spring Training tour, the band embarked on the *Signals* tour starting in Green Bay, Wisconsin in September 1982 and concluding in New York in July 1983. As well as North American shows, the band again visited Europe, playing eight shows on the continent and 10 in the UK.

THE CHECKERDROME

12 OCTOBER 1982, ST LOUIS, MISSOURI

I WAS THERE: JEFF DEUTSCHMANN

I saw them on every tour from 1982, only missing the 1988 and 2012 tours. It all started when I was in high school in St Louis aged 15. I heard about Rush from some of the stoners in class. When they put out *Signals* I got the LP. I heard they were coming into town for a concert so I got tickets. I was into AC/DC at that time but once I saw Rush live I was a firm believer. I went with friends from school. Just seeing them for the first time made every song stand out, particularly 'Countdown', and I loved 'Broon's Bane', which they played before 'The Trees'.

UNIVERSITY OF ILLINOIS ASSEMBLY HALL

13 OCTOBER 1982, CHAMPAIGN, ILLINOIS

I WAS THERE: PENNY MCCULLOUGH

It was the very first concert I ever went to. I went with a group of friends. It was amazing, and loud. I kept thinking of these three guys and wondering how did they make all of that noise? I really loved Geddy's synthesisers on that tour, and the sound of 'Subdivisions'. I've spent some time looking at old YouTube videos of Rush and remembering what it was I loved about *Signals*. I found my original concert ticket and also an ad for their concert. Also, I named my pet hamster Rush. I found her pictures in the same scrapbook as the ticket.

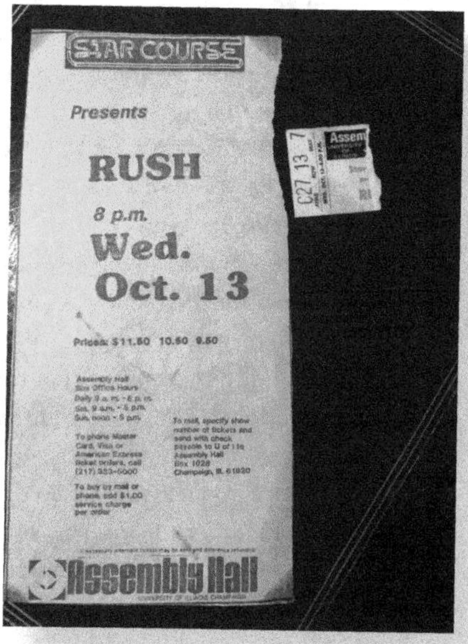

Penny McCullough saw Rush in Champaign, Illinois

ROBERTS STADIUM

31 OCTOBER 1982, EVANSVILLE, INDIANA

I WAS THERE: TIM WARGEL

The first Rush song I ever heard was '2112: Overture' on an over juiced car stereo in and I was like, 'WTF?' I didn't really start getting into them until *Permanent Waves* and *Moving Pictures*. Being from Southern Illinois and small market radio stations in the area you didn't get to hear a lot of their music. I lived three to four hours away from any big city. If you were lucky in the evenings, you could pick up a college or a St Louis or Nashville station.

In my senior year, September 1982, some buds and myself drove an hour and a half to Roberts Stadium in Evansville to see John Cougar (before he was Mellencamp) open for Heart. People were handing out flyers for upcoming shows. They handed one to my best friend Tony and he just stopped in his tracks and said, 'No fuckin' way!' We all read it and it said, 'October 31, 1982, Hallowe'en Night – Rush!' We went to school the next day and the caravan began. The show just happened to be on a Sunday so with it being church night for some and a school day the next day, a lot of crew going had some convincing to do with their parents.

At one time we had close to 30 people going but by the day of show there were 16 to 18 of us that drove up. We had a van and three or four cars drove over together. One guy even made a trip over to Southern Illinois University to score some hash and some kind of Hawaiian weed. The beer coolers were packed and the joints rolled and dispersed throughout the caravan and the road trip began.

We arrived at the stadium with time to experience our first ever tailgate. We smoked and drank with all different kinds of people (our age group was 15 to 19 years old). A little later we went in and hit the floor for the opening act. From seeing some earlier concerts, some of us knew to hang back and even sit in the chairs while everyone else is killing themselves getting to the stage. Opening act over, most of the people came crawling out of the pit so we walked up to about 15 to 20 feet from centre stage. By the time the show started the beers and weed were kicking in.

We were blown away by Neil's drum set and how it never ended. We saw the keyboards and were thinking that this was supposed to be a three man band. They came out and started the show and minds were blown! Just watching them perform with the sound that came out of the speakers was phenomenal. By the time the show was over, most of the crew was stoned numb or overwhelmed by the whole trip.

What I remember the most was when they performed 'Red Barchetta' and the picture screen running while they were performing it. I fell in love when they performed 'The Trees' and then went into Xanadu. It was a year or so later when I came across *Exit... Stage Left* and it was like I was at the concert all over again. *Exit...* is still in my car player and in my garage. Sadly that's the only show of theirs I ever saw.

HAMPTON COLISEUM

30 NOVEMBER 1982, HAMPTON, VIRGINIA

I WAS THERE: JOHN GABRIEL

Back in 1982 I was attending college at Old Dominion University in Virginia where I loved attending basketball games. During timeouts the

John Gabriel first heard Rush at a basketball game

band would play this catchy jam which I found to be 'YYZ'. Certainly different than anything else they played during the whole night. A friend was having troubles with his girl and had an extra ticket to a band called Atlanta Rhythm Section who were playing at the ODU campus one evening. I was into Boston, Foreigner and arena rock but I was amazed by the performance of that band. So when my friend Constantinos (and may God bless him, wherever he may be) suggested I also join him to go see a band named Rush, as he had an extra ticket for that show too, I trusted his taste. It changed my life. I only knew 'Tom Sawyer' and 'Limelight' that were being played on the radio and was certainly looking forward to the jam on 'YYZ'. I had a couple of beers to get in the mood and then the band announced they were going to play a few songs from *Signals*. They played 'Countdown', an amazing live song, where the Space Shuttle was ready to launch during the song and in the video background the stage filled with smoke as if the Shuttle was launching in front of us. My jaw dropped.

My jaw dropped again when 'Red Barchetta' was performed. Showing the cartoon vehicle in a winding road in the background with that amazing music was it for me. '2112' dropped me to my knees... and then they played 'Subdivisions' and I was thinking, ' Where the hell have I been, missing this band for so many years?'

I ran to the record store and purchased *Signals*, *Moving Pictures* and, at the advice of the clerk there, *Permanent Waves*. 38 years and 56 shows in five states later, I feel I am as devoted to this band as any.

MADISON SQUARE GARDEN

3 DECEMBER 1982, NEW YORK, NEW YORK

I WAS THERE: PHIL SAPIENZA

December of 1982 was a Rush-packed month for anybody living in the Tri-State area with five incredible shows. But one show was very special for this drummer and fan of the band since the age of 10, when my brother had come home with *Fly by Night* in 1975.

Phil Sapienza caught Rush at Madison Square Garden

Rush played two nights at Madison Square Garden with Rory Gallagher opening. Geddy was doing the bass section of 'Digital Man' right in front of me on the first night as I was up against the boards. That sonic bottom end pounding in my chest, taking me back to the feeling I had watching my older brothers in drum corps before I was old enough to march myself. It set me on my own non professional musical journey.

Day two was a Friday and my friend Jeff who had the connections knew they were staying at the Berkshire Place Hotel on 52nd Street. We avoided school and camped out in front of the hotel for several hours hoping to meet them to no avail. I did however meet Nick Nolte (with two very expensive-looking friends), so I scored an autograph for my girlfriend Patti. I also met The Smothers Brothers who were hosting *Saturday Night Live*, and Pam Dawber and Andy Gibb who were starring in *The Pirates of Penzance* on Broadway, so it wasn't a total bust.

Jeff and I went to the second show, but left about three quarters of the way through to get back to the Berkshire. Adjacent to the Berkshire is a restaurant called The Rendezvous. There were maybe 12 to 18 of us just waiting. One couple and their kids asked what we were doing, so we told them. The dad offered to camouflage me in with his clan to get me inside the hotel. I made it through the first set of doors before the doorman stopped us and informed my 'dad' that, 'He's not with your party, he's been here all day sir.' I stuck out in that family just a little bit, being a skinny little kid with a leather bomber jacket and denim cut-off Rush mural on the back.

Back out on the street and Geddy's limo pulls up. A guy gets out and says that Geddy will be happy to sign autographs if we 'made a nice line and didn't take any pictures.' A photographer was lurking who had pissed the band off earlier in the day, but he kept his distance while Geddy kept his head down (to avoid pictures), signed our stuff and headed into the hotel.

Neil's limo pulls up and we scurry over to him. He didn't seem overly annoyed as I expected. I was well aware of the band, and Neil especially, cherishing their privacy. He's signing away and I was about two or three people away from getting my autograph. I asked Neil if he would settle an argument and properly pronounce his last name to which he very cordially responded with what we now know to be the proper pronunciation. Then the photographer steps up and starts popping pictures, almost in Neil's face. Neil immediately stopped signing and bolted into the hotel.

We waited for Alex. Then someone noticed that all of the guys - including Alex - and their entourage were seated at the circular booth right up against the window of The Rendezvous. We were pressed against the window watching them try to eat and unwind after the show. Hoping Alex would stop what he was doing and come out and sign autographs, someone pounded on the glass. Alex looks at us very annoyed with a mouth full of food, gesturing towards his face as if pleading with us to leave him alone because he was eating. Which he was, and I don't blame him.

I felt horrible guilt at this point, so we ventured back to Queens. No autograph from Neil, but I can say that I spoke to the man, and he politely spoke back when he very well could have done otherwise. What a week of shows!

JOE LOUIS ARENA

7 & 8 DECEMBER 1982, DETROIT, MICHIGAN

I WAS THERE: PATRICK MONLEY

'Freewill' and 'The Spirit of Radio' were getting played on the radio. I was still in high school and didn't care much for Geddy Lee's voice so I never really paid them much attention. *Moving Pictures* came out the following year and piqued my interest with 'Tom Sawyer' and 'Limelight'. Detroit was a pretty good rock 'n' roll environment. But I didn't get a chance to see that tour. The *Signals* tour was the first opportunity I had to go see them

I went with high school friends who were bigger Rush fans than I was. Seeing them I was just totally, totally blown away. I heard songs like 'The Camera Eye' which I didn't know because I didn't have the *Moving Pictures* album at that time. It had a huge impact on me. They played 'Countdown' with a great video backdrop presentation while a lot of the new music that they played off *Signals* really enraptured me. I went in search of their back catalogue.

I'd been playing the drums since I was about 12 years old. When I discovered what Neil Peart was all about that made me want to be a drummer all that much more. When *Exit... Stage Left* came out I remember learning 'Xanadu' and 'La Villa Strangiato' and 'Jacob's Ladder' - all these songs I hadn't heard. It was love at first listen.

After the *Signals* tour, I saw them for every tour up until *R40* and a couple more than once. They came to the Toledo Sports Arena in Ohio, close to where I was living. It was pretty small compared to Joe Louis Arena, which held about 20,000. I saw them 25 times altogether. Once I got into them I couldn't be kept away.

VETERANS COLISEUM

11 DECEMBER 1982, NEW HAVEN, CONNECTICUT

I WAS THERE: WILL KUENZEL

I met a kid in junior high. Jeff and his family had moved from Texas and we became friends. One day he asked, 'Do you like Rush?' 'Who?' I asked. 'No, Rush!' He let me borrow *Hemispheres* and *A Farewell to Kings*. I was captivated. The first album I purchased was the newly released *Permanent Waves*. I started sharing my love of Rush with all my friends. My bedroom was 95 per cent Rush posters, photos and other collectables. I think what really made me an instant fan was the precision of their music. I started playing every album from *Fly by Night* on and reading all the lyrics from beginning to end. I found something I could relate to in almost every song.

Moving Pictures was the album that made many pay attention. 'Tom Sawyer' was getting all kinds of airplay. People would see my t-shirt or stickers on my locker and skateboard and say, 'Dude, you like Rush? Those guys are awesome!'

I went to every show from *Permanent Waves* all the way through to the *Time Machine* tour. I saw them in New Haven for the *Signals* tour. I was front row, smack in front of Geddy. Being a bass player, he was a god to me. Towards the end of the show they played 'Spirit of Radio' and Geddy sang 'one likes to believe in the spirit of baseball....' I pitched an 'air ball' towards him as he happened to look right at me. He swung at the ball with the neck of his bass and then quickly put his right hand up to shield his eyes as one would do to watch the ball fly off into the distance! How cool was that? I interacted with Geddy Lee!

No band has ever held my attention like Rush. When they played their last show it was something that was full of emotions. Knowing that Neil was dealing with serious foot pain and Alex was dealing with arthritis in his hands, I was relieved for them to go out while they still sounded as tight as ever.

I listen to Rush frequently and find myself saying, 'Man, I wish I could have seen just one more show.' I am as much a fan now as I have ever been.

Steve Savo saw Rush 126 times

I WAS THERE: STEVE SAVO

I saw Rush 126 times from 1982 to 2015 and became friends with them.

My older brother gave my childhood best friend *Hemispheres*. I remember playing it and said, 'Where did you get this?' He said, 'from your brother'. When I saw the band performing 'Limelight' on video I just fell in love. *Moving Pictures* came out and I was 10 years old. I was too young to go to the show and I remember crying.

My very first show was December 1982 at New Haven Coliseum. Then they played Hartford in April 1983 and that was it – I was all in. I was 16 when they toured *Grace Under Pressure*. I was driving by then and I had friends who could drive. I started going over the border into New Jersey and New York. If you really loved a band you could easily see them six or seven times on a tour. That was the first tour where I got front row seats.

They had a week of rehearsals in Florida because it was an extension of the *Grace Under Pressure* tour. I'd hang around the hotel like any other fan. As I got older I realised they wanted to be left alone; don't invade anybody's privacy. But at the time I was 16 and I didn't care. Geddy walked by and he said 'hello' and signed an autograph.

For *Power Windows* I took a road trip to Florida. And it was on that tour in Massachusetts when I first met Neil Peart. For *Hold Your Fire* I started travelling to places like Detroit. With each tour, I was getting closer to the crew and then getting invited into sound check. As long as I was willing to do that stuff alone, and I knew my place and I was respectful and quiet, they would let me hang around. I could quietly enjoy all the perks I was getting from the guitar tech, the drum tech and the road manager.

When they were coming to Connecticut and they had a night off, I'd take them out. For crew who are out on the road, having a friend in the city was an attraction. It was more fun than sitting in a hotel room. And sometimes they'd say, 'Oh, we're all going off to dinner' or 'we're all going to a hockey game – come with us!' so I just got invited to a lot of stuff.

Every town I would go into, I'd run into other fans, and we'd stay in touch. I remember saying to Geddy, 'I have so many lifelong friends because of your band and your music.' When I was in Chicago for the *Hold Your Fire* tour, this one friend was on crutches and Jimmy, Alex's guitar tech, brought my friend on stage before the sound check and let him look at the drums and all the pedals and see all the ins and outs of the production.

Presto was 1990. I was 19 or 20 years old. I rented a car. I got to be really tight with Howard Ungerleider, who was their tour manager and lighting director at the time. Because I was a young kid, and because I was on my own and it was easy to look after just one guy, they'd take me under their wing and look after me. After one of the shows it was, 'Listen, if you want you can follow the tour bus.' I remember going to Jacksonville, Miami and Orlando. I'd follow the bus and I'd get to the hotel and stay in the same hotel. I was very respectful when they were getting their keys. I'd stay back. It wasn't like, 'Hey, what room are you in?' Once there was no room for me and Howard wouldn't go to sleep at night until they found me another hotel where there was a room. He really looked out for me.

Later on that tour there was a day off in Miami and I'm having lunch with Howard when Geddy and Alex walk by, and they see Howard. I go, 'Wow, I've never met Alex!' And Geddy and Alex came and sat either side of me. I'm 20 years old and shaking in my shoes, but I kept it cool and reintroduced myself to Geddy and introduced myself to Alex, and they sat there for half an hour. Rush are not an easy band to get close to. It's like the Rolling Stones, you know, it's not an easy task. I was lucky enough to have that moment. Next day the band were getting off the bus and walking through security to soundcheck with the band. Howard was with them and security stopped me. Howard said, 'Hey, he's with the band!'

At show time I'd go back in with the fans. I'd have a pass and could walk wherever I wanted so I could go in and out of areas. Meeting people in each city and mingling was my favourite part. 'How many times have you seen the band?' So if someone said, 'It was my 60th show!' and I'd got a guitar pick from Alex, I'd give it to them. It would be, 'I can't bring you backstage but I got this.' Or if someone was crying and saying, 'Oh, I was waving at JJ and he was supposed to give me a pick and he never did,' then if I had a few extras I'd give them one. I enjoyed doing that and it was fun to share that experience.

Howard wasn't on the *Roll the Bones* tour so my main connection was gone. But at the end of the day, it was about the music and I was happy just to see the band. Howard was back for *Counterparts* in '94. By that point I had stopped buying tickets. I was getting into all the shows for free and I'd stand at the lighting board with Howard.

On the *Test for Echo* tour, I'd show up five hours early and go and watch the sound check. That tour was really special for me too because the drum technician, Larry Allen, would let me sit behind Neil's kit. He let me do it again on the *R30* tour.

At Jones Beach, I was talking to this girl for a little while and telling her that I got to talk to Geddy and Alex and I never get to talk to Neil, and I was telling her about the history of Jones Beach, and then she said, 'Oh, I'd better go - he's looking right at us.' And she walks up on stage and gives Neil a kiss and I'm like, 'Oh my god, I was just talking to Neil's daughter Selena!' After the show I talked to her for a few minutes more. The next month she was killed in a car accident. They were waiting for a phone call saying, 'I made it, I'm at my dorm' and instead they were told that the car flipped over. And then Neil lost Jackie. That was really tough.

Five years without Rush was really horrible for us die-hards because when Rush went on tour it was like baseball season or hunting season for the people who have those hobbies. When they finally got back together for *Vapor Trails*, the first show was in Hartford, Connecticut, where I'm from, so of course I had my front row seat. I took my six-year- old son Kevin with me. I have a picture of him backstage with Geddy and Alex, with them smiling because 'this six-year-old really knows our material.'

I saw 17 shows on that *Vapor Trails* tour. For the *R30* tour I spent a week on the road. My younger son Rocky was four and Kevin was closer to nine. We spent the week together on the road. During '2112', Geddy joked around with the lyrics, singing 'we are the pirates' instead of 'we are the priests'. He had a little parrot on his shoulder and they had a Jolly Roger on the screen. And I said to Kev, 'Wear this pirate's patch on your eye and a pirate hat,' and every show that week there's Kevin on the screen! During that whole week he got to hang out with the band. He said to me, 'Why do you walk away when Geddy comes up?' And I said, 'Because he knows me. He wants to say hello to you. I've had my time with them. Now this is your time.'

At one show, Geddy had thrown shirts out during the encore and held up his finger like, 'Wait a second.' This guy comes over with a shirt and I say, 'This is a small. This ain't gonna fit me. He said, 'It's not for you, it's for Kevin.' The next day we're backstage and Kevin has the band sign the shirt. He goes up to Alex and says, 'Alex excuse me, can you sign this shirt?' and Alex says, 'Absolutely Kev.' And Kevin says, 'I'm gonna let you go, cause I can see you're talking to a friend.' Even my kids have this great backstage etiquette.

Pennsylvania was my 95th Rush show. We got to watch it from stage right, on Alex's side, and that was really cool.

R40 was closed off to almost everybody. It was hard to get myself into some of these shows. There weren't a lot of passes. I got into a couple with all three kids. I was going through a divorce and didn't have a lot of money then. It would have been over 500 bucks to take all four of us to a show. I remember telling Howard I was going to split up the kids for the shows I was attending and he said, 'I know you're going through a tough time. I've got you passes for you plus your three boys. You're all set.' At one point Howard let my youngest son, Marc, do the lights for 'Spirit of Radio': 'Press this. Now press that!' That was cool.

THE SPECTRUM

13 & 14 DECEMBER 1982, PHILADELPHIA, PENNSYLVANIA

I WAS THERE: CHRIS SHELDON

Chris Sheldon saw the Signals tour

I grew up in a small town outside Philadelphia. We had two FM rock radio stations. I started getting into music and taking up drums around the time of *Permanent Waves* when I was 12 or 13. 'The Spirit of Radio' was the single they were spinning off that record. I was really into reggae so liked the little reggae twist they did at the end of the song. I asked for that record for Christmas that year and a family friend gave it me. I would sit with headphones on, listening to it and reading the liner notes and just obsessing about the record and the recording techniques. I made it a goal then to go see them next time they were in town, which was the *Signals* tour.

I was taking drum lessons at the time. I took the *Signals* record to my drum teacher and had him help me through some of the more technical parts that I couldn't get. I used to sit and play along with those records with headphones on.

They were unlike anything I'd seen before. Rush was my third concert after the Kinks and the Cars and it just took everything up to a whole other level. Once I got past the bombast of Neil's ginormous kit and his technique, I started homing in on what Geddy was doing and what he was able to pull off, playing bass and synth and bass pedals at the same time, and Alex's technique and his parts. Neil's way of playing melodically and not just rhythmically is what I incorporated into my own playing style as a drummer.

I WAS THERE: PETE BRAIDIS

I was in seventh grade and only 13 years old, living in Haddon Township, New Jersey - a lovely little suburb of Philadelphia, and I knew it was now my destiny to see my first concert. My mom and dad were very good at making my sister and I happy, and if we asked for things within reason, we usually did pretty well as long as we did chores and got good enough grades. However, the idea of me and my friends going to a concert took some serious work on my part as far as convincing her that this was a great idea to expand my horizons. Her sarcasm roared loudly: 'You're 13 years old, you have no horizons yet!'

'Ah, but I do,' I declared. My first attempt was a massive show being headlined at the decrepit but legendary JFK Stadium and headlined by Genesis with a supporting bill of new wave acts. Genesis was playing the nearly 25 minute long masterwork 'Supper's Ready' for the last time. But my mom said, 'There is no way in hell I'm dropping you guys off at a show with over 100,000 stoned rockers!' She also said no to The Who on their 'Farewell Tour' at JFK with Santana, The Clash and The Hooters.

My friends and I set our ambitions lower and decided that an arena show would surely get the green light. But Judas Priest with Iron Maiden opening was also shot down. I was devastated. Next time I grovelled and pleaded. It was Rush, and my mom knew this was my favourite band. Thus on 13 December 1982 my Dad volunteered to drive me and nine of my friends to Philly for the concert. 10 thirteen-year olds were packed like sardines in that Subaru, but none of us cared if we had an elbow in the ribs or a foot in the face. Once we started walking up the steps to the Spectrum and saw all the other concert-goers we got very excited. It was cold out and we could see our breath as we neared the entrance. We didn't give a damn. Once we were seated, we saw the stage being set up and when the lights went down around 7.30pm it hit me. We were ready to rock!

Rory Gallagher was the opener. He opened with 'Moonchild' and I was floored. I also noticed how damn loud it was, but I loved it. Rory probably played about 45 minutes or so and left to solid applause. Between bands, a stoner behind us made fun of our group saying, 'Isn't it time for bed yet, you little creeps?' I started getting nervous because he and his pals were much older and bigger and reeked of bad weed and even worse breath from cheap-ass beer. But one of the dudes leaned over and said, 'The hell with him, man. I think it's cool you guys are here, so enjoy the show, dudes.'

When the lights went down and the intro music of the *Three Stooges* theme came on, my heart started racing. And once Alex Lifeson blasted the opening riff of 'The Spirit of Radio' the place went nuts, as did we. The infamous 'concert hall' line belted out by Geddy Lee, where the house lights briefly went up showing the entire crowd, had me in awe. There were 17,000 other people here that felt just like I did about this music.

'Tom Sawyer' took me by surprise as I didn't expect to hear it so soon. And I felt totally free to play air drums (and still do). 'Freewill' was jaw-dropping as Alex, Geddy and Neal Peart all nailed that complex mid-section jam with aplomb. The first song from *Signals* was next with an excellent version of 'Digital Man', followed by my favourite song ever, 'Subdivisions'. We lived in suburbia and had just started high school and were tiny little mealworms at our school compared to all the bigger kids. The video was heavily played on MTV and accentuated what it was like growing up in such a town and not knowing your place, with the added bonus of video games (it was the Atari game *Tempest* in the video, and I sucked at that!).

'Vital Signs' was followed by the 11 minute epic 'The Camera Eye', which would not be played again after this tour until 2011. 'Closer to the Heart' had everyone feeling good and singing along with lighters in the air, and then it was 'Chemistry' (only played on this tour) and 'The Analog Kid'. Both were stellar. Alex Lifeson offered up some acoustic guitar work on 'Broon's Bane' before segueing into 'The Trees' which was amazing to hear for this first time concert-goer. 'Red Barchetta' then took me away and 'The Weapon' was dead-on, just like the album but with the added bonus of the hilariously lame vampire from SCTV's *Count Floyd* doing an intro on the video screen.

The band's lone Top 40 US single 'New World Man' was up after that, followed by the euphoria of 'Limelight' (still some of the greatest lyrics ever written) and the ode to NASA and the Space Shuttle that was 'Countdown' which would never be played again after this tour. The band left the stage to a deafening roar, but even we knew the show wasn't really over yet.

They returned for a packed encore beginning with '2112 Part 1: Overture' and 'The Temples of Syrinx'. I can still see all those lights and lasers as the keyboard intro to 'Overture' began and it connected in a big way. 'Xanadu' and 'La Villa Strangiato' were a musical orgy. How did these three guys reproduce all this complex music so flawlessly in concert?

It was back to the debut album from 1974 for the rollicking 'In the Mood', and oddly 'YYZ' finished things off and Neal Peart (God bless his soul) performed his infamous drum solo with class, panache, skill, dexterity and musicality that still defies true description. And that's how my first Rush concert ended. We walked out into the pre-Christmas cold feeling like Santa had visited us a little early with this musical gift.

I had in my clutches my ticket stub ($9.50), my tour programme ($4) and my New World '82-'83 tour t-shirt ($8). Wearing that t-shirt to school the next day was my declaration to the kids at school that I was cooler than they were.

I would end up seeing Rush 23 times right through to the final tour in 2015. Many of the friends I went to that first show in 1982 with were with me at all the shows that followed, all the way to the end. It was a bond between us and the music that could not be broken. Some people still think you're a nerd if you're a Rush fan, but if that's the case, then call me an extremely proud nerd.

I WAS THERE: JOHN VERICA, AGE 14

I had grade school friends who introduced me to several bands around 1976. Several of them were into Kiss but I really did not connect with Kiss. However with *2112*, I discovered Rush in earnest. I lived within walking distance of the Philadelphia Spectrum, where Rush often played multiple days on the same tour until the early 1990s. My first time seeing them live was on the *Signals* tour, with my cousin who was heavily into Rush. He was from Southern, New Jersey where vast numbers of Philly suburban kids and teens were into the band, more so than Philly proper. Most people while growing up in South Philly were not into rock unless it was radio FM-friendly AOR such as Journey.

It was an epiphany experiencing Rush live. I felt like an ethnographer, cognitively recording the experience, observing Rush fans air drumming in time to 'YYZ', getting a laugh out of the Dracula sequence skit being projected onto a screen propped up behind the band during the start of 'The Weapon'. It felt like a communal, collective vibe, with the band feeding off the crowd and vice versa.

I went onto see Rush 15 times. The first time I saw them do a behemoth three hour set, with a brief intermission outdoors, was at the Tweeter Center in 1997. My girlfriend and I at the time purchased six tickets; it was triple date of Rush couples! The weather was a beautiful summer evening. I felt that Rush communal sensation, and even more so with a sold out 20,000 plus fans outdoors. Many were singing along to several Rush songs, air drums going off at random.

That five year gap between tours and not knowing if Rush would ever reform, if Neil was up to it after his personal tragedies, was a trying time for fans, as well as the band. Respectful of whatever the band decided to do, or not do, I was on board. It was pure elation when they reformed for *Vapor Trails*. That sense of wonderment returned at that live show along with a sense of relief mixed with joy that Neil was going to be OK. The band reinvented themselves in the new century with modern sounds, yet so familiar, so very Rush-defined sonic sensibilities and poetic-meaningful lyrics. Rush returned, indeed.

And then, it was, 'Hey everyone, we are calling it a day, we are retiring. Neil cannot deal with chronic muscle pain, Alex has tendenitis, etc. We are boomers and we are going out with a bang!' That final tour was bittersweet on so many different levels. The tour was brilliant, pure genius, going back in time through their vast catalogue, changing clothes and instruments to match the relating decade to the live song, a fantastic end to a fantastic trio of friends.

I often went to shows solo. No girlfriend was interested, no friends were into it any longer. Whatever the shallow or lame reason offered, it never stopped my dedication to and interest in the band. They defined their own sound and brought progressive rock to new levels and a wider audience. They stayed the course and left us with a plethora of cherished music for future generations to come.

TINGLEY COLISEUM

11 & 12 FEBRUARY 1983, ALBUQUERQUE, NEW MEXICO

Paul Southward saw Rush 31 times

I WAS THERE: PAUL SOUTHWARD

I saw 31 Rush concerts in nine states and 11 cities with many friends.
My first rock concert was not Rush but Aerosmith in January 1983. The sound in Tingley Coliseum in Albuquerque, New Mexico, a rodeo arena for the state fair, was so loud and so bad it was hard to discern which song they were playing. The highlight of the show was at intermission when it was announced that Rush would be playing Tingley the following month. Back then they didn't sell tickets a year ahead of the show.

I bought tickets the moment they were available. Sales were so brisk they promptly added a second night and I bought tickets for that too. The first night, Chris and I went directly from school to wait for the gates to

open so we could run to the front of the stage. We ended up maybe 10 people back. There was a problem, however. I was maybe five feet five inches tall and Chris about the same; we played trumpet in the band, we weren't on the basketball team. We held tough and made it to about three or four people back until Rush started playing. It sucked. Of course, the band was great, but the constant press of people and staring at the back of people's heads wasn't the experience we had envisioned. After maybe six Rush songs, we agreed to get out of the crowd and watch the rest from the seats around the venue.

We chose a different approach for the second night. Around the beginning of the opening act, Golden Earring, we started at the edge of the floor crowd and kind of just slowly made out our way towards the front. Not long after Rush started, we reached the barrier in front of the band. I ended up with a big tall guy behind me, reaching his arms against the barrier on either side of me and bearing the press of the crowd behind us. I just stood there with just my fingers, nose, eyes and top of my head above the barrier. Geddy stood on the edge of the stage in front of me and looked right at me during 'YYZ'. I've always imagined he thought I reminded him of 'Kilroy was here'. He had the 'I (heart) you to (Darth Vader's helmet)' pin on. Chris was also able to find a pocket, and we enjoyed the rest of the show from the barrier. This was the experience we had hoped for!

Rush kicked off their *Grace Under Pressure* tour in Albuquerque on May 7th, 1984. My salient memory of that was Geddy goofing up his opening bass riff to 'The Body Electric', the first time he played it live. It was the only real mistake I remember from him in 31 concerts.

For the opening night of the *Time Machine* tour, once again in Albuquerque, my wife arranged us a VIP experience including third row centre seating. My next door neighbour also had VIP tickets. He knew I was a Rush fan but always saw me as a pretty reserved guy. In the VIP area, he was amused to see me excitedly jumping up and down like a pogo stick but was polite enough not to say anything.

Paul Southward

I took my two oldest daughters to the *R40* Phoenix show, the band's third from last, and my last Rush concert. I had four tickets. My oldest daughter was 12 and my middle one 10. I struggled over whether I could conscientiously also take my 7-year-old. In the end I offered the ticket to my old friend, Rodney.

I initially looked into attending the ceremony for their star on the Hollywood Walk of Fame, but remembered my first Rush concert experience and envisioned being behind the tall dude. There were too many uncontrollable unknowns, so I decided against it. I also looked into attending the Rock and Roll Hall of Fame ceremony. Experiencing the profound wave of applause when they started to be announced would have been worth the expense alone. Also, I didn't attend their last concert in LA. Given the events that followed, it would have been cathartic and historic. I was able to see Alex interviewing Geddy at the Hall of Fame and Geddy signed his book for me. Meeting him was so fantastic, and spending the day (and evening) with like-minded Rush fanatics was so much fun.

THE FORUM

17 & 18 FEBRUARY 1983, INGLEWOOD, CALIFORNIA

I WAS THERE: JAMES GALVIN, AGE 15

Before Rush, I listened to KISS, BTO, April Wine and Sabbath - mostly heavy metal. Golden Earring opened up the show I saw. I went with my best friend, Louis Hidalgo. We also saw the *Grace Under Pressure* tour. I went nuts when 'Red Barchetta' and 'Tom Sawyer' were played. Rush are so good that they sound live like they do in the studio. I was going to a doctor's appointment when I heard on the radio that Neil had died. I had to pull over into a McDonald's parking lot to regain my composure. We have lost the greatest drummer around.

SAN DIEGO SPORTS ARENA

21 FEBRUARY 1983, SAN DIEGO, CALIFORNIA

I WAS THERE: DAT NGUYEN

I first heard them during high school and fell in love with them. I remember going to their *Signals* and *Grace Under Pressure* concerts and it was a blast. Just watching my idol, Neil Peart, play was the best thing ever. I also remember buying the tour shirt and smelling a lot of marijuana!

PAN AMERICAN CENTER

26 FEBRUARY 1983, LAS CRUCES, NEW MEXICO

I WAS THERE: MYSTIC MERREM, AGE 16

It was late winter 1979. I was 13 years old. One of my two best friends was Laurie. One night we spent the night at Laurie's house and she snuck into her brother's room and came back with *2112*. We started the music up and were blown away by 'Overture' and the entire album. We were too young to be dating, so spent our Friday nights 'air performing' to 'Overture'. Sharon was Geddy, Laurie was Alex and I was Neil. We did this for months and it was some of the happiest times of my life.

In 1983, Rush appeared in Las Cruces at the Pan American Center, an hour out of town. I lived in El Paso, Texas and wasn't allowed to take the car out of town. I did it anyway. I was with my boyfriend. We made it to the venue, no problem. Our seats were up high near the rafters, but we didn't care. They opened the show with 'Spirit of Radio' and we were on our feet, moving to the music, and on my feet I stayed for the entire show. They had a huge screen behind the stage which showed many things, like photos, art, graphics and even shots of them performing. It was super cool because I had never seen anything like that. When they played 'La Villa Strangiato' as part of their encore, I cried tears of joy. By the time the show was over, I barely had a voice left from so much singing and cheering. The night was truly magical and one I will never forget. I bought a concert jersey to remember the evening.

But the night was not over yet. When we went to start my car, it wouldn't start. Boy, did I panic because - remember - I wasn't allowed to take the car out of town. Now I was busted for sure! My poor boyfriend worked on it for over an hour and finally got it started. We were safe, and would make it home.

REUNION ARENA

1 MARCH 1983, DALLAS, TEXAS

I WAS THERE: KYLE THOMAS

The first time I heard Rush and paid attention was in my brother Scot's Toyota SR5 pickup truck. It had a wonderful sound system and 'Tom Sawyer' was all over the radio.

It was what Neil Peart did with his kick and snare, their location in the mix, and their relationship with the song that hooked me. I thought, 'Why in the hell aren't all the songs on the radio like that?' (Full disclosure; I am a drummer). An immediate obsession with Rush began.

That show on the *Signals* tour was my first big rock show. It was the second of two shows, from back when rock acts routinely played multiple consecutive dates in 15,000-plus capacity arenas. Adult-types, friends and older siblings of friends had warned me I might encounter anything from an Altamont-flavoured riot to being made to ingest PCP while in the bathroom. At the very least, I could expect to be passed a joint. None of these happened, of course. I didn't know about these things, I wasn't even old enough to drive. But I had to arrange a ride with a friend of a friend and he smoked weed and drank Jack Daniels as he drove us the 30 or so minutes from the suburb of Garland to downtown Dallas. I was only marginally certain we would make it unharmed to the show. My driver assured me we were all good – he said the crank (biker speed, 1980s methamphetamine) he did before he picked us up would counteract the booze. Hey, it was 1983 and we arrived safely.

Inside the arena, my friend and I sat in our lower balcony seats and waited for Golden Earring to do their set. I knew the smell of weed and it was everywhere. I didn't realise until much later, when the smell of weed no longer ubiquitous at rock shows, what an integral part of the experience it was. The arena was nearly packed before the opening act began. Long-haired guys and girls in faded olive drab three quarter-sleeved concert shirts walked up and down the aisles and on the floor of the arena with purpose. A rocking playlist was on the PA. I felt I was at the centre of the universe of everything cool.

As it was my first rock show, I wasn't aware of the ritual. The signal of the house lights snapping off caught me off guard. Honestly, I didn't know the house lights would come down at all. Boom, it happened. Golden Earring rocked. I didn't go in as a fan, but they converted me. I couldn't believe the volume. I couldn't believe the lights. Again, I wasn't aware of the difference in volume and light show between opening acts and headline acts.

Intermission. The energy, the anticipation in the arena was… man, I lack the vocabulary to adequately describe the feeling. Then - oom, house lights and house music off and 15,000-plus Long-haired guys and girls in faded olive drab three quarter-sleeved concert shirts roared and screamed with a common voice. Just, unbelievable.

Rush opened with 'The Spirit of Radio'. The sound, the lights – damn! I loved it but didn't realise how exceptional their production was in the big rock touring business. Rush was not the only great production on the road in the early 1980s, but they were at the very, very top. We sat at the opposite end of the arena from the stage. We were an entire NBA basketball arena away from the stage and PA but it was as if we had the world's largest, most badass stereo 20 feet in front of our faces. Everything could be heard; every drum, every guitar part, every bass, keyboard/synth and vocal. Everything could be heard - and felt! Of course, this was before one could endlessly dial up performances of one's favourite act 24/7, and good luck seeing Rush on MTV, or hearing them on the radio before *Moving Pictures* and 'Tom Sawyer'.

The records were wonderful but this – this was Rush in person, at the same place, at the same time as me and everyone there. It just felt extraordinary.

I don't think Rush was the greatest band of all time. They were something better; they were Rush. They created something else. Very few artists of any stripe, in any medium, can achieve their own thing. There's the feeling, the one I get, that tingly skin energy in the gut, the 'yeah, man! Right on' feeling when, after the amazing guitar solo in 'Freewill' on *Exit... Stage Left* and the crowd erupts and you know - you know inside - that something real and heavy has just gone down and you know the crowd that erupts knows it too. Those three guys did that. And they did that at my very first big rock show. And I'm grateful to them for it.

CONVENTION CENTER ARENA

2 MARCH 1983, SAN ANTONIO, TEXAS

I WAS THERE: RONALD BIRKELBACH

I grew up in a small town in Texas in the mid-70s. I spent my time buried in the ethereal sounds of Bach, Mozart, and Beethoven, ironically much to the dismay of my parents. Mrs Potter, my sophomore English teacher, was a no-nonsense woman who seemed even less likely than I to know anything about rock music. One of my classmates asked to bring in a record and play it in class . We listened to the entire A-side of *2112*. It was the most interesting thing I had ever heard. I could sense the wonderment in the music.

In high school and college I looked forward to an upcoming album and tour and bought whatever album the day it came out. A Rush concert was an event, an experience. You knew every song, every riff, every word, because you listened to it a thousand times. You didn't want it to end, and just soaked it all in as it happened. I have a thousand memories.

My first Rush concert in San Antonio, Texas on the *Signals* tour was an awesome experience. I saw Rush again on the *Hold Your Fire* and *Power Windows* tours, mostly from the cheap seats. My wife and I moved to Rochester, New York in the late 1980s. We drove across the border to Hamilton, Ontario for the opening concert of the *Roll the Bones* tour in 1991. I recall some of the great songs although there were some growing pains as expected on the first concert of a tour. A roadie ran on stage and exchanged Geddy's Taurus pedals in the middle of a song. There were a few other glitches that night. We had front row seats on the side. The next night we saw them again in Rochester from the very last row of the War Memorial. I loved the giant rabbits on the *Presto* and *Roll the Bones* tours!

We saw them many times over the years. We saw the *Test for Echo* concert from the front row, 20 feet from Alex. It was an amazing experience to be that close. He walked to the edge of the stage and made silly faces at the security guard who was sitting facing the crowd.

After the tragedies that befell Neil in the mid 90s, I and so many other Rush fans took it seriously when he said he was an 'ex-drummer'. I was so excited when *Vapor Trails* came out and they toured again. We were fortunate to score yet another pair of front row seats for *Snakes & Arrows*, this time in front of Geddy. A roadie who was supposed to come out in a chicken suit and do some silly stunt on stage while the band played. Out of nowhere three or four other roadies tackled the poor guy on stage, hog-tied him, sat him up, ripped off his chicken head mask and propped up a sign that read 'Happy Birthday!' Geddy and Alex stood over him, playing and laughing, but the guy was obviously humiliated and pissed off!

In early January 2020 I was on a business trip in New York City when I received a text that told me the news that Neil Peart had passed away. I was shocked and stunned. I was 57 years old, and I began crying in the back of a taxi in midtown Manhattan. My immediate thought was that an important part of my life passed away with Neil. I watched videos after I returned home and could not stop the tears. That profound sadness has subsided, but I will never forget what Rush has brought to me and what an important part of my life they are.

HEMISFAIR ARENA

2 MARCH 1983, SAN ANTONIO, TEXAS

I WAS THERE: JONATHAN HERBERT

Jonathan Herbert with Chromey

Rush was played regularly on the local hard rock radio station KISS from the time of their first album. Joe Anthony and the station are thanked on the first live album. Joe would play new bands before most of the country got wind of them. The first time the band played in San Antonio was at a place called Randy's Rodeo, either on the *Fly by Night* or *Caress of Steel* tours. Later on bands such as the Sex Pistols would play there. Joe also owned an Italian Restaurant called Mr Pizza. The station offered a chance to have dinner with the band and ride to the show in the limo with them. I have no idea who won, but a friend of mine got to play Neil's kit while he did sound check.

I could not stand their music. The chipmunk vocals drove me nuts! It wasn't until *2112* and a ride in the back seat of a friend's car with a fantastic stereo - and a hit of acid – that I was enlightened. Holy shit!

I got to see the band for the first time on the *Signals* tour. When Rush hit the stage it was amazing. There was so much sound from only three guys, and this was before they started flying in backing tracks. Neil was suddenly promoted to equal status with my then favourite drummer, Keith Moon.

I next saw them on the *Time Machine* tour. A dear friend and my band's bass player at the time, Dave, bought a pair of tickets and said we were going. The seats were in the balcony. Even in the rafters the sound was so clear and crisp! What magic they used I am not sure as those seats were known to suck, sound-wise. The stage set up was almost as entertaining as the band.

I was working in a music store the day of the *Clockwork Angels* show, thinking of the several people who'd said they'd hook me up with a ticket. Nobody had come through. My day was almost over. The phone rang. It was a friend who was also the rep for Roland musical instruments. 'Hey Drumbo, what are you doing tonight?' Tim asked. 'Well I'm going to the store and pick up some cat litter and beer on the way home.' 'Wanna go to a concert?' Duh! 'I'll pick you up at 5.30. We have to get our tickets at will call.' We were on the guest list. Tim had been in touch with Lorne Wheaton, Neil's drum tech. Since Neal used Roland V-Drums, Tim was a welcome individual. We needed to get there early as there might be backstage passes. Boy, had my day changed its tune!

When we got there, Lorne apologised that he couldn't get us back stage. A camera crew were filming the show that night and nobody else was allowed in the back. Damn! So we get our tickets and head in to our seats. I saw many friends as we passed them, heading down to the front. Dead centre, eleventh row. When the show started you saw Neil's jowls jiggle with every hit he made. To see the interaction of these guys that close was stunning. The string section they used added to the sheer brilliance! This show is in my top ten concerts of all time, and I have been to a lot of great concerts!

My final Rush show was the *R40* show in Austin, Texas. Before the tour dates were released, a friend who worked for Drum Workshop said they were building a special kit for Neil, a replica of the Slingerland kit he used in the beginning - Chromey revisited! I was not allowed to share the information. Off to Austin we went. Friends from as far away as Georgia and Dallas hit Austin and preceded the show with BBQ and many beers. There was a mix up about my ticket and I would not have made it through the gate but for a guy who sold me a spare for half the face price.

The sound at the outdoor venue wasn't so great. All the magic sound devices were no match for the wind. The really tall drunk guy standing directly in front of me singing at the top of his lungs (off key to boot) didn't make it any better. Even though the band had said this was to be the last tour, we were pretty sure they'd continue. Surely there would be more music, maybe a Las Vegas string of shows, just no more tours. Farewell never seems to be forever in the world of rock 'n' roll. The second half of the show, where they went in reverse order of their music, was full of memories. And after all these years, Geddy's voice had finally changed. It made it easier to sing along (in key for some of us). And then it was over.

MYRIAD CONVENTION CENTER

4 MARCH 1983, OKLAHOMA CITY, OKLAHOMA

I WAS THERE: MARK FINLEY

I grew up in Oklahoma and went to college there. In 1981 I was back in my hometown for the summer from my freshman year in college. A former high school classmate and I took his pickup to cruise Main Street. He popped in a cassette and the intro to 'Tom Sawyer' blared from the speakers. About 30 seconds in, I was hooked. I said, 'Who the hell is this?' He said this was Rush. I remember a couple of people having the 8-track to *All the World's a Stage*, but I never paid any attention. My buddy and I drove around a while longer and I listened to the whole album. I was blown away.

Mark Finley (left) with head Rush Rat Lance Kasten before the opening nig of Rush's R40 tour in Tulsa, Oklahoma

The next day, I went to our nearest music store and bought *Moving Pictures*. I listened to that cassette non-stop for the next week, and then went back to the music store and got my hands on three more of their albums. The lyrics, the music, the voice, it was all there. I couldn't believe three guys could produce this kind of sound.

My first live show was in Oklahoma City. I'd see five shows out of the next four tours, each more impressive than the last. After *Roll the Bones* , it would be 16 years before I would see them again - career, marriages and children put that part of my life on hold.

In 2007, an old college buddy invited me to their first *Snakes & Arrows* show in Phoenix, and in 2008 I saw them twice on the second leg, one with my stepson.

When they announced the *Time Machine* tour, performing *Moving Pictures* in its entirety, I was so excited because I would get to hear 'The Camera Eye', for me the quintessential Rush tune. The musical theme perfectly goes with the lyrics. It also blends some of their past work into an epic 11-minute piece that puts each member on display with their individual talent. You hear each instrument throughout the song, and I had never really heard that before from any other band. I saw Rush five times on that tour.

I was at Dallas show on the *Clockwork Angels* tour that was filmed and recorded for the DVD and CD. The string section was a great idea; it brought another element to their live shows.

I was there on opening night in Tulsa, Oklahoma for *R40*. I took my sister, who had never seen them and wanted to see what all the fuss was about. She finally admitted to me that I was right in saying Neil Peart is the greatest rock drummer!

My final show was in 2015 at the Key Arena in Seattle. My girlfriend (now wife) came and we met some English friends I'd made during a show in Las Vegas years before. It was emotional for me as the show crept toward the end. By the time of the final strains of 'Working Man' I was in tears, knowing this was the last time I'd see them. But I was happy for the band that they were retiring and glad they went out on their own terms and still sounded great doing it.

In January 2020, my wife and I were in the middle of downtown Seattle when she got a text from a former colleague about Neil's death. My wife gasped and I said, 'What's wrong?' She told me and I was stunned. I tried to find a place to pull over so I could get on my phone for more news. I was heartbroken. We continued on. I realised I was only six blocks from the venue of my last Rush show. As we drove on, the clouds parted and a rainbow appeared. I started to cry. I know this sounds made up, but this is a true story.

THE SUMMIT

6 & 7 MARCH 1983, HOUSTON, TEXAS

I WAS THERE: JACOB VALVERDE

I was in middle school in Houston, Texas, I had a coach and English teacher named Coach Porter. Coach Porter was very cool. He was from Washington State and rode a chopper to school. He listened to the same rock music as most of the students . We'd talk about music and he knew I was a huge Rush fan. One day, my good friend Chance and I commented to him that Rush were playing two shows in Houston and that tickets were going on sale.

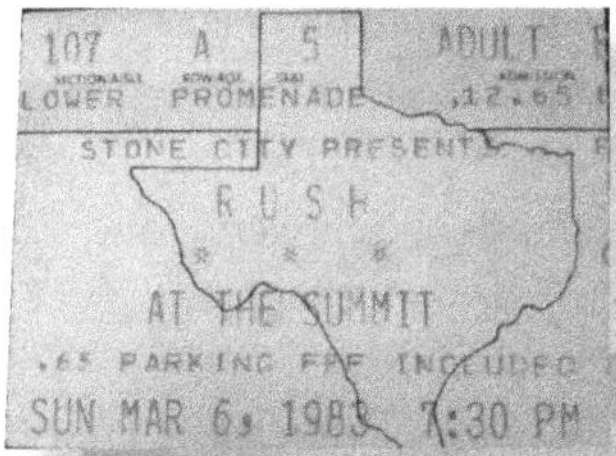

Jacob Valverde's ticket stub

Jacob Valverde went to The Summit with his cool high school coach

We halfway joked with him asking if he wanted a ticket. His response was 'sure'; if we bought him a ticket he'd pick us up and drive us there. We were blown away. We were going to the Rush show with the coolest teacher in school! My friend Chance and I camped out overnight at the local mall with a Ticketmaster outlet and obtained great seats in the lower level.

Coach Porter picked us up as promised and we all three went to the *Signals* show. To this day, when I am talking with others about our cool concert stories, I always mention this show. I will cherish the memory for the rest of my life and still think I will *never* be as cool as Coach Porter.

I WAS THERE: MARK FLETCHER

I had seen them about a year and a half before. But for this show I remember them showing a digital video of the red Barchetta cruising down the road, which was very new tech at the time. It sounded so exact, as if I had put on the album to listen to at full volume. I mean these three guys were amazingly tight and it was just sheer perfection. I had never been to a concert where it had been so closely matched to the album, and I had been to many concerts; big named ones. They performed very professionally, to the point of perfection!

HOLLYWOOD SPORTATORIUM

17 & 18 MARCH 1983, PEMBROKE PINES, FLORIDA

I WAS THERE: ANTHONY ANDREOZZI

I saw them 43 times, every tour from *Signals* forward. I was a sophomore in high school. At my friend Kevin Fury's house, he said, 'Did you ever hear Rush?' I said, 'Probably, but I don't know if I know any of their songs.' He put 'Limelight' on and that was me hooked. When *Signals* came out my parents bought me the album. The Sportatorium was a dive, an absolute bombshell of an arena. It's since been torn down. I went with Kevin and my friends Toby Oliver and Felicia Falso. Back in those days, Neil used to ride his bike from city to city. He got a flat tyre and was late and they wouldn't open the arena. Thousands of fans were standing outside the Sportatorium and starting to get a little crazy. The police had to use tear gas to keep people at bay. But it was an amazing show!

Through the years I've seen them in Fort Lauderdale, West Palm Beach, Tampa and Atlanta. For my 40th birthday my wife got us tickets, tenth row centre, at Madison Square Garden. That was one of the few shows that my wife went to. But she enjoyed it. You just can't help but appreciate the music and the musicianship. I took a friend to the *Time Machine* tour in West Palm Beach who had never really got into them. We had sixth row seats and he didn't know what to expect but for three hours he was sitting there in absolute amazement. His mouth was just open the whole time. He's a musician himself and appreciated the work behind the music. It turned him into a die-hard fan.

At high school I was never a terribly popular or social person. Their music, their lyrics spoke to me. When you hear 'Subdivisions' - the outcast - that's how I felt. I hated high school with a passion. The music just helped me get through those days. I'm a big fan of Yes, Led Zeppelin and Iron Maiden. But at the end of the day nothing compares to Rush. Probably 80 per cent of what I listen to is Rush. I just don't think anybody compares. Another endearing factor for me is that they're just regular guys. They don't think of themselves as rock stars. They don't put themselves up on a pedestal.

Neil lost his wife and daughter. After I read Neil's book *Ghostrider*, it seemed like it was the end. I was grasping at straws to try and find new music to listen to but nothing resonated with me. I listened to the old albums. But there was a glimmer of hope and get back out they did. They made some incredible music during those years.

My last show was on the *R40* tour in Denver. I went to a lot of shows by myself and enjoyed going alone because it doesn't matter where you are at a Rush concert, everybody's on the same wavelength. Even though you've never met these people, they're friends! They really poured their heart and soul into that show. I didn't know it was the last tour. The whole Rush community knows that Neil was never a big fan of touring. But it was only a 30 date tour. Generally, when they went on the road, it was 60 or 70 shows. I figured that they would be back in some way, shape or form. I was hoping it wasn't going to be the last show.

I was at work work and right next to the copy machine making some copies when my friend Adam texted me about Neil. Adam had been to some Rush shows with me. I had to sit down because I was in absolute disbelief. I still haven't come to terms with it.

Neil was a super private guy. It's such a shame that he was never able to enjoy the retirement that he deserved. It's a huge, huge loss to the whole music world. When I think about the world's greatest drummers, I think of Neil, John Bonham and Buddy Rich. Those three people really left a mark on the world. I have younger boys and they're starting to get into the music. It breaks my heart that I'll never be able to take them to a show.

I WAS THERE: MIKE FLETCHER

I saw them 46 times, going back to the *Signals* tour, with 14 front row centre and countless second and third row shows. I became a fan when I was just five years old. My buddy Johnny Lee's older brother Raymond was obsessed with Rush. He passed in a motorcycle accident when I was 10. 45 years later

Mike Fletcher and son Michael

Alex in action - photo Mike Fletcher

Mike Fletcher caught the Time Machine tour - photo Mike Fletcher

Johnny and I are still friends and have seen every show together. We often take his brother's Rush concert shirts, tickets, banners and other memorabilia to shows.

We took our sons to their first Rush concert on the *Time Machine* in West Palm Beach Ampitheater. Rush was our first concert too. My dad took us to see the *Signals* tour at the Hollywood Sportatorium. My dad wasn't a big fan but became one after that show. It's a true testament to how the band has crossed generations and been extremely inspirational to all.

R40 in Tampa was comical in the sense I took my wife after 18 years of marriage and spending thousands of dollars on tickets and travel to see the power trio. We were front row and Alex comes over to me during 'Distant Early Warning' and hits me with a pick and starts one of his goofy conversations he has with fans which lasted about a minute but felt like a lifetime. My wife has been a believer ever since. She couldn't believe she got to witness my 'bromance' with one of my idols.

Mike Fletcher with his son Michael, his buddy John and John's son Johnathon

Lyrically, the Professor just knew how to get into my soul, and musically the band is second to none. I took a lot of shit as a young guy for idolising the band but I wouldn't change it for the world. They have been instrumental in my make up as a person.

CHARLOTTE COLISEUM

25 MARCH 1983, CHARLOTTE, NORTH CAROLINA

I WAS THERE: DEBORAH DEATON WILSON

The first album I had was *Caress of Steel* and it's still my favourite. I saw them 12 times. Every tour was exceptional. They always had a very cool light show and the songs sounded just like it did on the album. It was a family thing for us. My mother, brother and sister have all been to see them with me. My first Rush concert was in a small place in Charlotte called Park Center. I fell in love with their music. My mother was glad I wasn't blasting Black Sabbath and other heavy metal anymore. I was blasting Rush and she started really liking them. She went to four shows with me and my brother started going to see them too. My mother was with me at my most memorable show, on the *Signals* tour. She was really sick and taking chemo and I was pregnant with my son. It must have been sold out because we couldn't find a seat so sat on the steps. Some guy threw up on the steps behind me and my butt got soaked. I guess that's why I remember that one most!

CARRIER DOME

2 APRIL 1983, SYRACUSE, NEW YORK

I WAS THERE: SCOTT PERRY

I've seen every US tour starting on the 1983 *Signals* tour in Syracuse, New York (my first ever concert) and ending in 2015 on the final *R40* tour at Madison Square Garden. I discovered Rush while in middle school in 1980. I was 13. A friend had a copy of

Scott Perry's Neil tribute is his drum rig

Hemispheres. I thought the pull out pictures of the band and Neil's drums were so cool, what with me being a drummer! But I had never heard their music. I was into Styx and ELO. That all changed when *Permanent Waves* came out.

I can listen to an album and remember where I was and what I was doing at that particular time in my life. *Counterparts* was released the day my first son was born. I am very proud to be a Rush fan. I am also very fortunate to have been able to bring my wife and three kids to shows. I never had to worry about raucous crowds or be embarrassed. My kids are fans too.

RHEIN-NECKAR HALLE

11 MAY 1983, EPPELHEIM, WEST GERMANY

I WAS THERE: ANDY HARTARD

I'm a German female Rush fan, both characteristics most people think don't exist. For a long time I thought I was the only one. Until the early 90s, when US GIs were still stationed in Germany, Rush came to unknown cities like Böblingen or Neunkirchen. So my first concert was in Eppelheim. There were a lot of American soldiers - and so dedicated Rush fans – stationed there at the time.

The son of a GI introduced me to Rush. He got me *Moving Pictures* for my 13th birthday.

Andy Hartard was introduced to Rush by the son of an Amer stationed in Germany

It was my first party ever and I got this album! I was blown away from side one but then I listened to 'The Camera Eye' and all my guests had to hear it again and again. I was a party killer!

I had no Rush buddy. My friends didn't get it. I saw one show on the *Signals* tour, two shows on *Hold Your Fire*, four shows on *Roll the Bones*. And then I had to wait 12 years. In Germany Rush had no radio presence and the music magazines didn't write much about the band. After *Test for Echo*, I heard nothing. I had no idea what had happened and wondered if the band still existed. At the end of 1997, I got the first private access to the internet, and guess what the first word was that I put into the Altavista search engine? When I heard about Neil's losses for the first time, I thought it was over.

On September 17, 2004 I stood in the front row of the Arena in Oberhausen, heard the first notes of '2112: Overture' and cried. I never thought that this would be happening again. Over the years I saw 10 more shows, mostly travelling alone, but making a lot of Rush friends in a lot of different countries. And I realised that there are a few German and female Rush fans out there!

In 2001, 18 years after my first Rush concert, I gave birth to my son. I wanted him to be named Neil, but his dad didn't agree….

NATIONAL EXHIBITION CENTRE

14 MAY 1983, BIRMINGHAM, UK

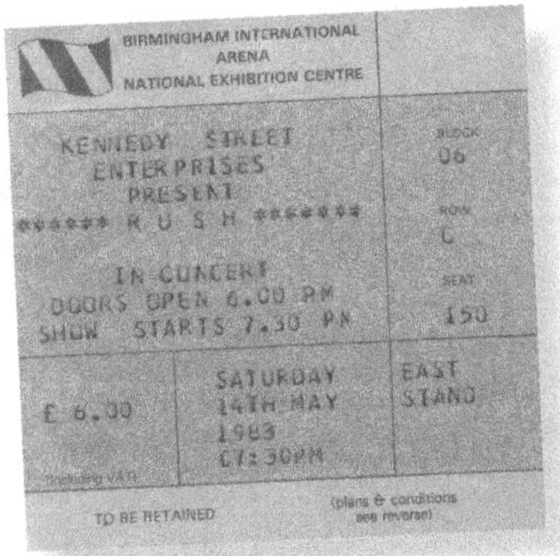

Steve Potter saw Rush in 1983 at Birmingham's NEC

I WAS THERE: STEVE POTTER

I've got a bootleg of the second show I saw. Alex broke a string just as he was starting the solo on 'The Analog Kid'. He took the guitar off and I remember him throwing it to his roadie at the side of the stage and strapping on another guitar. Neil and Geddy continued playing and Alex just picked up the solo where he had stopped when the string broke!

I WAS THERE: RAZA RIZVI

My parents were immigrants from Pakistan so listening to rock music wasn't top of their agenda for their children. I went to a grammar school in Newcastle. That meant it was

Raza Rivi's mother didn't approve of her son liking Rush

pretty small, and because it was the 1970s and the north of England, there was tons of racism. But you just went with the flow and you gave as good as you got if you wanted to get anywhere. And because everybody who went to grammar school in Newcastle had to come from absolutely miles away, your friends weren't the people that lived around you. They might live 10, 20 or 30 miles away. You congregated at school and then you didn't really see them in the evening because they were just too far away. You had to get home afterwards and that was a right faff with buses and whatever.

But I started listening to Rush because my best mate at school got a Rush album in April or May 1979 and said, 'Come round my house and listen. It's absolutely fantastic.' I went round and he dropped the stylus on *Hemispheres*. I thought it was absolutely fantastic. It was the first record I bought. I think I've got nine copies of it now – the US version, Canadian, Japanese, picture disc and so on.

My dad had a fairly archetypal Asian-in-England upbringing so he'd saved his money, worked double shifts, bought a house, then bought a number of houses. He was uneducated so he bought a shop because that's what you did. You could look after yourself that way. He and my mum would work in the shop until 9pm. In 1980 Rush were touring and they were coming to Newcastle. There was no chance of me being able to sneak out of the house and come back from a gig at 10.30 or 11. So I had to tell them. My mum said absolutely under no circumstances could I go. I was doing my O levels. I had to get my head down and study, go to university and become a doctor. But the local pub owner's son was a huge Rush fan and he got me some memorabilia from that tour.

After hearing *Hemispheres* I bought a couple of Rush bootlegs. I'd have them delivered to my local newsagent and I would collect them when I got home from school. I'd play the record, record it to cassette and sell the cassettes out of the back of *Sounds* for a fiver a time. The advert in *Sounds* used to say 'ring before 9', because that's when my parents got home!

I was at Leeds University when I first saw them. They played the NEC. In those days you applied for a ticket by post and sent a stamped addressed envelope. My tickets were delivered to the wrong house. Luckily, someone eight doors up from me knocked and said, 'Oh, I think this is for you.' It turned out it was a front row ticket, right in front of Geddy.

Of course, being an Asian, there was a catch. The gig was on a Saturday in Birmingham and there was no direct service after the gig from Birmingham back to Leeds. I had to be back by 2pm on Sunday because that was when my parents expected me to ring every week. I had to work out this complicated route which involved going from Digbeth bus station at four in the morning to Manchester and then getting a bus from Manchester back to Leeds so I could be back in time and not get a bollocking from my mum. I ended up sleeping on New Street Station until I got kicked out and then walked around Digbeth until 4am, which was an utter hole.

You'd see me around university in Rush gear. I was treasurer of the Progressive Rock Society so I snuck Rush in whenever I could. If you were a Rush fan, you might gravitate towards other Rush fans but they would probably be just as coy as you about mentioning the fact, because it wasn't really very cool. Liking rock music wasn't really cool anyway in the 80s. Everybody wanted to be punk or New Romantic. There were lots of rock-orientated people at university. But liking Rush - all those lyrics? What's that all about? It was a counter culture within a sub culture.

I've seen them on every tour subsequently. I've seen them multiple times since 2007. On the *Clockwork Angels* tour I saw them on nine out of their 10 European dates. My wife said, 'Just get on with it.' She has no idea how big my Rush vinyl and memorabilia collection is, because it's all hidden away in boxes in the garage. I've got about 1,600 ticket stubs from shows around the world. I even have a stub from Neil Peart's first show, on 14 August 1974.

All three of my sons have been to a Rush gig. If you asked the older two if they liked Rush, they'd say yes. The younger one would say no. As Meatloaf said, two out of three ain't bad.

My brother followed them around England in 2007 and saw them in 2015 in Boston and Toronto. I just could not wangle it with work. My brother puts his love of Rush down to the fact that I drummed it into him. I was 15 and he would have been seven. He was hearing it around the house. There was no escape. I didn't turn out the way my mum wanted. I'm not a doctor and I still listen to Rush. But she knows now that I listen to Rush. My brother is 47. He was getting a bollocking off my mum recently and he said, 'Yes - but at least I didn't follow Rush around Europe.' To get himself off the hook he put me on it.

WEMBLEY ARENA

17, 18, 20 & 21 MAY 1983, LONDON, UK

I WAS THERE: DAVE PHELAN

I've been a fan from the first time I heard 'Spirit of Radio'. Then one of my mates got *Permanent Waves* and I was hooked. Ireland in the late 1970s was a

Dave Phelan was a fan on hearing 'Spirit of Radio'

gloomy place; the Catholic church held sway over society, the economy was in the toilet and for a 15-year-old lad, it was a pretty crap place to live. I loved music, but Rush seemed to speak to me like other bands didn't.

In October 1981 and *Moving Pictures* was touring. They weren't coming to Ireland, but a trip to London was hoped for, till my mam put the foot down and wouldn't let me go. In mid-1982 *Signals* was released and I saw in *Sounds* the ad for the upcoming tour in May 1983. In the days before low cost carriers like Ryanair, the only option was the boat and train to London. Simple choice - air fare £179 or boat and train £44?

Fast forward to Tuesday 17th May 1983 and our trip began with a bus across Dublin to Dún Laoghaire ferry port to catch the 9pm Stena Sealink to Holyhead. It was pretty rough and ready on board and we arrived around 1am. After a 90 minute wait, the train for London Euston departed at 2.30am, arriving in London at 7.30am. The 40 minute Tube journey to my uncle's place meant a 12 hour journey in total, door to door.

That afternoon we headed for Wembley. Doors wouldn't open until 7pm but with the excitement building, we were there by 4pm. I had never been to a big rock concert before, let alone one by my favourite band. From the moment the doors opened the evening was a bit of a blur. I was buzzing with almost child-like excitement.

The show was all I expected and more. In those pre-internet days, I hadn't a clue what to expect and the backdrop videos were a complete shock. We were sitting beside some guys from Manchester, who told us that if we went round the back after the show, autographs were possible. We couldn't stay after the show, but we also had tickets for the Friday night show.

The Friday show was equally good, and sitting beside the same lads, we went round the back with them. A crowd steadily built and we patiently waited. After what seemed like hours, and several episodes of considering heading home, the gates opened and we were allowed in. Marshalled into a queue we waited to be called forward. I had my programme with me. The clever guys who knew the score had brought their album covers with them and looked to get a different one autographed each night. Finally, it was my turn. Walking forward and almost stuttering a 'hello' to each of the guys, I was so star struck my mind went blank and I couldn't speak.

Afterwards, as the buses and Tubes were finished for the night, we had a two hour walk home to my elderly uncle's in Northolt. As he was quite old, he was well delayed in his bedtime by our late night escapades. So, unlike in 'Red Barchetta', we didn't get to sit with him by the fireside.

The following night we trooped into Euston Station for our 12 hour journey home. What a couple of days. 37 years later, I still remember it like yesterday.

I saw them 15 times. Each was special in its own way, like their one and only date in Ireland in May 2011. All that week I felt that same level of excitement as in those heady days of May 1983.

I remember that terrible moment in January 2020. My sister texted me to ask if I'd seen the news about Neil Peart. I felt a wave of sadness, the like of which I had only ever felt for family, etc. It was the end of an era, as I knew I would never again see Rush. But their music will always be an inspiration in my life.

ROYAL HIGHLAND EXHIBITION CENTRE

24 MAY 1983, EDINBURGH, UK

I WAS THERE: PAUL BIRDSEY

That lunch time I would walk through the school gates for the last time and be a free man, with my entire working life and dreams ahead of me. My buddy Stuart was helping with my daily milk round. Stuart had recently passed his driving test. He had access to his mother's Mini (his parents were on holiday) and he and our friends Alan and Michael were that afternoon setting off to see Rush play Edinburgh. I'd need parental permission to join them. We parted company on the understanding that I would contact Stuart later to finalise our arrangements.

Dad had reservations about the inexperienced Stuart driving the four of us 125 miles up to Edinburgh and decided he needed to contact my mum at work. She knew how disappointed I was at missing the *Exit... Stage Left* tour the previous year, was of the opinion we were all sensible guys and that I was due a reward for my hard work in undertaking my finals. I had the green light!

On the two and a half hour trip north to Edinburgh we debated what might be on the set list. They'd played 102 shows on the tour and been out on the road since September but none of us knew what songs they might play.

When we arrived the show had already started. From the lobby we could hear 'The Spirit of Radio' being played. A young guy, dressed like us in denim jacket and jeans, exited the double doors of the hall with a female acquaintance. In his strong Scottish accent he advised us not to bother going in - 'it's a load of shite' – and stormed off. They hadn't even finished the first song! We were not deterred. I had waited for so long to see the band playing live and here I was only feet away from fulfilling that dream. We found the box office, parted with our five pounds each and burst into the hall, high on adrenalin. The excitement was thick. I stood transfixed by the sight before me of 5,000 people going crackers in cattle shed. The whole crowd was bouncing, they just looked fluid.

The video screen behind Neil's drum kit must have been 25 feet tall and seemed to span the width of the stage. My eyes fell on the lighting rig suspended above Neil's head and then down to the drum set which sat up high centre stage with the candy apple red Tamas with the twin bass drums, each with the Starman logo painted on the drum heads. The drum set was huge, just how I remembered it from the *Exit... Stage Left* video. It seemed all the more impressive with the amount of percussion instruments laid out around the sides and rear of the kit. Tubular bells, wind chimes and temple blocks all had their place.

The show was general admission and standing on the floors. We squeezed our way through the heaving crowd as best we could and ended up on Alex's side of the stage, about a dozen rows back from the front. I wasn't getting swamped like the guys down the front and was far enough back to be able to take it all in. My senses were alive. Eyes were out on stalks trying desperately to see and absorb everything on stage. Ears wide open being assaulted for the first time by Geddy's pounding bass lines and Alex's wailing guitar licks. I was in heaven; I could not stop myself from grinning like some demented lunatic. I could not believe I was actually there at the show in the same room as my heroes.

In no time at all it seemed they were into their encore. But not before they had thrilled us all with every song except 'Losing It' from the *Signals* album. 'Freewill' was the only song they played from *Permanent Waves* album. However *Moving Pictures* was better represented with 'Tom Sawyer', 'Limelight', 'Red Barchetta', 'Vital Signs' and 'The Camera Eye', along with 'Closer to the Heart' and 'The Trees'. But to this day my one overwhelming memory of the show is when they played 'Countdown'. The chills ran down my spine at the start of the song when Alex lay down the lead guitar and with each strike of the chord a huge spotlight from the Columbia launch site was illuminated on the video screen behind him. We were transported straight to the Houston launch pad. The entire hall seemed to vibrate when the shuttle eventually lifted off. It was just how I had imagined a launch to be and exactly what Neil had conveyed to us in the song lyric. And then the medley encore of '2112 (Overture and The Temples of Syrinx)', 'Xanadu' and 'La Villa Strangiato'. The show was closed out with 'In The Mood' and finally 'YYZ', interspersed with the Professor's drum solo. I was a very happy boy; all my wish list boxes had been ticked.

After burgers, fries and Cokes in the car park we set off on our return journey, still pumped from the show. We had only driven an hour south down the A1 when we ran out of fuel. We had not refuelled on the journey north and were now stuck in the middle of rural Northumberland, miles from any filling station. The car became cool and then cold fairly quickly. We were all dressed in denims and new Rush t-shirts. Sitting it out until sunrise was not the answer.

We could see a light on in a house across heavily ploughed fields. The mud was over our shoes by the time we got there, by which time it must have been 2am. The guys in the house had just moved in and no phone (so I couldn't ring my parents) and no fuel. But an old VW Beetle was parked on the drive, a long abandoned restoration project. They produced a length of flexible hose, a funnel and a fuel can. We could siphon any fuel from the Beetle.

We filled the can and returned to the Mini. The gallon of fuel wouldn't get us home. We limited our speed to 40 miles per hour, only driving up the longer uphill stretches. On the shorter ones, three of us would push the car and we'd freewheel on the downward gradients. We soon tired of this. But our fuel conservation efforts got us into the town of Alnwick where we parked up near the castle, still 30 miles from home.

It was 4am. The only public pay phone was out of order. The local police station did not want to know about our problems. We tried siphoning fuel from a couple of parked cars, but stealing was not really our thing and no one wanted a mouthful of petrol again.

We made ourselves as comfortable as we could in the Mini until the filling station opened. As dawn broke, we caught the milkman on his morning round who sold us a breakfast of milk and Mars bars. We pushed the car onto the petrol station forecourt just as it opened and scraped together the cash for fuel to get us home.

Mum had already left for work. Dad had been up all night, phoning emergency services, police headquarters and hospitals from Blyth to Edinburgh trying to locate us. I don't think I've ever run short of fuel since.

I WAS THERE: GEORGE SUMMERS, AGE 17

It was a Friday night in September 1978. Me and a mate snuck into his big brother's bedroom where he put on *A Farewell to Kings*. At the age of 12 this was something I had never heard the like of before and I was blown away! I went in search of the back catalogue just like everyone else who had been snared by their creativity.

George Summers first saw Rush in 1983 but he and his family were also at the second to last Rush show

I have lived most of my life in the north east of Scotland. The double header in Edinburgh in May 1983 was my first chance. The crush for the shows was nuts. A wee spindly 17-year-old had no chance and Geddy kept appealing to the crowd to step back. I was pulled over the front and sent to first aid where my chum had also been hauled out. We were both fine, and I spent the rest of the evening enjoying the magical experience beside Howard U's mixing desk. He even said 'hello'. I was near the desk again for the second and last night of that tour. Despite the crap venue – a cow shed – their musicianship was outstanding and only cemented my admiration of the band.

At the time, I was calling SRO/Anthem every few months. One of the staff there would send across bits of memorabilia or promo material and even albums by all of the bands on the Anthem label, one of which was a signed *Power Windows*. On one phone call I had an extremely brief 'hello' from Neil Peart – it lasted seconds! I asked if he would sign the book *Anthem* by Ayn Rand for me. I sent it over to Canada from Scotland not expecting anything back. To my astonishment, the book was returned with Neil's signature and the phrase 'A big hello to George' on the inside cover.

I lost touch with SRO/Anthem at the end of the decade as I worked away in remote places for a few years but returned in the mid-90s, missing several UK tours. I attended the second Rush EuCon in 1997 with a few pals. I managed to get the funds together to see them in Chicago on the *Test for Echo* tour at Tinsley Park. Sadly, tragedy struck for Neil Peart after the *Test for Echo* tour and the guys were on hiatus while Neil recuperated. A personal tragedy of my own was to strike a few months after when I was involved in a fatal car crash and in which I was seriously injured.

Vapor Trails in 2002 was the comeback tour. Despite still recovering from the crash and having mobility issues, I had to go. Two Rush buddies came along despite only having met virtually on the forum t-n-m-s. We met at Schiphol airport and flew to Chicago. We saw the guys there, in Milwaukee and on to Toronto. SRO/Anthem had learned of my near fatal accident and so I got a meet and greet. A photo with Geddy and Alex was taken with a disposable camera so getting that developed was an anxious wait. I could not believe just how large both of their hands were, like spades! It must have been years and years of muscle growth!

After *Vapor Trails* we got *Snakes & Arrows* and I met a bunch of folk at an organised fan meet on the opening night of the tour in Atlanta. I had fantastic seats. *Clockwork Angels* changed my life again. When the tour was announced I got flights from Glasgow to Toronto with a couple of other fans, Steve Heath and Pamela Amos, who I'd met seeing the Scottish Rush tribute, Moving Pictures, at the Lemon Tree in Aberdeen a few months earlier. Pamela and I got on very well that trip and I asked her out for dinner a month after getting back to Aberdeen. We got married at Fyvie Castle in Aberdeenshire on 20th February 2016. Our first dance was learned by our band, The Kilts, who played a fantastic slowed down version of 'Time Stand Still'.

We saw Rush on the *R40* tour in Toronto (both nights), Irvine (with my 12-year-old daughter Alice) and the last ever show at The Forum in Los Angeles. Pamela got a meet and greet in Toronto because of her charitable fundraising via RUSHfest Scotland. We could actually hear them rehearsing 'Losing It' three times whilst waiting for the meet and greet and knew they would play it live for the first time - and with Ben Mink no less.

I was interviewed in Toronto and Los Angeles for a new Rush documentary, *Time Stand Still*, about my car crash and my experience from almost dying to walking again. When I was 'encouraged' to go to Toronto for the world premiere I could not resist. We were sat at the front of the movie theatre on Dundas Square with fellow fans while the VIPs sat up the back. When I appeared on screen my jaw dropped wide open. I had no idea they had used so much material, putting me on after Neil Peart, talking about my determination to keep going on. At the end we were in the atrium chatting to Terry Brown. Then Geddy's sister introduced herself and their mother to me, explaining to Geddy's mother that I was the guy in the documentary.

The awful news of Neil Peart's death in January 2020 came as a complete shock. The fact that he had such a short time with his family is so sad. I feel privileged to have the experiences I've been able to enjoy and I've helped out at Rush EuCons in the past and recently stepped down as one of the organisers of RUSHfest Scotland. I have friends all over the world because of this band, I met my wife because of this band and I believe they helped me in my determination to get as fit as I could after my accident in 1998. Surely, a garden to love and respect.

The *Grace Under Pressure* tour kicked off with five shows in New York in September 1983 before getting underway proper on 7 May 1984 in Albuquerque, New Mexico on 7 May 1984. It concluded in November 1984 with two shows in Hawaii and focussed exclusively on North America, save for four shows in Japan.

RADIO CITY MUSIC HALL

18, 19, 21 – 23 SEPTEMBER 1983,
NEW YORK, NEW YORK

Dave Millman saw Rush at Radio City Music Hall

I WAS THERE: DAVE MILLMAN

It was the summer of 1982. I was a 13-year-old boy at sleep-away camp when I stumbled upon some older kids listening to music on their boom box. I never heard such a sound and unique voice. It was 'Tom Sawyer'. I got home from camp in August and the first thing I did was go to the record store and buy every Rush album they had.

My best friend, who I got hooked on Rush, wanted to see them in concert with me. We were two 14-year-old kids growing up in northern New Jersey. Back then, parents let us do things. So we took a train into New York City to see Rush at the Radio City Music Hall. To this day I will never forget it. In the course of my life, since my first tour in 1983, I never missed a tour. Sometimes I would see them multiple times on a given tour.

What was it like seeing Rush? I thought about it and compare it to going on a cruise. You buy your tickets. You are so excited for months, weeks and days leading up to the event. The day arrives and you are so excited you can only think about the event. You get to the venue, everyone is there for the same reason, and everyone there has an unexplained love for these three men that have given you years, or decades, of joy. Although we all come from different cities and towns, we all have the same thing in common and that alone makes us friends.

We are all about to experience a show that is going to blow us away. The sights, sounds and smells will take us to another place. We know every song and we sing along with Geddy. We know every riff and play air guitar with Alex. And of course, we know the timing of every beat and play the drums with Neil as we stand in amazement and wonder. How can he play those drums with exactness and precision the way he does?

For much of the concert, you do not sit. You give these men the respect they deserve and stand. You stand and when they are done performing a song, we all scream and applaud. We want them to know that they just took us to a place and we love them. I have seen Rush over 50 times in my life and with every show I experienced a feeling of completeness and bliss. I've sweated and I've cried. I never left empty, just physically drained from three hours of participation.

Rush has given me a lifetime of music. I graduated high school in 1987. In my yearbook, under my photo we were required to write something. I thanked my parents: 'Blah, blah, blah.' But I also wrote two quotes by, in my opinion, one of the greatest songwriters of all time. I lived by these quotes: 'The suburbs have no charms to soothe the restless dreams of youth' and 'I will choose freewill'.

As a teenager in the 1980s, I grew up in North Jersey, the suburbs of New York City. We were bored kids going to the mall on weekends. So at a Rush concert, during 'Subdivisions', when the screen showed kids our age walking through a mall and having fun driving around….? That hit home and we were able to relate.

In 1993, I was working as a part-time security guard for Metropolitan Entertainment. I had the opportunity to work the after show. My job was to stand outside the dressing room checking credentials and, when the band was ready, walk them to the waiting limo. I will never in my life forget telling Geddy how great the show was and him replying, 'Thanks man.'

Going to a Rush concert was not just going to see a band perform music. It was more of an experience lasting a lifetime. You can expect to leave a show physically and mentally drained. Your legs will be exhausted and your throat will be sore. We always made sure we had water or soda waiting for us at the car.

I cried on my way home from the last show. I understand the reasoning for their retirement, but I selfishly wanted them to take one more go at it. Damn, I am starting to tear up now as I write this and I reminisce about all the shows I have seen.

I WAS THERE: HERMAN PARKER

My family came from Ukraine to the United States from back when it was still the USSR. I was nine years old. I didn't even know the language. It was really challenging for the first couple of years. I was 11 when I went to my friend's house. He was playing this record and he said, 'Somebody just gave me this record and I absolutely love it.' I started listening to it too and I said, 'That's a great orchestra.' He said, 'It's not an orchestra. It's three guys.' I said, 'Come on, three guys can't make all that noise!' It was *2112.*

A week later WHT, a cable TV station in New York, had an hour long concert on and I fell in love. I first saw them at Radio City Music Hall. It was me, my best friend at the time and his uncle who was in his mid-20s. After that I had my parents get me the rest of the albums and I was listening to them around the clock.

I saw every single tour they ever did, 72 concerts in total. The summer after I graduated college back in the early 90s, I travelled with two of my friends and we followed the whole tour around the United States. I saw 30 shows on that one tour.

I had a lot of connections back then. I pretty much put myself through college by scalping tickets. Scalping was a popular thing to do. Tickets were extremely cheap for most concerts, and I had a huge consumer base through my college. Everybody liked different music - Michael Jackson came to town, Madonna - and I was living in New York City, so Madison Square Garden was the mecca for every big show there was. So I was fortunate to get tickets to all these Rush shows really, really cheap. It pretty much didn't cost me anything, because I was scalping direct.

I WAS THERE: ERICK LYNEN

Erick (second left) saw Rush at Radio City

I was 13 or 14. I was with my Canadian friend Jamey Corrigan at his house in Bonao, in the Dominican Republic. Our parents worked for Falconbridge, the Canadian nickel producer that operated a mine in Bonao. Jamey, myself and others loved to get together and listen to music. Every time he or my older brothers returned from Canada or the States, they'd bring back the current music and we would all hang out and listen; intently. We couldn't get enough music it seemed, and in particular, Rush's music. I can remember playing air guitar and drums to *2112*, *A Farewell to Kings*, *Hemispheres* and *Permanent Waves* and constantly commenting and thinking about how complex and full a sound they had considering they were a three-piece band. I was so taken with their music that I would listen to them every day, for hours, and I learned to play their songs on guitar by ear. It was a difficult feat but one that I enjoyed completely and this 'work' helped me become an accomplished guitar player. After some time playing along to their records I felt an even stronger connection to their music - they had become my favourite band.

In June of 1983, I moved back to Hackensack, New Jersey to finish high school there. My older brother Richard had moved back in 1981. We both had hopes of seeing Rush live but bands didn't make a tour stop in the Dominican Republic back then. As fate would have it, Rush were going to play Radio City Music Hall later in the year and my brother surprised me with a ticket. I couldn't believe that it was actually going to happen. I ran around our house screaming, 'I'm going to see Rush live!'

Time could not move fast enough. September seemed like years away but playing their music held me over just fine because, before I knew it, it was time. I was so excited. I wanted to see how they played their songs, how they sounded live, if they played things the same way as on the record, if they played the songs faster, and on and on. My mind was racing all day and I had to hold it together because this prize of seeing them live came with one more sacrifice. I had to get myself to Radio City Music Hall and meet my brother Richard there. I had never been to Radio City Music Hall or even alone to New York. This was well before cell phones, GPS and Siri so a leap of faith was involved. We agreed that we were to meet out in front of the venue; that is all. Richard went to college in New York so the commute to him was easy. Me? I'd never taken public transportation or gotten around in New York City. I was freaking out.

So there I was, all of 16 years old on Hudson Street in Hackensack, waiting for a bus to take me to the Port Authority in New York. The bus I could handle but the Port Authority? It's massive, I'd read. I was scared that I would make a wrong turn and never make it home. Richard's instructions were pretty straight forward: 'Walk out and when you get to the sidewalk, make a left and walk up to 6th Avenue.' At least that's what I'd remembered. The bus arrived and I kept telling myself that it would be fine. The ride on the bus was fine but my heart began racing like crazy as we got to New York. Now I had to walk and conquer this granite beast of a city when I was only accustomed to a green, lush valley, surrounded by mountains from my little town of Bonao in the Dominican Republic. It was nerve wracking. I walked through the massive crowd of commuters in the Port Authority and was constantly getting bumped by people walking with conviction while I was walking as if on a precipice. After what seemed like a day-long walk, I made it to the sidewalk and I froze. The massive buildings were crowding me. I couldn't see green anything - no valley or beautiful mountains or even the clean air I was accustomed to breathing. All of this was replaced with people shouting, cars zipping in and out of lanes, horns blaring and police officers re-directing traffic. Me? I was still frozen in place. I mustered up the courage to ask a police officer for help. He immediately asked me if I was OK (I imagine the look on my face cried out 'help'). I explained to him where I was trying to go and he told me to take a deep breath, which I dis. He directed me to Radio City Music Hall and I thanked him repeatedly. Off I went with what to me seemed like an angry mob, walking. Again, I was getting bumped and even yelled at because I was walking too slowly. I took my measured steps and tried to stay focused. Thankfully I ran into people wearing Rush t-shirts who were taking the same path as me. I breathed some sighs of relief and kept walking, now accompanied by new Rush brothers and sisters. Shortly after, I arrived.

Now I'm standing outside Radio City Music Hall and again - fear. I'm not alone. There are what seems like a thousand people around and it's crowded to the point that I'm thinking, 'there's no way Richard is going to find me and its almost time to go in' and I'm freaking out. I'm looking around for him a bit desperate now and I feel a tap on my shoulder and – it's Richard. Whew! After I vent to him what it took to get to the venue, we both have a good long laugh and we go in.

We find our seats and we meet up with a family friend and his girlfriend. We are seated on the floor on Alex Lifeson's side of the stage, about 20 rows back. I'm incredibly excited because I know once they hit the stage I've got a straight view of my idol. As we're waiting, I comment about what a unique place Radio City is and our family friend Tom explains how he used to go there to see movies when he was a kid. This is all fascinating to me. The crowd is still working themselves in and the lights dim and Marillion come out on stage.

Marillion played for about 35 minutes. Then off the stage went Marillion and the lights were back on. The venue was now full and the air electric. My anticipation was reaching new heights as I couldn't contain my excitement. After what seemed like forever, but was really only three or four years, I was going to see Rush live. As I watched the road crew get the stage ready, I couldn't stop looking and pointing and practically jumping in my place. This was it. I was here!

The lights dim and the *Three Stooges* theme plays. We're all laughing and loving the moment. The theme ends and Rush open with 'The Spirit of Radio'. The noise of the crowd is deafening and the music is secondary for about half a minute. It's clear that the crowd in very into it and the sound man turns the band up louder. Now it's on and you can feel the music properly. I'm fixated on Alex's fingers, on Geddy's vocals and on Neil's power. All I can think is 'wow!' The song sounds like the record and the experience has my senses firing on all cylinders. I can hear everything clearly and I can see their hands on the guitar necks and where they're playing the respective chords. They end the first song and they go into 'Tom Sawyer'... and the crowd goes to 11. Now you've got the entire audience singing along. I'd never seen or heard anything like it. The band has this control over a sea of humanity. I am in heaven.

The band was as precise as on the record and to put it mildly, I found myself in disbelief that they were human. All the while they're playing, they looked to be having fun and to me that spoke volumes. Music is even more enjoyable when you're having a good time playing it.

They played with precision and power. The band was so on that I didn't walk out of Radio City that night - I elevated out. It was such an experience I can transport myself to 1983 in my mind and relive it easily. Rush have been my favourite band since back then. I've seen them multiple times and every time it's an incredibly memorable experience. I even got to meet Alex Lifeson and Geddy Lee in West Palm Beach some years ago before a concert, on Geddy's birthday. They were very gracious and it's yet another moment I'll never forget.

THE SALT PALACE ARENA

14 MAY 1984, SALT LAKE CITY, UTAH

I WAS THERE: CLINT MCRAE MUIR

They have been my favourite band since I was 10 years old. I saw them live 20 times, along with both my brothers, and we have all always loved Rush.

The best one was my first time, seeing them on the *Grace Under Pressure* tour. The last time was the *R40* tour. But I will never forget the *Snakes & Arrows* tour. The day of that concert I was one of very few people that got to meet Neil face to face. I shook his hand and he talked to me for a few minutes and signed a CD for me. At the time my sister worked at a BMW motorcycle dealership in Salt Lake City. Neil had to get his bike serviced and she found out the day before that he would be stopping in there. So I made arrangements with the company I was driving for to reroute that day, so I could make it there when she called me to say he'd arrived. He was very polite and thanked me for being a fan. I didn't get to talk very long because they were taking care of stuff there but before he left he gave my sister six front row tickets for the concert that night.

We of course already had our tickets from the day they went on sale so we gave our tickets to some friends to sit in the front row. In his book, *Ghost Rider*, Neil thanks that dealership for the great work they did and it's a privilege knowing I was there that day and got to meet him.

BOISE STATE UNIVERSITY PAVILION

15 MAY 1984, BOISE, IDAHO

Michael Seefeldt was at BSU Pavilion

I WAS THERE: MICHAEL SEEFELDT

The BSU seated around 13,000 people and was filled to capacity. There are a lot of Rush fans in Boise, Idaho. When Rush took the state, the Pavilion erupted. I really loved *Signals* and was excited to hear the new material off *Grace Under Pressure*. To hear the opening of 'The Spirit of Radio' and that distinct guitar riff sent everyone into a frenzy. What amazed me most was the musicianship. The band sounded incredibly tight, especially when you consider that they are a trio. Alex Lifeson's guitar playing was crisp and simply spectacular. Geddy Lee's bass was so melodic and his keyboards were 'hemispherical' – for lack of a better term! But nobody could outperform the Professor – the best drummer, percussionist and showman in the history of rock music. His drum set was immense. It completely surrounded him. One half was acoustic, the other half electric. He played with such precision and speed that it was simply one 'wow' moment after another. He flipped drumsticks into the air while playing, caught them and never ever missed a beat. The supporting laser light show and fog show was really cool as well.

I had heard beforehand that Rush would just be three guys, standing around on stage and playing music. Nothing could be further from the truth. Geddy and Alex were very animated and energetic. Neil was an incredible showman. The concert moved way too fast and I didn't want it to end. 'Closer to the Heart' was a clear fan favourite as everyone seemed to know the lyrics and sang along. 'YYZ' really showed off the musicianship of the band. Neil's drum solo was stunning, amazing and mind-blowing. The bass sound in 'YYZ' was so incredibly loud and almost intimidating.

I became a Rush fan when I first hear 'Limelight. However, I really started being a die-hard Rush fan when I discovered *Signals* and the song 'Subdivisions' in particular. The video was cool and the chorus, 'Subdivisions… in the shopping malls…' was really cool, but the supporting drumming by Neil Peart was simply mind-blowing and the best I had ever heard. It's my favourite Rush album and my fandom simply grew from there.

COW PALACE

24 – 26 MAY 1984, DALY CITY, CALIFORNIA

Douglas Whelan took his son Mike to one of the 52 Rush shows he saw - photo John Arrowsmit

I WAS THERE: DOUGLAS WHELAN, AGE 14

I was a short 14-year-old, standing on my chair in the fourth row and centre stage. I felt the heat of the lights, the mechanism of the music was perfection and the sight of Neil's candy apple Tamas required chamois from the drooling. I lived through the 'Fear Trilogy' before it became a wishful list. The encore came, 'Red Lenses' into Neil's solo and the random tossed sticks out into the audience. I caught one and behind me, a monster with bad acne and bigger arms stole it from me. I still curse him to this day.

Music was a new world to meI. My dad insured San Jose Box Office at the time and came home with tickets to Rush (so I blame my parents!) A few months before my first show I was with my best friend, Aaron, and we went to his cousin's house. He pulled out *Moving Pictures,* skipped 'Tom Sawyer' and dropped the needle on 'Red Barchetta' and I literally wanted to be Neil Peart. Drum lessons began and when I didn't have sticks in my hands, I was 'air drumming' - no easy task.

After the *Test for Echo* tour ended, I was one of many who believed the band was done. Thankfully, they roared back with *Vapor Trails* and I was one of the lucky dads that got to take his kids to a show. On July 2, 2004 I took my son Mike to his first show and again July 2, 2011 at the beautiful Gorge Amphitheater on the night Geddy dropped the F-bomb. A few years later, I took my daughter, my 'Rush chickie', to *Clockwork Angels* in Portland, Oregon. To see my kids' faces light up, just as mine did the first time, will always be great memories and 'some memories last forever'!

I saw 52 magical shows in three states and seven cities. No show was ever the same, as Geddy and Al would interact with the fans and the trio would go back and forth with each other. But the music was always the same, if not better. Rush raised the bar on what can be done in the studio and multiplied it on stage.

I WAS THERE: MARK SHAW, AGE 16

I was in eighth grade and I was at my friend's house. He was a drummer and had *All the World's a Stage* and I was captivated by the drum solo. I also remember listening to 'Red Barchetta' at his house and later having the 45 single with 'Tom Sawyer' and 'Witch Hunt' on it. Another friend was a more hard core fan and a bass player. He told me all about going to the *Moving Pictures* concert and meeting up with the band during soundcheck at the Oakland Coliseum. At that time you could just walk into the arena.

Mark Shaw saw Rush play three successive nights at the Cow Palace

Over the next year, I got totally into the band. Then *Signals* came out. 'Subdivisions' is still up there as one of my favourites because I got to crack open the brand new album and listen to it with headphones on my old stereo. They never came to my area on that tour and I had to wait three more years for *Grace Under Pressure*. They ended up playing three shows in the SF area on that tour and I went to all three. I got eighth row seats for the first show. I've seen 20 shows since in different parts of the country and on different tours. There were several points along the way where I thought they would call it quits, as many bands tended to just break up or fall apart at some point. But they kept trucking to the end.

I was at the second to last show ever in Irvine, California on the *R40* tour, where they went backwards in time. That was really emotional and nostalgic, even though I didn't know it would be their last tour. At that point I considered every show I attended to potentially be their last, or at least the last one I might see. I still get fired up when I listen to their music. And I still uncover new meaning in the lyrics.

I WAS THERE: WILLIAM WAYNE WOOD, AGE 23

The first time was at the Cow Palace in San Francisco. They had a big screen behind them that showed the band and also played a video with the song 'Red Barchetta', which was awesome. The second time was the *Clockwork Angels* tour in Vancouver, Washington. On our way back to the car after the show my son Robert said, 'Father, I had no idea.' I told him that us old classic rockers could still get it done.

William Wayne Wood and his son Robert Nunn

PAN AMERICAN CENTER

5 JUNE 1984, LAS CRUCES, NEW MEXICO

I WAS THERE: APRIL TAYLOR, AGE 16

The first time I saw them live I went with two friends. The band were beyond awesome, extremely talented, and there to perform their best for their fans. I write poetry and have had a few poems published so I appreciate their song lyrics as they talk about things relevant to our lives here on earth, for example their song 'The Trees'.

COTTON BOWL

10 JUNE 1984, DALLAS, TEXAS

I WAS THERE: CLELL TICKLE, AGE 14

Clell Tickle plays bass with his band The Nobodies

The first time I saw Rush my older sister took me. I couldn't believe it. It was 105 degrees and girls in bikinis were on guys' shoulders in the general admission area in front of the stage, being sprayed with fire hoses to cool everyone down between shows. I remember being speechless and not blinking when they played 'Red Barchetta'. The song came to the pause, with Alex still playing the harmonics, and Neil threw a drumstick what seemed like 30 feet into the air - the height of a telephone pole - and it came straight back down, landed in his hand perfectly and effortlessly and right on time for about a half beat pause before they all dived into the song again at the exact same split second, never missing a beat. I remember thinking that it was an open stadium and what would have happened if the wind came along and knocked it off course a bit? He would have looked mighty silly.

It was a huge stage about the width of a football field. Even though Rush had only three musicians they used the stage well. As headliners they were the only ones that played at night when it was dark, which was great because they were known for their spectacular light shows.

I saw them numerous times afterwards, the last being in 2012. They were one of the very first bands to play in the new Barclays Center, the new home of the Brooklyn Nets, on the *Clockwork Angels* tour. There was never a dull moment - every show had lots of energy.

MONT HORIZON

29 & 30 JUNE 1984, ROSEMONT, ILLINOIS

I WAS THERE: ERIC REMLINGER

I saw Rush 20 times starting with the *Grace Under Pressure* tour and then saw every tour,

When Eric met Geddy

some more than once, except the *R30* tour - which drives my Rush OCD crazy!

In my youth I spent the night at a friend's house. Mike had just lost his older brother in a car accident and he inherited his brother's record collection. This was right around the time of *Signals*. I'd heard 'Subdivisions' a time or two on the radio, related to the lyrics and loved the song. Mike and I had picked up the guitar around the same time, with Mike having a distinct knack for picking it up. We went to his room to play our guitars and he said, 'Eric, you've gotta hear some of this music that my brother Mark had!' He put on *The Lamb Lies Down on Broadway* by Genesis and my reaction was, 'Wow, that's pretty interesting. I've never really heard anything like this before!' Then he put on *2112*. We listened to 'Overture' and then 'The Temples of Syrinx' started. Game over. Life changing moment. Growing up on Queen and REO Speedwagon, I'd never heard singing like that before. I was terrified, intrigued, exhilarated, inspired and euphoric all at once as soon as I heard, 'We've taken care of everything, the words you use and the songs you sing, the pictures that give pleasure to your eye.'

I bugged the hell out of my poor mother to take me to the mall the next day so I could buy *2112*. I bought *Exit... Stage Left* that day as well. And it's been a hell of a ride since. I met Geddy at his book signing in Chicago in 2019, a dream come true. My 18-year-old daughter, who was leaving for her freshman year of college, bought me the ticket as a surprise.

ST LOUIS ARENA

2 JULY 1984, ST LOUIS, MISSOURI

I WAS THERE: DOUG PRIEFER, AGE 14

A friend played the album *2112* for me when I was 11 years old and I fell in love with the band. I saw them for the first time on the *Grace Under Pressure* tour and 16 times in total, every time they came through St Louis. I also drove to Chicago twice. The only tour I missed was *Power Windows*. My favourite tour was the *R30* tour!

RICHFIELD COLISEUM

5 & 6 JULY 1984, CLEVELAND, OHIO

I WAS THERE: PATRICK W BECKER

I 'found' Rush in eighth grade. I had started playing drums a year earlier and my best friend told me I just had to hear the drums in this song called 'Limelight'. I went out and bought *Moving Pictures*, listened to 'Limelight' and then started at 'Tom Sawyer' and listened to the entire album. I was hooked!

My parents wouldn't let me travel two hours away with the 'rockers' from high school to see the *Signals* tour so I had to await the *Grace Under Pressure* tour. I saw every tour thereafter, and the *Test for Echo* tour twice. My second *Test for Echo* show was an outside arena and I got to hear my favourite song at that time, 'Losing It', as they did it as part of the soundcheck.

My favourite tour memories are the giant *Presto* bunnies bouncing up and down on the sides of the stage, the release of all the red balloons on the *Hold Your Fire* tour and seeing the *Clockwork Angels* string ensemble. I loved the depth and fullness they added to the band's live sound.

My only 'road trip' show was when I got to fly from Phoenix to Las Vegas to see the *Time Machine* tour at the MGM Grand. That was the best sounding show I ever saw. It was a great venue, the tour and songs were awesome and the band were at their pinnacle.

I am now enjoying one of the Rush cover bands, YYNOT. They do an amazing job on the Rush tunes but also have their own unique style and sound on their original music.

THE COLISEUM

16 JULY 1984, QUEBEC CITY, CANADA

I WAS THERE: SYLVAIN LAVALLÉE

I first saw them on the *Grace Under Pressure* tour. I never missed a show since and last saw them on June 21, 2015, at the Bell Centre in Montreal, Canada. I saw them twice during the *Snakes & Arrows* tour.

Sylvain Lavallée and his son saw the Clockwork Angels tour

MAPLE LEAF GARDENS

20 – 22 SEPTEMBER 1984, TORONTO, CANADA

I WAS THERE: SHAWN WAGSTAFF

I saw both the *Grace Under Pressure* and *Power Windows* tours in Toronto. They were using a lot of synthesizers and technology. But the concerts were brilliant. One thing that stands out to me about the *Power Windows* show was Geddy's disdain for the roar of the crowd. Isn't it funny the things we remember?

I WAS THERE: DANIEL HARBOUR, AGE 21

I was living in a small town in southern Ontario. I'd already heard of Rush on the radio and through the grapevine. It wasn't until I watched a local show on a local channel that I saw the videos for 'Closer to the Heart' and 'Xanadu'. When I saw the kimonos they wore and the mystical look it reminded me of Yes. They were just a little heavier, with the double-necked guitars. They had the pyro for 'Xanadu' and it was like, 'Fuck – I'm hooked!'

The first album I bought was *A Farewell to Kings* and as far as I'm concerned it's still one of the best they ever made. Everybody criticised it because it's only got six songs on it but they're all like seven, eight, nine, ten minutes long. They weren't looking to go on the radio. They were doing what they felt, which I liked about them.

I saw them at Maple Leaf Gardens for the *Grace Under Pressure* tour. Rush played there a lot and did a lot of New Year's Eve gigs there. They filmed it for the DVD. I remember a lot of cameras being set up and cameras on booms, and cameras on cables that go flying from one end of the arena to the other. And we got these free 3-D glasses. It was packed. I was on the right hand side and up a couple of sections. I remember Alex Lifeson with his camouflage pants on.

I saw them on the *Power Windows* tour too, at the Copps Coliseum in Hamilton. That was a really good show too. I was a little further away from the stage for that one but it was good and that was another great album.

They attracted a very male audience. Women tended to follow the music of the day, not the music of a band. Guys had a tendency to follow bands more than girls did. Girls would listen to what's on the radio and get into that – 'Footloose' or whatever.

BRENDAN BYRNE ARENA

29 SEPTEMBER 1984, EAST RUTHERFORD, NEW JERSEY

I WAS THERE: SCOTT ESPOSITO

So it all began for me back in the early 80s with MTV. I was in grade school and everyone had their musical favourites. I never really gravitated to anyone in particular until I saw the video for 'Tom Sawyer'. As they released more hits off of *Moving Pictures* and put them on MTV I was hooked. That's by far my all time favourite album, and 'Red Barchetta' my favourite all time song.

When they released 'Subdivisions' off of *Signals*, I was totally won over - for ever. It's such an epic song with amazing lyrics that hits home with every teenage kid in the States. I was still pretty young at this point, in fifth or sixth grade. As I got older and went to the stores at the malls with my friends, we would go into the music stores and look at cassettes. That's when I discovered Rush had been putting out music since the early 70s. As I saved my money I'd buy each album one by one and play it over and over on my Walkman. I'd get lost in my own world, reading the lyrics along with the music. The stories that go with the songs were these epic journeys for our hero, Starman. Being so young I didn't realise how political the songs were. But I loved learning about them as I got older.

My first time seeing them live was in eighth grade. I never saw anything like it, with an amazing laser show. Over the years I saw them for *Hold Your Fire*, *Roll the Bones*, *Presto* and *Counterparts*, each show was better than the last.

Alex to me is an amazing guitar player, up there with all the great players from the 70s and 80s. Geddy playing bass and keyboards and singing - who today can do that? And Neil on the drums – I can't say enough about his drum solos. Just three guys making all that sound!

As the years went on it was harder and harder to see them live. But I never got tired of the music. I read a few of Neil Peart's books, and I am not a reader by any stretch. I just wanted to get into his mind. He was such an amazing writer. When I learned of his passing, it felt like I got kicked in the balls. I don't think a celebrity's passing ever affected me the way Neil's passing did. It was like part of me died along with him.

HAMPTON COLISEUM

3 NOVEMBER 1984, HAMPTON, VIRGINIA

I WAS THERE: THOMAS DEATON

Thomas Deaton got into Rush via 'YYZ'

My best friend, a drummer, introduced me to 'YYZ'. The third lick where Neil is 'trading eights' with Geddy blew me away. Starting on the six inch tom and descending down that beautiful red Tama kit changed my world. I asked, 'Is this the same band as that 'Tom Sawyer' band?' I was in ninth grade and 'Tom Sawyer' was on heavy rotation so it had saturated the airwaves. Then I gave it a closer listen; the nuances of the 7/8 measures leading up to the drum solo enlightened me to the brilliance of this band. Notably, the intricate part Neil played originated as a mistake that somehow worked.

Being a fan of the 'largest cult band' pre-internet was an insular experience, no Facebook, message boards, etc. No man is an island indeed; I was completely stranded there. These were truly the days of Rush being the nerdist band. I mean, a naked dude or pentagram on album covers? The thinking man's band? What say you? Give me 'four on the floor' with lyrics about boozing and women vs enlightenment, freewill and short-lived galaxies! I was in a punk rock band, but my solos were 50 per cent Neil's solos including the cowbells… so punk - false!

When *Grace Under Pressure* came out, I didn't quite get it but they were still my intrepid heroes. My first concert was in Hampton, Virginia for $13.50 per ticket on the front row of the balcony with my best friend. You rarely got to see their videos or performances on MTV as Rush weren't the MTV darlings that some bubblegum pop rock bands were. So the *Three Stooges* music came on and suddenly I am screaming my lungs out with 13,800 of my best friends. Alex's 'The Spirit of Radio' opening riff comes searing out of the speakers... lights... and there they are! Living, breathing Rush! A friend on the other side of the Coliseum said he could see me losing my mind.

That was the first year Neil added the electric kit to the back and when it spun around in his solo - with those familiar cowbells - I nearly passed out. It was a total surprise – there was no one posting spoilers on a non-existent internet. From that night Rush held the bar for all other bands I witnessed. Some came close but the complexity of the music performed flawlessly, the visuals and integrity of every gig (no cussing to ever be heard) and genuine fun they seemed to always have will never be surpassed. I never missed a tour from that day.

SPECTRUM

5 NOVEMBER 1984, PHILADELPHIA, PENNSYLVANIA

I WAS THERE: BENJAMIN BARLETTA

In 1976, a friend who introduced me to a lot of music made the statement, 'You're a drummer, right?' and then proceeded to play 'Working Man' from the recently released *All the World's a Stage*. When it got to the drum solo, I wet my pants and drooled simultaneously! I never heard anything like that. When I got home that night, I looked for the Columbia Records catalogue and tried to find anything Rush-related. I begged my mother to order *All the World's a Stage* and *Caress of Steel*. When they showed up, I immediately put the live album on my turntable on side one. By the time it got to the parts my friend played for me, I was a fan.

I was more of a Beach Boys, Beatles, etc. player. But Neil pushed me to a higher level of drumming. Listening to everything from *All the World's a Stage* pushed me to do more than I've ever done and love it! Yeah it hurt, but it made me a better musician. When I joined a drum and bugle corps, I was already on a better level than most and was able to fit in and hang with the older players.

I saw my first live Rush concert in Philadelphia on the *Grace Under Pressure* tour, and 14 shows altogether, which isn't many compared to some people. The last time I saw them was on the *R40* tour in Philly. About the only thing that really would have made it more complete would have been 'La Villa Strangiato' and the entire 'Cygnus'/'Hemispheres' suite. Other than that it was a perfect show. I finally was able to hear 'Jacob's Ladder' live and in person, and see them do the entire 'Xanadu', complete with double-necked guitars and Neil playing real orchestra chimes!

Another highlight was hearing them do 'Losing It' during soundcheck. After that I wandered over to the merch table to get my tour book and t-shirt. I considered the $600 leather jacket but I value my marriage so I abstained. The friend I went with said I should get a matching jacket for my wife to ease the pain.

We had decent seats. The pre-show music sounded like it could have come out of my music collection… all sorts of great stuff like Yes, ELP, Jethro Tull, etc. This is a band that knows its audience. The lights dimmed and the intro movie started and we were treated to 'The Anarchist'. The rest of the first half of the concert followed suit, and the band played admirably. Being a fan of the older music, I was enjoying myself, but I knew what was coming, and really didn't feel overly enthused about the first half.

When 'Roll the Bones' was playing, I was enjoying the video of the rappers. Then 'Distant Early Warning' started and I was ready to start getting into it. Towards the end, Neil had a bad miscue and went into the last verse of the song rather than the next section and looked totally lost. It was odd to see him miss this bad. They got out of it, and went into 'Subdivisions' and ended the first set.

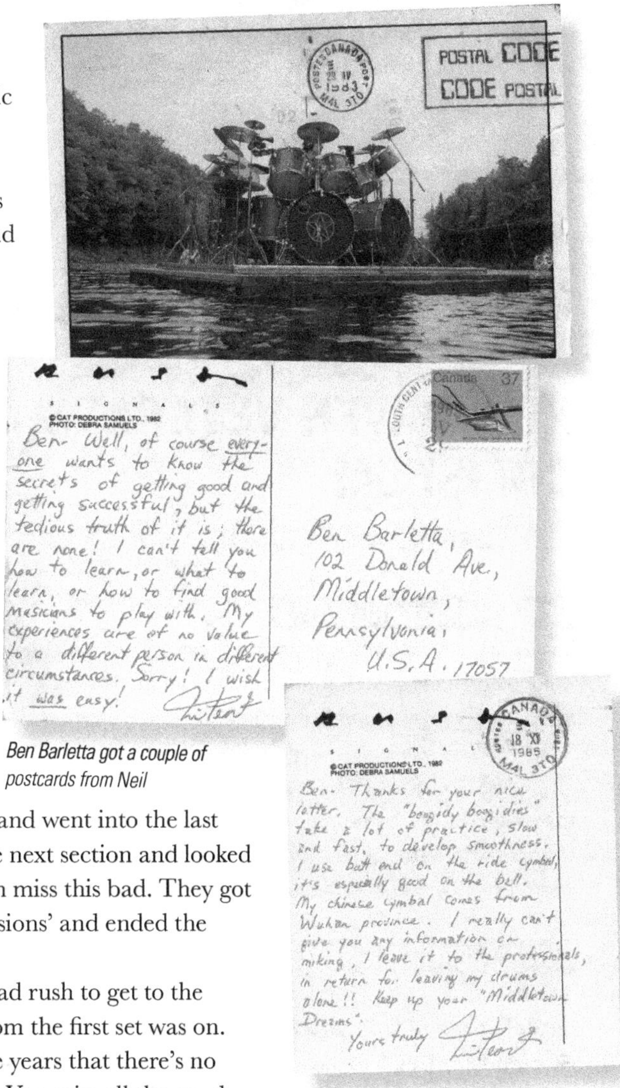

Ben- Well, of course every-one wants to know the secrets of getting good and getting successful, but the tedious truth of it is; there are none! I can't tell you how to learn, or what to learn, or how to find good musicians to play with. My experiences are of no value to a different person in different circumstances. Sorry! I wish it was easy!

Ben Barletta,
102 Donald Ave.,
Middletown,
Pennsylvania,
U.S.A. 17057

Ben- Thanks for your nice letter. The "boogidy boogidies" take a lot of practice, slow and fast, to develop smoothness. I use butt end on the ride cymbal, it's especially good on the bell. My chinese cymbal comes from Wuhan province. I really can't give you any information on miking, I leave it to the professionals, in return for leaving my drums alone!! Keep up your "Middletown Dreams".

Yours truly

Ben Barletta got a couple of postcards from Neil

The lights went up and the mad rush to get to the bathroom to unload the beer from the first set was on. Thankfully I've learned over the years that there's no need to get trashed at a concert. You miss all the good stuff, and spend most of the night trying to figure out when to hit the bathroom!

The beginning of the second set's video started, and we were soon getting Cartman's count in to 'Tom Sawyer'! 'YYZ' was next, 'The Spirit of Radio' and then probably one of my favourite songs, 'Natural Science'. I admitted to my friend on the ride home that when *Permanent Waves* came out, the two that always stuck with me were 'Freewill' and 'Natural Science'! I was thrilled then they brought that one back out of retirement for a few tours.

Next up was 'Jacob's Ladder' which I listened to many times in the 80s on *Exit... Stage Left* in my friend's foggy bedroom. Snippets of 'Hemispheres' were next, into some 'Cygnus' and another drum solo and then some more 'Cygnus'. This was a satisfying bit of these tunes, but I still would have loved to see these the whole way through. 'Closer to the Heart' gave everyone a little break mentally and - BAM! – 'Xanadu'. Double-necked guitars, chimes, fog, lights… this was one of those 'dream come true' dream sequences. What a great performance!

After the fog rolled out, '2112' started and we were treated to a little more than the last few tours' worth. Alex had some guitar issues during parts of the song, and apparently ripped his tech a new one each time he swapped guitars.

After the grand finale we were treated to another intro video, and another song I never got to hear live – 'Lakeside Park'. 'Anthem' came up next, and after the tease of it on the *R30* tour, we got a lot more and lyrics! Then it was 'What You're Doing' and into 'Working Man' with a 'Garden Road' tag on the end.

NEW HAVEN VETERANS MEMORIAL COLISEUM

9 NOVEMBER 1984, NEW HAVEN, CONNECTICUT

I WAS THERE: KARL WATTS

Visually this was awesome with a great light show. They played so well and reproduced their recordings as well if not better than anybody I've ever seen. I do remember how amazing they were and how excited I was to get that ticket. It was a sold out show.

The *Power Windows* tour was two-legged, taking in North American 70 dates to promote the album of the same name. It started on 4 December 1985 in Portland, Oregon and wrapped in Costa Mesa, California on 26 May 1986. The band also played a handful of warm up shows in March 1985 some nine months before going on the road.

I WAS THERE: PAUL SKATTUM

The first time I got stoned my cousin had me put on a pair of those big bass 1970s headphones and listen to *2112*. I was basically flying around with Syrinx priests through caves, discovering a strange device with wires that vibrate. It's still the most memorable trippy music moment. That moment is what hooked me. After that I wanted to know what they were singing about. It sounded so magical and strange. From then on I would be more excited about opening up the lyrics to each new album. The music was usually second for me. Neil eventually became my most important school teacher. His description of everything he wrote about helped open my eyes to outside perspectives and more thorough views of human nature. My other memory is sneaking out of my home as a teenager after bedtime and cycling to the other side of the country lake to sneak into my girlfriend's window. We were young, so we would just lie together and kiss a bunch. Those rides were on dark roads, with moonlit and beautiful lakeside scenery. I listened to a bunch of music on those rides, but memories of *Power Windows* and *Caress of Steel* blocks out all the rest.

HOLLYWOOD SPORTATORIUM

15 MARCH 1985, HOLLYWOOD, FLORIDA

I WAS THERE: ROBERT PRINCE

My first Rush show was the *Exit... Stage Left* tour, which was pretty much a continuation of the *Moving Pictures* tour at the Omni in Atlanta in December 1981, and probably the best concert I've ever seen.

In later years I became friends with the band and spent most shows backstage or on the stage or at the side of the stage. One special memory was the second tour of the NADARS. The story goes that Geddy wanted to catch baseball spring training in Florida so the band did a few shows as a warm up for *Power Windows*. It was either the first or second time the band had played 'The Big Money' and 'Middletown Dreams'. That really stuck with me, because of all the times I've seen them, I can't really remember them demoing new material from an upcoming album.

I WAS THERE: RODRIGO SEPULVEDA

A friend of my older cousin gave him *Exit... Stage Left* on vinyl. We listened to it over and over; I could not believe how awesome and cool the music was. When 'YYZ' came on with Neil Peart's drum solo, my jaw dropped. This nine-year-old kid was in total awe. I was hooked! Needless to say, that album stayed at my house. I listened to it obsessively, memorising lyrics and studying the drum parts. One year, my dad told me he had not gotten me a gift for my birthday, but he would take me to the store to buy me a gift of my choice. I told him to take me to the music store and I got my very first cassette tape, *Moving Pictures*. Eventually, over many years, I owned all of Rush's albums on cassette.

Rodrigo Sepulveda saw Rush in 1985 and again 30 years later with his sister

I went to my first Rush concert with my older brother and cousins. I was 10 years old. We got there late. It was loud, dark and a few drunk fans were standing by us. I was scared and wanted to leave, but my brother said we had to stay; I'm glad we did. I finally settled down and we had a great time. I was mesmerised by the lights and by the laser beams that travelled from the stage and seemed to reach every corner of the Sportatorium. The sound was massive; I felt every beat reverberate on my chest. After that concert, I saw every Rush tour that came close to my city. I saw them as close as the eighth row, to as far as the last seat in the upper section. I didn't care - I just had to be there. Certain songs would always leave me with a lump in my throat. Singing along to beautiful and meaningful lyrics, along with thousands of other fans, always brought out overwhelming emotions.

When the *R40* tour was announced, the closest venue was over four hours away in Tampa, Florida. I had decided to wait and see if a closer venue would be added but my sister insisted we go. The concert in Tampa would be the day before her birthday. It was one of the best Rush shows I have ever witnessed. They played songs that I had never seen them play live before; 'Jacob's Ladder', 'Losing It' and 'Lakeside Park' to name a few. That night the lump in my throat would not go away. I was very emotional. I was so happy to have listened to my sister and gone to that concert. That was the last time I ever saw my favourite band of all time perform live. It was the last time I saw the Professor play. I taught myself to play drums because I wanted to play like him. He is my idol. His lyrics helped me cope with difficult times in my life. I could always find solace, advice or encouragement in his lyrics. He and his work will truly be missed.

CAPITAL CENTER

16 DECEMBER 1985, LANDOVER, MARYLAND

I WAS THERE: MICHAEL KINSTLINGER, AGE 17

If you were an American teen in the early to mid-80s, Rush was the coolest band around. Liking Rush was like gaining access to an afterschool club. For a band that seemed to cater to outsiders, it was the most inside you could be. The then Capital Center in Landover, Maryland was about an hour's drive and my dad took me. Since it was a school night, he wanted to make sure we didn't get home too late. We had a designated spot and time where he would meet me. When it was time, I left the show. Little did I know that the next song would be '2112' - their concert show-stopper. I had to wait until later on the same tour, in spring 1986, to experience that song live - first the visuals, then the synth, then the crunching guitar and the voices of the audience yelling 'hey'.

My memory of those early Rush shows I saw is that it felt like joining a river mid-stream. All the other concert-goers seemed to know when to cheer, when and what to yell, when to stand up, which songs preceded which. They were the most intimate events I would attend with 14,999 other people. Later on, after I had seen them a few times (15 in total) I remember attending a show with a then-girlfriend or friends who hadn't had the chance to see them perform yet and reviewing with them: 'Here's what you do during '2112', and this is when you cheer during 'Spirit of Radio'.'

In June of 2015, I caught them with another frequent concert goer in Bristol, Virginia. We knew it was their last tour - the last time we'd be seeing Dirk, Lerxst and the Professor. The beer tasted a little better that evening, the audio a little better, the memories a little fresher, the shirts we had worn since 1996 a little messier.

THE SUMMIT

16 JANUARY 1986, HOUSTON, TEXAS

I WAS THERE: SAM KOVAR, AGE 13

Sam Kovar's dad worked the first Rush show that he saw

I was seven years old when I went to live with an aunt and older cousin. My cousin Richard was a huge Rush fan and turned me on to Rush and other bands. I remember going to bed with my headphones on listening to *2112*. The intro made me turn on the lights. It still does.

My mom allowed me and a friend to go see them at The Summit. My father was a stagehand, working the spotlight on Geddy Lee that night. My friend and I had tenth row. It was epic. Rush has been the soundtrack to my life, even in the mid-80s when some people (older usually) kind of faded away once the keyboards came in. But I was a young teenager. It was all new to me and I was young enough to not have that judgement. I loved *Grace Under Pressure*, *Power Windows* and *Presto* and saw the *Power Windows, R30*, *Time Machine* and *R40* tours. When Rush made it into the Rock 'n' Roll Hall of Fame I cried. Like the day my daughter was born. When Neil passed away I cried. It felt as though I lost my cool uncle.

ERWIN SPECIAL EVENTS CENTRE

18 JANUARY 1986, AUSTIN, TEXAS

I WAS THERE: CLAUDIA ALARCÓN

They were a huge influence on my teenage years and have remained a companion, not necessarily unobtrusive, throughout my life. I grew up in Mexico City and learned to love rock at an early age - I became interested in learning English so I could understand The Beatles. By the time I was in high school, the first true rock-only radio station sprouted. One of their signature 'call' tunes was the intro to 'The Spirit of Radio'. I loved it, but I didn't know what it was. There was no Rush on radio at the time.

Around the same time, a friend lent me his Walkman during school recess and the tape was *All the World's a Stage*. Wow, did that blow me away! My boyfriend at the time was the singer and bass player in a band and he would play 'In the End' for me. He lent me *Fly by Night* to listen to at home, and the discovery happened… 'Rivendell'! Here

Claudia discovered Rush via 'The Spirit of Radio'

was a band singing about my favourite book, about which I was obsessed at the time. It just couldn't be true!

The rest, as they say, is history. I took a listen to *Hemispheres* and was hooked. Then I discovered that intro on the radio was 'The Spirit'! By the time *Moving Pictures* came about, 'Tom Sawyer' was on heavy rotation. My brother and I were smitten with anything and everything Rush. Sadly, concerts in Mexico at the time were considered dangerous and neither promoters nor bands were comfortable with the idea. It took until 2002 for Rush to make their only appearance in the country - on my birthday. Alas, I was living in Texas at the time and could not afford the trip back home.

But they played in Austin or San Antonio on every tour. My first was *Power Windows*. I remember standing in line outside the venue in the cold to get tickets. My brother had come to stay with me and we went to the show together. As the lights went down to the intro to 'Spirit', we ran inside glowing with emotion and screaming at the top of our lungs. We just ran, disregarding the ushers or our seats or the other 30,000 people there. It was our moment. Nothing mattered. We were finally experiencing the band that moved us to tears.

Before my brother and I became estranged five years ago, I decided we should go to the last *R40* show in LA. I had seen the one in Austin and I refused to let that be the last. I cashed in my meagre savings and bought us plane tickets, scalper tickets to the show, and even attended Rushcon, where we met so many new friends with whom I am still in touch in all corners of the world. It was magical. Hell, we even ended up appearing on *Time Stand Still* as we boarded the bus to the LA Coliseum, a ride full of excitement and expectation.

On the way back, everyone was quiet, teary eyed, spent. We shared beers together at a pub around the corner from the convention hotel. I sat next to a kind man who had flown from New Zealand just for the show. Through the magic of Facebook we have remained friends and when I had the opportunity to travel to Aotearoa, we met up wearing our Rush *R40* shirts at the top of One Tree Hill.

Rush has never been just a band for any of us fans. It's an extended family, a vehicle to discovery, a solace in trying times. Neil's beautiful words have touched so many of us deeply, and the music created by Alex and Geddy is beyond compare spectacular. While I favour some periods of the band's catalogue over others, I find true gems in every single album. And when a painful divorce after an 18-year relationship sank me deep into despair, a line from The Pass kept me going:

All of us get lost in the darkness, dreamers learn to steer by the stars...

ARIZONA VETERANS MEMORIAL COLISEUM

8 FEBRUARY 1986, PHOENIX, ARIZONA

I WAS THERE: GRACE MITCHELL, AGE 16

I was 12 years old when I heard 'Limelight' for the first time and *Moving Pictures* is still my favourite album. I saw them for the first time with my ex-husband. The second time I was 27 on the *Test for Echo* tour - and my son was conceived that night! And I saw the *R40* tour in Phoenix in July 2015, which was the greatest show ever, encompassing their career as a band. Neil's passing was a sad day, knowing that was the end of an era. But we will always have his words to carry on. So many of their songs are so profound and speak to moments in everyone's lives.

MCNICOL'S ARENA

14 FEBRUARY 1986, DENVER, COLORADO

I WAS THERE: TROY STERLING KNAPP, AGE 14

I saw them 98 times before they retired. My first show was on the *Power Windows* tour. My mom drove me down to Big Mac in Denver, Colorado and picked me up after the show, very cool. I made every tour after that. When *Snakes & Arrows* came along I had made it professionally and spent most of the summer touring along with the band. It was fascinating inasmuch as it was exhausting and I was only watching. It really made me respect that stamina of the players, especially as they were much older than me! I really wanted to make it to 100 shows as I thought it would be cool to say I did it but it was not in the cards. I saw the last one in LA. I really thought they would do a second leg....

I WAS THERE: RICK MCCABE

I saw Rush live many times but some of my fondest memories are the three times I was fortunate enough to see them at Red Rocks Amphitheatre in Morrison, Colorado. The first time was on the *Power Windows* tour when I was only a kid on a holy crusade. Then there was *Test for Echo* when I missed out on the opportunity of a lifetime by getting so drunk that I forgot to meet up with the stagehand that I had bribed with a big bud of red-haired weed to get back stage. And the *R40* tour, when my girlfriend went to the bathroom right as the lights went down and disappeared into the dark and I couldn't find her and ended up missing the entire show while looking for her.

MAPLE LEAF GARDENS

6 MARCH 1986, TORONTO, CANADA

I WAS THERE: JOHN HAINEY

I've witnessed Rush 47 times and seen every tour starting with *Moving Pictures* at Maple Leaf Gardens. On the *Power Windows* tour, my younger brother Michael and a couple of our friends were consuming a few ales before the show. We weren't sitting together but had planned to meet up after the show. Mike was sitting half way up in the middle of the arena. My friend Paul and I made it up to front row in front of Alex. After seeing Rush a few times in the past, I knew the encores they were going to play. I waited until the last song and then attempted to jump on stage.

John Hainey's stage invasion attempt failed badly

The barrier in front of me wasn't mounted and it gave way when I hopped up and pushed off. Picture a 20 year old kid with long curly hair in a black leather jacket and jeans, flailing in the air and landing on a row of stage lights that lined the entire length of the stage. These lights pointed straight up and made a curtain effect when lit up. The one I landed on shifted to the right and was way the fuck off. Immediately security was dragging me away and as I looked up to Alex, I waved to him and he was laughing his head off.

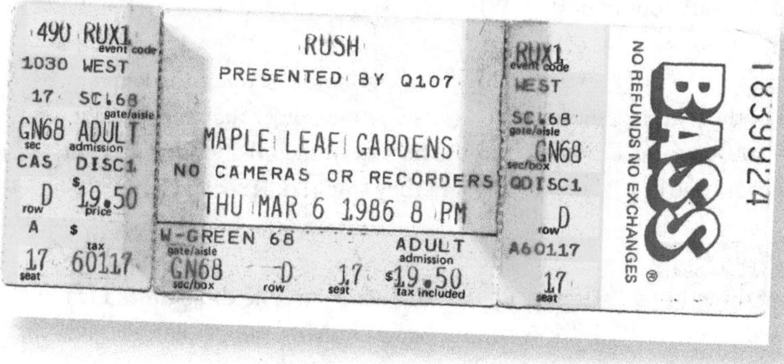

After the show Mike said to me, 'I saw you try to jump on stage, ya numpty! I was watching you through my binoculars and your hair stood out! I said to Chris, 'Hey, that's my brother John. He's being dragged out!" Mike told me that I started something. A couple of other fans got excited like me and did make it on to the stage. He also said every time they used that row of stage lights after that, the one I landed on pointed way off to the right!

NASSAU VETERANS MEMORIAL COLISEUM

4 APRIL 1986, UNIONDALE, NEW YORK

I WAS THERE: PAUL ESPOSITO

My friend played 'Tom Sawyer' on a one speaker mini cassette boom box. I was 12 or 13 years old and I bought the cassette. I didn't get MTV so I asked the person at the counter about this song with a girl lead singer. Since there were no photos on the cassette, I didn't know that Geddy was a guy until *Signals*.

My first show was *Power Windows* at Nassau Coliseum. I was with some good friends and my brother. They played 'The Trees' and my brother, who is four years younger than me, sang every word! I remember being blown away by the musicianship and the fact that they sounded just like the records. This was maybe my sixth concert overall, and the first of many Rush shows.

My last time seeing them was at MSG on the *R40* tour. We knew it was the last time. I loved the way the set list went from present to past, and the stage de-evolved as well, starting with chicken machines and what not back down to a few amps on an empty stage. My favourite Rush songs are 'Red Barchetta' for the imagery and uniqueness , 'The Trees' for the lyrical content (I am a teacher and I have used these lyrics for many lessons, including one about the colonies vs the British), 'Subdivisions' because it's the first Rush song that was in my vocal range as a singer in a cover band, and 'Time Stand Still', which has taken on new meaning since Neil's passing and since hearing the US Army band version.

SPECTRUM

14 & 16 APRIL 1986, PHILADELPHIA, PENNSYLVANIA

I WAS THERE: THOMAS WOLF

I was runner up in Neil Peart's *Modern Drummer* magazine drumkit giveaway. Neil had tickets for me and my family to meet him. We thought it would be after the show and we missed seeing him. After he wrote me a nice letter apologising, we got to meet him before the *Power Windows* show at the Spectrum. I was runner up in a contest that really only was intended to have one winner. A guy called Adam Roderick of won the set Neil used for *Moving Pictures*. He already had a big set and Neil asked him if he would give them to me, which he did. I had a trucker we knew pick them up and bring them to Pennsylvania. Neil bought cases for me!

HAMPTON COLISEUM

19 APRIL 1986, HAMPTON, VIRGINIA

I WAS THERE: STEVE CHINNIS

On the *Power Windows* tour Blue Öyster Cult opened for them. I also saw the *Roll the Bones* and *R40* tours, the latter in Bristow, Virginia. I loved the *Three Stooges* theme that opened the *Power Windows* show, followed by an amazing 'Big Money'. The *Roll the Bones* show was probably my favourite of the three. It's one of my favourite albums by them and the live version of the title track was excellent. They had the video of the skeleton rapping on the big screen. 'Dreamline', 'Bravado' and 'Ghost of a Chance' were also highlights.

The *R40* tour was special. I didn't know it was the farewell tour when I bought tickets. I'm a teacher and took one of my students who I'd introduced to Rush that year. It was his first and only Rush show, making it extra special. They played for almost three hours, starting with two tracks from *Clockwork Angels* and gradually working their way back through their catalogue. It was great to hear 'Natural Science', 'Jacob's Ladder' and 'Xanadu'. Of course, everyone has their own favourites that they didn't play (I would've loved to have heard 'The Camera Eye') but it was a great show overall. I was also glad that they put out the live CD and DVD which included some songs they didn't play at the show I attended.

I WAS THERE: BRENT WOOLARD, AGE 20

I wasn't really a fan but had heard 'Big Money', bought the cassette and thought the bridge and solo would be impossible to replicate live. I was wrong. I somewhat ignored them after that and became more of a hair metal fan. Five years later, I met a new set of friends at a new job and one of them invited me over for some beers on a Friday afternoon. Ronald was a huge Rush fan and had a book on his coffee table. We started talking about it and he'd play a song and discuss its meaning. It started to click with me that these guys were something different. From then on I attended every tour.

Brent Woolard met Geddy at a book signing in Seattle

ST LOUIS ARENA

28 APRIL 1986, ST LOUIS, MISSOURI

I WAS THERE: KEITH DART

2112 was one of the first albums I ever owned and I loved their sound. The line 'and the meek shall inherit the earth' resonated with my Protestant Sunday school upbringing. I saw them live on the *Power Windows* tour and several tours after that. For the *Clockwork Angels* tour I saw them at the United Center in Chicago and at SummerFest Grounds in Milwaukee. Lerxst left me a second row seat for Milwaukee and both he and Ged each gave me a bow and a wave during the show, which my friend saw from mid-crowd. The nicest folks ever, including all their staff.

CAL EXPO

24 MAY 1986, SACRAMENTO, CALIFORNIA

I WAS THERE: MARK SALOWITZ

I may never remember the date without looking it up. I may never remember the set list without looking it up. But I will never forget my first concert: my first experience with Rush. Fence boards pressed against my chest, I saw music performed live, 15 feet away from Alex, I never thought possible. 'Manhattan Project' in particular blew me away. At one point Alex and I made eye contact, he smiled, and I knew three things: he was fulfilling his destiny, he once stood where I was, and I would be following these three guys forever. I still have the guitar I bought immediately after the concert. I have not missed a tour since.

Mark Salowitz with the guitar Rush inspired him to buy and his Red Barchetta

Alex was walking around the *R40* parking lot at Bristow, Virginia. My wife and I were there in our red Miata with the license plate, BRCHTTA. Alex saw the plate and said, 'Barchetta... Red... Barchetta! I get it!' and smiled and walked off. I wish that I could live it all again!

The *Hold Your Fire* tour started with shows in Canada in October 1987 before continuing into the North Eastern United States. The second leg of the tour began in January 1988 in the US and continued through to May 1988, concluding with 10 European shows.

PROVIDENCE CIVIC CENTER

6 & 7 NOVEMBER 1987, PROVIDENCE, RHODE ISLAND

I WAS THERE: HEATHER ALLARD

My brother Sean was a drummer in a band and obsessed with Neil Peart. I grew up listening to him and his band play Rush songs down in our basement. As 'YYZ' rattled the dishes in our china cabinet over and over, I began to know every Rush song by heart. I received *Permanent Waves* for Christmas in 1980 - the first album of my very own - and really started getting into Neil's lyrics. I got every album after that and the first thing I'd do after tearing the plastic off was pull out the booklet with the lyrics and pore over them.

Heather Allard's kids got to see the R40 tour

I saw Rush in concert half dozen times, beginning with the *Hold Your Fire* tour in 1987 when I was a freshman at Providence College. My brother and his friend invited me to go with them, and I remember getting such chills when I heard Geddy belting out 'Mission'. After that first concert, I saw the *Test for Echo*, *Vapor Trails* and *R30* tours.

Years later, my son Brendan started drumming and like my brother became obsessed with Neil Peart. I smile ear-to-ear hearing him play Rush songs too. In 2013, my husband and I took Brendan to the *Clockwork Angels* tour when he was only six, and all three of our kids to the *R40* tour in 2015.

Every time I saw Rush in concert, they were amazing from the first note to the final encore. The lights, the special effects, and the funny videos were totally awesome! They were the greatest and most gracious showmen I've ever seen. I'm forever grateful that Rush was such a big part of my life, and so glad I got to share them with my husband and kids.

THE OMNI

25 NOVEMBER 1987, ATLANTA, GEORGIA

I WAS THERE: MICHAEL DUNCAN

I've seen Rush 11 times in two states at five venues, starting when I was 16 with the *Power Windows* tour in Atlanta at The Omni. Almost every time I went, I was with someone different. It kind of became a tradition to take someone new each time, each in varying stages of fandom, from newbie to full fanatics like me.

I was raised by a couple of rock 'n' roll-loving hippie-types. My mom took me to the Omni to see David Bowie when I was 6. For my second Rush show, *Hold Your Fire*, also at The Omni, I was able to return the favour and take her. She had the best time and she absolutely fell in love with Geddy's feet. When we would watch *A Show of Hands* together she would exclaim, 'His feet are so cute!'

BRENDAN BYRNE ARENA

7 DECEMBER 1987, EAST RUTHERFORD, NEW JERSEY

I WAS THERE: ROMAN DOLINSKY

I was 16, impressionable and had recently discovered this mega trio called Rush. I spent weeks before the concert listening to all my cassette tapes, namely *All the World's a Stage* and *Exit... Stage Left*, and I knew I was in for something special. When those lights dimmed promptly at 8.30pm, the roar of the crowd practically overpowered the *Three Stooges* theme song, which played as their intro back then. Then the sudden opening chord of 'The Big Money' overtook the arena. Hundreds of arms around me were air drumming in unison, in attempts at capturing the precision of every beat that Neil expressed from his giant kit. I was out of my own body with admiration, excitement, goose bumps, and sheer awe.

Geddy's voice pierced the air, his bass counter-balancing the vocal cadence with fierce attack, as Alex spoke from his guitar, his blond mane covering his face. Neil's drums sounded like nothing I ever heard before. The overall sound was almost too perfect for a concert. With a powerful stare, almost angry, The Professor executed his parts note for note as I remembered them being on the album. They were not even human! No three musicians can sound this good! As Geddy belted out 'Big Money, got no soul', the opening riff was played one final time up to the pause. Up, up, up and away goes Neil's stick, almost touching the overhead lights above the stage. He craned his neck backward, backward, leaning back from his drum stool to almost lose his balance. The drum stick eventually succumbed to gravity and landed somewhere behind the drum riser, almost off stage. Wearing a sheepish smirk, Neil quickly shrugged his shoulders, dipped his head sideways, and already had another stick in hand, ready to come in after Alex's guitar riff. My drum hero was a human!

This concert goer's respect for Neil went through the stratosphere that night. If you are going to make a mistake, go big or go home, but don't let it interrupt the song. Well played, Mr Peart. Precision, power, and grace under pressure. I will never forget that moment.

SPECTRUM

13 DECEMBER 1987, PHILADELPHIA, PENNSYLVANIA

I WAS THERE: NATE GERARD

Moving Pictures had made its way to the airwaves of B104 in Baltimore. I had a small boom box that could record songs from the radio and I recorded it so I could listen to the details. I went out and bought the album and later *Exit... Stage Left*, which exposed me to songs previously released.

By the time *Grace Under Pressure* cane out I was a fully fledged fan living in South Philly and two Rush singles would be played daily during the *Top 5 at 5* on WMMR 93.3. In the early days I didn't listen to lyrics much. I just loved the music.

By the time *Power Windows* was released I was living in Gordon, Pennsylvania - also known as 'The County' or 'The Skook'. There were tons of Rush fans in rural PA. One of my best friends was a drummer and a huge Rush fan.

Jump forward to fall of 1987. I was a freshman at Shippensburg University and *Hold Your Fire* was released. I had gotten to know a guy in my dorm who had some connection to WMMR and had 12th row tickets to see Rush for the first of two shows. I had two finals the next day and... let's just say I was no longer the straight A student I had been in high school. I was concerned I might flub the finals and end up with a below 2.0 GPA for my first semester. But the ticket was free and my friend drove us so how could I not go? When Rush came out they played the *Three Stooges* opener and launched into 'The Big Money' and the Spectrum went nuts!

They had these green lasers that, when standing, would basically hit us in the chest and you could see a plane of smoke between us and the stage that looked almost thick enough to walk on. Lots of weed was being smoked! There were some really great fans around us and one who was too drunk or high or something. He tried to keep himself up, holding onto the shoulders of anyone he could, but eventually he crashed to the floor and people had to help him out of the aisle. We didn't see him again.

Early in the set, they played 'Subdivisions' and 'Marathon', two songs that would become some of my favourites. I remember seeing the video screen during 'Manhattan Project' and wondering if nuclear weapons would ever be used again. I was a pretty serious 18 year old kid. Yet I felt at home there and not nervous as I always felt in South Philly. The set list seemed as if I got to pick the songs myself. It was a truly magical night.

We drove a little more than two hours back to McCune Hall at Ship. I got As on both my finals the

BIRMINGHAM JEFFERSON CONVENTION COMPLEX

17 JANUARY 1988, BIRMINGHAM, ALABAMA

I WAS THERE: GARY WILSON

I was 13 in the spring of 1981 and I was sitting on the tailgate of my buddy's truck when the radio DJ said that this was the new song and this would be a classic people would be listening to hundreds of years from now. I'll be damned if he wasn't right. It was 'Tom Sawyer'.

The *Hold Your Fire* tour with Tommy Shaw opening was my first Rush show. I was living about 100 miles from the BJCC so it was always a decent road trip to see a show. My brother and several friends attended the show with me, and we raised quite a bit of hell that night. Many people say that this was during Rush's synth phase, and although they were prevalent during the show, the sheer sonic force of Alex definitely was on display. And Neil's pink drum kit... wow!

MID-SOUTH COLISEUM

21 FEBRUARY 1988, MEMPHIS, TENNESSEE

I WAS THERE: SEAN JOHNSON

My cousin introduced their music to me about 1983. In high school I felt I didn't fit in with everyone else. I could really relate to their lyrics and loved the music. It blew my mind that a three piece band was that good. I've been a hard core fan ever since. I had a seat on the floor centre, half way back, for this show. Everyone was standing so I stood on the armrests for three plus hours - the entire show. Neil's solo was 3 minutes and 16 seconds long. I wrote each song on my forearm in order to write down later to remember that show and that night.

ROSEMONT HORIZON

25 & 26 FEBRUARY 1988, ROSEMONT, ILLINOIS

I WAS THERE: MICHAEL PRIBYL, AGE 25

I started listening to them when *2112* hit the market. Then I went back and listened to every thing before. I have every single piece of music either on album, cassette or CD. I've replaced the early stuff on CD. The group of friends I hung around with did not like them so it was nice having a group of my own. The music was hard to understand when Geddy Lee's voice was at its peak until you listened to it over and over. On later albums it was easy.

The *Hold Your Fire* tour was an amazing show. The age span of the audiences was already showing up, from very young to 35 year olds. The Chicago crowd was looking for a greatest hits show, playing songs off of the earlier albums, but they were touring to sell *Hold Your Fire* and they played a five minute greatest hits set and that was it.

I felt their music went stale on the later albums. After about 10 years I had time to listen to those albums again and fell in love with them. It just took some growing up and seeing life through Neil Peart's eyes....

NATIONAL EXHIBITION CENTRE

21, 23 & 24 APRIL 1988, BIRMINGHAM, UK

I WAS THERE: RICHARD CHARLESWORTH

The first Rush song I ever heard was 'La Villa Strangiato' on a minibus cassette player on a school skiing trip to Windishgarsten in Austria in 1985. I asked my class mate to rewind the tape so he put the whole of Side 2 on. Then I asked to hear the other side, 'Cygnus X-1: Book II'. I was already a rock and metal fan but I loved this. On my return from Austria it was straight to the record shop to buy the vinyl. I still have it, complete with £4.99 sticker.

I saved up to buy the entire back catalogue up to *Grace Under Pressure.* I eagerly awaited the new album. I remember 'Big Money' and 'Territories' airing for the first time on the Tommy Vance Radio 1 *Friday Rock Show.* I bought the album the day it came out.

Birmingham NEC clashed with school. But Birmingham University was having an open day the day after the concert. We were allowed to be off school for these open days so I got the time off with another class mate. His auntie lived in Birmingham so we got a free night's B&B as well.

For some reason, Rush always had seated floor arrangements for concert - unlike, say, Iron Maiden who make the floor a standing area. Our seats were at the back so we sauntered up to about 12 rows from the front, avoiding the stewards, found a row with no people in and stood there, shifting around as people arrived. Despite the seats everyone was standing anyway so we managed to avoid getting moved and got to see the show 30 yards from the stage.

I saw them again in Birmingham in 1992. My friend forgot to bring the tickets with him, remembering after an hour as we drove down the M6. We arrived just as they were getting on stage but in the rush (pun intended) we forgot where the car was parked so spent two hours looking for it after the concert.

They didn't tour the UK again *R30.* I was living and working in London so saw them at Wembley Arena. This was the best set list of any tour. As in 1988 my ticket was way back but I found a place to stand near the stage.

I saw them once more at Wembley in 2007. In 2010 I moved to the Middle East so did a three day return trip for the 2011 UK tour to see them in Birmingham. I did the same in 2013, this time at Manchester Arena.

When my first daughter began to talk she used to ask me to sing songs. I'd ask, 'What kind of song?' She would say 'a dog song' or 'a cat song' or whatever she saw. One day she said she wanted 'a tree song' so I sang her 'The Trees'. Even though my singing is awful she loved it. Her little sister has been the same. Very recently I actually played the real song in the car. They know all the words and now want to hear more of the 'loud rock music that Daddy likes'.

I WAS THERE: STEVE LEE

It all started with a 12 inch vinyl, the *Rush Live!* EP, and three great live tracks: 'Tom Sawyer', 'Red Barchetta' and 'A Passage to Bangkok'. I was 11 years old and the record wasn't even mine!

My sister was responsible for creating a Rush monster. I discovered other tracks and became addicted to 'The Trees', especially preceded by 'Broon's Bane'. I knew this band were a true force to be reckoned with 'in the theatres and concert halls'. I rented the *Exit... Stage Left* VHS tape for a weekend and watched it over and over. I missed the release of *Grace Under Pressure* but, in true rock fan cliché moment, was waiting in my local record store on release day for the delivery of *Power Windows*. The same probably happened for the release of *Hold Your Fire*, with me skiving off Sixth Form.

I was old enough and had the requisite funds to purchase a concert ticket. Way Ahead rock tours of Nottingham provided transport and the ticket. A selection of friends, introduced to Rush by me, came along. But I would have been perfectly happy going alone. I would not have missed Rush live for the world. To know the whole event was being recorded for live video and audio releases was just the icing on the cake – the ability to relive this special night as many times as I wished.

The trio did not fail me. From the first chest-thumping opening blast of 'The Big Money' my attention was fixed on that stage, albeit on the far side of the arena from my elevated seat. Time did indeed stand still for several hours as the music washed over me. Alex entertained with his on-stage antics, Geddy was the consummate professional who sang and played multiple instruments. And Neil. Metronomic, powerful, perfect - the solo. I had finally experienced the Professor's pièce-de-résistance. I'm not religious but the gig had that sort of effect on me, a confirmation of love for those three Canadian gents.

I WAS THERE: DAVID SANDERSON, AGE 20

I was still at school when I heard *2112*. People had to go into record shops then. At the time people were either punks, Mods or heavies, back in the day when people sewed patches on denim jackets. The 'heavies' tended to like Rainbow and AC/DC and the NWOBHM (New Wave of British Heavy Metal) was just emerging which meant it wasn't unusual to see Madness, Iron Maiden, The Stranglers and George Benson on the same *Top of the Pops*. Our only media back then was Tommy Vance on Radio 1 and *Kerrang!* magazine, which was fortnightly. Geddy's vocals took some getting used to but by *Permanent Waves* the sound and his voice were more mainstream.

My first impression on seeing them live was that no band could create their studio sound as well on stage. Pink Floyd did, but that extra musicians and backing singers on stage.

I think there was a stampede at Detroit's Cobo Hall when Rush tickets went on sale to the public and fans stormed the building. Living in Grimsby, I never had that problem.

Back then, coach companies did travel and ticket packages and until the mid-80s you could take alcohol on board, but 50 hyped up rock fans drinking on a coach can be a bit colourful. They introduced a strict alcohol ban. It didn't deter some people.

They didn't tour the UK for *Grace Under Pressure* or *Power Windows*. Every year they were rumoured to be headlining Donnington but never did. I think they avoided those types of shows and insisted on safe seating after people were trampled at the Who concert in Cincinnati. One stand out show was Sheffield Arena in 1992 with Primus as support. It was the Friday after the 1992 UK General Election and the only time I've heard rock fans discuss politics in the pub before the show! Yes Rush are that kind of band. Over the years I even tried reading Ayn Rand but that's another story….

I WAS THERE: STEVE POTTER

The *Hold Your Fire* tour in 1988 was a highlight. The first UK shows were going to be the Saturday and Sunday at the NEC, on 23 and 24 April. I had the first ticket that was sold on the tour - block A, row A, seat 1 on the Saturday. That ended up being the main filming night at which *A Show of Hands* was recorded. I'm on the DVD very briefly – if you know where to look!

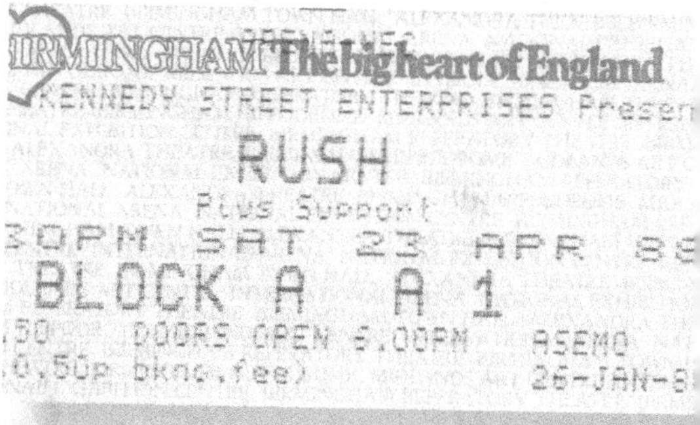

Steve Potter bought the very first ticket for the 1988 European tour

After those shows I met Alex and Geddy. They were stopping at the Metropole Hotel in the NEC grounds. You were allowed one autograph each. I got my programme signed by both of them and a couple of picture discs each signed by one of them.

They cancelled a show in Paris the Thursday before, so they ended up putting on an extra night at the NEC. They used it for the camera crew to see how the hall would worked for the main filming night. They did a bit of filming on the Sunday but just from the side of the stage. The track in the pit between the stage and the audience wasn't there on the Sunday.

I WAS THERE: NEIL RYLANCE

When I was nine years old, my brother Chris sat me down with *2112* and a pair of Dad's headphones and forced me to read the sleeve notes and lyrics and listen to the album again and again. He told me that I would get beaten up if I started high school and didn't like Rush! On that day I probably pretended to like it. Now I can say that Rush have been the soundtrack to my life. Rush have always been there, always been my number one. On the rare occasions they come on mainstream radio it lifts my day and I feel proud, like it's 'my' band.

I met them several times. I've waited outside record stores for the doors to open to buy their latest album, I've seen them in concert many times (but not enough), I'm captured in the crowd on the *A Show of Hands* video and I've collected all sorts of merchandise and some rare collectors' pieces. I have all their genuine autographs - twice. Being a Rush fan is like being part of a cult - only we understand.

WEMBLEY ARENA

28 – 30 APRIL 1988, LONDON, UK

I WAS THERE: STEVE PLEDGER

Power Windows had not long been out. A friend of mine who was heavily into Rush asked me if I'd make a copy of his cassette of the album on my Dad's new 'tape-to-tape' hi-fi system - state of the art stuff! I agreed. I figured I should probably give it a listen because friends kept going on about how amazing this band was. So I did. And then my world changed! For the better. Forever.

My musical tastes have grown and altered. But one constant since that autumn day in mid-80s England has been Rush. Within their canon of work there is a style; a lyric; a groove; an indefinable 'something' for any and every occasion and their songs continue to find me in times of need or of joy and provide the perfect accompaniment to the moment.

My first Rush show was at Wembley Arena on the *Hold Your Fire* tour. It felt as if I'd had to wait a lifetime to see them since first hearing their music two and half years previously. It was a glorious night.

I WAS THERE: PAUL TIPPETT

We're hitting the red button on the GeFilter machine and heading back to the first of Rush's three night residency at London's Wembley Arena on the *Hold Your Fire* tour. It was the first time I'd see my heroes in the flesh. My brother had introduced me to the music of Geddy, Alex and Neil and it's him I blame for my ongoing addiction and Rush-induced overdraft. Having ordered the tickets several months in advance, gig day eventually arrived - excitement so thick, you could cut it with a knife.

London had everything an 'analog kid' could possibly require to soothe the restless dreams of youth, so I decided to make a day of it while I waited for my brother to finish work. My first port of call was the fabulous Imperial War Museum in Lambeth. As you approach the very impressive building you're met with two imposing 15 inch guns from HMS Ramillies and HMS Resolution. Hold your fire!

Having spent several hours exploring, the pub beckoned and as I headed through the cavernous space towards the exit, I spotted a very familiar figure admiring the Sd Kfz 173 Jagdpanther. I immediately recognized that distinctive blond combed-over fringe, upon which I had modelled my own. It was Alex Lifeson! Now this was a time before camera phones and selfies and, as a 17-year-old kid, I was too shy to say 'hello'. As a polite young English fellow, I also didn't want to intrude on his private time with his son. In hindsight, perhaps I should have. From what I now know of Alex, he's a very friendly, warm and accommodating chap to his fans.

That completely unexpected encounter just about made my year. As for the gig I was completely and utterly blown away. As Rush hit the stage with the *Three Stooges* theme and 'The Big Money', the place just erupted and I thought my heart was going to explode with feelings of admiration, pride and excitement. This was the greatest live band I had ever seen in my life. They remain so, and the memories of that day in 1988 will last forever.

AHOY SPORTPALEIS

2 MAY 1988, ROTTERDAM, THE NETHERLANDS

I WAS THERE: ARJAN MULDER

Arjan Mulder was introduced to Rush by his Uncle Henri

It was February 1981 and I was 10 years old and visiting my grandfather and grandmother when my Uncle Henri, seven years older than me, played me side A of *Moving Pictures*. It was as if I heard it thunder in Cologne. 'Tom Sawyer' hit me like a bomb - those drums, bass and guitar parts surrounded by those fantastic signature keyboard parts. I started to learn more about Rush. I didn't have a record player and had to make do with my cassette recorder. I got everything my uncle had by Rush on tape and I turned all those tapes completely grey. At 13 my parents thought I was too young to go to the *Signals* tour. I had to wait five years for the *Hold Your Fire* tour until my dream finally came true.

I went to see Rush with my Uncle Henri and his friends. It was truly wonderful! The next day I went to my local record store. In one fell swoop I was seven Rush LPs richer and of course a great experience richer. I was now a diehard Rush fan.

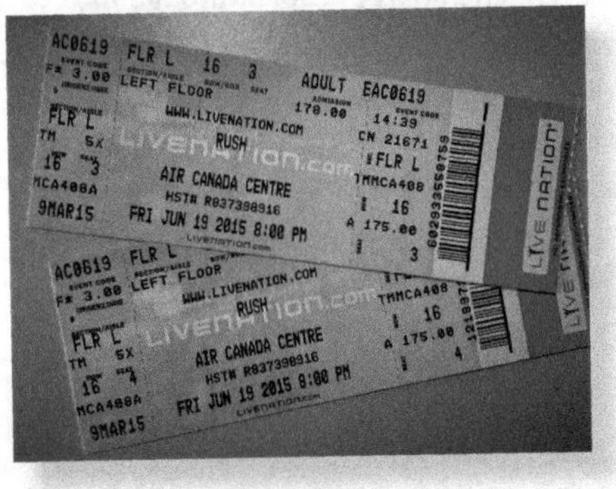

I saw Rush live a total of 20 times on eight different world tours in four different countries – The Netherlands, Great Britain, Germany and twice at the Air Canada Center in their hometown of Toronto, which were the most memorable. The first time was very special because it was the *Vapor Trails* tour and after

Photo Arjan Mulder

five years of silence over the terrible personal tragedy in Neil Peart's life, Rush had finally made another album and eventually went on tour again. How touching it was to be there. I remember just crying with happiness.

And I saw their last concert at the Air Canada Center, together with my friend Alex van Loon. That was a very emotional night. I knew it would be the last time I saw Rush play live and because Rush played 'Losing It' live for the very first time, with Ben Mink on violin. That evening I had come full circle. I put on the tour t-shirt from the *Hold Your Fire* tour in 1988, the first tour I ever saw. And it still fitted!

Rush - with their joy of playing, their musical qualities, the friendly personalities of the band members, the hard work on stage, the ever-beautiful light shows and their own, great authentic sound - will remain in my heart forever.

The *Presto* tour started on 17 February 1990 and ended 63 shows later on 29 June 1990. It was an exclusively North American show, with seven Canadian gigs and the remainder in the United States.

BAYFRONT CENTER

20 FEBRUARY 1990, ST PETERSBURG, FLORIDA

I WAS THERE: JOHN KANA

I was in a friend's car as we were traveling to a shopping centre when I first heard Rush. The album was *Hold Your Fire*. I immediately bought that, and *Moving Pictures*, *Hemispheres* and *Power Windows*, at my friend's suggestion. I skipped school to get tickets for the Bayfront Center *Presto* show and missed school the day after the concert too. It was well worth it.

MIAMI ARENA

22 FEBRUARY 1990, MIAMI, FLORIDA

I WAS THERE: MIRANDA SHERYEL

I was 29 when I saw them at the Miami Arena. 'Xanadu' and 'Closer to the Heart' are my favourite songs.

ORLANDO ARENA

23 FEBRUARY 1990, ORLANDO, FLORIDA

I WAS THERE: MATT MACDONALD

I spent the late 70s and entire 80s spent listening to *Moving Pictures*, *Permanent Waves* and *Exit... Stage Left*. I raided my brother's record and cassette tape collection. I came of age during *Hold Your Fire*, *Power Windows* and *A Show of Hands*. *Presto* was the first tour I saw in person, and then *Roll the Bones* – twice. Growing up in suburbia in Orlando, Florida, 'Subdivisions' really spoke to me.

KEMPER ARENA

3 MARCH 1990, KANSAS CITY, MISSOURI

I WAS THERE: SEBASTIAN E MENDEZ

Having moved from my homeland to finish high school in the Midwest, the music of *Power Windows* and *Signals* helped me to cope with the anxieties of making new friends and a new environment on top of the regular dose of high school stressors. A few of my new friends and I secured tickets to the *Presto* tour. That weekend, we crammed into my friend's Bohon's cheap version of the A-Team van and headed for the gig. The excitement was palpable. I remember the lights going down, the *Moving Pictures* animated scene and knowing what was coming – 'Tom Sawyer'! When that low synth note and bass drum hit, I was in the moment 100 per cent. It was one of those few times where you are one with the moment, fully embracing the present. I cried.

Going back, the van broke down on the highway. We sat in the van and shared our Rush experience and our memories from that perfect night over and over again as we downed beer after Keystone beer. We fell asleep and were woken up by a highway patrol officer asking 'Are all these empty beer cans yours?' 'No, officer!' He gave us a sly smile and said, 'OK then, I'll call you guys a tow truck.' The perfect ending to a perfect weekend.

PALACE OF AUBURN HILLS

8 MARCH 1990, AUBURN HILLS, MICHIGAN

I WAS THERE: JOE DISANO

Joe Disano saw Rush in 1990 and took his son in 2015

If I could wave my magic wand, I don't know if I would go back in time to the first time I saw Rush simply because I remember it so vividly. Anticipation began months before as my friend Kurt and I slept overnight at the mall to make sure we were first in line to physically buy tickets. As we waited, we chatted with an old hippie who regaled us with tales of seeing Rush in the mid-70s. We were jealous.

We beat the scalpers, made a new friend, and scored two pretty decent tickets to the famous *Live from the Rabbit Hole* show at the Palace of Auburn Hills - at the time a brand new venue, but recently razed. The Palace also hosted Rush's last show in Detroit on the *R40* tour, to which my wife and I took our bass-playing, Rush fan son.

Beyond the songs, stellar musicianship, and spectacular light show, the example of three individuals working together to create something unique and uncompromising stayed with me. Rush challenged its audience by always playing a large selection of their latest release live. 'Show Don't Tell' and 'The Pass' became classics but when played live for the first time on the *Presto* tour they were cheered alongside the rest of the catalogue. Few Rush fans took new music as an excuse for a bathroom break.

Rush were vital. Always responding to the current of the times but never imitating or treading old ground. In concert. In life. In total.

I WAS THERE: KEVIN THOMPSON

It seems impossible to believe that three musicians could be so gifted. I believe Eric Johnson opened for them on guitar. They have brought so much joy to so many people's lives with their music. As a drummer myself, I was deeply saddened to hear of Neil Peart's passing. He was without question a magician on the drums.

I WAS THERE: SANDY ATKINSON

I was a fan of their music from the *Fly by Night* album. I didn't know much about them, only that I liked their music. When they started performing and I only saw three guys on stage I asked my date, 'Where's the rest of the band?' I was amazed by the different age groups that attended and almost everyone near the stage knew every beat that Peart put out... even the little ones!

I can picture the huge bunnies on either side of the stage for the *Presto* tour. I remember the dryers with the shirts showing the video of tumbling clothes. And the rotisserie chickens cooking on stage. I saw the tour with the choral singers (Geddy kept apologising and thanking us for 'putting up' with this show). I didn't like that one as much. I know most of the songs that Neil threw his stick up in the air to and when he caught it to not miss a beat... and I do it when those songs come on.

ARCO ARENA

28 MARCH 1990, SACRAMENTO, CALIFORNIA

I WAS THERE: TIM ONIONS

In 1977 our math teacher in the eighth grade let us bring an album to listen to every Friday. He would pick a couple each week. I remember my friend bringing Rush's *2112* in and he was so into it - but most of the class was not! That album did not fit into the pop culture of the time, but to this day is still my favourite album. In 1982, when *Moving Pictures* came out, it was a 'must have' for every rocker out there. Neil with his overly syncopated drumming and Geddy with those incredible bass lines meant Rush were like no other band at the time. And they were like that since day one. You couldn't put their music in a box or ever know what the next album would bring.

All through the 70s Rush was talked about as a 'must see' live band. I did not get to see them until late 80s but I saw them five times and enjoyed every show. They always had big screens, videos, pyrotechnics and the most awesome drum set of any band, and I have seen hundreds of rock shows. And the laundry machines? Well, I always thought they were for the acid heads. My two year old's first concert was Rush. I saw them after they got back on the road after Neil's loss and I noticed the life had gone out of him but he still played perfectly. Rush are the most eclectic band ever and live they bring us all together.

VETERAN'S MEMORIAL COLISEUM

8 APRIL 1990, PHOENIX, ARIZONA

I WAS THERE: GRAEME HUNT

It was my junior year in high school. A good friend made me a mixed cassette that contained Led Zeppelin, Pink Floyd - and a band that called themselves Rush.

The internet forum set up by Graeme Hunt (right) led to Joe & Cindy marrying & having daughter Cassie

I was drawn to all three bands, but the three Rush songs from their recently released *Hold Your Fire* album struck something within in me. I couldn't help but listen to 'Time Stand Still', 'Force Ten' and 'Lock and Key' over and over again. When my friend later brought me VHS tapes of Led Zeppelin's *The Song Remains the Same*, as well as Rush's *A Show of Hands*. I must have watched the Rush concert two or three times that weekend, and was just astounded by Rush's skill, their humour and their music. And because my father was a jazz drummer (and I was a mediocre one myself), I was blown away by Neil Peart.

Rush immediately became my favourite band, and I began purchasing their albums one by one as fast as my meagre high school job's salary would allow. I bought *Presto* on the day it was released and listened to it on repeat for hours, with 'The Pass' being an emotional favourite.

When Rush announced their *Presto* tour, my friends and I sat by their phone and took turns calling the venue box office, praying we could get tickets. My friends ended up getting front row seats on Alex's side, but I wasn't as lucky. Still, I was overjoyed to get two tickets near the back of the Veteran's Memorial Coliseum . I could barely wait until the show. It would it be my first Rush concert and my first concert, period!

When the day arrived my younger sister (who I had turned into a Rush fan) and I were beside ourselves with excitement. With me being 17 and my sister 14, my parents volunteered to drive us there. Pulling up to the Coliseum before the doors opened, my parents dropped us off and wished us a good show. My sister and I walked the length of the parking lot, amazed at the gathered fans next to their cars and all blaring different Rush albums. The energy was electric.

After saying a jealous goodbye to my friends who headed up to the front row, we found our seats near the back and chatted with fellow fans. I barely remember the opening band, Mr Big, other than them playing a couple of Led Zeppelin riffs and wanting them to end so we could see Rush. Then the lights went out, and the crowd exploded. The opening chords of 'Force Ten' after the animated intro vibrated my chest so deeply I coughed. I will never forget that concert, from the dancing bunnies to the incredible drum solo, hundreds of air drumming arms in the air, clouds of pot smoke and lighters being held aloft - and just how loud it was!

My parents picked us up afterwards. We were exhausted, exhilarated and with ringing ears. Coming down from the show high (and probably a little secondhand pot high too) my sister and I both fell asleep in the car on the two hour drive home, knowing we had school the next morning.

I am now 47 years old, with a wife and two young sons. I still have my concert *Presto* t-shirt, now faded to grey, as well as my ticket stub. I made it a point to see every tour since, from *Roll the Bones* through *R40*. As clichéd as it sounds, Rush truly has been a soundtrack to my life, and I am forever grateful to Alex, Geddy and Neil for sharing their music with me.

ROCHESTER COMMUNITY WAR MEMORIAL

19 APRIL 1990, ROCHESTER, NEW YORK

I WAS THERE: GARY CONSTABLE

I won a contest during the *Presto* tour which included a limo to and from the show, two CD libraries, seats at the sound stage and meeting the band before the show. The show was cancelled because Geddy got sick but at the makeup date he was very apologetic knowing how much I was looking forward to it.

THE SPECTRUM

24 APRIL 1990, PHILADELPHIA, PENNSYLVANIA

I WAS THERE: JOHN B BROWN

During the early part of 'Xanadu', it sounds like winds are blowing. During that part of the song, it sounded like the winds were not only blowing around us but also over us! Somehow they rigged part of the sound system directly over the audience in the ceiling.

I WAS THERE: MATTHEW PHILLIPINE

My brother is six years older than me. We shared a room. He played 'Tom Sawyer' when it first came out. I wanted to hear it over and over again so he put it on a cassette and I wore that out. When *Grace Under Pressure* was released he played that cassette over and over too. Those songs just became ingrained in my brain.

In the late 80s, I decided to go and get a couple more Rush albums for myself. I didn't quite gel with the first album, *Rush*, but *Power Windows* and *Hold Your Fire* hit me instantly. I was in junior high school. If I listen to those albums now, they take me instantly back to that time.

My brother came back from college and he said, 'Do you still like Rush? They're coming into Philadelphia to support *Presto*. Would you like to go?' I was in tenth grade and had to beg my mother and father to let me go. We had nosebleed seats. They had these giant 20 foot rabbits that inflated halfway through the show and started dancing around to the songs, and they played just about every song I wanted to hear off *Power Windows* and *Hold Your Fire*.

I signed up to all these different newsletters that would send you information about Rush. *The Necromancer* was one. It came out monthly. It looked like it was typed up by some kid in their room and then photocopied, but it was the only thing you really had during that time. You'd buy different bootlegs that people had. You'd write to them and exchange bootlegs. I acquitted all kinds of memorabilia.

In my twenties Rush took a back seat. When they came out on the *R30* tour, I said to my wife, 'Rush is coming out again and I really want to go and see them.' That reintroduced me to my obsession. I had more disposable income and could travel and from then on I'd go and see them at every opportunity.

I saw them on the *Clockwork Angels* tour at the Taj Mahal in Atlantic City with my brother. I think it only sat about 8,000 people. We had second row seats. They were shooting out t-shirts near the end and I was able to snag one from Alex. When they get to the words 'concert hall' in 'The Spirit of Radio' the house lights go on and they always take a picture of the audience. It showed me clear as day on the second row, with my hands up in the air. My brother had that photo blown up and I have it hanging up in my home to this day.

For *R40*, my gut was telling me the touring was probably coming to an end. Their visit to Tampa lined up with spring break and I said to my brother, 'If you can come visit me down in Florida and maybe bring the kids, I'll pick up the tickets. This could be the last time we ever get to see them.'

I got front row tickets, Alex's side. My brother didn't know that until he got down there. I took loads of pictures. It looks like Alex was posing for me when I was taking the pictures. It was a really expensive decision but one I'd do again in a heart beat. To have my final show being on the front row with those guys is as memorable as it gets.

My wife told me about Neil. She called and asked, 'Did you hear?' And I said, 'Hear what?', because I'm all over the Rush groups. 'Neil died.' I just could not fathom it. I always thought that we'd hear that he was working on a book, or there'd be a sighting of him somewhere.

I got out a bottle of Macallan, went out back and poured myself a big glass. They'd been with me all my adult life. I felt I'd lost a family member. I cried for probably three hours.

THE CAPITAL CENTRE

5 MAY, 1990, LARGO, MARYLAND

I WAS THERE: SKIP DALY

I first recall hearing Rush at William Salb's house when I was in fifth grade via the *Exit...Stage Left* video on MTV (back when they played, you know, music). At the time, Rush was akin to background static – the 'cool stuff' that the older brothers of my friends were into. The long hair, Alex in that red sports jacket, and the heaviness of the music that just made me feel as though

Ad for the Largo show - photo Skip Daly

darker things were happening here. Stuff meant for older kids. A few years would pass before I 'got' popular music, and it wasn't until my junior year of high school, in the spring of 1988, that I would be reintroduced to Rush in a meaningful way. During a particularly tedious history class (a subject I usually enjoyed – sorry, Mr. Alden), I noticed that the kid next to me (Eric Kircher) had a Rush *Hold Your Fire* cassette and I asked to check it out.

I started reading through the lyrics and was just floored. Far from the typically vacuous 'girls and cars' topics that dominated the airwaves, this was poetry! I borrowed the tape and that was it – I was all in. Those next few months were a glorious immersion study in the back catalogue as I bought used cassettes, album by album, from the local Record & Tape Traders shop. There were 'only' 12 twelve studio albums at that point!

Unfortunately, my 1988 conversion came about four or five months after the *Hold Your Fire* tour had come to town, so my first Rush concert didn't come until the Capital Centre stop on the *Presto* tour – over two years later. In that time I had devoured the catalogue, eagerly purchased the new 1989 live release, *A Show of Hands*, and even started learning bass guitar (an instrument that I had no appreciation for prior to hearing its magical presence in Rush's soundscape). My good friend, Andy Yarrish, scored us tickets, and away we went. Our seats were neither great nor horrible, being in the mid-tier, about halfway up the arena, and halfway back, on Geddy's side of the stage. Mr. Big warmed up the crowd, but when the lights went down for Rush, I recall the surge of adrenaline as the opening notes of 'Force Ten' pulsed through the arena. Song after song went by and, after two years of enjoying the recorded catalog, it was amazing to finally be experiencing the band live. It's funny the things we remember, and for some odd reason I vividly recall the moment the band began playing 'Manhattan Project'. It's not a bad song, but at the time I remember it being the first tune in the set list where I thought that they could have made better use of the time, and a soft 'ugh' must have escaped my mouth. Andy, ever vigilant, looked over at me, pointed toward the aisle with a grin, and said, 'Uh, you can leave at any time!' We shared a good laugh, and it remains one of those little quirky moments I'll never forget. (I choose not to dwell on the more sensible things that this brain space could be occupied with.) Truth be told, the gig was magical from first to last, with 'Mission' being a particular high point. There is nothing like the first time…

MAPLE LEAF GARDENS

17 MAY 1990, TORONTO, CANADA

I WAS THERE: JOHN TABAKOS

I heard 'Tom Sawyer' in 1981. In the summer of 1982, 'Subdivisions' definitely got my attention. It had that new wave ' thing' in addition to a nice rock feel. Soon after I purchased *Signals*. I appreciated the variety of songs on *Signals* – synth rock, reggae/ska, etc. There were a lot of musical styles to digest.

John Tabakos was at Maple Leaf Gardens

Grace Under Pressure was an enjoyable listen, with the new wave influence still there but heavier, with more angst and hard rocking. Purchasing the back catalogue I appreciated the shift from the prog rock, space and sci-fi themes to more down to earth subjects. With *Power Windows* the synths were still prevalent but the guitar, bass and drums sounded clearer than on *Grace Under Pressure*, and from *Hold Your Fire* to *Clockwork Angels*, different albums and different styles but awesome music and lyrics.

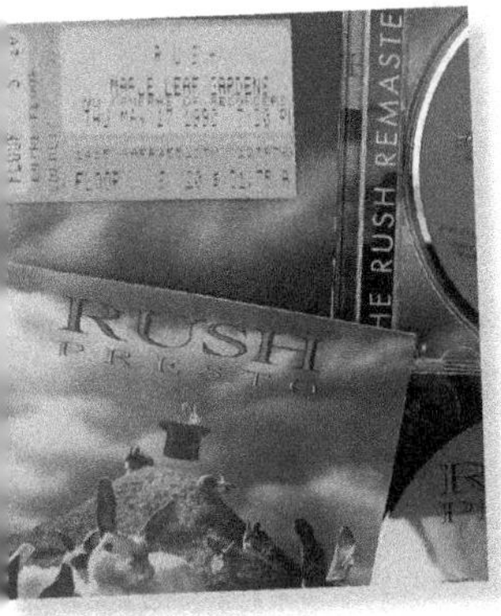

My first Rush concert was the *Presto* tour in 1990 and the last one *R40* in 2015, 13 times altogether. At the *Presto* show, I recall a buzz in the crowd and the excitement, the wonderful sense of anticipation. I recall 'Force Ten' as the opener, just as the lights dimmed. Then 'Subdivisions', 'Freewill', 'Distant Early Warning'... songs I've known for years. The material from *Presto* was well received too.

The concert albums and DVDs are the next best thing to being at a Rush concert.

OMAHA CIVIC AUDITORIUM

20 JUNE 1990, OMAHA, NEBRASKA

I WAS THERE: ROB MALLORY

My very first concert was in 1979, nearly five months before my birth! My dad talked my mom into catching the band on the Lincoln stop of the *Hemispheres* tour. I was kicking my mom the entire show.

I grew up with Rush. I can remember staring at the albums for hours at a time, being lulled into a peaceful sleep by their music. In 1990, my dad took me to the Omaha, Nebraska stop of the *Presto* tour. The setlist was very similar to the *A Show of Hands* album, with many *Presto* songs thrown in

Rob Mallory's first live show was before he was even born

to showcase the band's newest masterpiece. I was also taken to the Omaha stop of the *Roll the Bones* tour in November 1991, and remember enjoying the setlist more than the *Presto* tour.

Throughout the years I was able to catch the band on the *Vapor Trails*, *R30*, *Snakes & Arrows*, *Time Machine* and *R40* tours. I took my three oldest kids to see the *Snakes & Arrows* stop. My youngest was only seven months old. She had a blast. My son Robbie is the biggest Rush fan amongst them and caught them with me three times.

Seeing the band on the Lincoln, Nebraska stop of their *R40* tour, so many years after my first in utero Rush show, was something I'll never forget. It was magical watching the band tear through their catalogue, and even though we all knew it would be our last time seeing the band, the tears were happy tears. And though all of the shows I caught, and all of the time I spent watching my favourite band live are now just memories, some memories last forever.

FIDDLER'S GREEN AMPHITHEATRE

22 JUNE 1990, ENGLEWOOD, COLORADO

Ross Maak and ex-wife Julia remain friends through a mutual love of Rush

I WAS THERE: ROSS MAAK

I had two older brothers, one who introduced me to *Exit... Stage Left*. I can still air drum most of the solo tucked into the middle of 'YYZ'. And this song about a car, called 'Red Barchetta', remains my favourite Rush tune to this day. When the dust settled, I'd seen the boys 27 times. Most of my friends look at me like I'm completely nuts when I throw that number out there. It's cool. I probably am.

My first show was the *Show of Hands* tour in Denver. You never forget your first. I saw them again on the *Presto* tour, of course. The *Roll the Bones* tour may be my strangest memory. For months I received a book each month in the mail. There was no return address and no note inside. Just one paperback, typically one that was right up my alley... a good spy novel, usually. The day after Denver's *Roll the Bones* tickets went on sale, a single ticket showed up. Again, no address, no note, just one single ticket.

I went to the show (12th row on Geddy's side - great seat!) expecting to finally get the chance to meet my secret admirer. Alas, it wasn't to be. The seats on each side of me were occupied, but not by anyone I knew. Books had continued coming leading up to the show, but that was it. No more books and no idea who sent the swag. To this day it remains a mystery.

A few years later a buddy of mine lived in a tiny little apartment and was awakened every morning by his next-door neighbour blasting Rush, Queensryche, Dream Theater, etc. in the shower. She always apologised to my buddy for waking him to which he replied, 'Keep playing kick-ass music and we'll never have a problem. But...' he continued, 'I got this buddy of mine you need to meet.'

She and I were married a few years later. She saw the same *Roll the Bones* show after hearing a radio announcement saying Rush was playing in Denver that night. She didn't have enough money to go to the show and get home to Colorado, so had her mom to wire her some cash. She bought a ticket at the window, hit the show and drove home after. We enjoyed talking about how that was our first Rush show together, alone. We made many a road trip to see Rush. Illinois. California. Iowa. Always via the road trip, never by plane.

During the *Counterparts* tour we decided on Moline, Illinois. Six of us packed into two cars at 2am on Saturday morning and headed out across Nebraska. I got a speeding ticket, lost my favourite sunglasses, left my favourite pillow in the motel in Illinois and left my daytimer (remember those?) with $400 cash and my chequebook and credit cards in a McDonald's bathroom stall in Des Moines. 'I love me some Rush, but I didn't realise I was going to have to tithe to see them!' became the quote of the trip.

Rush afforded me so many priceless memories with incredible friends and the exuberance of youth ... and beyond. Sadly, the marriage didn't withstand the test of time, but we remain good friends and still love to talk music on a regular basis.

I WAS THERE: DAMEN ZIER

I was nine or ten when MTV played the live 'Tom Sawyer' video. It was very dark. The music was distinctive but I preferred Journey, Loverboy and a few other early 80s bands. By the time I was in my junior year of high school in 1988 I was more receptive to their music. I was in a friend's car and he had a cassette of *Moving Pictures*. I put it in and played it and it grew on me.

The *Presto* tour was my first ever concert. 'Manhattan Project' hooked me for life. I'm a huge history buff, and to hear those lyrics timed with the video they back-screened was unbelievable. Only Pink Floyd, who I saw in a 75,000 seater stadium, can touch Rush live.

Damen Zier was hooked by 'Manhattan Project'

I went to their last show in Denver. Like a lot of fans, I couldn't believe that it had ended. You always held out hope that they would take a break and they'd put out some tracks and maybe they wouldn't tour but the music would live on. That came to an end in January 2020. It was January 10th when Neil died. My wife served me with divorce papers on the 15th and I met a new girl on the 13th. That week was bittersweet.

IRVINE MEADOWS AMPHITHEATER

29 JUNE 1990, IRVINE, CALIFORNIA

I WAS THERE: RICK REEVES

I did not have tickets. Without funds there was no hope. My birthday rolled around and my girlfriend, now wife, gave me two third row centre tickets. So my best friend and I were ready for the show. Unbeknownst to me, my girl wanted me to invite her. I have yet to live it down.

Ushered to our seats, I was really excited to get the show rolling. For the next almost three hours I was transfixed by the drum kit and the maestro behind it. Being a drummer, I was drawn in by Neil's amazing playing. I barely noticed Geddy or Alex. Being 20 feet from the stage I could see his playing up close for hours and it couldn't get any better.

The crowd was a group of old friends we had never met, with handshakes and high fives all over when a particular part of a song was played and screams went out for more. A certain substance was being passed around when I noticed Alex looking over at our area with a smile. With the encores done, Alex threw out a couple of drumsticks. Just my fingertip touched the stick as it was caught by the guy behind me, with several others trying to grab it from him. Despite that it was one of the best birthdays ever.

Tickets to the *Presto* show were scarce, being the last show of the tour. But they were being given away on the local Rush friendly rock station, KLOS. You had to stump the morning guys with a sports trivia question and I was successful with 'who were the original Pittsburgh Steelers' Steel Curtain?' They couldn't solve the question and we won two tickets. The show was that night. We had to get to the radio station in downtown LA but we fought traffic into town and out again before heading south, getting there before the band hit the stage.

We were on Alex's side of the stage and on our feet for a great portion of the show. I didn't care one bit because the show was electrifying. All the shows I saw had their flow and this night they were having fun and it showed. It rubbed off on the crowd. The show ended with a huge encore and a long walk back to the car. For the drive home, and the rest of the night, it was show talk.

I WAS THERE: VICKI FLIER HUDSON

I was 14 years old and striding to a friend's kitchen to get a snack when I heard an incredible song drifting in from one of the bedrooms. That song was 'Natural Science'. My soul was never the same.

My first tour was *Presto*. I went to three shows on that tour. When they played 'Mission' at the Irvine show, a gentle California breeze blew across the outdoor venue as Alex closed his eyes and played his soaring solo. That memory is burned in my mind forever.

In 2013 I had a client who was related to one of the members of the *Clockwork Angels* string ensemble. He arranged backstage passes for me and a friend to have dinner with him before the show in Saratoga Springs, New York. In an insane coincidence, I also won the meet and greet contest to meet Alex and Geddy. They couldn't have been kinder. I gave Alex a letter that explained his impact on me as a musician and told him what he meant to me. He seemed quite touched. He thanked me, put the letter in his pocket and went off to do the show. I figured he read it and then threw it out. Then on January 7, 2020 I received a package. It was a *Clockwork Angels* tour book autographed by all three of the guys. Inside was my letter to Alex. The package had been mailed to me by the president of Rush's merch company, ShowTech. He'd found the letter and tour book in an old box of tour stuff. Alex must have given my letter and the signed tour book to someone to mail to me. Somehow that never happened. Until seven years later.

The items arrived on my doorstep the day Neil Peart died, just when I needed them most. Every time I look at the tour book I am blown away by this sweet miracle. I now play in a Rush tribute band called The Spirit of Rush out of Atlanta. We have been together for seven years and I get great joy out of bringing the music of Rush to people of all ages. Nothing uplifted me more than seeing Rush live. Now I feel that inspiration from the inside as I perform and look out at the faces of our fans.

The *Roll the Bones* tour comprised 103 shows, starting in Hamilton, Ontario in Canada on 25 October 1991 and finishing at Tinley Park, Illinois on 28 June 1992. It included European shows, the last tour to do so until 2004.

CIVIC ARENA

28 OCTOBER 1991, PITTSBURGH, PENNSYLVANIA

Aidan Monaghan saw Rush in Pittsburgh in 1991 and their third to last show, in Vegas

I WAS THERE: AIDAN MONAGHAN

Pittsburgh's local rock station WDVE played 'Freewill' from the newly-released *Exit... Stage Left* over my sister's very powerful stereo system. This then 13-year-old had never before heard a more intense and action packed song or the sound that only band members Lee with his Rickenbacker bass, Lifeson with his various guitars and Peart with his snare and various tom drums and cymbals, recorded. Life changed forever.

I campaigned for my mother to buy me the record. She came home with *Hemispheres*, a record I hadn't heard of. I less than enthusiastically began to investigate it. After regular plays I was impressed, albeit for different reasons from *Exit... Stage Left*. I'd never heard such complex lyrical and musical arrangements from what I assumed was just another high-living group of rockers. Rush had a lot more to offer.

Although their subsequent releases never impressed quite as much, I always waited with anticipation for new material that might revisit the potential I knew they had.

In 1991, from the third row floor section of the Pittsburgh Civic Arena, I saw Rush for the first time. One could literally feel an energy not present during a mere record playback. All my favourite late 70s and early 80s Rush material was revisited that night including a 'Xanadu'/'Hemispheres - The Prelude' medley, with dry ice mist drifting from the stage.

In 2015 I got to see Rush's third to last show ever, in Las Vegas. I remember a pre-show glimpse of a t-shirt worn by a woman that read, 'I May Be Old, But I Got To See All Of The Good Bands.' And I remember Neil's drum solo and the sustained energy and use of his acoustic kit during that evening's solo. It crossed my mind that Neil too may have realised this was going to be one of his very last ever drum solos before a major audience and he wanted to exit on a memorable note.

THE CAPITAL CENTRE

4 DECEMBER, 1991, LARGO, MARYLAND

I WAS THERE: SKIP DALY

Roll the Bones had been released in September of '91, and I loved that album. It sounded so fresh and vital, and had a lightness and optimism to it that really resonated with me at the time (I was 20 years old, in my third year of college, and life was generally good). The tour had kicked off in October and I had managed to catch a show in Normal, Illinois of all random places), so this Capital Centre show was my second of four on that tour. I had floor seats, 15th or 16th row centre. Earlier that afternoon, I had actually gotten autographs from Geddy and Alex at a local hotel, about two minutes from my house. It was well known that artists performing at the Cap Centre would stay in the Greenbelt Marriot, so I went and read a book in the lobby for a little bit and, sure enough, Geddy strolled through.

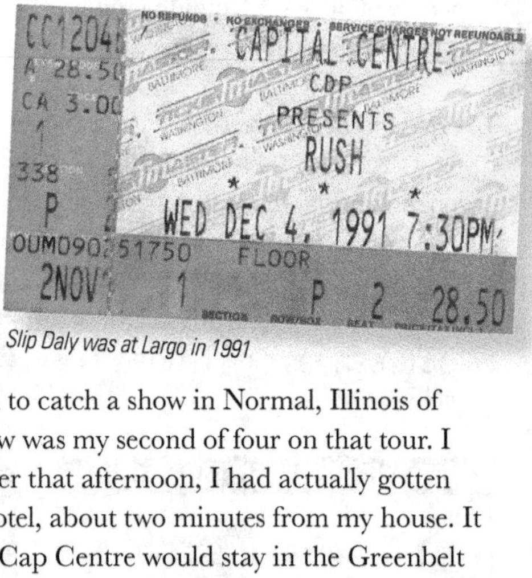

Slip Daly was at Largo in 1991

I liked the new album but that tour was even better. The set list touched on many of my favourite songs at the time, and struck a nice balance between contemporary material and older classics. I vividly remember the goosebumps of standing in the arena when the house music would fade, the lights would go down, the crowd would roar and the intro video would start. You'd catch a glimpse of three silhouettes running onto the darkened stage, and then another roar from the crowd as the opening notes of 'Force Ten' rang out. This show saw the live debut of 'Ghost of a Chance', which sounded great. Geddy experienced some bass difficulty during 'The Pass' (a broken string?) and he had to swap to his backup (black Mk1 Wal) bass mid-song, while continuing to sing. 'Xanadu' was pure magic, and the encore on that tour was a thing to behold – a six song medley, and a fun romp through Rush's early discography. Oh, to 'live it all again'.

MADISON SQUARE GARDEN

6 & 7 DECEMBER 1991, NEW YORK, NEW YORK

I WAS THERE: ROSS BROWN

Ross Brown saw Rush at MSG in '91 and on R40 in Vegas

I heard 'Tom Sawyer' at a roller skating rink I went to for a birthday party. I didn't know what the song was about but was drawn to the music. Then, aged 16 and in high school, I was at a friend's house and he was playing *Exit... Stage Left*. I immediately recognised 'Tom Sawyer' so I borrowed the CD and listened to it over and over. That CD really jump started my connection to the music.

I saw the *Roll the Bones* tour at Madison Square Garden. I was very high up. It was the second ever show I saw, after the Grateful Dead in front of 80 or 90,000 people at Giants Stadium. Madison Square Garden was 18 or 19,000, so a very different experience.

As I was transitioning into college, my parents separated and ultimately divorced. Rush became my outlet, my comfort blanket. I started to read the lyrics and what the songs were saying resonated with me. There wasn't a topic that Rush didn't cover, whether it was nature or technology or space or our judicial system. When I sat down and read the lyrics of 'Red Sector A', that was a very pivotal moment. But they were always very balanced. They never sang anything about politics.

I was always very moved by the fact that they weren't a mainstream band. They weren't always on the radio but when they were, you almost wanted to call the Rush fans you knew and say, 'Wow, they're finally getting some air time!'

When you wanted tickets, you'd have to dial and redial to get through. It wasn't like today where everything is just a click of a button on the phone. It didn't matter to me what the cost was, I just wanted to get as close to the stage as possible. For a very long time I never went a day without listening to them. You could not put a price on seeing them live. I saw them 56 times, mostly in the north eastern United States and pretty much anywhere on Highway 95. When I started working in a job where I could travel I'd try to connect with friends and colleagues in other parts of the country when Rush were on tour.

I was there for the music. The lighting was great, the pyrotechnics were great and the videos were always so interesting. And they would use those videos again in future tours. It was always a very solid thing in my life that I could always rely on. It felt like a piece of home.

I met Geddy briefly when he promoting his solo album in malls. And I met Alex at a children's cancer benefit in New York my friend organised. I got there and my friend introduced me to the CEO who took me upstairs to a private room with the CEO of a wine company and Eddie Murray, a Baltimore Orioles Hall of Famer. I started to talk to the two of them and out of the corner of my eye I saw Alex coming over. It was the four of us talking and we all had a glass of Chardonnay. I ended up talking to Alex on my own for about 30 minutes and I probably forgot every single question I wanted to ask him. In my head I was arguing, 'Dummy, wake up! Think of something intelligent to say to show you're a Rush fan!'

An item in the silent auction was a meet and greet for the *R40* Las Vegas show. I got into a bidding war with somebody at the back of the room. I decided I had to have this, no matter what it cost. In the end the auctioneer said, 'If you guys want to split it, we will put an extra one in there.' So I got the chance to meet Geddy and Alex in Vegas.

Later in 2015 they did an interview with Michael Moore on SiriusXM at New York Town Hall and a friend won two passes to go see them. There were 40 people tops in the studio, listening to the interview, and afterwards they did photo ops.

I was at the end of the bar in my favourite Italian restaurant when I got an alert on my phone saying Neil had died. My phone started blowing up as my friends started texting me. One thing I've always respected about the band is that they were always very private. They weren't lavish or partied or got themselves in trouble. They were family oriented. They performed and they went home. When the rumours started about Neil giving up playing, was that the start of his illness? Is that why they gave up playing? It was devastating because it was the confirmation of the end. Even if Alex and Getty collaborated and did something together it's not going to be a Rush concert.

MAPLE LEAF GARDENS

16 DECEMBER 1991, TORONTO, CANADA

I WAS THERE: LISA CARRANO

It was 2am on October 25, 1991. My friend Chris and I were still debating whether or not to do the Hamilton and Rochester shows. It was late and frankly I was ready to hit the sack, but it was still 'a good road trip for Rush'.

Lisa Carrano got to meet her hero Alex as he arrived at the Toronto show

After a 12 hour drive we arrived in Hamilton on a rainy, dreary afternoon. I went in search of somewhere to stay while Chris went in search of good tickets. I went into the arena beforehand and directly to my usual spot, stage left in front of Alex's equipment. I spoke with JJ (Alex's guitar tech) for a while and saw a guy with about 100 pins tacked to his jacket. His name was Kevin. We started talking about various shows we'd been to and he was impressed a female had come all the way from Long Island to see Rush. I told him how much I loved Alex and Kevin replied, 'Oh, I've been to his house a couple of times and met him as well.'

We exchanged addresses and phone numbers and talked frequently. When I bought front row centre tickets for Madison Square Garden Kevin came down from Toronto to see both shows. Those were the best two nights of my life. I never thought I'd ever be that close to Alex. I came out, with no voice as usual (I wonder if he heard me?) and bruised arms and hands from hanging over the barrier.

They were playing Buffalo and Toronto. Kevin promised that if I came up to see them I'd definitely see Alex. The Buffalo show was great. We saw Ged in the limo while it was stopped at a traffic light and we ran after it for two blocks – in ten below zero weather! I had gotten both Alex and JJ a Christmas card and written Alex a letter. JJ had always been great to me and had always given gifts to Alex for me. When JJ gave me the thumbs up from the stage I knew Alex had received the letter.

We arrived at Maple Leaf Gardens in time for soundcheck. I had brought a single red rose and a card for Alex, and a folder containing two photos for him to sign. We were standing in a little doorway next to where the crew, etc., come in when Kevin turned and said, 'Don't look now, but here comes Neil down the sidewalk.' Sure enough, all bundled up with hat, hood and sunglasses, was the Professor himself. Kevin walked right up to him but Neil went straight for the door, business as usual. But that's just Neil and I loved him anyway.

Five minutes later, Kevin said, 'OK Lisa, be calm – here comes a white limo down the street.' I looked over and, sure enough, it was heading straight for us. We walked very quickly to the corner. It had its right blinker on and it was going to use the other entrance. The limo pulled up to the kerb and I could vaguely see Alex's silhouette through the tinted glass. The limo made a three point turn and headed for the ramp. I was right there… jaw frozen and heart racing.

Kevin yelled for me to hold up my bag so Alex would see I had something for him. I held up the bag with the rose and card, walked straight towards the limo and it came to a dead stop. Oh my god, this was it… after 10 painful years, this was finally it!

Down went the window and there, sitting right in front of me, was my beautiful angel. 'Hi – what's this?' 'Hi Alex, this is for you.' I somehow muttered. 'Oh, thank you so very much.' The first thing I noticed were his eyes. There were so blue, so beautiful. I had my head and a half of me through the window. The limo was so warm inside. He put my package next to him on the seat and smiled. I asked him if he would sign a photo for me and he happily obliged. He even had his red Scripto marker ready! When he had finished I asked him if he had read the letter I had given him the night before in Buffalo. He looked me straight in the eye and said, 'You're Lisa, right?' I thought my legs were about to give out. 'Yeah, that's me!' 'Yes, it was very nice. I really appreciate it, thank you.'

I was about two inches from him the entire time. I've never seen anyone so beautiful. I don't remember exactly how long I was there, but the security guard came over and tried to shuffle the four of us who were there away. Alex signed a couple more autographs and we told him how much we enjoyed the show in Buffalo. Alex thanked us again, rolled up the window and disappeared behind the garage. I think I slipped 'I love you Alex!' in there too.

Kevin and I returned to the car to recover from what just took place. He looked over at me and said, 'Now do you believe me?' I looked at my two autographed photos, then back at Kevin and suddenly tears streamed endlessly down my face. 'Thank you so much. I owe you my life.' 'Don't worry,' he said. 'It was no problem.'

I ended up sitting second row on Alex's side. I screamed. I screamed so loud my insides hurt. Do you think he heard me?

THE FORUM

22 & 23 JANUARY 1992, LOS ANGELES, CALIFORNIA

I WAS THERE: HAYLEY HERSH

Hayley Hersh was in a Rush tribute band called Chronicles

I must have been nearly 10 when I occasionally heard that synth growl at the beginning of 'Tom Sawyer' on the radio. The next time I remember hearing of Rush was walking into my older brother's room. The video for 'Big Money' was on MTV. My brother pointed out, 'That's Geddy Lee, he's super talented, he plays bass and keyboards and sings.'

At high school, one of my best friends was Jeff. He had a huge drum kit made up of several mismatched drums, complete with roto toms and a glockenspiel. I had been progressing as a piano player and was into synthesizers too. Jeff had a Roland Juno 106 synth and wanted to see if I could play the synth part to a song called 'Subdivisions' so we could jam together. He showed it to me a little bit then sat down to play it through on drums. I was totally amazed by the song and especially the drum part. I thought, 'Finally some cool keyboards in a rock song!' I was bitten. He showed me some more by playing along to the *Show of Hands* VHS and I was hooked. I'd never been so excited about a band.

We'd jam and I'd learn the synth parts but realised they were only in the parts of the song when Geddy wasn't playing bass. That's when I decided to start learning bass. Over time we found a guitar player and jammed often, forming a Rush tribute called Chronicles.

My first concert was at The Forum in Los Angeles for the *Roll the Bones* tour. I was so excited to finally be seeing my music gods live. I remember being outside the building about to go in and feeling astounded that they were actually inside about to play. The concert was amazing. I knew I'd be going to every Rush concert I could.

For the next several years I listened relentlessly and practised bass, pushing myself to grow as a musician. I took great pride in being able to play many of their songs and aimed to nail every note and nuance. It was 2015 when another good friend of mine hit me up to get Rush tickets for *R40*. The rumour was it might be their last tour. We got decent seats for about $400 each, the most expensive concert ticket I ever bought.

The Forum was the same place I first saw them. The arena was packed and the energy palpable. The show was great; they were really giving their best. Near the end my friend led me up to the fifth row. I'd never been that close before and it was so loud! I was in a sea of cheering fans and we flashed each other smiles, all of us in our happiest of places, seeing our favourite band rule the stage. After the last note we saw Neil come forward and wave and we were all surprised since he never did that before. We left buzzing, not sure if that was really it. But if it was, what a way to go out!

The day I heard of Neil's passing I felt a shadow cross my heart. I've never cried over a famous person's death before but this time it was different. I cried a lot that day, and over the next several days. It was all so unfair. He gave so much of himself to us, he deserved better. He had already suffered so much. Suddenly you were gone, from all the lives you left your mark upon.

Rush has brought me endless joy and fascination. They're a huge influence on my life and have taught me so much about music. I know everyone says it but they really are the soundtrack of my life.

ARCO ARENA

27 JANUARY 1992, SACRAMENTO, CALIFORNIA

I WAS THERE: PAUL JACOBS

Having seen Rush every tour since *Moving Pictures*, I was not about to miss the *Roll the Bones* tour. I lived 140 miles north in Redding, California. My buddy and I arrived just as Rush started playing. The show was sold out and there were no scalpers in sight. I told my buddy to save himself - he'd never seen Rush - and to go in without me. Sad, depressed and sulking next to the entrance, an angel from heaven appeared literally from I don't where, handed me her one extra ticket and said 'enjoy'. I got in by the third song and I had learnt my lesson. I never missed a tour and after that I made sure I always got my ticket right away.

SEATTLE CENTER COLISEUM

4 FEBRUARY 1992, SEATTLE, WASHINGTON

I WAS THERE: MICHAEL KIRLIN

I was introduced by my brother to Rush. He is four years older than me, and when he was 16 years old he had a part-time job at a grocery store where he could easily afford lots of cassette tapes. He introduced me to *Moving Pictures*. We became hooked, especially on the song 'Limelight'. He and I shared a bedroom and on the wall of the bedroom was a poster of a Rush concert. It looks like it was taken from the video of *Exit... Stage Left*. My brother eventually moved out of my parents house and found his own place but I still wanted to obtain anything I could on Rush. The first cassette tape I purchased was *Signals*. 'Subdivisions' was an early anthem to me while 'The Analog Kid' resonated with me because I was wondering where I would be and when I would be moving on with my life the way my brother did.

After three years I finally had enough money to go to a Rush concert, and the *Roll the Bones* tour that played in Seattle in 1992 was the first one I could attend. I paid $24 for that ticket and probably had the single worst seat in the entire venue but I never left a concert with such a feeling of wonder. When Rush had been on for 30 minutes, Geddy said they had a couple more hours. I started asking myself if this was going to be as good as the first 30 minutes. It was everything I could ever have dreamed it could be.

Over the years I saw Rush six more times, including twice at the Gorge Amphitheater in Washington State, which Neil Peart once described as the most beautiful venue he's ever played at. With every concert the visuals got more and more spectacular. Going to a Rush concert was very much a pilgrimage or maybe a religious experience. At the very least their music made me sensitive to being human. Rush had a song for just about everything. Even if their sound as a band was fairly similar, the lyrics made each song unique.

SHEFFIELD ARENA

10 APRIL 1992, SHEFFIELD, UK

I WAS THERE: HASSAN RIVI

My love of Rush started from my brother Raza. He's eight years older than me so it was classic big brother syndrome. I was only 4 or 5 years old in 1976 or '77 when I started getting into Rush. Unlike kids today with all the things they have, we didn't have anything other than music. Mum and Dad weren't really there because they were working 12 hours a day. So me, my brother and my sister were in this little flat above Mum and Dad's shop and all we had was music and a telly.

My dad bought us a record player. Raza had a great way of getting mum and dad to agree to stuff that they wouldn't have ever agreed to do for me because he was the eldest and the first born. Dad bought two albums. My sister chose Abba's *Greatest Hits*. We got

Hemispheres. I remember Raza dropping the needle onto Side A and that big swirling intro coming in. We were huge fans from there on in.

If we'd even suggested going to a concert, our parents would have said, 'And then you're going to start drinking and then you'll be on drugs, and then I'm going to lose you.' So we missed a lot of those early tours, which is frustrating because they played Newcastle City Hall fairly regularly.

In '88, Raza scored eighth row tickets at Wembley Arena. It was during the Easter holidays and I said, 'Will you take me?' but he took his friend instead. I didn't see them until 1992 but they were my band throughout that time. I'd buy the records and collect all the press clippings. They're still my band now. I grew up with them. Every significant event in my life can be traced back to what Rush were doing at the time. I don't have that connection with any other band.

When I saw them it was the first time they'd played the UK since 1988. Newcastle City Hall used to run coach trips to any band that wasn't playing in Newcastle. I got on a bus full of other Rush fans at Central Station. It was bizarre because you thought you were the only Rush fan. I chatted to three people on the bus who were seeing more than one show. That seemed really extravagant.

My ticket was awful. It was right at the very back in the corner. But for years and years that was my favourite concert. The sound was phenomenal. They had a quadrophonic sound system on that tour.

But then I thought that would be the last time I'd see them because they didn't come for years afterwards. For the *Vapo*r Trails tour there was a date online with 'tickets coming soon' for Paris Zenith but then it got pulled. I don't know if they were planning a European tour in 2002?

I did all the UK dates on the *R30* tour and then flew to The Netherlands and saw them in Rotterdam, the final show of that tour. The next tour started three weeks after my daughter was born. I still managed to catch six shows. And I flew to Dublin with Raza and a friend in 2011. A huge group of us went, and we were front and second row. In 2012 I went to Toronto for *Clockwork Angels* and four or five shows when they came over in 2013. I saw 21 shows altogether, so I managed to get my fill. But if I had a time machine I'd go back and see all the early Rush shows.

I listen to Rush every week. Since January 10th they've probably taken up 95 per cent of my listening time.

I WAS THERE: RICHARD STAINFORTH

I was just coming out of my punk rock phase so I liked the speed and fury of the likes of Iron Maiden and Motörhead. I was round at a friend's house and this song came on and I was instantly attracted to it, then another and another. The band was called Rush and the album *Exit... Stage Left*. This band was something new and very different to what I had been listening to.

The first opportunity I got I purchased *Exit... Stage Left*, closely followed by *Moving Pictures*, *Permanent Waves* and *All the World's a Stage*. Hearing '2112' for the first time I was blown away, first by the live version and then the studio version.

The *Roll the Bones* tour was my first real opportunity to see them. I'd already purchased a ticket for the Glasgow gig but I worked on a farm and it was right in the middle of lambing season. My boss said he couldn't let me go. But we compromised – I could go to the Sheffield gig at the weekend, he'd milk the cows and his kids could help their mother with the lambing.

I went on the coach with other Rush fans. I remember trying to take everything in. Watching the intro on *A Show of Hands,* and the guy with his ticket walking into the arena, I so wanted that to be me. This time it was me – I was seeing Rush for the first time. We were on the 14th row from the stage so I had a great view of everything. I wasn't that fussed about what they were going to play. I was just glad to be there. I could barely take my eyes off them. As the concert rolled on, so came the inflatable rabbits for 'Tom Sawyer'. They were moving about like mad. Well, our side was. One of the lads from the coach was running up the aisle shouting, 'Our rabbit is more lively than yours!'

NATIONAL EXHIBITION CENTRE

12 & 13 APRIL 1992, BIRMINGHAM, UK

I WAS THERE: PETER QUIGLEY

I started listening to Rush around the time of the *Chronicles* release. It was the first CD I ever owned. I was 13. I already had a tape copy of *Fly by Night* and remember taking it to my friend's house and praising 'Anthem' and the drums in particular. It sounded so new and fresh, even though it was nearly 20 years old.

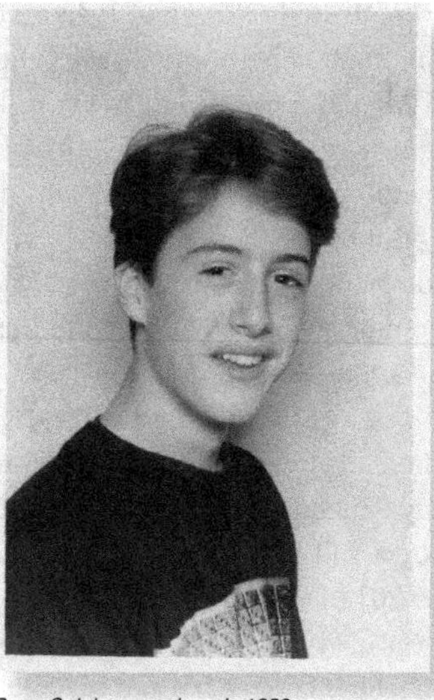
Peter Quigley was there in 1992

I went to the *Roll the Bones* tour with my older brother and his friends. The NEC was where *A Show of Hands* had been filmed. It was like attending the VHS concert in the flesh, although we were right at the back and I had a drunk guy shouting out to the band the whole way through. I saw the title track rap and the drum solo, and the introduction film was just as I had pictured it might be.

I'd spend the last part of my evening in my room drifting to *Permanent Waves* and fall asleep to the sound of the waves lapping against the shore that had been recorded to add effect. This was soon replaced by evenings drifting to *2112*, turned down low enough not to disturb the rest of the house, my bed on the floor and pillows in front of the speakers. The acoustic guitar of 'Discovery' and the beautiful sound of the rain featured on that particular recording.

It was years later on the *R30* tour before I saw them live again. *Rush in Rio* was my training for the *R30* tour, celebrating the band's 30 years together. With my brother and our band mate bass player, we did our own mini-tour and caught shows in London, Birmingham and Manchester. I bought too much merchandise including the bobble head dolls. It was bliss at that time to witness their performance, the vibe and the atmosphere. It was musical cleansing at its best.

There followed the *Snakes & Arrows* shows in Manchester and Sheffield - both amazing nights with the lights and the ever increasing short movies. The evolving drum solos were documented on further educational DVDs. Peart just got better as his skills matured.

The *Time Machine* tour was followed by *Clockwork Angels*, both in Manchester, the latter my last show. I so enjoyed singing along, especially to the 80s material, and miming bass (even though I drum usually). The songs later on came across as very easy to dance to and so loose, yet knitted strongly together at the same time.

One of the most unexpected things at a Rush concert was Neil throwing a stick and missing catching it. That was something close to unbelievable for me. But I got over it. Geddy appeared like an elf wizard on the bass, bouncing around the stage. His voice always seemed higher live and so much clearer than on record. Alex was always just an amazing guitarist, so talented. All three of them were so talented. I was lucky to see one of the best bands in rock. I've heard it said the live experience stays with you. And it does. Just magic. The Spirit of Rush. The Spirit of Radio.

I WAS THERE: STEVE LEE

I acquired a pair of tickets but my fiancée was not interested – she was dubious having heard Geddy's early singing! A lucky friend got the ticket as a birthday present. The seats were much closer this time, stage right and about halfway back. Rush were perfect again. I remember they played 'Bravado'. I liked that track before the show, it became my new favourite afterwards and still sends shivers down my spine to this day – especially the extended live version.

I WAS THERE: STEVE POTTER

I was on the sixth row for the 12th and second row for the 13th on the *Roll the Bones* tour. Great shows both and it was such a pity that they didn't tour the UK for another 12 years. Their production was getting bigger, so some of that was down to costs and whether bringing the show to Europe made sense financially. The big arenas in the UK were only just starting to appear at that time.

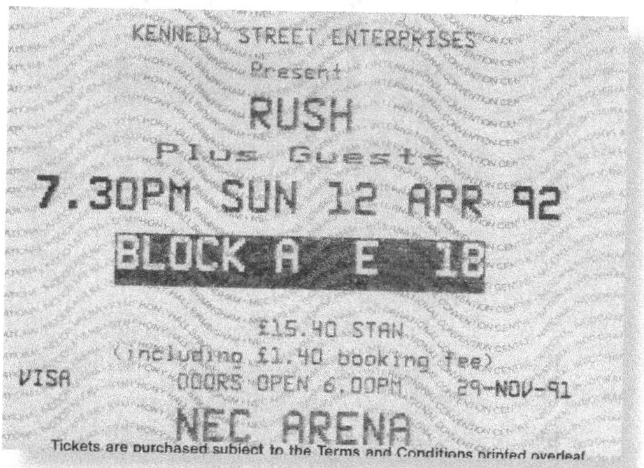

Steve Potter was back at the NEC for the Roll the Bones tour

SECC

15 APRIL 1992, GLASGOW, UK

I WAS THERE: WILLIAM WINSBOROUGH

William Winsborough was introduced to Rush by his best friend's dad, big Andy

As a young lad, I had a best friend called Andy who lived along the street from my house. Most days Andy and I would go out and kick a ball around or play hide and seek. When we got computers (ZX Spectrums) for Christmas we would always be in each other's houses playing games.

Andy's dad was also called Andy. He was a big music fan and he loved playing his vinyl records. And one day back in 1988 when I was 13, I went along to Andy's house to see if he was coming out for a 'kick about'. Big Andy came to the door and said, 'Wee Andy is not ready yet, Willie, but come in and wait for him.' I went into the living room and sat on the settee. Big Andy had his hi-fi system on and was playing one of his records. While we were chatting - 'How are you today? What have you been up to? How's your mum and dad?' etc. - and waiting for wee Andy to come downstairs, I couldn't help but hone in on the music I was hearing from the record player.

'Who's that playing? I really like that.' He replied, 'It's a band called Rush.' My ears pricked up. I was really digging what I was hearing. He was playing 'The Spirit of Radio'. So I'm enjoying the music when wee Andy comes into the living room. 'Are we going out to play football?' he asked and I said, 'Yes, but let me hear a bit more of this music first.' Wee Andy had grown up with Rush as his dad was a big fan. I was so taken by 'The Spirit of Radio' that I wanted to hear the rest of the album. Big Andy played the whole of *Permanent Waves* and wee Andy and myself were just sitting there, open-jawed at what we were listening to.

We spent the whole afternoon just listening to big Andy's Rush records. I browsed the *Grace Under Pressure* album cover. The back cover showed a picture of the band. I thought to myself, 'Surely there are more to this band that just three guys?' There was no way that only three guys were playing all this wonderful music. I knew other bands like The Police had only three members, but the music of Rush was on a whole other level. The more songs I heard, the more I was loving it.

Much later in the day, I was asking big Andy to put on 'The Spirit of Radio' again as that was my introduction to them and it hit me in such a way that it became my favourite song so I wanted to hear it again and again. Big Andy said, 'Watch this, Willie. You'll love this…' and put a VHS video cassette into his video recorder. It was the *Grace Under Pressure* live concert and of course the first song on that concert video was 'The Spirit of Radio'. I could not believe my ears or my eyes. There were indeed only three musicians on the stage creating this fantastic music. My head was completely blown!

That day completely changed my life. Both wee Andy and I listened to more Rush on repeat and eventually we got the bus to Edinburgh and I bought my first ever Rush vinyl album, *Moving Pictures*. It remains my favourite Rush album to this day.

In early 1992, big Andy told me that Rush were touring their latest album, *Roll the Bones*, and were coming to Glasgow. Little did I know that he had got wee Andy and myself tickets to the show at the SECC. On 15th April 1992, I actually got to see this wonderful three piece band create their music live right in front of my eyes. It was a beautiful thing to behold. I'll never forget that night.

WEMBLEY ARENA

17 & 18 APRIL 1992, LONDON, UK

I WAS THERE: MICHAEL PAYNE, AGE 23

For the *Roll the Bones* world tour, two rows from the front. I stood and watched Rush play a blistering set from the moment they launched into 'Force Ten'! I had a perfect view of Neil Peart's hands between a tom and his snare drum. As a drummer, I stood and watch the blurred brilliance and precision in awe. I remember thinking, 'Why can't I do that as good as him?' I was sat almost under Geddy's mic stand. Every time he walked over and pressed the bass pedals it almost blew me to the back of the arena. It was so good I got a ticket for the following night's performance.

Michael Payne saw two nights at Wembley

THE CAROLINA COLISEUM

5 MARCH 1992, COLUMBIA, SOUTH CAROLINA

I WAS THERE: ROBERT NOAH

In 1976 I had a ticket in my hand to see Rush in Shreveport, Louisiana but had to turn it down due to moving to Dallas, Texas and my not being a big fan. Then I listened to the album *Moving Pictures* and have kicked myself in the ass every time I hear *Fly by Night*. In 1991 a radio station offered tickets to the Columbia *Roll the Bones* show if you were the eighth caller. And if you were, you were also entered into a draw for a chartered bus ride with the other winners. Well, I was and I also won tickets on the Rush bus. It was a great show and we had front row balcony seats, right on top of them.

Robert Noah's e-bike

I didn't have another opportunity to see them until the *R30* show in Dallas, Texas. Wow, what a show - three and one half hours of Rush. It was great, and being the tail end of that tour they were at their peak. I sure wish I could find the guy sitting next to me with Bushnell binoculars with a digital card who was recording the show. He has my e-mail address and hasn't sent me the show yet!

FIDDLER'S GREEN AMPHITHEATRE

27 MAY 1992, ENGLEWOOD, COLORADO

I WAS THERE: JIM BLUM

I was 12 years old and my musical taste was pretty much limited to Kiss. My dad and I were on a road trip through the Nevada desert. It was the middle of the night because that's when you drive through the Nevada desert during the summer time. I had been asleep in the passenger seat when I awoke to the radio blasting 'Tom Sawyer'. My dad liked that song and cranked it up. It was pitch dark outside. There was no light in the car, save

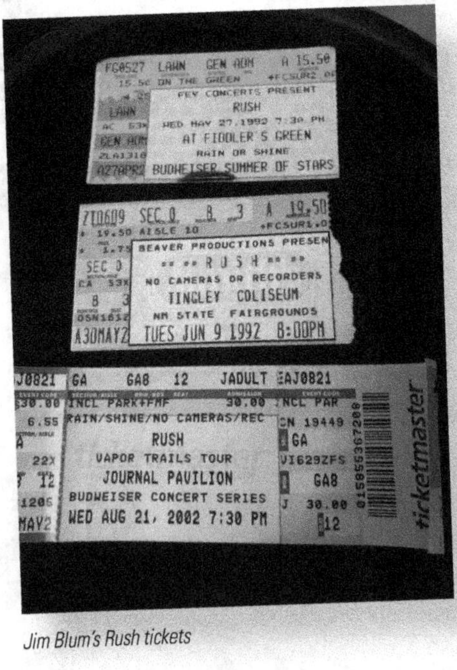

Jim Blum's Rush tickets

the glow of the radio and the instrument panel, and I was completely immersed in the music. For the first time ever, I had heard a song that I fell in love with that wasn't a Kiss song. 'Tom Sawyer' had branded me with a vivid memory of what I was doing and who I was with whenever I heard it from that day forward. 40 years later, I always keep a copy of *Moving Pictures* in my car and whenever I am driving on a lonely road in the middle of the night, I can pop it in and return to that night in my childhood.

The following year was my freshman year of high school. *Signals* had just come out and Rush announced two dates in my home town of Albuquerque, New Mexico. I had my ticket in hand and couldn't wait to attend what would have been my second live concert (of course, Kiss was my first). The only problem was that the dates coincided with the release of first-half report cards, and I had a D- in math. My other marks weren't anything to brag about either. Naturally, my parents made me sell my ticket. This was a day that would haunt me forever.

When Rush announced a date in Las Cruces, New Mexico in support of *Roll the Bones,* I was broke and unemployed. I passed on making the three hour drive from Albuquerque. While the concert was in progress 225 miles away, I sat in my studio apartment listening to *Exit... Stage Left* and suffering from a severe case of kicking myself in the ass.

I called a friend of in Denver, Colorado and asked her to let me know if Rush announced a date up there. Less than a week later, she called and said that a date had been set for May. I promptly invested in two tickets. A date was then announced in Albuquerque for June. Since the venue for the Denver show was Fiddler's Green, a beautiful outdoor amphitheatre, and the Albuquerque show was Tingley Coliseum, a structure better suited for rodeos and motocross, I decided to stick to my plan to see them in Denver.

On the day of the show, I left early to make the six hour drive taking a small quantity of smokeable contraband to enjoy on the trip. As fate would have it, I was enjoying said contraband when a member of the state's law enforcement community observed me traveling at an unacceptable rate of speed. Alas, I was forced to ditch my contraband on the side of the highway. The officer presented me with a behavioural modification document for doing 70 in a 55 and sent me on my way.

I arrived in Denver just in time to pick up my friend and head to the show. She was extremely pregnant at the time so we abstained from our normal concert behaviours, found a comfortable spot on the grass and had an amazing time enjoying the best band ever.

The next day I hit the road home. Despite the extreme pressure the experience put on my limited budget it had been well worth it. As soon as I arrived home, I went straight to the nearest Ticketmaster outlet and picked up a ticket to the Albuquerque show. The entire experience remains my fondest concert going memory 28 years later. I am forever grateful to be able to say that I was there!

THOMAS AND MACK CENTER

6 JUNE 1992, LAS VEGAS, NEVADA

I WAS THERE: RUSSELL VAN DRIEL

It was fantastic. They did 'Time Stand Still' with a video on a giant screen behind the stage of a speed boat going up a river. The boat would slow down, then go to a high rate of speed, and repeat through the song. I have seen a lot of concerts. This was one of the best!

MERRIWEATHER POST PAVILION

16 JUNE, 1992, COLUMBIA, MARYLAND

I WAS THERE: SKIP DALY

This was my fourth and final show on the *Roll the Bones* tour, and the only time Rush performed at Merriweather, an outdoor concert shed about midway between Baltimore and DC. I had okay seats – under the pavilion, about halfway back - and went to the show with my good friend, Andy Yarrish. It was a beautiful summer night, and this was my first time experiencing a Rush show at an outdoor venue. This third-and-final leg of that tour featured some welcome and exciting changes in the setlist, as 'The Pass' and 'Subdivisions' had been dropped and replaced with 'Vital Signs', 'The Analog Kid' and 'The Trees'. This had the effect of making a great setlist even better. I had heard of these changes in advance, but Andy, always seeking to remain 'unspoiled', had not. As the concert approached that part of the programme, I recall looking over at him and saying, 'Wait until you see what's coming.' His jaw dropped when the band launched into the one-two punch of 'Vital Signs' and 'The Analog Kid'. The band was on fire at this late point in the tour – a well-oiled machine (though there was a slight gaffe during 'The Spirit of Radio', where Neil transitioned to a chorus too early).

The *Counterparts* tour ran from January 1994 to May 1994 and focused exclusively on North America.

THE SUMMIT

26 JANUARY 1994, HOUSTON, TEXAS

I WAS THERE: JOHN HILL

I go backstage and do the usual meet and greet with Geddy and Alex and, after a lengthy conversation and a deal struck with Geddy, I am to

John Hill got his photo taken with Neil

meet Neil in Houston two nights later and get my picture with him. I show up early at The Summit as per Geddy's request. I'm so nervous I can hardly breathe. Finally, after all these meeting and concerts I am going to get my photo taken with Neil! I walk into the arena and through backstage with Michelle, my girlfriend at the time. The band's assistant, Peter, is waiting for me. My nervousness is a bit out of control. Geddy comes out and tells me Michelle has to stay back in the hallway. She isn't too happy but I don't care much about that. Geddy walks me in to Neil's dressing room and there Neil is, wearing blue shorts and a white t-shirt and socks. He is sitting on a couch with a book and with a fake tall plant with a light on it shining down, so he can read I guess. It's totally not the vibe I was expecting.

Geddy takes my camera and we get the photos out of the way. Geddy was my photographer - imagine that! The photos turned out great. It helped that I brought two cameras and got Geddy to take two photos with each. Neil just chuckled and said, 'You must really want this photo to turn out', and I said, 'I sure do. When was the last time you took a photo with a fan?' and he simply said, 'I understand!'

We talked drums for a few minutes and we got along so well Neil told Geddy he could go if he wanted to. Geddy was happy that Neil was happy and comfortable and so left. We talked drums and life in general for 30 minutes until someone poked their head in and told Neil it was time to get ready for the show. He made his tech at the time, Larry Allen, make sure I got the sticks he used after the show. I have to say, Larry Allen was not very cool at all and he was kind of rude to Michelle and I. I had the satisfaction of telling Geddy after the show what a jackass Larry was and he was told to apologise. It was a perfect night.

ARCO ARENA

10 FEBRUARY 1994, SACRAMENTO, CALIFORNIA

I WAS THERE: CHRISTOPHER J SCONZA

I saw them live four times on the *Counterparts*, *Test for Echo*, *R30* and *Snakes & Arrows* tours. I took my 75-year-old mother to the last one. All four shows were simply amazing. What I'm left with most of all is their level of professionalism individually. Alex Lifeson is an amazing guitarist. Geddy Lee is amazing on bass guitar, keyboards and bass pedals. As if that's not enough his vocals were unmatched and such a huge part of what made Rush great. But above all? Neil Peart. I could say nothing about this man's abilities as a musician that hasn't already been said. He was such a great drummer and the driving force that allowed Alex and Geddy to shine. Pinch yourself and also realise that Neil Peart has written the lyrics to nearly every Rush song, lyrics that were so perfectly delivered through music written by Alex and Geddy and with the vocals delivered by Geddy.

COW PALACE

11 FEBRUARY 1994, SAN FRANCISCO, CALIFORNIA

I WAS THERE: FERN GULLY

The first night we were stuck in the back of a stadium. The music was distorted and the band the size of peas. The second night we rolled change for gas and were running late, but it didn't seem too bad as Grandmother prepared 'to go' random food wraps as we rushed off to the Cow Palace. All the ticket windows had lines, so we picked the shortest. To our luck, the fellow before us talked away as we watched the other lines move. We started worrying we were screwed again. Then we heard someone behind us say, 'Looks like this is your lucky night!'

We turned around as if it was another usual creeper line, only to see two tickets in his hand. He placed them in ours, as he explained he won them and wanted to give them to what he thought might be big fans. We clobbered him with hugs and ran off to get our seats. Only then did we realise, while locating the seats, they were for the 13th row. Turned out they are the first row, elevated above the first 12 and in a half circle layout, placing us even closer to the stage. The playlist was everything we could have ever wanted to see live. We still talk about that night as if it was yesterday. We felt so lucky to experience Rush, even if we were just adolescents in the late 90s.

ROSEMONT HORIZON

29 & 30 MARCH 1994, ROSEMONT, ILLINOIS

I WAS THERE: JEFFREY SCOTT BURTON

My very first album was the first three Rush albums in one spit - *Rush*, *Caress of Steel* and *Fly by Night*. I just fell in love with them. I was in high school when they brought out *Moving Pictures* and it took my heart, soul and brain. I don't care what the album or song is. All of them are number one for me. People either really liked Rush or they hated them. Half of my friends liked to listen to my albums. The other half were, 'Turn it off, change the channel.'

I was in the 25th row on the ground for the *Counterparts* tour. Primus were the warm up band. That was the last tour that they had a warm up act. At that point they turned into a three plus hour concert. I saw them eight tours in a row. I only missed the *R40* tour because I had AVM brain surgery. I died three times in surgery.

BRADLEY CENTER

7 APRIL 1994, MILWAUKEE, WISCONSIN

I WAS THERE: BOB KREMER

Rush crept into my consciousness over the course of time, from my grade and high school years into college and beyond into adulthood. I have my late best friend, Brian,

Bob Kremer saw Rush on the Counterparts tour

to thank for exposing me to music outside what I had been listening to at the time. As a kid, I was into pop and Top 40 hits, although I did grow up listening to the jazz and big band records my dad would play on our stereo. Brian taped some of my records so I could listen to them on my boom box and in the car and added stuff by 70s groups his older brothers gave him such as Triumph, April Wine, Jethro Tull, Pink Floyd, Yes - and Rush.

Their music didn't really resonate with me at that time. A couple of my college roommates were hard rock and metal fans so they broadened my musical horizons with artists like Iron Maiden, Queensryche and Metallica. It was then that I recognised that Rush had finally planted a seed in my brain.

It was around the time of *Presto* that I started seriously becoming a fan. When *Counterparts* was released, my wife and I went see the boys at the late Bradley Center in Milwaukee. Our seats were toward the back and the backing music came from the suspended speakers above us so while I was trying to focus on what Rush was playing the sounds coming from the speakers above was very distracting, but I still enjoyed my first Rush concert. My wife thought it was 'ok'.

We didn't go to another Rush concert for another 12 years, mainly due to family and work things, but I kept up with Rush's output. I was also fortunate to be able to listen to Geddy and Alex on *Rockline* once or twice, which of course I taped for posterity! Our next concert was during the *Snakes & Arrows* tour. We arrived at the Summerfest grounds near Milwaukee's Lakefront in a downpour. The rain eventually quit and we were able to enjoy the show. The Amphitheater has excellent acoustics and good seating, making it even better.

The *Clockwork Angels* tour was the last tour I'd see, although we didn't know it at the time. I took my oldest son and Brian took his two oldest sons. The weather was beautiful and we all had a fantastic time. The new music sounded amazing, especially since Rush had brought along their incredible string ensemble, and also since I had yet to hear the album in its entirety. Sharing this concert experience with my son and my best friend made it truly unforgettable. As I write this, I am reminded of both good and not so good times and I think my life is much more interesting and much richer thanks to the guys in Rush. Journey well, everyone.

CIVIC ARENA

20 APRIL 1994, PITTSBURGH, PENNSYLVANIA

I WAS THERE: SCOTT HAINES

Instead of having an opening act they billed it as *An Evening with Rush* and played two sets. After about an hour they took a 20 minute break and then came back for a second set. I was attending this concert with the members of a band for which I was the soundman. They were all 10 to 15 years younger than I am. We had great seats, fifth row back and dead centre. The crowd around us also had some older fans with their teenage kids with them.

After playing two or three songs in the second set, the band said how glad they were to be playing at the Civic Arena as it was the first place they had ever played outside of Canada. They then said they were going to do something they had not done live for over 20 years. With that the stage went black and the picture of the naked little kid standing on the pentagram from the *2112* album came on behind them. All the people my age who had bought that album all started cheering wildly, and all the younger people looked at us wondering what we were cheering about. Then they commenced playing the entire '2112 Overture' non-stop. It was incredible.

The *Test for Echo* tour saw Rush perform without a support act for the first time. Starting on 19 October 1996 in Albany, New York and concluding on 4 July 1997 in Ottawa, Canada, the tour focused entirely on North America and took in 68 shows.

UTEP SPECIAL EVENTS CENTER

30 NOVEMBER 1996, EL PASO, TEXAS

I WAS THERE: MARCOS LUJAN

My two best friends and I, all 16 years old, decided sort of late to check out Rush, who would be performing that evening in our hometown of El Paso, Texas. We had our high school rock band, and were somewhat familiar with some of Rush's work, having heard them a lot on the radio. I was discovering more progressive rock and metal at this time and had no idea just how impactful and defining a moment this show would be for me. Moreover, it was to be my very first rock concert!

The *Test for Echo* title track was played on the radio a bit, and I immediately loved it. What really struck me was the great chord progression, the dynamics and the musicianship of all three members. Being a new bass player myself, I was of course drawn to Geddy Lee's thunderous basslines. Seeing them perform this in person was absolutely breathtaking!

We walked to our seats right as the band was playing the first song, 'Dreamline'. I was surprised at just how loud it was. After the next several songs, my friends and I were all entranced. This group was undeniably incredible live! The songs that they played in the first half included 'The Big Money', 'Red Barchetta', 'Driven', 'Half the World', 'Animate', 'The Trees' and - most amazingly - the entire '2112' suite. I was in absolute awe.

The second half of the show featured more of their classic tunes from the early days on through to the present. Highlights were 'Test for Echo', 'The Spirit of Radio', 'Freewill', 'Resist', ' Natural Science', 'Closer to the Heart', 'Roll the Bones' and 'Tom Sawyer'. We exited the arena not fully processing the sheer musical spectacular that we just experienced. If I wasn't a full Rush fan before that, I most certainly was now. My parents picked me up to take me home and I recall raving to them about the awesomeness I had just witnessed.

I was able to see Rush again twice more: with a group of friends on a blistering summer day in 2007 in Phoenix, Arizona on the *Snakes & Arrows* tour, and by myself in Austin, Texas on what would be the band's farewell tour in 2015. I knew it would be the last time I would ever see them play together again.

I consider myself extremely lucky and honoured to have witnessed them make musical magic in three very different stages (see what I did there?) of my life. My goal is to introduce my three-year-old daughter to the gift and wonder of rock music, and most notably Rush.

UNO LAKEFRONT ARENA

6 DECEMBER 1996, NEW ORLEANS, LOUISIANA

I WAS THERE: LEWIS D'AUBIN

I've seen Rush live 11 times, starting with the *Hold Your Fire* tour. The *Test for Echo* tour in New Orleans stands out as their first tour with no opening act - which was fine, as it meant more Rush music. It was a thrill to see all of '2112' performed live; transposed down a couple frets to accommodate Geddy's maturing voice, it seemed even more powerful than the familiar studio recording.

The *R40* show at the New Orleans Arena in 2015 will also stay with me. The set list was littered with my personal favourites: 'The Wreckers', 'Far Cry', 'Animate', 'Between the Wheels', 'Subdivisions', 'The Camera Eye', 'Jacob's Ladder' (I was almost completely overwhelmed by that one), 'Cygnus X-1', 'Xanadu', 'Lakeside Park' and 'Anthem'. It was as if they read my mind. They could have played all of *Caress of Steel* and I couldn't have been more pleased sonically. And the visuals, regressing the instruments and staging back to the beginning, was a masterstroke. Seeing the *Moving Pictures*-era acoustic drum set and the double-neck guitars was particularly moving. My biggest regret? Spotting lighting director Howard Ungerleider after the *R40* show and not running up to thank him for all the decades of wonderful illumination.

THE OMNI

11 DECEMBER 1996, ATLANTA, GEORGIA

I WAS THERE: DYLAN PAYNE

I was casually familiar with Rush from listening to classic rock radio as a kid. Once I started college in 1995 I started to explore music more and started to dig a bit deeper into Rush. When my good friend David offered to get me a ticket to the *Test for Echo* tour, it was the first big arena concert I had been to and the experience was pretty mind blowing. I saw them twice after that, both times at Madison Square Garden in New York, on the *Vapor Trails* and *R40* tours. At the *R40* show my friend David, who took me to that first show back in 1996, was visiting and so we got to see the last Rush concert together. It was made extra special because it was one of the shows where they played 'Losing It' with Jonathan Dinklage on violin.

SANDSTONE AMPHITHEATRE

7 JUNE 1997, BONNER SPRINGS, KANSAS

I WAS THERE: JOYCE WENZINGER

Joyce Wenzinger caught the Test for Echo tour and was there for R40 with her husband Jack

My first Rush concert was on the *Test for Echo* tour. I heard a guy from a couple rows behind me say 'sit down!' I glanced around and realised he was talking to the woman behind my husband. As pretty much everyone was on their feet - who sits during a Rush concert? - I didn't pay much attention. I heard the guy complain a couple more times, but ignored it. I was completely enthralled with the magic of seeing Rush live. Later, my husband told me that the woman behind him got fed up with the guy complaining and took a swipe at him. She ripped his t-shirt completely open down the front.

Another memory is from their *Time Machine* performance at Red Rocks, which is a fabulous venue and where I got to see them perform 'Marathon', my favourite. When they started playing the opening notes, I could feel the hairs on my arms rising. I had to fight back tears of joy, but told myself that crying would blur my vision, and I didn't want to miss a second of seeing them perform my favourite song. As I sang along, I felt like Geddy looked right at me a couple of times. After all, I was one of the 'seven chicks'!

I was also fortunate enough to see Rush's final performance. My husband and I flew to California to see them as a wedding anniversary gift to ourselves. We'd heard the rumours that Rush would be retiring after that tour and didn't want to miss it. When they finished the encore, I was surprised to see Neil come out around his drum kit and run over to Alex. He tapped Alex on the shoulder and motioned for him to follow, then ran over to Geddy. As Neil put his arms around them both, I realised he was saying 'goodbye' and my tears started flowing. I applauded so hard that my hands hurt and my arms ached, but I couldn't stop.

KLPX RADIO

14 NOVEMBER 2000, TUSCON, ARIZONA

I WAS THERE: JEFF RUSHFAN

I was in Tucson when Geddy released his solo album, *My Favorite Headache*. The KLPX morning show DJs announced they would be having a telephone interview with Geddy. They knew me to be a big Rush fan. They told me if I called in early when the show started, they would keep me on hold when he called so I could speak with him. I took the day off work and called first thing in the morning. Sure enough, they kept me on hold well over two hours. They told Geddy how long I was waiting before connecting me. I of course told him how much I admired his music and how excellent of a solo album *My Favorite Headache* was. I asked him what it was like doing lyrics without his band mates (I forget what he said in reply) but then I inquired what it was like trying to record 'La Vila Strangiato'. He complemented the question and answered it exactly how they described it later in *Behind the Lighted Stage* documentary, that they were really reaching beyond themselves as artists at that time. They tried relentlessly to do it live in one take but eventually had to settle for three takes. It was great to have a full three to five minutes on the phone with him.

The Vapor Trails tour was the first the band undertook after a five year hiatus following the twin tragedies in Neil's life, events which put the continued existence of the band both as a touring outfit and as a recording act in doubt. The tour started in Hartford, Connecticut on 28 June 2002 and concluded 66 shows later with a performance in Brazil's legendary Maracanã Stadium in Rio de Janeiro on 23 November 2002.

MEADOWS MUSIC CENTRE

28 JUNE 2002, HARTFORD, CONNECTICUT

I WAS THERE: WAYNE M UGLIONO

The hiatus was horrible. Neil lost his daughter and then he lost his wife. I've met a lot of Rush fans and the five years they were off the road was a long five years musically for us. You didn't know if they were coming back. I drove up to the first show in Connecticut on the *Vapor Trails* tour. Grown men and women were crying once they got on stage. It was unbelievable. People had brought their kids, and the kids were watching their parents cry with happiness that the band was back together. And they sounded phenomenal.

I drove three and a half, four hours to Connecticut and I didn't care. I wanted to see them right away. It was like a drug addiction with this band. The Grateful Dead had a similar kind of following, with not much air play. It was personal to people. I've never seen an empty seat in the house with Rush and I've been following them since I was 16. And it's killing me that they're not going to be able to tour again.

After *R40*, rumour had it they were going to go a Vegas-type kind of thing because Neil lived out in California. Rumour also had it that they were going to finish some unfinished songs and that they were at least going to record.

When Geddy said in an interview that Neil didn't want to play drums anymore and had retired, I didn't buy that. It was only after he passed that I figured out that he was already sick. You don't just stop playing as a musician.

They weren't a band like Mötley Crüe with the broads and the drugs and all that 80s shit. Rush were the good guy band. And they weren't pompous. They were very humble musicians who appreciated that somebody actually liked what they produced. What they produced, from the first album to the last, was something different and unique: Geddy's voice; Neil's drumming when they were coming up. You didn't see another drummer like that; and Alex was just a great guitar player, period. He was born with a guitar in his hand.

They had their own unique sound. Gene Simmons said it best when he said, 'What's Rush? Rush is Rush.'

And that's the best way to explain it. There's only one Rush. Growing up in the 70s a lot of bands started sounding the same. But Rush always sounded different. Even when they got on the radio you were like, 'Wow, that made it to the radio?'

I WAS THERE: DAVE ARNOLD

I am fortunate to live 30 minutes from Grand Meadows where the boys came back from hell for their first show. My buddy and I were about nine rows from the stage. It was such an electric show, even more than most because of the hiatus. They were incredible as usual and Ray Daniels said it best. It would be a shame if that never happened again. I'm always grateful that show was near me and to be there. It was a night I'll never forgot and was easier than usual to RUSH on!

Dave Arnold saw the first show after the 'hiatus'

I WAS THERE: STEVEN WHITE

All the Rush shows have been great, but there are some stand out moments. The *Vapor Trails* show I saw in Hartford, Connecticut was the very first of the tour and the first tour since the hiatus. While not being privy at that time to what Neil had gone through with the passing of both his wife and daughter, I noticed that during the show Geddy walked over to Neil between songs and asked if he was all right. Only because I was so proximate to the stage was I able to catch that. On learning after the show of what Neil's life had been like during the hiatus, I was so very touched. It was clear to me that the three of them were not just bandmates, they were brothers.

My second stand out memory was during the *R40* tour. Knowing that this was billed as the final tour, there was no way in heck I was going to miss it. One of my best friends talked me into getting really, really good floor seats - yet again! During a particularly long instrumental near the end of the show, I could not help but notice that Alex was doing nothing but smiling out into the audience for a rather long time. After all these years and all the tours, he was still absolutely enjoying what he was doing and both his stage demeanour and playing absolutely showed that. The length of that smile and the way he was looking out into the audience brought an extra measure of joy to a show that was already joyous to begin with. The gentleman standing right behind me on the floor just summed it all up in a perfect way: 'If I never see this band again, I walk away satisfied.'

MONTAGE MOUNTAIN AMPHITHEATRE

29 JUNE 2002, SCRANTON, PENNSYLVANIA

I WAS THERE: NATE GERARD

Nate Gerard got pretty wet at a Rush show - and it wasn't raining

In 1997 I moved to Minnesota and eventually married my girlfriend, who was from there. One of the reasons I was willing to move was that I would always spend a long weekend back in Pennsylvania visiting with my high school and college friends - Todd, Mac and Cris - who love Rush as much as I do.

Many of my trips would get planned before I'd find out Rush were playing the weekend I already was flying there. We saw Rush in Philly mostly but also in Hershey and in 2002 we saw them outdoors at the Pavilion at Montage Mountain. This turned out to be one of the coolest venues to see our favourite band.

They made the permanent structure in 2000 so it was still fresh for our experience in 2002. Like all PA concerts, we showed up about four hours early and began to have some beer. There were lots of other fans who were all drinking too, so after a while the edge of the parking lot became a de facto bathroom. I made the mistake of taking one step onto the pee covered vegetation and slipped out of sight onto the ground. I counted myself lucky not to break anything and washed the pee off my arms with some wet napkins that my friend Mac had in his car from getting carry out wings. Mac gave them to me, after doubling over from laughing about my story.

Everyone paid me the money for their tickets on our way in. We saw where our seats were and decided to go for more beer. The 32oz cups of beer were $15 and the line was long so we grabbed two each. This would turn out to be a rookie mistake. When we went to pay, my friend Todd exclaimed that he gave me all his cash for his ticket. A brilliant move since that now meant I was buying him beer with the money he used to 'pay' me. 'No problem,' I said as I plopped down $100 for six beers including a tip for the girl who was furiously trying to serve 14,000 guys and 500 girls in attendance. (I'm kidding about the number of girls but this ratio became significant within about 45 minutes).

There wasn't an opening act so as soon as we heard *The Three Stooges* we knew what was coming. They opened with 'Tom Sawyer' and while that song had been the gateway to Rush for all of us, I was glad it was the opener so it wouldn't be an encore song.

The venue was amazing and I remember getting to watch the sun set while Rush was playing. That was an experience I only had once. We also had a great time getting to know the fans in front and behind us.

At the time I knew nothing of what had happened to Neil, but I did see a sadness on his face. I would later learn about the two tragic events that led to that look and until recently I don't think I ever understood what kind of person Neil was. This was only the second stop on the first tour they had done since those events.

As we were each holding two 32oz beers, we agreed to place three full beers in a little triangle under my seat. When they started 'YYZ', Cris - who is a drummer - started jumping around, and then it happened. A splash and a small tidal wave of beer poured over my sneakers. I got the look of disgust on my face since I knew that was a lot of wasted money on the ground. But Cris agreed to buy for the rest of the night, and we had all been friends for 15 years, so it wasn't worth getting upset over.

At the end of 'Natural Science' we were about ready to burst and decided to head to the men's room. We had no idea that there were only four urinals and even fewer stalls. We also had no idea it would take 45 minutes to get to the end of the line.

Once we were out of the bathroom we got back to our seats about the time they played 'Red Sector A', which for us was a high school album and part of our collective experience. We also got to see 'Limelight', 'La Villa Strangiato' and 'The Spirit of Radio' all in a row. After the encore, most of the fans stayed for about 15 minutes and tried to get them to come back. We had no idea they were probably 15 minutes down the road to Charlotte already!

We were on top of the world when we got back to Mac's car. Cris and Todd promptly went to sleep and I sat in the front seat and talked to Mac while he drove us back to his house in Allentown. It was the kind of conversation you can only have with an old friend you trust. We talked about our wives and jobs. His marriage would eventually break up and I would eventually get out of advertising.

I tried to think of the most supportive thing I could say so I told him I was his friend before he got married and I'll be his friend if he stays with her or if she's gone in a few years. He always gave me great job advice, and once told me any job was better than the one I had, which cracked me up and gave me the push I needed to find a better one. And that's the real ingredient I've had at every Rush concert since. I saw them with amazing friends and made great memories that strengthened our friendships, people who are still important to me today.

NISSAN PAVILION

9 JULY, 2002, BRISTOW, VIRGINIA

I WAS THERE: SKIP DALY

After a five-year hiatus (for the darkest reasons imaginable), Rush was back! In the wake of Neil's well-documented, personal double tragedies, the band had quickly and quietly faded into hiatus. Aside from the 1998 release of *Different Stages*, and the later release of Geddy's solo project, it started to feel as though Rush was over. But in late 2000, word had begun circulating that Neil had remarried and the band would be entering the studio in early 2001. I still recall the feeling of joy, not merely because my favourite band was coming back, but at a more fundamental, human level there was the sense of wonder that someone could survive such tragedies and return to 'the land of the living'.

In the fall of 2001, in anticipation of the tour, myself and another fan (Al Horta) had launched RushPetition.com, as a way of polling the fan base for songs that they'd like to hear represented on the upcoming tour. The band's management (and the band members themselves, so we were told) liked the idea and 'found it extremely useful'. Thousands of 'votes' poured in, and sure enough, when the tour launched in Hartford, Connecticut, the set list reflected some of the requests. (Alas, I was unable to attend that Hartford show, but the internet was now in full flight, making it easy to keep tabs on what was going on). Songs like 'New World Man', 'By-Tor and the Snow Dog', 'Cygnus X-1' and 'Working Man' – which hadn't graced the stage for many years – were all polished up and brought forth to shine.

A pleasant side-effect of our 'petition' website was that Pegi Cecconi at Anthem/SRO very kindly hooked me up with meet and greet passes and fifth row centre seats for the Saratoga Springs, New York and Bristow, Virginia shows, which I attended with my cousin, Pat, who is basically like the older brother that I never had.

I still recall our good-natured arguments from my high school days, where he tried to convert me to Bruce Springsteen and I tried to convert him to Rush. I'm pleased to say that we both succeeded, and this was Pat's first Rush show. It was a hot summer night and a storm was brewing – both onstage and off. The band hit the stage with more energy than I had ever seen, and it was a barnstormer of a show, with one of my favourite set lists. At times, rain would be coming down and blowing in under the pavilion, but it only served to increase the palpable sense of excitement at this gig. It is always a blast to experience the 'reflected light' of watching someone else experience something that you love for the first time, and I'll never forget the sight of my cousin finally 'getting' Rush.

TWEETER CENTER FOR THE PERFORMING ARTS

12 JULY 2002, MANSFIELD, MASSACHUSETTS

I WAS THERE: DAVID EGAN

I was going to see Rush in the USA, catching them in Holmdel, New Jersey and Mansfield, Massachusetts. Taking the time off work and spending the money to travel 4,000 miles to watch a bunch of ageing rock stars strut their stuff takes some comprehending. I only made the firm decision to go ten days before I flew and had no accommodation booked, no travelling companion and no one to meet up with when I got there. I didn't even know if I would be going north or south from the airport when I got there. I picked the tour dates 'nearest' to home and booked my flight. I then spent five days surfing the internet for accommodation without success, apart from one night in a hotel in Manhattan. Hotels prior to at the cheaper end of the market simply weren't there. Or they were well hidden.

I stepped out into bright midday mid 80s Fahrenheit sunshine in my all black t-shirt and black jeans. After hearing a brief explanation of my proposed itinerary the lady at the information / booking desk, with body dimensions to match her surly attitude, advised me that I could get a shared taxi to Holmdel for $31. 'May I have your reservation details?' 'I haven't got one.' 'Well you must have one if you want to go in the taxi. The drivers will only drop you at a specific address.' The lady directed me to 'up and along' where 'they' would help me get a reservation.

'They' proved to be two older guys in charge, one of whom looked like someone's granddad who had lived alone for too long, with his open necked shirt, poorly shaved face and bits of food dotted on him. I explained my travel plans ('Rush? What does he play?') and predicament and they provided me with maps and information about the towns surrounding the Holmdel area and the best places to find accommodation, and where to get an $11 train ticket to a town called Hazlet.

My 45 minute train ride ended at a ground level platform station in the town of Hazlet. Directly opposite the station was a wooden building with a large sign on it telling the world that it was a 'Greek Deli'. Even better was the fact that there was a police car outside. Two Chinese men ran the deli. In my best polite English I said, 'I need to find a motel near the PNC Bank Arts Centre. Could you help me?' The first Chinese man pointed me to the second, who was at a table eating spaghetti bolognese. He pointed me to the policemen sat drinking coffee and unashamedly browsing girlie magazines. They casually directed me 'up to the main road'.

So here I was in Smallville, USA and looking for a room to stay. The North Shore Motel had a queue, so like a good Englishman I joined it. At my turn I asked for a single room only to be told that there was only one double room left. I took it. After a Happy Meal from the local McDonald's and a visit to the PathMark supermarket to stock up on fruit, biscuits and water, I cheered the timid man at the motel office by paying for a further night's accommodation. A taxi driver had pulled up outside my hotel and I asked how much it would be to get to the PNC Bank Arts Centre. '$11. Who you going to see?' 'Rush, tomorrow.' It was at this point he figured I was not from these parts and asked me where I got my 'Brooklyn accent' from. 'Brooklyn? I'm from Bolton, England mate!'

There wasn't much to see at the PNC Bank Arts Centre next day as the place is built into the hillside and at the front is nothing but a ticket office and a huge car park. Walking around would have meant going beyond the huge security fence into the big woods and thus seeing nothing. I walked up a hill adjacent to the venue and got a view of the roof.

After sitting under a tree for a while taking in the view, I went back to the box office area where a few people had gathered. Until then, I thought I was a pretty hard core Rush fan, but these were seriously hard core. Almost all had seen some of the earlier shows and seemed to be intent on following the boys as far across America as they could. Some were hassling the box office for news on late release tickets to upgrade their seats. It was still mid-afternoon and hot and I was hungry so I decided to go back to my hotel, freshen up, and get something to eat then return to the venue for show time.

When I did return to the venue there were a lot of cars parked up with people milling about, drinking beer, talking, cooking on barbeques, listening to Rush and generally having a good time. I started chatting to people. Getting on with strangers straight away can be quite difficult at the best of times but this was effortless. We were all in the same zone. I spoke to some who had met the band, had sat in on radio interviews with them, got their pictures taken with them. A lady I spoke to told me the band were OK about people taking photos with disposable cameras and she had a spare so I bought it from her for $10.

I went made my way up nearer to the entrance as I didn't want to miss hearing the soundcheck. I got talking to a couple who were on holiday from Oldham of all places, and we talked about Rush and our travels. They had decided to get married whilst in New York a few days earlier. It was then that we heard them play 'Earthshine', 'New World Man' and half of 'Distant Early Warning'. To hear them again after ten long years and all they had gone through was just glorious.

At 5pm I was able to collect my ticket from the 'Will Call' window and then I immediately moved along to the ticket window and upgraded my ticket to about 20 rows further forward. I was learning fast. I decided to enter the venue at about 6pm, having first shoved the camera down my shorts. The security folks were frisking everyone and anything not allowed, such as food or even bottles of water ('you can buy ours inside') went into the voluminous bin bags set up at each gate. Once inside, I chatted briefly to a guy who seemed to have bought everything there was to buy from the merchandise stall and he told me that he was on his 143rd show. I was on my tenth!

Show time - and Rush came on with Alex waving his arms about in a mad frenzy. The crowd went wild. A beach ball appeared in the crowd and bounced around the excited audience for several minutes until it landed on stage and was quickly scooped up by a roadie.

As ever, Rush played a storming set. During 'Resist' I got a little more brave with the camera but a woman steward caught me taking pictures and summoned a colleague who was so big he would have put Hagrid in the shade. He calmly and politely asked me to hand over the camera and follow him. This did not look or feel good at all. I was escorted out of the seating area to the back of the venue to a small kiosk where he handed the camera to the 'kiosk lady' who gave me a ticket for my camera and told me I could retrieve it after the show. He then said, 'OK, you can go back to the show.' Phew!

Post-show, I needed to get back to the motel. Using up the last of my small change I rang my taxi driver's office and gave his name. They said as I hadn't paid in advance they would not send a taxi for me. With no money, no idea how to get home and alone in the dark, what was I going to do next? I turned around and the very next person I saw said in a cheery voice, 'Alright Dave. Remember me? I'm Mark, we went to the Rush conventions in Crewe.'

We chatted briefly and discussed the gig. I asked him if he had any change for the phone. Mark rummaged through his pockets and gave me a handful of silver and I managed to get a taxi back to my hotel. Back at the motel I did what all right-thinking people do after a great concert. I went to the pub. I thought my days of having to prove my age before buying a drink were long behind me but the policeman on the door, who was younger than me, was having none of it.

Next morning, I had to be at the train station for 6.30am and with no alarm clock it was a small miracle that I woke up in time to get up and get gone. It wasn't helped by a heart stopping moment when I realised I had left my *Test for Echo* t-shirt in the room. Arriving at Penn Station, New York I enquired about trains to Mansfield, Massachusetts. 'Mansfield?' said the lady. She advised me to phone Massachusetts tourist information but as the operator wanted $4 of change slotting into the payphone I gave up and bought a ticket to Boston. My five hour train ride took me north through New York, Connecticut, Rhode Island and on to Massachusetts. Some way into the journey, I asked the guard when we stopped at Mansfield. He replied, 'We passed it ten miles back and we don't stop there anyways.' His advice was to get off at the next stop; Route 128. The man in the ticket office at Route 128 advised me that the next train to Mansfield was at 5pm. It was now 3pm, just over four hours to show time, and I had to find a hotel, get something to eat and get to the venue.

I ordered a taxi and agreed a fare of $40 to Mansfield. My driver was keen to know why I was in the US. We had a great conversation about Rush. He went on enquire if it was true the F- bomb wasn't used much by the English. I thoroughly disabused him of this notion.

The man at the Mansfield tourist information desk pointed me in the direction of a Red Roof Inn where I got my room for the night. Food was next on my 'to-do' list but across the car park was a Super Stop and Shop where I bought a bland but filling sandwich. On my way out two guys spotted I was wearing a Rush t-shirt and they struck up conversation with me about the evening's concert. For me this was another sweet miracle as I managed to catch a lift to the venue in their truck.

The second and final show of my tour was equally outstanding despite having only managed to get seats at the rear of the venue. After the show I had a far better taxi ordering experience, but due to the volume of traffic leaving the venue I was instructed to walk to the main road where I could meet up with the taxi. Walking along an almost pitch-black road I was acutely aware that I was catching up to a lone female and felt concerned that I may be causing her concern. I decided to ask her if she was going to pick up her taxi and hopefully reassure her that I was no threat. Of course, when two Rush fans get chatting, there is no stopping them.

The taxi driver, it turned out, was due to collect both of us, along with two guys already in the taxi. (Note to non-English readers - strangers do not generally share taxis. They are called 'Private Hire' for a reason). Talking to my travelling companion, I discovered that she was a freelance rock journalist. Having a shared passion for Rush we traded email addresses and stayed in touch. Two years later, during the *R30* tour, she interviewed Lerxst and asked him to sign a copy of *Feedback* for her 'friend', David. Lerxst being Lerxst, he took the album and returned soon after with three signatures on the cover. She posted the album to me with no advanced warning. When I opened the parcel I nearly exploded with joy! Thank you Rush.

JONES BEACH THEATER

15 JULY 2002, WANTAGH, NEW YORK

I WAS THERE: TONY FERRARI

Tony Ferrari got to meet Geddy, Alex and (briefly) Neil

I didn't really think of the tragedies in Neil's life meaning the end of the band, but I remember very vividly when Neil lost his daughter and the exact date of it. On July 10, 1997, I lost my mom to a single car accident that she had. A couple of weeks later I was back to work on the road and after work in my hotel room on August 10, 1997, exactly one month later, I saw the news online about Neil's daughter. It hit me deeply at the time and I felt for him. Maybe it was because it was in certain respects identical to what happened to me with my mom, it hit home even more.

Word spread about the band recording a new album (*Vapor Trails*), sparking a new hope and appreciation that myself and the fans were extremely happy to hear. A friend's girlfriend was working at Atlantic Records at the time. Alex and Geddy had flown into New York to play some of the songs that were completed to some of the execs there. She grabbed the CD and made a copy and to this day I have a CD of some of the

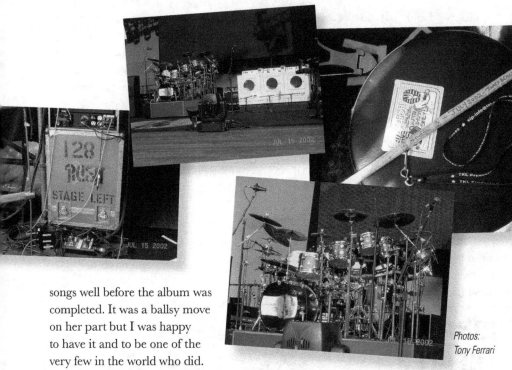

Photos: Tony Ferrari

songs well before the album was completed. It was a ballsy move on her part but I was happy to have it and to be one of the very few in the world who did.

In the summer of July 2002, with the knowledge of having now been working around the country and the world for years as a roadie, I was able to get myself into the venue that day and meet up with my friend on the Rush crew. He personally showed me every bit of equipment on the stage and explained much of his job duties and behind the scenes production that happens during a show. We spent time in Neil's dressing room and I met Neil for a second as he arrived by motorcycle. He was a bit late by his standards due to some trouble with his bike on his way to the venue.

I also met and had my photo taken with Alex and Geddy. I stood on stage right for the band's soundcheck and I was given a drum stick that Neil had used. Having dinner backstage Alex invited me over to sit with him and who he was talking with. I wanted to tell him my story of him tossing the pick to me in New Jersey years earlier, but I was nervous like a little kid.

MOLSON AMPHITHEATRE

17 JULY 2002, TORONTO, CANADA

I WAS THERE: DARYL CROSS

I saw them a few times. I was 15 the first time, on the *Hemispheres* tour, and went with five friends. My first album was *All the World's a Stage*. I saw every tour in Toronto except the last one, and *Permanent Waves* when they played outdoors. The *Moving Pictures* show was good but the first concert back when Neil came back, at Molson Amphitheatre, was a standout, as was one song – the acoustic version of 'Resist' after Neil's drum solo.

I WAS THERE: ROBERT DUTCHMAN

The 2002 Rush concert at the Molson Amphitheater changed my life. I met my partner Jen at that concert, which ultimately led to me emigrating to Canada so we could be together. Rush has been my favourite band since I was about 10 years old, growing up near Winchester in England. Rush was like a secret club in the UK, almost never on the radio and passed by word of mouth and pirated cassettes from friend to friend. I was mainly into heavy metal as a kid, but also punk, 80s pop, reggae, prog like Pink Floyd, even some classical music; basically all kinds of things.

Robert Dutchman and partner Jen fell in love thanks to Rush

I was instantly drawn to the complexity and virtuosity of their music, plus their lyrics and stories are so intelligent and thoughtful, actively encouraging and rewarding close consideration. Rush seemed to defy classification into easy categories, which appealed to my own sense of not being defined by a specific genre or clique. It's always felt like Rush were almost custom designed for me and my interests. Even when a new album didn't immediately click because of some change in direction, it was always worth persevering with it, until its (usually considerable) charms were revealed.

As the internet age has revealed so much more information about people, it has been of great comfort to discover that the three guys in the band (and even their management, collaborators and road crews) really do seem to be the decent, thoughtful, humorous and genuine fellows that they appeared to be on record. Of course I'm biased, but there have been no jarring revelations of racism, wife beating, or heroin addiction and inner self-loathing that seem to plague so many celebrities and musicians; they've never let me down. While I still listen to a wide variety of music, they remain my favourite band and the one I most closely identify with.

When they appeared to have retired in the 90s, I regretted only ever having been able to see them live once: the *Roll the Bones* tour at the Birmingham NEC in 1992. I promised myself that if they ever toured again I would make a pilgrimage to their home town and see them in Toronto.

I did the full Rush Nerd trip, visiting a bunch of Toronto locales: Lakeside Park, the Ontario Legislative Building from the cover of *Moving Pictures*, the obligatory YYZ baggage tags from the airport, a selfie at the corner of Danforth and Pape. But the main event and primary purpose of the trip was the show at the Molson Amphitheater.

I was sat next to a girl called Jen and a couple of her buddies from Northern Ontario. They'd driven several hours for the concert. She loved my British accent and the fact that I'd travelled all the way from England just for a Rush show! Being Rush fans gave us plenty of common ground for small talk. I learned Jen had also been a lifelong Rush fan - as a Canadian her experience of the band was rather different to mine: she had already seen them several times and was used to them being a regular fixture on rock radio. After the concert Jen and her friends had to leave right away to make the long drive home, but we exchanged email addresses.

18 years later, here I am in Canada. Jen and I have been together through thick and thin in those years, facing life's challenges large and small. We have managed to see Rush many more times: all the tours they played in Toronto, a couple of times in Montreal, with a group of my old friends at Wembley in London on the *R30* tour, and for the very last time in Madison Square Garden. We miss having new music and concerts to look forward to, and deeply mourned the death of Neil - a wonderful man who deserved a far longer, happier retirement than he received. We still have all their music and innumerable fond memories to cherish - not least that wonderful summer night in 2002 when we were introduced to each other by our great buddies, Rush.

I WAS THERE: RANDY RUMSBY

I saw them five times. I became a fan during their hiatus after Neil's wife and daughter died, so seeing them in concert during the *Vapor Trails* tour was pretty emotional. Neil is from the town next to mine. He's from St Catharines, I'm from Welland. I go to Lakeside Park often.

Randy Rumsby has one shelf in the family home for his Rush artefacts

It all began for me in the late 90s in high school. I signed up for BMG Music Club, where you get nine CDs for one dollar and then need to buy nine or 10 more at regular price. One of the CDs was *Test for Echo*. After listening to this CD over and over, something about Rush really sat well with me.

The next CD that I bought as part of the music club was the *Different Stages* set. After listening to this over and over, it became clear that Rush was my favourite band. In the meantime I had researched on my slow dial-up internet everything there was to know about Rush. Unfortunately at this time, they were on their hiatus due to Neil's back-to-back family tragedies. I was okay with the fact that I may never see them play live.

When their *Vapor Trails* tour was announced, I got tickets to see them in Toronto with my buddy, a Rush fan and drummer and naturally a huge Peart fan. This show was incredibly emotional. They opened with 'One Little Victory' and it truly was. Thinking and coming to terms with the idea that I'd never see them perform through to actually seeing them was almost too much to handle.

I saw them next, again in Toronto, in 2003 but under different circumstances. Toronto had been hit hard by a SARS epidemic and tourism was suffering. The Rolling Stones put together a one day benefit concert and Rush was added to the line up at the last minute. It was, and may still be, the largest single day ticketed event as around 500,000 people attended. The media predicted pandemonium but nothing bad happened.

Randy Rumsby's ticket collection

I then saw them at their 30th anniversary tour in Darien Lake, New York in 2004. I went again with my drummer buddy. This was a fun outdoor concert and we were in the unreserved grass section. Then I saw them in 2012 on the *Clockwork Angels* tour in Buffalo, New York. My wife bought two tickets for my birthday, and my brother drove. It was first (and last) Rush concert. For my last concert, in Buffalo on the *R40* tour, I again went with my drummer buddy. This one had a sombre feel to it, as it was rumoured to be their last tour. It was a great concert and I felt at peace once it was over.

I WAS THERE: WILL TOTH

My Rush story officially began as a child growing up in Willowdale. Near my school there was spot where people cut stone. It was surrounded by trees. It was a cool place and we liked to sneak onto the property and look at the various rocks. There were bits of white quartz on the ground, green jade bits and other things to see. There was a grumpy old man who either ran the place or was security. He would chase the kids off the grounds. We used to sneak in over recess to smoke cigarettes and hang out. Years later I heard 'The Necromancer' and I always associated that song with my childhood memories of that stone yard, the old man being the Necromancer and the line, 'The three travellers, men of Willowdale' being us kids sneaking onto the property.

Grade 8, 1980. I was at a party and there were a lot of older boys there. One ran in and said, 'I have the new Rush LP!' They disappeared into the basement, probably to smoke some weed, and to preview the new release, *Moving Pictures*. I then heard

Will Toth with his son at the opening of the Lee Lifeson Artpark in 2016

something so astounding and powerful. I remember thinking 'Wow, I am not sure what that is but it's incredible.'

Officially I became a fan at the age of 13 when my neighbour played me 'By-Tor and the Snow Dog'. I was fascinated by the sounds, the growling bass line, the guitar riffs – and the drums. The nearest I had ever heard to this were some Sabbath songs. Then I heard 'Fly by Night'. The opening riff blew me away once again.

I went right out and purchased *Fly by Night* and *Caress of Steel* and, a week later, *All the World's a Stage*. I played it in full every day for an entire year. I'd begin and my day with Rush. Later, *Exit... Stage Left* was played for endless hours. For a teenage boy trapped in his room, Rush provided an escape.

Rush was there for me through the 90s. As soon as I hear *Roll the Bones*, I am back in 1991 in my buddy's car heading someplace and listening on cassette, or on the bus with my Walkman. Rush was touring for *Bones* and this was the last tour I saw before they took a five year hiatus.

I saw the *Vapor Trails* tour twice. Rush was back, on fire with sonic brilliance. A hot summer night in Toronto, they played at our local outdoor venue. They played hard and fast. It was a perfect night with my Rush pals. Highlights were all the material from the new album and the best version of 'Natural Science' I have ever heard.

2007 marked the release of *Snakes & Arrows*. Something about this CD did not catch on with me right away. But a couple of songs make my playlist. 'Armor and Sword' speaks to me and the musicianship is incredible. The tour was one of their best. The live sound was excellent, the drums outstanding and the guys played very well.

The *Time Machine* tour featured the inspired idea to play an entire LP, in this case *Moving Pictures*, as the second set of their show. Many bands were following this format at the time. I loved it, although a friend in the UK said they were very tired and going through the motions by the time the tour hit Britain. I caught the show fresh in Toronto as I always do.

When I first heard an orchestra was going to be on stage with them for the *Clockwork Angels* show, I was not sure what to think. But the live presentation of the songs matched the production level of the LP. I prefer the live band only, just the three guys jamming it out, but this was a special thing and it was cool to see Rush performing (and having fun) with other musicians in a live setting.

They pulled out all the stops for the *R40* tour, a de-evolving stage setup from the current time back to their beginnings in a high school gym with paisley guitars and a disco ball. What's not to like? The double-necks for 'Xanadu', a new video for *Roll the Bones* featuring various celebrities such as Peter Dinklage of *Game of Thrones* fame and Paul Rudd and Les Claypool to name but a few. Jonathan Dinklage and Ben Mink both performed 'Losing It', a song Geddy had to write an excellent bass part for. That was a stellar moment in the show.

I don't think anyone really realised that this was 'The End' in every sense of the word; the end of Rush playing live, the end of Rush recording and, for many of us, the end of our youth. A band like Rush only comes along once in a while and takes you on a lifelong journey, through trials and tribulations, to a graceful closure. Time moves forward but for Geddy, Alex and Neil, time caught up with them and Rush went out with grace. All the best to our three travellers. Thank you for all that you have done to impact our lives. Time stand still….

UMB BANK PAVILION

2 AUGUST 2002, ST LOUIS, MISSOURI

I WAS THERE: PAUL MILLER

From hearing *Permanent Waves* on vinyl as a tween at a family friend's house in Utah to walking up at show opening with a best friend from Utah at an outdoor concert in St Louis when they were playing 'Distant Early Warning', the ever increasing sonic energy was like a dream. Looking over at my friend Ben, in the same thought thinking, 'Here we are again, ready to witness the best live band ever perform for us and for thousands of others.' I watched them live from every release after *Moving Pictures* if they toured to my current location. I loved every album, a next chapter in life to complement and excel us to the next level. My other friend Scott, a fine guitarist, went for his first and only Rush concert, said it started out good, got even better and then it got great! He and I went to the Amphitheater in St Louis and I remember Geddy saying, 'Glad to be back on this sultry evening, we've got a lot of songs to play for you tonight – here's 'Earthshine'', and that powerful Lifeson guitar just put you back on your heels.

SHORELINE AMPHITHEATER

20 SEPTEMBER 2002, MOUNTAIN VIEW, CALIFORNIA

I WAS THERE: DAVID HUGHES

I saw them twice with my concert buddy at the Shoreline Amp in Mountain View, on the *Vapor Trails* and *R30* tours. They were both three hour shows with no opening

David Hughes caught the Vapor Trails and R30 shows at Mountain View, California

bands and a 30 minute intermission. I remember the *Vapor Trails* show opening with 'Tom Sawyer'. Both shows were outstanding but Rush normally were!

PHILIPS ARENA

13 OCTOBER 2002,
ATLANTA, GEORGIA

I WAS THERE: MICHAEL NIBLETT

Michael Niblett's Mustang had a custom tag reading 'Bravest'

I saw Rush seven times. My first memory of them is listening to my brother's *Exit... Stage Left* on vinyl in the 80s when I was 10 years old. 'The Spirit of Radio' just captivated me. My first show was the *Vapor Trails* tour in 2002. I went with my brother. They were really loud... but I knew every word by heart and I got really excited when they played my favourite song, 'Animate'. I jumped up and down!

I went to two shows on the *R30* tour, two on the *Snakes & Arrows* tour and one each on *Clockwork Angels* and *R40*. My brother and I would catch them in Atlanta on one leg of the tour and then somewhere in Tennessee on the other leg. I even got a custom tag on my Mustang GT. It said 'Bravest' from the song 'Bravest Face' from *Snakes & Arrows*. I remember they played for three hours and how the place about came apart when they played '2112'. People would clap in rhythm with the song during '2112'.

TARGET CENTER

2 NOVEMBER 2002, MINNEAPOLIS, MINNESOTA

I WAS THERE: GARY LAWVER

I saw them nine times, starting with the *Roll the Bones* tour. My best memory is when I first heard the news that they were indeed back in the studio to record what would eventually be *Vapor Trails*. I really thought they were done before that. And it was topped off for me with seeing them live again on that tour!

ESTÁDIO DO MORUMBI

22 NOVEMBER 2002, SÃO PAULO, BRAZIL

I WAS THERE: ALEXANDRE VIGANO

In 1987 a school friend lent me the double vinyl album, *Exit... Stage Left*. I'd heard Rush on the radio before, but this was the first time I was going to listen to a full album. It was remarkable. There was nothing we could compare Rush to at that time. They were different from other bands. I am not a musician and I do not know how to describe it, but my ears know.

Alexandre Vigano saw all three shows Rush played in Brazil

Rush performed three times in Brazil and I was there every time. The first time was in São Paulo. I believe the 60,000 crowd was the largest show they ever headlined at. The concert finished and I went home, took a shower, slept for two hours and took a bus to Rio de Janeiro – 282 miles - to watch them again the next day at the Maracanã Stadium. This concert is the DVD *Rush in Rio* recorded on November 23, 2002 with a crowd of 40,000. The best moment of the concert was the performance of 'YYZ' when everyone was jumping and singing together, following the band.

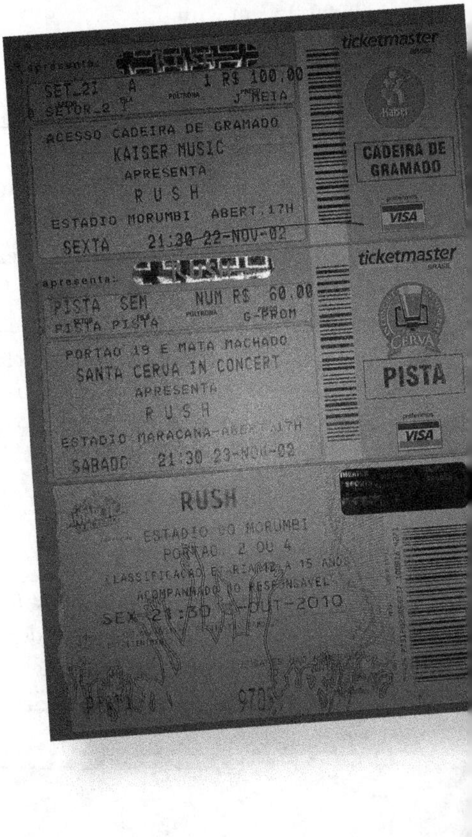

The third and last time I saw them was again in São Paulo, at the Morumbi Stadium in 2010 in front of 38,000 people on the *Time Machine* tour. They played *Moving Pictures* in its entirety.

THERE: DANIEL MILNER

I was 16 or 17 when my brother, who is two years older, brought me a cassette tape and said, 'Listen to this. You'll like it.' It was the first U2 album. We then bought it on vinyl. I am Brazilian and by listening to records I learnt English. At school we had a teacher who really loved The Beatles. I said, 'Why The Beatles? Bring me some good stuff. Bring me some Led Zeppelin. Bring me some other stuff.' And that's when my brother brought me *Moving Pictures*.

The lyrics blew my mind. Neil's lyrics were amazing and complex. I wasn't 100 per cent sure I was understanding what he was trying to tell me. We wanted to learn English better in order to understand the lyrics better.

They played three shows in Brazil on the *Vapor Trails* tour. I went with my brother to the São Paolo show. The show was fantastic although the sound wasn't great. They had the washing machines running on the stage. Geddy Lee and Alex were crazy about the crowd. The stadium was packed out. It was a real crush. It took five hours to get home when normally it would take 20 – 30 minutes after a football match there.

The R30 tour marked 30 years for Rush as a band with Neil on the drummer's stool. Starting off in Antioch, Tennessee in May 2004, the tour encompassed 57 shows and concluded in Europe in October of that year.

STARWOOD AMPHITHEATRE

26 MAY 2004, NASHVILLE, TENNESSEE

I WAS THERE: GARY WILSON

My wife and I made the pilgrimage from our hometown of Tuscaloosa, Alabama to Nashville for my first Rush concert since 1987. This being the opening show of the tour was very exciting for me. We would be the first audience to witness 30 years of Rush history. It was godawful traffic. I had not purchased tickets, thinking I might have time to score at the box office when we arrived, but ended up in a huge line with people who obviously were thinking the same thing. Stupid. We were in line for no more than two minutes when a young lady asked if we would like some free lawn passes. 'Um, yes please!' We happily took our tickets, went through the gate and made our way to the lawn. Then the houselights went down and the crowd erupted....

I WAS THERE: EMERSON TAYLOR HIXSON

They've been my favourite band since sixth grade when my dad showed me 'YYZ'. I used to unwind listening to their music when I was feeling sick to help me feel better. As a musician they have always helped me to be better. My dad took my twin brother Caleb Tanned and myself to the *R30* tour opener in Nashville, where they opened the show with 'The Spirit of Radio'. I had the opportunity to catch them four more times. The last show I caught was in Atlanta on the *Time Machine* tour with my brother and good friend. It was my friend's first Rush show. They always blew me away live and I realised that not only did these amazing musicians know how to play but they worked pretty intensely while doing so. They have made some of the best memories through their music and continue to do so.

MARCUS AMPHITHEATER

7 JUNE 2004, MILWAUKEE, WISCONSIN

I WAS THERE: QUINN WUTKE

Quinn Wutke and her brother Adrian bonded through a mutual love of Rush

I grew up the youngest of five siblings, the only girl with four older brothers. Naturally I wanted to be like them and to like the things that they liked. They dabbled in all kinds of music but one of the common threads among them all was Rush. While other kids my age were watching Disney movies on repeat, I was the kid watching *A Show of Hands* on repeat. Those were the songs that became my anthems growing up. I remember in high school walking down the hall with my brother's hand-me-down Walkman blasting 'Subdivisions' through my headphones and just relating so much to those lyrics. It was exactly how I felt at that time.

My middle brother Adrian and I related to their music the most. I finally got to see my first live show on the *R30* tour in Milwaukee, Wisconsin just north of where we lived. It remains one of the most memorable concerts I've ever seen. I was so in awe finally getting to hear all these songs I grew up with live, and with the catalogue of music they had by that time it was all the favourites. The lights, the onstage rotisserie and dryers - I remember it all so vividly.

I got to see them three more times before they hung it up for good and I will cherish the memories for the rest of my life. Now Adrian and I periodically meet up to see the Rush Tribute Project perform (as far as tribute bands go they are top notch) and try to capture some of that nostalgia from a bygone era. I am 36 with two young children (6 and 8) I am passing the Rush torch to. When we get in the car and they ask to listen to Rush, I know I must be doing something right.

CYNTHIA WOODS MITCHELL PAVILION

26 JUNE 2004, WOODLANDS, TEXAS

I WAS THERE: AMY DAVID VALENTINE

Driving by the sugar cane fields and levee systems of southeast Louisiana, the green, yellow, beige and browns ablur amidst the summer dusk evening sky, my young eyes stare out of the car window taking it all in. At times the blurs whip by my window, reflected in my wide-eyed gaze, the forms swaying in what little summer breeze might be available, in time to the staccato West African drum beats.

The rhythm pounds into my very soul, and I know I am a witness to something quite special. Although I have heard this song before, the raw emotion will elude me for some years, after which I will understand the meaning and the rhythm. But for now my young mind is content with watching the sun go down across the levees, the colourful graffiti blurring into a musical crescendo in time to the music. The brown fences passing us by on highway 71, I watch my mother's fingers busily drumming along to Neil Peart's impossibly fast beats, as my dad concentrates on the road ahead. The cassette recorder, for during this time, this is how new music is being released, blasts more of the African rhythmic sections as the base booms a completely different beat, opposing yet perfectly complementary. 'I get this feeling…'

The voice of Geddy Lee echoes to the synthetic bass generated to complement those hypnotic drums. The mood is set for the sky, now full on dusk. Not a cloud in the sky. As we travel to visit my grandfather in Patterson, Louisiana, I will ask for the album *Presto* to be played again. My innocent young mind can't seem to get enough. A different track on the same album offers a glimpse of the ability for Rush's music to be passed on to the next generation, something that some 20 years later I will pass on down to my own daughter. The line 'reflected in another pair of eyes' that references a natural weather phenomenon known as 'Chain Lightning'.

Although I will go on to venture into many pop phases, including Mariah Carey, Ace of Base and grunge bands like Nirvana, Hole, Soundgarden and Pearl Jam, I'd come back to Rush and they would become my favourite band. Circa 1997, as a sophomore in high school, I came insanely close to winning tickets to see them in my home state in New Orleans for the *Test for Echo* tour. Sadly, I was caller #8 (ha, those were the days!) and I needed to be #9.

Once I started college, I would use many of Neil's lyrics in English essays, always ending with college professors either questioning what musical group wrote this (an English professor I made a cassette mix for) to those questioning if I was a Rush fan. It was my psychology professor and turns out they were too. Neil's words of wisdom, which aptly seemed to sum up life events and society, would follow me through my childhood and adolescence into adulthood and the formative years of my own child. The magic spell that took hold back in the early

Amy David Valentine saw Rush in Texas

1990s has never quite run out. I intend to pass the magic spark along, and continue the Rush legacy.

My first Rush show was three days before my first wedding anniversary. I still remember the anticipation waiting in line, and walking near the stage of the outdoor venue to see The Processor's throne and gorgeous black with rainbow hologram accents. That drum set was a work of art and a sight to behold!

A light misting rain started during 'Leave That Thing Alone'. I vividly recall goose bumps, especially during Lerxt's solo, and was so psyched to hear it live. They did 'The Seeker' from the *Feedback* album and 'Summertime Blues' and 'Heart Full of Soul'. Neil was such a machine that I would in later years remark that he may be a cyborg, programmed to rock us mere humans into progressive stratospheres unknown!

HOLLYWOOD BOWL

6 JULY 2004, HOLLYWOOD, CALIFORNIA

I WAS THERE: ROBBIE GENNET

When I was too young to go to a concert, the first I heard of Rush from some older kids made them sound much more dangerous than they turned out to be. On the warm-up run for the *Moving Pictures* tour, the band came to the Hollywood Sportatorium in South Florida, a legendary shed in the middle of the swamp where, in November 1981, Mr Peart was late to the show and a riot ensued, the crowd throwing rocks and bottles at guards and officers. When the doors opened, people started climbing the walls and running towards the gates, where they were tear-gassed and mostly subdued. To a young kid, this seemed pretty wild and crazy. Eventually seeing the band live, I could sympathise with the enthusiasm of the gate crashers.

Robbie Gennet caught the R30 tour at the Hollywood Bowl

In 2004 a friend got me backstage and I got to watch the encore from side stage and then wait while the halls were cleared for the band to walk through coming off stage. Geddy came down the ramp and, as he passed me, he made eye contact over his glasses, just a brief moment. I must have looked rather rapturous as I saw him give me a knowing smile and then continue on down the hall. As a devotee and hardcore fan, that one glimpse meant so much without a word exchanged.

Having seen the final show at the Forum, it made me profoundly grateful that these three people connected and brought such incredible art to all of us. With the scarcity of that kind of magic these days, I can only look back with wonder that they managed to exist at all. Farewell to Kings indeed.

SPAC

9 AUGUST 2004, SARATOGA SPRINGS, NEW YORK

I WAS THERE: JACK J BRITTON

At the age of 17, my stepfather introduced me to Rush. When I heard they were coming to my area for their 30th anniversary tour I had to see them. They weren't great seats but I still had a great view of the band. In exchange for a ride I bought tickets for me, my mother and stepfather. It was an excellent show. No amount of money can put into words the feeling of excitement and energy I got from being surrounded by fellow fans and seeing my favourite songs coming to life before my very eyes.

Another time, me and two college buddies had tickets to see the *Snakes & Arrows* tour, also at the SPAC. We knew the food at this venue was expensive so we decided to eat at a good sit down restaurant. We were waiting for the check when my buddy said, 'Guys, I left the tickets at my house!' I hit the freeway at 110 miles per hour. I broke the strap on my muffler but we made it to my buddy's house. He then had to drive us to the venue. Somehow, we made it to the show on time.

MOLSON AMPHITHEATRE

22 AUGUST 2004, TORONTO, CANADA

I WAS THERE: JANET WEIR

Listening to the first album I instantly fell in love with 'Working Man'. The *R30* tour was memorable as it was the first time I ever saw them. I grew up in Toronto and so they are very special to me. They played music from all of the albums. We were sitting up on the grassy knoll in the outdoor stadium and when they played 'Subdivisions' I thought I'd died and gone to heaven. I saw them again a few years later in Hamilton and it wasn't anywhere near as good.

WEMBLEY ARENA

8 SEPTEMBER 2004, LONDON, UK

I WAS THERE: KARL J ZAMMIT

I saw Rush 30 times in total, including on their unforgettable *R30* European tour. It was the

Karl Zammit caught the R30 tour in London

best three weeks of my entire life. It started at Wembley Arena in London. My best friend and I eagerly set forth from our London hotel to the venue. We had purposely gone there earlier in the day, before the commencement of the live performance, in order to be able to take our own photographs. This was a momentous and self-gratifying one-off musical experience for both of us.

I WAS THERE: STEVE PLEDGER

On that September evening in 2004 all the wondering and waiting, the sadness and the hope of a return to the European stage evaporated when the lights in Wembley Arena went out and the intro music began.

The noise from the crowd was like nothing else! One spot light, stage right, hit Alex as he stepped from the wings and struck that opening riff from 'Finding My Way'. The roof came off the place: they were back! And when the lights went up on the whole band and we saw the Professor back on that stage, behind his kit, well… there have been few moments in my life that get close to the rush of adrenaline and emotion that coursed through my veins right there and then.

I WAS THERE: DEREK COLLISON

Rush have been my favourite band since 1976 and the *2112* album. I eventually got to see them for the first time on the *R30* tour. I also managed to see them on the *Snakes & Arrows*, *Time Machine* and *Clockwork Angels* tours and was gutted when they bowed out after the *R40* tour without visiting the UK. My biggest memory is losing my alcoholic mate at *R30* (I went on my own after that). We went straight to the bar and then took our seats. My mate went to get another pint and I never saw him again until after the gig and couldn't get him on the mobile. I found him afterwards loitering outside in a rather drunken state. He'd managed to get right to the side of the stage and even showed me a pic of how he'd got to within 10 feet of Geddy before security saw him.

I had a Starman tattoo done. The snakes and arrows underneath was just an idea I had while chatting to my tattoo artist. It's one of my favourite tattoos now.

I WAS THERE: RAY SMITHSON

I saw them for two nights at Wembley on the *R30* tour. I saw them in Sheffield a few years later and in Dublin on the *Snakes & Arrows* tour. I could not take my eyes off Neil Peart the whole night. What a drummer. But the man was more than that - he was a genius. I was always aware of them but it was a local businessman who ran a record shop in Omagh who really got me into them. I remember vividly the second Wembley Arena show as I was so close to the stage. There was a young up-and-coming British band behind us going absolutely mental, playing air guitar and air drums. I met Ross Halfin, the famous photographer, too.

I was on the balcony for the Sheffield Arena gig and, again, just could not take my eyes off Neil Peart. And the venue for the Dublin show had a balcony which went round the venue in a semi-circle, so no matter where you were, you got a good view. I loved the fact that Rush didn't take themselves too seriously. They got the *South Park* characters to count them into 'Tom Sawyer'. And they weren't afraid of using the pyrotechnics when it was needed. They were brilliant live.

I WAS THERE: RICHARD MILLER

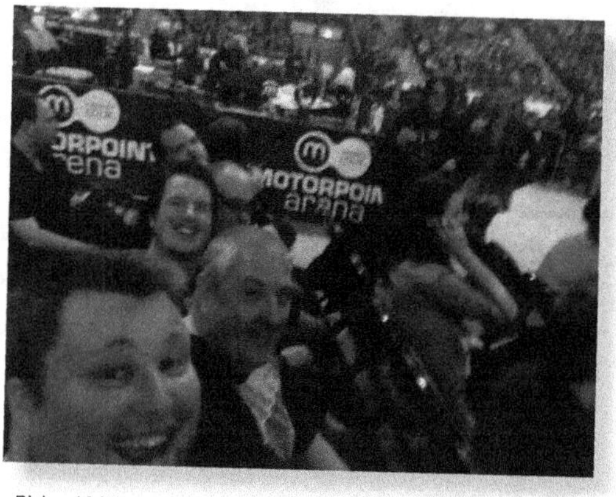

Richard Miller was introduced to Rush by his dad

I grew up in a house where music was always playing. My dad was a big fan of bands such as Led Zeppelin, Black Sabbath, Pink Floyd, Yes and Genesis. But one band in particular resonated with me and that was Rush. I can recall hearing 'The Spirit of Radio', 'Closer to the Heart' and 'Tom Sawyer', and my dad buying *Roll the Bones* and *Counterparts* on CD. I was 12 and watched his VHS of the *Grace Under Pressure* concert when my interest really started to grow. This was the first time I'd actually seen any of the members of the band performing rather than just hearing them, and I was utterly captivated. I sat open-mouthed as Geddy effortlessly switched from playing intricate bass lines to synths all whilst singing on 'The Enemy Within', and as Neil threw his sticks in the air and caught them in time in the intro to 'The Weapon'. But it was mainly Alex with his Flock of Seagulls haircut

and white blazer jacket that caught my attention, with his awesome guitar work, particularly on the solos for 'The Spirit of Radio', 'The Weapon' and 'Witch Hunt'. Alex was my new idol, and I asked for a red and white Squire Strat for Christmas.

In my teens I bought the entire back catalogue on CD, and spent hours on the internet reading everything I could about them. I'd picked the worst time possible to become a Rush fan. They had been inactive since 1997 due to the tragedies in Neil's life and I resigned myself to never seeing them live and there being no new music.

Things all changed in 2002 when I read on the internet of a new album on the way. I remember going to HMV in Darlington to buy *Vapor Trails*, taking it home and listening to it over and over. Being 17 and having just left school, this album became a massive part of my life. I was gutted that the *Vapor Trails* tour didn't include any UK or European dates. But soon enough the band announced the *R30* tour, including their first live dates in the UK and Europe in 12 years.

The opening night of the European leg in sold out straight away. But they added a second Wembley date on September 9th, the day before my 19th birthday, and my dad got tickets for him, me and my friends Mark and Martin as my birthday present. In return I bought us tickets for the Manchester show three days later.

Living in the North East of England I'd only seen a handful of live bands and never been down to London before, so travelling down to see Rush seemed like a wild adventure. We took the train from Darlington and then the Tube across to Wembley. Outside the arena was a sea of people wearing Rush t-shirts. I'd never even seen anyone else wearing a Rush t-shirt before! A group of people had gathered together

Richard Miller's tickets and (above) his Alex Lifeson ES Les Paul

and spontaneously started to perform a vocal rendition of 'Tom Sawyer', complete with air drumming along to Neil's parts. The atmosphere was electric, and I'd never felt excitement like it.

We went inside and took our seats, high up on stage left. As the lights went out, an intro film started to play on the large screen behind the stage, starring the comedian Jerry Stiller. I recall him complaining about the band never playing 'A Passage to Bangkok' before rousing the band to take to the stage. Suddenly Alex was on the stage in front of us playing the opening riff to 'Finding My Way' and the whole place erupted as Neil and Geddy joined in. The song led into a medley of other older Rush classics such as 'Anthem', 'Bastille Day', 'A Passage to Bangkok' and 'Hemispheres', before launching into 'The Spirit of Radio'. It felt surreal to finally be seeing live this band that I'd pretty much idolised since watching that *Grace Under Pressure* VHS several years prior. Actually seeing Alex perform the solo to 'The Spirit of Radio' was something I'll never forget.

The setlist continued with classics such as 'Red Barchetta', 'Bravado' and 'The Trees' along with 'Earthshine' and 'One Little Victory' from *Vapor Trails*. The band mixed things up by adding some of their favourite covers, including 'The Seeker' by The Who. One highlight was the rendition of 'Between the Wheels', which sounded absolutely incredible throughout. Alex's guitar roared and soared, with the solo in the outro giving me goosebumps. The setlist continued with Neil's incredible drum solo, followed by renditions of older Rush staples such as '2112', 'Xanadu' and 'La Villa Strangiato', Alex goofing around and ranting about forgetting how to play the song. The concert concluded with a spine-tingling rendition of 'Limelight', again with Alex sounding sublime on the solo.

All too soon it was all over and the house lights came back on. My ears were ringing, but I felt on such a high from what I'd just seen and heard. I remember heading to the merchandise stalls after the show and buying two *R30* t-shirts, one in red with the tour dates on the back, and one in black with the *R30* logo on the front.

Three nights later, my dad and I were in Manchester to see the band again. I'd read online that it was Neil's birthday, which added an extra excitement to proceedings. At one point in the show the camera zoomed in on a birthday cake on top of the dryers on the stage, which got a very loud cheer from the crowd. This time we were sat towards the back of the arena with a great central view of the stage. The set list was pretty much identical to the show in London which as far I was concerned was a good thing, as it meant I got to relive the whole thing once again!

NATIONAL EXHIBITION CENTRE

11 & 15 SEPTEMBER 2004, BIRMINGHAM, UK

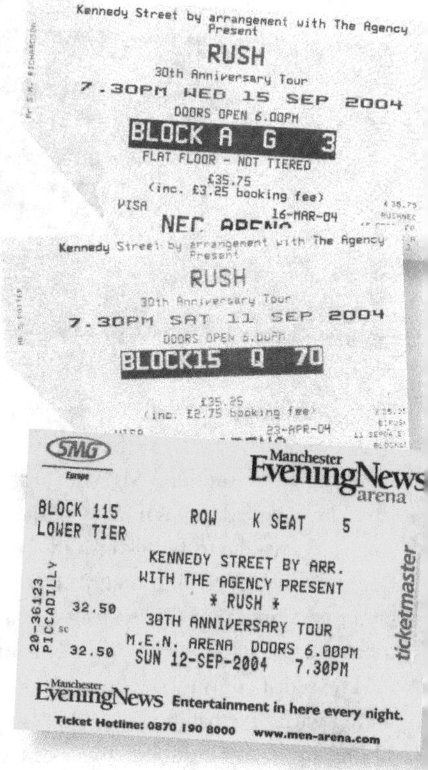

I WAS THERE: STEVE POTTER

I was there for two shows in Birmingham, one of which I was sixth or seventh row for, and one in Manchester. The first Birmingham show was also the date of the first Rush convention I went to at the NEC. It started just after lunchtime and was on all afternoon with tribute bands and a Rush karaoke. That's when I realised I was just a small fry when it came to being a Rush fan.

I WAS THERE: PAUL TABBERER

I saw them three times, on the *R30*, *Snakes & Arrows* and *Time Machine* tours. I've been playing drums since 1983 so Neil was a real hero for me… although I will never be able to play as good as him! My favourite album has to be *Exit... Stage Left*. In 2004 we were late and they'd already started playing. We had seats around 10 rows back, so had to run down to them. Neil hadn't incorporated the 'big band' bit into his drum solo at that point but I remember just watching him in awe. The second time I saw them we were to the right of the stage and again had an excellent view of all three of them. The last time, in 2011, I took the wife and I think the booking agent was having a bad day as we were right at the back. The sound wasn't great either.

Paul Tabberer was at Birmingham's NEC

I WAS THERE: STEVE LEE

While Rush weren't touring the UK I became a parent, twice. The first, a boy, was named Alex after you-know-who, the second is a girl with no real Rush names available – she thinks their music is weird anyway. *Rush in Rio* came out and graphically showed what I had been missing. Then the news came out about the 30th anniversary tour. *R30* was coming to the UK. I acquired a pair of great tickets, at Birmingham again – Mrs Lee would accompany me this time, a compromise deal struck by my attendance at an Alanis Morissette gig. Our seats were stage right again. However, this time we were in the block almost directly next to the stage, maybe ten to twelve seats back from stage front and not too far up. My wife and I both spotted Alex arrive in the blackout, taking his place next to the steps that would deliver him on stage.

I loved that gig. Not just because it was Rush, but also because I saw the joy on my wife's face as she enjoyed the spectacle. She could finally experience that essence, that camaraderie, that aura of spirituality that accompanies the live Rush event. It was also my favourite Rush concert in terms of the setlist: a snatch of 'Bangkok', 'Earthshine', 'Red Barchetta', 'Bravado', 'The Trees', 'Red Sector A', '2112', 'By-Tor and the Snow Dog', and all the others. In terms of perfection, it beat that first concert from 1988. The first time is always special, however, this time I was with my wife and the set, the performance… it just all added up to near ecstasy.

MANCHESTER EVENING NEWS ARENA

12 SEPTEMBER 2004, MANCHESTER, UK

I WAS THERE; PHILIP LONGSHAW

I saw Rush six times in all, twice in the 80s and four times in 2004. The reason for the gap is that my ex held the purse strings. All the gigs were superb but my favourite was the *R30* tour at Manchester Arena in 2004, my first Rush gig as a free man. It was a gap of 20 years and I'd forgotten how awesome they were live. I really liked the production. The show was well over three hours. What got me was how crazy the fans were, very intense. I was also surprised to see a good 25 per cent of females in attendance!

I WAS THERE: MARK APPLETON

I was excited to take my son, Christopher, to his first Rush concert on the *R30* tour. He was only three years of age when I had last seen the band so now at age 16 (almost the same age as I was for my first Rush concert), and a very talented guitarist/singer himself, I was anxious to introduce him to what I had been telling him about all these years. Thankfully, he loved the show every bit as much as I did.

I really tried to drink in the scene, the performance and the atmosphere, feeling that maybe this could be the last time. But I attended Manchester Evening News Arena on the *Snakes & Arrows* tour, taking Christopher and his brother Luke. What a thrill it was for me to be able to take my family to witness something which has been one of the absolute passions of my life through the years. We saw the *Time Machine* and *Clockwork*

Angels tours together too. I was especially paying attention to the lyrics of 'The Garden' at the latter show and really feeling that this was the end. It was.

FESTHALLE

24 SEPTEMBER 2004, FRANKFURT, GERMANY

I WAS THERE: MARTIN JANSEN

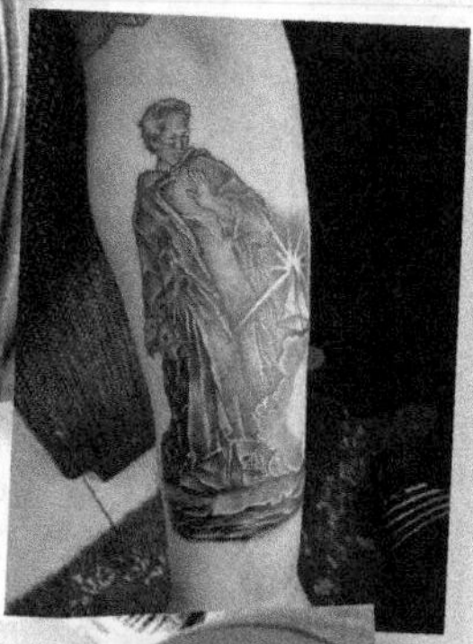

Martin Jansen's Rush tattoos

I drove down to Frankfurt to see them for the *R30* gig which was to be filmed. Bootleggers were selling t-shirts and posters and they had loud Rush music played from their cars and vans. We stood in line to get in but as we came closer to the entrance we noticed a sign saying everyone needed to leave their phones outside the venue. There were a few cargo containers placed next to the venue and you had to bring your phone there and you'd get a number to pick it up after the show. It was weird, because not many phones had good cameras at that point.

Before the show started there was also this public announcement that the show was about to get loud so you were able to get a refund if you wanted to leave before show time. We had also heard this message a week before in Oberhausen. The show was superb and the venue is a classic. The next week we also went to the Rotterdam gig.

The *Snakes & Arrows* tour was a two-legged affair commencing in June 2007 and running through to October 2007, and then recommencing in April 2008 and carrying on through to July 2008. The band played 114 shows. Only the *Hemispheres* tour was longer.

HIFI BUYS AMPHITHEATRE

13 JUNE 2007, ATLANTA, GEORGIA

I WAS THERE: GARY WILSON

I had been to two prior concerts - *Hold Your Fire* and *R30* – and those shows were absolutely outstanding, but I had my wife and two sons, who were 17 and seven then, with me for the opening night of the *Snakes & Arrows* show. It ended up being our only Rush show together as a family. Life threw us some curve balls later and unfortunately we never were able to attend another live Rush show together. But I still think back to those concerts and how lucky I was just to be there, with my family by my side.

TOYOTA PAVILION AT MONTAGE MOUNTAIN

29 JUNE 2007, SCRANTON, PENNSYLVANIA

I WAS THERE: DANNY WHITE, AGE 26

I had begun listening to Rush in the 1990s and was instantly hooked. I was unable to attend a show then because my folks would not have let me, plus the band went on hiatus following the tragedies in Neil's life. When I finally saw Rush - three more tours would follow - I was blown away by the group's performance. Despite the fact the band members were in their middle fifties, they performed like it was 1981 and they were at their peak. My favourite tour was the *Time Machine* tour when they played the entire *Moving Pictures* album and debuted two new songs, which appeared on *Clockwork Angels*. 'Caravan' and 'BU2B' proved that Rush still had something exciting to offer. I will always cherish their music. RIP Neil and long live Rush.

HOLLYWOOD BOWL

23 JULY 2007, LOS ANGELES, CALIFORNIA

I WAS THERE: DANNY HAIM

I've been to a few shows. My brother is a huge Rush fan. He's the one that always took me. I think he's been to half a dozen if not more shows. I'm not into rock but I love Rush. The last show I went to was at the Hollywood Bowl. We didn't have the best tickets but once Neil did his solo I told my friend, 'Follow me and we will sneak to the front row, but chances are we will get kicked out after.' I managed to get us to the front row and we were able to see the solo from start to finish before security did indeed come and kicked us out.

I WAS THERE: RAYMOND BOWEN

Raymond Bowen saw Rush at the Hollywood Bowl

I went with my youngest brother. What can I say? They were freaking awesome. I've always been a big Neil Peart fan because I played drums and he's one of my best drummers. I have two DVDs of him talking about his drumming, playing and explaining his entire drum set. I've got a few books by him too, including *Ghost Rider* which he wrote after he lost his wife and his daughter. He was a very interesting person. I just wish I could have met him in person. He didn't like the media or being interviewed or people in his face. He let Alex and Geddy deal with that. And just like Led Zeppelin could never replace John Bonham, Geddy and Alex will never be able to replace Neil Peart.

I was devastated the day Neil Peart went home to be with God. He was absolutely amazing - and to hear them live? They were absolutely the best three man band I have ever heard. Neil may be gone but he'll never be forgotten, not by other excellent drummers or by the fans. Rock the heavens, Neil.

VERIZON WIRELESS AMPHITHEATER

12 AUGUST 2007 SELMA, TEXAS

I WAS THERE: RAY PERME

I saw them live 22 times. Rush are the band that I had listened to after breaking the bonds on Kiss fandom. Being of a certain age and growing up in a suburb outside of Cleveland, Ohio, it's easy to see why my musical tastes formed the way they did. Rush had always been there. I knew of the legend and lore of *2112*, being the youngest of six children whose musical landscape reached from The Beatles, Steve Miller Band, James Taylor, Pink Floyd and Bread through to Led Zeppelin, Aerosmith, J Geils Band and Bobby Sherman.

In 1977 and 1978 the Kiss marketing machine was aimed directly at my age group with bombastic music, comic book character group members and tales of explosions and fire at their concerts. What's not to grab a comic book-reading kid just coming into their teen years? I was not only the youngest in my immediate family, but also the youngest person in my graduating class. Having the benefit (or curse) of having my birthday fall on the last date of inclusion and having a mother who was ready for her last of six children to enter into his primary public education and get out of her hair for eight hours of the day. Looking back, I can understand.

My older brother did a lot to shape my musical tastes beyond Kiss, mostly because he had a prized stereo and turntable and his own record collection. I learned that I liked rock music and gravitated to the guitar playing by the likes of Jimmy Page and Eddie Van Halen. In the middle of this, *Permanent Waves* was released. The infectious 'Spirit of Radio' was on heavy rotation on the legendary WMMS. It's a song I've never grown tired of.

My brother took me to my first concerts, with a lot of sweet talking and assurances to my mother. One was Rush on their *Permanent Waves* tour at Richfield Coliseum in February 1980. I don't remember much about the show. My second show was on the *Moving Pictures* tour in May of 1981. I vividly remember the opening number of *2112*'s 'Overture' and 'The Temples of Syrinx' and how the Coliseum erupted as the music started. I saw them every tour stop in Cleveland until I left for my own USAF odyssey in January 1988.

I didn't own a lot of their music. I had *Permanent Waves*, *2112*, *Moving Pictures*, *Exit... Stage Left* and 'Subdivisions'. I didn't own *Grace Under Pressur*e or *Power Windows*. This is when they started to lose me as a fan. I went to the shows but I'd hardly classify myself as a huge Rush fan. It's odd that they are the band that I have seen in concert the most, by a wide margin.

I saw them in England for the *Roll the Bones* tour. A friend had an extra ticket and I went because I liked them back when. There were quite a few songs I hadn't heard before. 'Dreamline' in particular stands out. I hated the song 'Roll the Bones' and laughed at the 'rap' section. I recall leaving that concert and, on the train back to Flitwick, thinking, 'That band is done.'

I changed my Air Force station from RAF Chicksands to Kelly AFB in San Antonio, Texas. My immediate supervisor and another new friend of mine were both Rush fans, and my new friend's wife was an even bigger fan. We bonded over the music, sharing tales of how we could relate to 'Subdivisions' and how certain other songs still held such personal meaning to us. I maintained that I didn't really care for the albums after *Signals*. They tried to convince me otherwise, but I liked what I liked.

Counterparts was released and the song 'Stick it Out' was getting heavy radio air play. I liked the song and bought the CD. When the tour was announced we all went to the show in San Antonio as a group. I remember hearing 'Analog Kid' for the first time in years and loved it.

Test for Echo came out, and we as a group went to that show in San Antonio too. The album wasn't as strong and certainly didn't age well. The song 'Driven' was much better live than on the studio release. The additional bass solo really set that rendition apart. It was a good show.

I was out of the Air Force by the time *Different Stages* was released. I remember reading about what had happened to Neil's daughter and wife. When *Vapor Trails* was released, I learned about the tour stop in Selma, a small suburb of San Antonio. My friend and supervisor from the Air Force had moved back to California years ago, but I went with the couple that were Rush fans. It was a subdued and triumphant return for Rush to be in concert. We were older, more established, and my own personal appreciation for the musicianship in their music had deepened. Rush's place on my musical palette had also grown.

My most memorable and favourite Rush concert was on the *Snakes & Arrows* show at the Amphitheater in Selma. I had been a member of a Rush message board (remember those?) and was looking forward to meeting a few of the local members who'd be at this show. I was excited to take my 19-year-old son to his first Rush show.

We had excellent seats on the fourth row, leaning towards Geddy's side but more centre stage. I'd also, for the first time, purchased the preferred parking pass. We had our own designated parking close to the entrance and, when we left the show, instead of the normal mad dash and gridlock, we had a cordoned lane that was orderly and straight to the highway. By the time my friends (that same couple) left the parking lot I was already pulling into my home some 20 miles away. I'd never go to a show without the preferred parking again.

We had a great view of the stage. It was a typically hot summer Sunday evening in Central Texas. The band came on stage just as the sun was about to set. In fact it didn't set until at least three songs in. I remember them jogging on to the stage to a big cheer and as Alex played the opening riff of 'Limelight'. This tour had the ideal set list. The crowd at Rush shows was markedly different from other acts. They were older, mostly male, and wanted to listen to the music. Sure, there are the air drummers and air guitarists. Even air bassists, unique to Rush as far as my concert going experience. Those that sing will sing every word along with Geddy, but not in an annoying or an obnoxious way. It's a very orderly crowd.

When they dovetailed immediately into 'Digital Man', from my personal favourite Rush release, I became the singalong guy! I knew it was going to be a special show. I liked the new album a lot. I avoided any set list spoilers posted online. I preferred to experience the concert like I did in the 1980s. I wanted to be surprised. I wanted to watch my son's reactions and share that with him at the same time. He had budded into a pretty big Rush fan by this point.

'Entre Nous', 'Mission', 'Freewill' and 'Main Monkey Business' left me breathless. This was one great set list. We got the 'Passage to Bangkok' encore and I can still clearly see Alex smile as he played the 'Chinese' part usually played by Neil. A perfect end to a perfect concert.

GERMAIN AMPHITHEATER

2 SEPTEMBER 2007, COLUMBUS, OHIO

I WAS THERE: CASSIE WEDGE NESSLEY

My dad played them my whole life. Most kids probably don't care for their parents' music but Rush hit me right in the soul. Their lyrics, their music, all so carefully thought out and painstakingly put together. I had the great joy of seeing that majestic trio twice in my life. It would have been three times if I'd had a little more money the third time around. I saw the *Snakes & Arrows* and *R40* tours. I also surprised my dad with *Vapor Trails* tickets. He took my mom as his guest instead of me. She had never seen them, so it was time! They were great every time. No matter how hard they may have been on themselves, Neil especially, if a show wasn't as good as they thought it could be, it was all magic to us.

MARCUS AMPHITHEATER

6 SEPTEMBER 2007, MILWAUKEE, WISCONSIN

I WAS THERE: EDDY SCHURING

I used to hang out with my cousins and they said, 'Dude, listen to this.' It was *Moving Pictures*. I thought then that if I was ever to be a dad I would take my kids to see this band. That's how impressed I was. They were precise and they were intricate. It wasn't your standard four bar stuff with power chords that's been done so often.

I took Tye, my 10-year-old, to the *Snakes & Arrows* show in Indianapolis. We were 12th row centre but got down front and this couple said, 'Our friend didn't show up. Would you like to sit with us on the second row?' So we were right in front of Geddy. A week later we saw them in Milwaukee and we're second row again. With

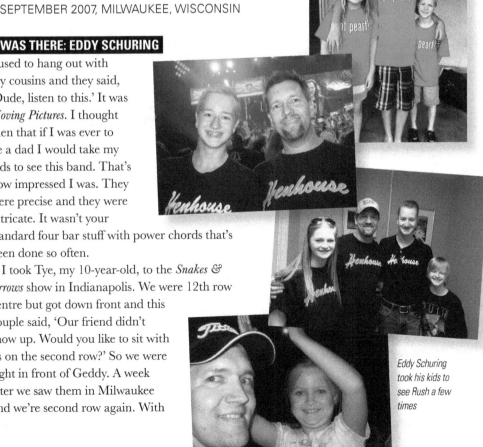

Eddy Schuring took his kids to see Rush a few times

about an hour left of the show a tech comes out, offers me a wadded up t-shirt and says, 'This is for him from Geddy' and we look up and Geddy is there on this little shoulder of the stage and we say 'thank you' and Geddy says, 'You're welcome'. While he's playing!

On the second leg of the tour, Tye wore the t-shirt that he got from Geddy. We're totally enthralled in their music and I said to Tye, 'Why don't you go and hang out up in the front row?' Geddy comes out and there's Tye - five feet tall, blond hair, with a Rush hat on, back to front. He points at his shirt with two fingers then points at Geddy and then back to the shirt to say, 'Dude, you gave this to me.' All of a sudden Geddy pulls his hand off his bass and points at him, and then at the end of the show Alex comes over and hands my son his pick.

I took all three of them – Tye, Aidan and Piper - to an outdoor show at Deer Creek. At the end of the show, Alex and Geddy came over and looked down at me and I shrugged my shoulders because I'm holding my two little ones. One's five and one's seven and we're front row. A tech comes out and hands all three a t-shirt. Because it was the last show of the tour they were throwing out all of their merch from the stage. They must have thrown out 50 pairs of drumsticks. And Geddy comes over with a stuffed animal and hands it to my daughter, Piper.

We saw the *Time Machine* tour in Chicago. Aidan was on my shoulders. The tech came out and said, 'Neil wants you to play with these sticks.' Not 'Neil wants you to *have* these'. It was '*play* with these sticks.' Aidan had been air drumming all night on my shoulders. And then, at the end of the show, when they're playing 'Working Man', Alex and Geddy come out and point to Aidan and jam with him for about 20 seconds. It's on YouTube.

MADISON SQUARE GARDEN

17 SEPTEMBER, 2007, NEW YORK, NEW YORK

I WAS THERE: SKIP DALY

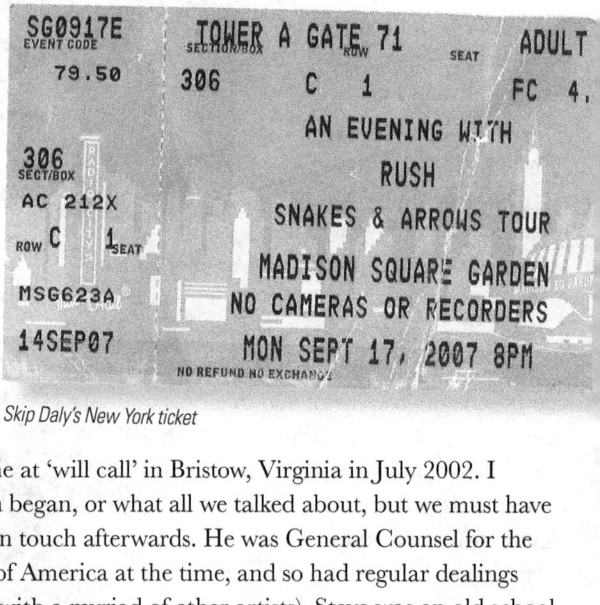

Skip Daly's New York ticket

Friendships can sometimes begin under the most random circumstances. My friendship with Steve Marks began when we were both waiting in line at 'will call' in Bristow, Virginia in July 2002. I don't recall how the conversation began, or what all we talked about, but we must have both enjoyed it because we kept in touch afterwards. He was General Counsel for the Recording Industry Association of America at the time, and so had regular dealings with Rush's management (along with a myriad of other artists). Steve was an old school Rush fan, having first seen them back in 1981. His first show was the infamous 'teargas gig' in Hollywood, Florida – a story that he delighted in relating. That concert had been the first one after a 10-day break in touring, and Neil Peart was late in arriving due to air travel issues. The venue manager didn't want to open doors until he was sure that the band had all arrived, lest there be a riot inside the building – so the crowd outside got more and more unruly, with the police department eventually unleashing teargas in an attempt to quell the unrest. In the end, Neil arrived and the band took the stage (albeit a little late). Why am I telling this story of Steve's first show here? Stay tuned....

After meeting in 2002, whenever Steve and I would catch up over the following years, I would always good-naturedly tease him about how his kids kept 'stealing' my 'plus one' slot. I was friendly with Pegi Cecconi, from Rush's management but Steve, through his job credentials, really had a class A hookup. Pegi kindly connected me with meet and greets and great seats, but Steve would get the coveted VIP laminate, which allowed him to catch soundchecks and travel anywhere backstage outside of the band's private dressing room. Alas, for all of the local gigs, he would inevitably take one of his kids as his guest (the nerve of the guy!). We hatched a plan – we would road trip to a show, to avoid those awkward familial attachments, and he could bring me as his 'plus one', guilt-free! It took us until September, 2007, but we made plans to travel up to New York for one of the last 2007 North American dates on the *Snakes & Arrows* tour. Steve was in New York on business anyway, so I took a day off work and travelled up by train to meet him. We met at Madison Square Garden (still my only trip to that famous venue) and retrieved our tickets and passes from Will Call. Alas, we were too late for soundcheck, but we briefly wandered backstage and found Pegi to say hello and thank her. Then it was back out front for the show (which was excellent).

After the show, we went backstage, and ended up being directed over to a group of five or six guys from Atlantic Records. Pegi was still around, as well as the ever-friendly Andy Curran. We were escorted into a small room with some food and drinks and then Geddy and Alex came in. They ended up spending about 20 minutes with the seven or eight of us, just chatting in this small room backstage. A few of the Atlantic guys ended up in one corner with Alex, while two Atlantic reps stood with Steve and I in another corner, chatting with Geddy.

At some point, one of the Atlantic guys starts in with, 'I remember the first time I saw Rush. It was...blah blah blah...' Geddy nods politely, and then the second Atlantic guy starts telling his introductory story. At this point, Steve and I make eye contact, and I just start laughing to myself, because I know he holds the ace card. He then says, 'The first time I saw Rush, it sucked, because I got teargassed!' Everyone goes quiet and Geddy looks over at him, peering over the top of his glasses, and says, 'Miami!' Steve and Geddy then tell the story for the others, completing each other's sentences at times.

Geddy then says, 'Guys, I actually have another story about that show. I was in France just a few years ago doing a tour of wineries, and we're catching cabs at the end of the night to go back to the hotel. My buddies went on ahead so I ended up in the back of this cab, in the middle between these two other guys who had been on the winery tour. As we're driving back, the oddest thing happened – a Rush song came on the radio, which is pretty weird in France. One of the guys in the back starts talking about how he liked this band, and the other guy says, 'Yeah, Rush! I saw them in concert years ago in Florida, and we got teargassed,' and he tells this whole story about it. They're going on and on and I'm just quietly sitting there. Finally, they finish the story and there's silence, and I just look over and say, 'Hey, I was at that gig too!'

AIR CANADA CENTRE

19 SEPTEMBER 2007, TORONTO, CANADA

I WAS THERE: BRETT DAVIS

Our high school had them booked during their early days with John Rutsey, but they increased their gig fee by $500 to $1,500, so we had to settle for Triumph. Fast forward many years....

During the late 70s or early 80s, I was working at Baton Broadcasting, Channel 9 (the precursor to the CTV network in Canada) when I literally ran into a very young but shy

Photos - Brett Davis

Alex Lifeson in the hallway. He was heading to the commissary for lunch and I was finishing my lunch break. I recall telling him to skip the meatloaf. Later, after uni and marriage, I was handling a client by the name of Al Weinrib. I noticed he looked like Geddy's twin. It turned out it's his younger brother and he was working on a Rush video, and we were shooting it and later editing it.

Shortly after my son James took up drums, Rush were on their *Snakes & Arrows* tour and I thought I'd take him to see the world's best drummer. James was 12 at the time and it was his first concert. We were both blown away. It was then that I regretted not going to more concerts during my youth and specifically more Rush concerts. We made their *Clockwork Angels* show at Copps Coliseum in Hamilton, Ontario. Our seats were on the floor but back a bit, in front of the mixing and lighting boards. They were great seats.

Brett Davis took his drummer son James to three Rush shows

For their *R40* tour in Toronto, my wife Laurie surprised us with fourth row centre. It was the biggest thrill for both of us, being so close to Neil, Geddy and Alex. After their finale Alex flicked his guitar pick right into James' lap! The only thing missing in that concert was Neil's drum solo. Back issues... As for my hearing, I think it came back nearly three weeks afterwards.

My younger daughter Von was the first to let me know of Neil's passing and she told me how sorry she was for me. Boy, kids do surprise parents at times. When I got word of Neil's passing I was truly devastated, as was my son when I told him. We both knew that Neil hung up the sticks after *R40*, but if there was to be a reunion tour, we'd be there with bells on.

Von never expressed an interest in seeing Rush but I snapped up four tickets to see the worldwide release of their *R40* movie. Just like going to their concert, we old folks had on our Rush concert tees. Mine was their *R40* shirt. Von got a kick out of this, and she didn't even mind her old man shouting out 'hey!' and pointing both hands into the air during the chorus of '2112'. That the film was edited from both Toronto shows was even more thrilling. I saw Alex flicking his pick into the audience. Was it the one that landed in James' lap?

SCOTTISH EXHIBITION & CONFERENCE CENTRE

3 OCTOBER 2007, GLASGOW, UK

I WAS THERE: GORDON SEMPLE

Gordon Semple gave Alex a Jack Nicklaus £5 note

Just as *Moving Pictures* came out, I spotted a competition in the local press to win this album. No-one else I knew was into the band so why the hell would this be in a local newspaper in rural Scotland? I duly filled in the questionnaire and sent off the answers. A fortnight later a bloke said to me, 'Your name is in the newspaper!' I had won the competition and was to collect the album at the local office.

Here was me thinking that the press would be out in numbers, taking my pic for the next week's edition, etc. I even had my best denim jacket on. I entered the office, to be met by an elderly lady, sat in the corner of the office with blue hair dye, wing-edged specs and a Woodbine hanging off her lips. The whole works.

I told her I was there to collect my prize and showing little interest she just handed me the album. I smugly asked, 'How many people were in the competition then?' Deadpan, she replied, 'Just you son, just you…'

The night before Rush played Glasgow on the *Snakes & Arrows* tour, my mate Hugh Fitzpatrick texted to say he'd won a meet and greet. I was naturally very excited to meet Lifeson and Lee, and we decided to go in the last of the groups, hoping to have a bit more time with them. However it was last in, first up for the meet. But Alex was running a bit late, we got a few minutes alone with Geddy for a wee chat.

I had brought a Jack Nicklaus limited edition Scottish £5 note to give to Alex as he has a love of all things golf. Alex holding the fiver I gave him is on the *Beyond the Lighted Stage* DVD, much to the mirth of my long term Rush mates, who still rips me to this day about giving cash to a multi-millionaire. My mate Baldie Pete also made it onto the DVD. He was caught rocking out with Mick Paz in the front row.

The 114 show *Snakes & Arrows* tour was Rush's second longest after *Hemispheres* and grossed nearly $65 million.

WEMBLEY ARENA

9 & 10 OCTOBER 2007, LONDON, UK

I WAS THERE: DAN TORDJMAN

Rush and France always seemed to have a love /hate relationship. Rush toured France just once, for *Roll the Bones*. There are not so many Rush fans in France as there are in North America. But this small number of fans is definitely as devoted as American or Canadian fans. My first encounter with Rush goes back to the mid-90s. It was late December and Geddy Lee was voted number one in a guitar magazine's 'best of the year' feature. I was intrigued. I didn't hear Rush until a few years later. The song was 'The Pass' and it was love at first hearing. I was 18 years old.

I began exploring Rush's discography with *Exit... Stage Left*. 'Jacob's Ladder' made me go, 'What the hell is that?' I knew I was in for an endless, fantastic ride. I got all the albums. Besides the quality of the band's music, the graphic design genius of Hugh Syme made it interesting to me. Being able to see them live was obviously on my bucket list.

Miracles can happen sometimes. Mine happened on the *Snakes & Arrows* tour. It was a rainy day in London. Maybe that's why the doors opened earlier than planned, to make sure we didn't get wet before show time. We were in the entrance hearing 'Subdivisions' during the soundcheck. I went nuts at the merch store. I just thought, 'It's going to be the only time I'll see them. Let's make it a day to remember, for me - and my credit card!' I was like a kid in a candy store.

I didn't want any spoilers on the set list. That moment had to be authentic. I had the blast of my life, especially when the chef came on stage to baste the chickens in the rotisserie ovens. I relate to one line written by The Professor: we're only immortal for a limited time. That was definitely relevant when I first heard about his passing.

I WAS THERE: STEVE PLEDGER

I was going to see them at Wembley and at the NEC. I was buying the tickets for Wembley and was thrilled to get eighth row. My friend Simon was impressed, but not quite as impressed as I felt he should. 'Not bad, eh?' I enquired. 'No, that's great.' I asked him how he had got on as he was buying tickets for the Wembley show I had decided not to go to. He had managed to get front row. I was happy for him, of course, but gutted that I was missing miss out on the holy grail of concert tickets. He called me the next day. He'd booked one too many tickets by mistake and did I want to buy the extra one, face value? Thankfully my wife recognised the magnitude of this and immediately gave the thumbs-up.

Slap-bang in front of Geddy's keys we witnessed the wonder of Rush live. One of my favourite memories is of us giving Geddy the whole 'we're not worthy!' bow and him smiling at us and humbly shaking his head. We did the same to Alex, of course, when he came over stage left and he smiled and gave us an arch look and nodded as if to say, 'Damn right!'

I wish they'd made it to the UK one more time. The *Clockwork Angels* tour proved to be the only time I didn't get to see them during my years following their music. The songs of Rush and the path they took have informed and accompanied me along my own way and their music moves and thrills me to this day. It's different now, now I'm older, now the band is no more. Now that Neil has journeyed on. But it's no less rich or rewarding, and maybe it's somehow even deeper because of those things. It's with me still and will remain so, until the candle is burned.

NATIONAL EXHIBITION CENTRE

12 OCTOBER 2007, BIRMINGHAM, UK

I WAS THERE: JORD NEALE

I was lucky enough to see them play on the *Snakes & Arrows*, *Time Machine* and *Clockwork Angels* tours.

I started playing drums at the age of eight. After discovering my dad's copy of *Fly by Night*, I became completely invested in and obsessed with the band and started collecting the back catalogue and immersing myself in it. Everything that makes them great on record comes alive in a live setting. The musicianship and delivery knocks you for six while the amazing stage show, production and sound complements the songs and

Jord Neale saw Rush three times at Birmingham's NEC

keeps you totally fixed on the band while they deliver every song with pin point accuracy and passion.

The three tours I was lucky enough to see them on were all absolutely electric and unforgettable experiences. To see my musical heroes do what they do best first hand was an honour and a privilege.

I WAS THERE: MATTHEW BOOTH

I got into Rush through my uncle, Peter. I was about 14 or 15 and he burned a CD rock mix for me which included 'Red Barchetta't. Then he gave me a few Rush albums and one of the first ones to grab my ears was *Show of Hands*. That was recorded in Birmingham, which is where I saw Rush three times. I dialled into their music in the 80s synthesiser age and then went forwards as well as backwards with their music. That first concert I went to, at the NEC with my uncle, had three generations of families there, both men and women. Rush didn't just write to the heart. They wrote to the head too, covering a lot of topics, making them different from the mainstream. They looked like they were playing for the joy of it. Some bands seem to do it just for a pay day. They kept their music fresh, even to the last album.

I WAS THERE: STEVE LEE

This was the last time I saw them perform live. I drove to the NEC alone. I had a floor seat, about halfway back and reasonably central. They played their socks off and included some rare tracks which was a real treat. I particularly enjoyed 'Mission', 'Freewill', 'Circumstances', 'The Trees' and 'Witch Hunt'. Only certain songs on *Snakes & Arrows* have properly clicked with me and although I loved the show and seeing the guys live again, I hadn't felt the desired emotional contact with certain songs.

I missed the release of *Clockwork Angels*. I had listened to snatches of 'Caravan' and 'BU2B' on Amazon and didn't make the purchase. I was on holiday and unaware Rush were in the UK in May 2013. Soon afterwards I purchased *Clockwork Angels* and fell in love with it. To this day I kick myself for not buying it on release day and not rescheduling that holiday! I have the live Blu-ray, which is great to watch. But there's no substitute for being there.

R40 never reached Europe. I was aware of Neil's thoughts and issues and I respected his reasoning. I felt I had a greater understanding of the man from reading his travelogues.

At 50, I sometimes fail to remember what I did five minutes ago. At 50, I can still play *Fly by Night*, *Moving Pictures*, *Presto*, or any other album, older or more recent, and know the words, solos, drum fills and basslines by heart. That is the hold Rush takes on you. Neil has passed – into legend – but the memory of Rush is undiminished.

I WAS THERE: STEVE POTTER

In 2007, I saw them in Sheffield and then at the NEC, on the front row with my brother and my wife, Emma. At the end of the main set, Alex threw his pick to Emma but it fell into the pit. The security guard picked it up, put his hands behind his back and faced away from us, the pick resting on the palm of his hand: 'Who wants it?' I didn't make a move for it because I thought Emma would but she was slow on the uptake and my brother got there first!

Steve Potter was front row again at the NEC in 2007

For the *Time Machine* tour I saw them in Manchester, Sheffield, Birmingham, London and Glasgow. It was great to see them up in Scotland. The Glasgow crowd are an amazing crowd.

MANCHESTER EVENING NEWS ARENA

14 OCTOBER 2007, MANCHESTER, UK

I WAS THERE: CATHY SHEARD

My late husband had been a Rush fan since he was a kid but never seen them in real life. I'd heard them in our house and seen them on DVD but wasn't that into them. When we went to the gig and all the crazy, amazing lights and strobes set off and the band appeared, I was star struck. They were proper musicians and Geddy's unique voice just made the whole thing a quite special experience. Neil Peart did a drum solo and it was amazing. All the cameras were at different angles and the images projected on the screens showed you his amazing talent. The concert was a crazy mix of short sketches, with the band dressed up, and amazing lighting. I am so glad my husband got to experience his favourite band before he died. I put something in the newspaper this year that he is with Neil Peart now that Neil has also sadly passed away.

COLISEO JOSÉ MIGUEL AGRELOT

11 APRIL 2008, SAN JUAN, PUERTO RICO

I WAS THERE: DEE VAZQUEZ, AGE 38

I've been a fan since *Moving Pictures* when I was aged 11. Finally Rush had come to Puerto Rico. I took my 20 year old niece. She didn't know anything about Rush at it was her first major stadium concert, and she never sat down or closed her mouth once during the concert. After the show she said, 'Screw these new bands. Those old guys are gods!' That night a new fan was born. One of her favourite records right now is *Permanent Waves*. She wasn't born when it was released in 1980. And my t-shirt from that night is framed, never to be used.

NEW ORLEANS ARENA

20 APRIL 2008, NEW ORLEANS, LOUISIANA

I WAS THERE: AMY DAVID VALENTINE

I had recently landed my dream job when I found out that Rush were playing New Orleans. *Snakes & Arrows* had dropped and I had been listening to it in my car constantly during lunch breaks. I brought my spouse to the show along with his two brothers. At one point during the show, as I was jamming out to 'Red Barchetta' and watching a father and young son staring in awe at The Boys, one of my brothers-in-law turned to me and said, 'Damn! I never realised this guitar player kicks ass!' I had to smile and do a 'thumbs up', because Alex is criminally underrated at times. I love sharing Rush and then watching them receive the recognition they so deserve. After the show, an older man saw us and asked had we just seen Rush. We all nodded, smiling, and he said he had to choose between seeing them and going to the Hornets game. For us, this was a no-brainer.

NOKIA LIVE

6 & 7 MAY 2008, LOS ANGELES, CALIFORNIA

I WAS THERE: ZAC IMPERIAL

This was going to be my first rock concert ever with my dad, with our favourite rock band of all time. As we neared the chamber, grabbing our drinks and seats, all I could hear was dull roars and the murmurs of the surrounding crowd. Anticipation was high; I was guessing what songs they would play the whole time, with my then-limited knowledge of their catalogue. I was asking my dad questions, since he had gone to several Rush concerts before, but he simply told me to be patient.

Zac Imperial saw his first Rush show – his first ever show – with his dad

The animations and lights, not to mention the overall performance from the legendary men of the craft, were all fathomable. The set was equally amazing: the likes of 'The Main Monkey Business', 'Spindrift', 'Far Cry' and 'Workin' Them Angels' (which I have always associated with my dad), were all incredible to see live, as well as songs I never thought I'd hear like 'Ghost of a Chance', 'Freewill', 'The Trees', 'Between the Wheels', 'Passage to Bangkok' and 'Witch Hunt'.

The penultimate moment of excitement was when Neil Peart performed his drum solo. Breathtaking as it was, what was more impressive was that this older master musician still had the fortitude to not only perform a very physically demanding act of a drum solo for over ten minutes, but do these three hour shows consistently with his measure of perfection in mind every night. I have never been so happy to not be able to hear for three days.

I saw them a couple of times more, always latching onto moments that made the experience so wonderful: the ten minute drum solos, the creative and thematic intros and transitional movies like in the *Time Machine* tour, Alex's acoustic improvisations, the adapted arrangements to some songs such as the length for 'The Camera Eye' or tempo for 'Analog Kid', the full orchestral accompaniment - and even my neighbour spilling his beer on my leg!

The whole thing was so magical, every strange and wonderful moment capping off one show after another. When they announced their *R40* tour, I didn't have money, I was struggling with work and school, and I thought I could see them another time. But something told me that it might be the last chance. Against all logic, I acquired two tickets at scalper prices and took my soon-to-be wife to Inglewood, California. I bought a poster, they played my favourite song off *Clockwork Angels*, I got to watch the original violin player for 'Losing It' perform with them, and most of all I got to watch Neil play three solos across two drum sets.

I was still sceptical whether or not it was actually done. When I read the article that they were no longer doing big tours, I started believing, but not until Neil's passing did I realise how truly lucky I was to be able to say I seen the legendary band, Rush, live in concert.

Jarrett Tupper's t-shirt was too small but he wore it anyway

BRANDT CENTER

25 MAY 2008, REGINA, CANADA

I WAS THERE: JARRETT TUPPER

Ever since hearing Rush at 12 years old, I'd always wanted to see them live. The first chance came during their *Snakes & Arrows* tour. I wore an original *Permanent Waves* 1980 tour shirt that night. It was too small but it didn't matter. I remember waiting outside the doors and chatting with a few people about how exciting seeing Rush would be. The doors opened and I found my seat. From the opening riff of 'Limelight' until the last notes of 'YYZ' faded away and Geddy announced 'good night', I was in complete musical shock. I had just witnessed my favourite band play for two and a half hours straight!

The second and final time was at the SaskTel Center in Saskatoon during the *Clockwork Angels* tour. It felt like I was the only person in the room. My eyes were on Neil for most of those shows. Watching him flawlessly pound out every rhythm and fill with precision confirmed his position as one of the greats. Geddy's pulsing bass and synth lines weaved in and out while Alex's stringed fury intertwined, making the musical landscape that is Rush. From the intro of 'Subdivisions' to the string section in the second set to the final sonic assault that is '2112', my dream of seeing my favourite band had been achieved twice over.

STARLIGHT THEATRE

7 JUNE 2008, KANSAS CITY, MISSOURI

I WAS THERE: DUG SHELBY

Dug Shelby rode 1,200 miles in 26 hours to see Rush

I looked at my haphazardly precarious creation one last time. My trusty motorcycle was loaded up with probably too much, and I wanted to make sure the tangled web of bungee cords was securing the load properly. It was going to be a long ride in general, but specifically today. If everything worked out, by tomorrow I would be in Kansas City - 1,200 miles away - listening to my favourite band in the world, and hopefully from inside the Starlight Amphitheater and not all alone in the parking lot.

I was moving back to the West Coast from Virginia Beach. Rush were on tour and were headed east from the west coast. I had been watching the dates and it became very clear: their date at the Starlight would be my only chance to see them on this tour. Things came together in a rushed and haphazard manner and I wasn't able to buy a ticket beforehand.

My last inspection complete, I slid into the saddle, adjusted my gloves and started her up. I had 26 hours until show time, and quite a few miles to go. My plan would be to roll into Kansas City, grab a hotel room, take a shower and make my way to the Amphitheater. I didn't have a ticket, but I had set aside $100 so that I could buy the cheapest ticket a scalper had in the parking lot. I just wanted to be inside. If I could be inside, I'd be happy. I would probably have enough left over for a shirt and a beer.

With this solidly unsolid plan, I pointed my two-wheeled friend westward. Neil would like this, I thought. The lyrics to 'Ghost Rider', about how 'nothing can stop me now', sprang to my mind easily, as they often do when I'm on a journey by motorcycle:

I wish I could tell you the ride was memorable, but it was just a jumble of interstate pavement, energy drinks, and crappy food. I only have two real memories that stuck with me: One, taking a quick 15 minute nap in the parking lot of a convenience store, sitting upright in the saddle, helmet and gloves still on. The other, waking up as I was heading into the slow lane of Interstate 40, and seeing another motorcyclist looking back at me slightly panicked as I approached him from behind, his left hand extended out frantically waving me off. Had I really just dozed off while riding my bike? How is that even possible?

I pulled off the road, furious with myself, stomping circles around my bike and audibly (and loudly) lecturing myself. I was embarrassed, thankful to be alive and severely disappointed in myself. That poor guy... he must have been panicked! 25 hours later, I rolled into Kansas City, hot, still alive, but exhausted. I had barely slept now for two days, I had just ridden 1,200 miles and I had one hour to check into a hotel, grab a shower, get to the Amphitheater and try to find a ticket to the show.

When I arrived at the Amphitheater, it was hot and balmy. I was surprised: not a single scalper selling tickets or even t-shirts! The Starlight Amphitheater was most definitely a family-friendly venue. I assessed the situation and headed immediately to the last option: the ticket office. I'd heard the show was sold out. Things weren't looking good. Just as I arrived at the ticket office, the pre-show video started. Oh no! Why did the boys have to be so punctual? I asked the gentleman in the ticket booth for the cheapest ticket he still had available. He said they had one, and said it was on the left side of the Amphitheater, almost at the very back row. I said I'd take it, ecstatic that I'd actually be inside! I love it when a plan comes together, I thought!

'What about that one ticket?' I looked up, and there was a girl poking her head around the corner of the ticket office. 'Oh, yes...' replied the ticket booth gentleman. 'There *is* one other ticket, it's a little closer, but it's more expensive. $94.50, if you'd like that one.' 'Closer? I'll take it! Thank you!' Anywhere closer than the very back row was fine with me! Although this all but assured there would be no t-shirts, beers or a hot dog, 'closer' is always worth it.

With the sound of the opening intro ringing in my ears (Jerry Stiller being hilarious as always, to be exact), I went to the entrance. This began one of the most surreal few minutes of my life. I handed the ticket to the lady at the gate, and she motioned next to head straight across. Well, I'm at least no worse than right in the middle, I thought. Awesome! I got to a spot in the middle, and wasn't sure where my next move was. Showing my ticket to another Amphitheater staff member, they motioned me down and forward. 'I'm closer than half way up?' I was ecstatic! I again presented my ticket to another staff person. He unlatched the rope partition we were standing next to, and motioned me down. Again. What's going on? I'm now within the first 20 rows. I take a few steps, turn around and look questioningly to the staff member. He motions to 'keep going, keep going.' So I do. I'm now at another roped off section. Row 5. Again

I present this ticket which seems to be infused with unheard of magic powers. The staff member glances at the ticket, unhooks the velvet rope partition and motions me through. I'm sure they're going to realise their mistake shortly and take me up to the last row, but no one approaches me. The numbers and letters on the ticket are starting to make sense now, as they more closely match the seats I'm standing next to. Fourth row? No. Third? Keep going. Second? Not matching.

I'm in the first row. What's going on? Did I actually crash my bike, hit my head and now I'm having some type of medicinally-induced coma dream in a Kansas City hospital? There's five sections to the front row. My ticket says I'm in section three. The middle? Fifteen seats in each row. My ticket says seat 8. The very middle seat in the very middle row of the very first row?

'What about that one ticket?'

I get to my seat...the guys are onstage, just getting into their opening song. I look on the stage in front of me. There's a '0' directly in front of me. To each side, there's increasing numbers from '1' and increasing. Stage markings for true centre! I literally pinched myself.

There were about 12 guys spread throughout the first few rows wearing orange movers jumpsuits, obviously an homage to 'Moving Pictures.' Standing next to and in front of several, we started talking.

'You made it! Good to see you! We were starting to wonder whose seat that was!' 'Thank you, good to be here, it's been a journey,' I replied. 'We've been securing as many of these tickets as we could for months, our group likes to hit as many shows as possible. We always dress up in the jumpsuits. We've been to about 60 shows like this now!' Jumpsuit Guy tells me. 'We've been getting as many tickets close together for months. How much was your ticket? We paid around $1,100 average for these, some more expensive....'

'Well, I just got...' I started. 'When did you get yours?' He yells over the song. 'I didn't have a ticket. I just rode my motorcycle 25 hours straight, 1,200 miles to get to the show, I came straight here. I got the ticket at the box office...it was $94.50.'

His face froze. The look told me he was calculating what I said, trying to figure out if he just misheard me because 'Limelight' was blaring at full volume, or if he had actually heard what he thought he had just heard. 'Just NOW? Ninety-five bucks? JUST NOW?' I nodded. My look must have displayed as much amazement as he felt, and he turned to his friends and told them what he had just heard.

At the intermission, the Orange Jumpsuit Brigade gathered around, and I told them the story. I told them I brought $100 because that's all I had, as I was moving back to the west coast, and this was the only show I'd be able to get to. 'We're buying you a beer! And something to eat! This is incredible!' The Orange Jumpsuit Brigade leader exclaims. And buy me a beer and a hot dog they did. I didn't get a t-shirt from this show, but I got so, so much more. I made new friends, and watched a few old friends from front row centre. Sadly, I never got the Jumpsuit Brigade's contact information, but I've paid it forward at later shows many times over.

I'll never forget the one time I got to a Rush show late, exhausted and weary, and heard those enchanted words. 'What about that one ticket?'

VERIZON WIRELESS AMPHITHEATRE

20 JULY 2008, CHARLOTTE, NORTH CAROLINA

Sam Dyar got to meet Rush thanks to the Make-A-Wish charity - photo John Dyar

I WAS THERE: SAMANTHA DYAR

I looked out to where 10,000 people would soon be standing to hear the band that I was about to meet. It was surreal. Ever since I was four, I had dreamed of meeting them. I had wanted to meet them for most of my life. As I grew, they became some of my heroes. Then when I was diagnosed with cancer in August of 2007, my world changed. The one thing that remained consistent was my family and their music. Three months into treatment, Make-a-Wish, a non-profit organisation, came to me and told me that I had a wish. I could do anything but get a car or a swimming pool. The things that I could do were numerous. I thought about it until the day they came to get my wish. Finally making my decision, I told them that I wanted to meet Rush.

The morning of July 20th, we went to the Verizon Wireless Amphitheater in Charlotte, North Carolina. We met with the head of security the band liaison, Kevin Ripa, who gave my family and I a tour of the stage, backstage and the dressing rooms. I got to meet the techs for the band: Bucky, the guitar tech, Gump, the drum tech, and Russ, the bass and keyboard tech. I even got to sit at Neil Peart's drum kit and hold Alex Lifeson's 1976 Gibson ES-355. After that we went to the back to wait for the band's arrival. I sat in on a security meeting and then I went back onto the stage to meet them. I first saw Geddy Lee. I was in awe. He smiled and gave me a hug. We started to talk a little when I saw a man in a white shirt and baseball cap come up. I did not notice who it was at first, I thought he was just some guy. Then I looked again. It was Neil Peart, one of my heroes. My emotions overcame me and I started to cry. At that point Neil gave me a hug.

The last to arrive on stage was Alex Lifeson. He was a good natured person and a fun person to talk to. I told him that I listened to the song 'Hope' over and over during my chemo treatments and the song meant a lot to me. That made him smile. After a little talking, the band went to their respective parts of the stage for the sound check. I went off the stage and to the rail at the front row. They played a few songs including 'Subdivisions', 'The Trees' and 'Ghost of a Chance'. I then took a moment to take in where I was and what I was doing. I engraved everything on my mind, forgetting all else. It was like being in a perfect world, filled with music.

I went back on stage and Alex played the song 'Hope' for me, which made me cry because of what it meant to me during my treatment. When the sound check was over, the band signed a few things including my copy of *Roadshow*. Neil signed it, 'To Samantha, You can get back on! Neil Peart.' I told him that my illness was like the lyrics in 'Far Cry' that go 'some days I feel I'm ahead of the wheel and the next it's rolling over me.' Neil also gave me the sticks he used for the sound check.

Alex and Geddy gave me a bunch of picks. Geddy also gave me a 'Henhouse' t-shirt, all generous gifts. I was also able to tell the band what their music has meant to me and my family, and also thank them for it. Then the meet was over. It was an amazing two hours for me and my family. But the night was just beginning.

We went to the concert where we had fifth row seats. During the first couple of songs, Kevin Ripa called me up on stage. After the song 'Ghost of a Chance', Geddy walked up to the mic to talk to the crowd for the first time. After saying hello, he mentioned that they had 'a ton of material' for the crowd. He then said, 'But first, we would like to dedicate this next song to my friend Sam. This is from *Hold Your Fire*, it's called 'Mission'.' 'Mission' is one of my very favourite songs and Geddy told me while we were talking that it was his favourite song to play. For the third time that day, I cried.

Watching the band play that song from on stage was overwhelming especially since they were playing it for me. The rest of the concert was phenomenal, and the day was one that I will never forget. My dad and I also attended the Atlanta show two days later. I met many people there that were also at the Charlotte show who asked me about the song dedication. I was nice meeting everyone. I just told them that Make-A-Wish and Rush made it all possible. It was an unreal couple of days. Thank you Rush and thank you Make-A-Wish!

I WAS THERE: JOHN DYAR

My daughter Sam started going to concerts with me when she was four. We saw Rush around 10 times, during which time Sam endured three bouts of cancer. In 2008, and thanks to Make-A-Wish, Sam got to meet Rush. We spent the entire day with the band, including the sound check, and had third row seats for the show. She got an all access pass and could roam around backstage any time she wanted. It was an extraordinary day. They treated our entire family very special. Seeing her so happy after seeing her so sick for so long was so unbelievably heart warming.

Alex sat on stage and played 'Hope' for Sam while she watched from five feet away. She sobbed. That was her theme song during her fight. Another highlight was Geddy dedicating 'Mission' to her while she was watching from the stage. I'd never heard Geddy dedicate a song before. And yet another was after sound check, watching Neil walk up to Sam and hug her and then hand her the sticks he used during sound check.

We ended up seeing them together around 30 times, the last couple of times in Toronto and Montreal for *R40*. We went to Le Studio together too. Sam is doing great with no reoccurrence of the 'c' word. She received a Masters degree from UGA and works as a social worker in a hospital emergency room. She was and still is a true fan. But the apple didn't fall far from the tree. I'm a fan too.

I WAS THERE: TIM KLINE

It was mid-March in 2008 when I learned tickets were going on sale. We lived in the Smoky Mountains so got tickets for the Charlotte, North Carolina show and were on top of the world. We planned a vacation for that week, starting with a Rush concert. There's no better way to start a vacation!

Come July we left home early morning so we could get a motel room close to the venue. Meanwhile, my brother-in-law had gotten a ticket the same day we did, and next to us - go figure! He brought brownies so we were definitely aboard the Thailand Express. We got to the Amphitheater about 30 minutes before show time. The excitement amongst the crowd was so thick you could cut it with a knife. The film began for the *Snakes & Arrows* tour and Alex came on stage and opened with 'Limelight' before going directly into 'Digital Man'.

This show was my only time ever seeing them play a full show. The highlight of the first half for me was when they played 'Ghost of a Chance' and 'Natural Science'. Of course, we ate more brownies during intermission! The second half movie was pretty awesome. The second half opened with 'Far Cry', 'Angels', 'The Larger Bowl' with Bob and Doug McKenzie, then the *South Park* short for 'Tom Sawyer' and then - Neil's solo! I've never seen synchronised air drumming before, but I witnessed it on that night.

The *Time Machine* tour took in 82 dates between June 2010 and July 2011. It saw the band play material from their latest albums going back to their earliest, with an innovative stage set up that was a tour highlight for many fans.

WHITE RIVER AMPHITHEATRE

7 AUGUST 2010, AUBURN, WASHINGTON

I WAS THERE: JOHN RIVERA

In 1982 I joined the US Navy. I bought *Signals* on cassette. It was a bit different from previous Rush recordings but I liked 'Analog Kid' and 'New World Man'. I lost touch with Rush due to military life, married life and several moves. In late 2009, AXS TV were playing *Rush in Rio*. I stood alone in the living room behind the couch watching these three older guys tearing up the stage in front of a throng of people, Alex shredding the guitar like a teenager, Neil hitting the skins with fervour and precision and Geddy playing bass while singing and playing keyboard. My jaw just dropped and I said aloud to no one, 'Holy shit, these guys got better.'

When the *Time Machine* tour was announced, I asked a friend to buy tickets for me and my then 16 year-old son. We arrived at the White River Amphitheater early enough to be the first car in line to park, what I dubbed 'groupie hour'. It's now affectionately the term we use to say we are arriving early to whatever event we go to. I walked to the ticket booth and if I could upgrade my seats. The attendant typed on her computer for a second and to disbelief said, 'How about section two… row… six?' My credit card literally flew out of my wallet. I don't think my feet touched the ground as I returned to my car to tell my son.

We got in the gate and walked 'down' instead of up to our seats. We took our seats and I noticed we were centre stage. We were one of the first ones in our seats and just took in that we were so close. And I took in the fact I was with my son and sharing with him a band who I have loved for years. Just before the band took the stage, I told my son, 'Look behind us. Everyone is behind us instead of in front of us. Oh, yeah!' Big smiles.

The percussion centre was draped in the now familiar black cloth. The lights went down and a video started. It was new to me. I thought to myself, 'If the video was this good then the show will be awesome.' I was not disappointed. The band took the stage and the cloth was removed. Neil's set was somewhat reduced but now included electronic drums. It still gleamed. I was again blown away by their playing. These guys *are* better. 'Subdivisions', 'Marathon', 'Spirit of Radio' and some new material were played. Wait, what, new material?

Geddy told the audience they were going to play 'Presto' for the first time live. It was magical. I found a new favourite Rush song. Another was 'Working Them Angels'. As a US military veteran, I appreciated the picture in the video of two soldiers in the field with angel wings. 'Marathon' was yet another new favourite. Then they played *Moving Pictures* in its entirety. 'The Camera Eye' and 'Witch Hunt' made the biggest impression. After an encore of 'Working Man', it was over.

When Rush announced a second leg of the *Time Machine* tour, with a tour closer at the Gorge in George, Washington, I took my son and his best friend, driving two and half hours east. While we waited for the venue to open my son and his friend crashed out in the car and I walked towards the street. I noticed a red motorcycle followed by two others riding our direction. The red motorcycle turned and stopped in front of me, obviously a wrong turn, then turned around and continued toward the venue. I stopped in mid-step and said, 'That was Neil!' I floated back to the car, woke the two sleepy heads up and told them of my encounter.

SHORELINE AMPHITHEATRE

9 AUGUST 2010, SAN FRANCISCO, CALIFORNIA

I WAS THERE: ANDREW DONLEVY

Choosing my favourite Rush concert is akin to asking me to name my favourite child. A flood of memories from the over 200 Rush shows I have attended: from *Permanent Waves* to *R40*; from almost every city in the United States to Toronto and Brazil. Each show not just a reflection in time and growth but also emotion. The exact way music was meant to be.

Andrew Donlevy has seen over 200 Rush shows

I discovered 'the boys' at age 10 when my older brother's friend lent me *A Farewell to Kings* on 8-track. To this day, I know when each song would fade out when progressing to the next track. Almost every possible feeling and event in my life is associated with a lyric or instrumental. I literally and figuratively grew up with Rush. The only people who seem to understand this type of strong bond are other Rush fans.

I was there whenever there was a tour to be had, Usually three or four each tour. The Grateful Dead had the Deadhead. Me? I was a Rushian. Rush was and has always been there for me and my daughters, each of them having attended at least two shows with me.

Which brings me to the *Time Machine* tour: I was only two weeks separated when I saw them at the Shoreline Amphitheater outside San Francisco with my oldest daughter, the only show where I sat for most of it because of the release of the pure emotion, sobbing as I tried to separate memories of a 25-year relationship and marriage from every song; Dallas, where I attended with a long and dear friend who would later move to Seattle where we attended my first show on the *R40* tour; and then Phoenix, where I joined my best friend from high school, his wife, and my youngest daughter. Who knew that in a few short years my friend of 38 years and my daughter, at age 21, would be gone? Yes, Neil, Alex and Geddy were there for me like a friend, brother, psychologist and, at times, bartender.

I am in recovery from alcoholism. When I drank, each day would end with the opening lyric to 'Middletown Dreams' which talks about the office door closing early and the hidden bottle coming out. I became sober soon after *Clockwork Angels* was released and 'The Garden' became my life song, a perfect association to recovery, taking each moment one at a time and daily tending to life. I use this song as recovery poetry, instilling the belief that life throws curveballs so we must only worry about issues we have control over and weed out the rest.

Then there was The Professor, transcending my life from such Kiss songs as 'Love Gun' and 'Detroit Rock City' to 'Xanadu', 'Closer to the Heart' and even 'I Think I'm Going Bald'. I identified with Neil's tragedies, going through the most hostile of divorces in 2010 to the sudden death of my youngest daughter in 2017. Neil's books, especially *Ghost Rider*, taught me the serenity of road trips and getting out of my own head. Having enough material to listen and contemplate to last an entire week's drive without repeating. I had my best friends with me, even if only in song. I grew up and matured with each album and concert, as if they knew what I needed to hear at that period in my life. If not for Neil, I would never have discovered the writers that I did. Rush is not 'nerd rock'. Rather, it is 'intellectual rock', opening one's mind to so many things, allowing growth through a musical perspective.

Yes, Neil, Alex and Geddy were there for me. Rush is the soundtrack of my life. I cannot think of any other way I would want it. Nor can I think of how to repay such a debt of gratitude other than keeping their music in mind, heart and sound.

VERIZON WIRELESS AMPHITHEATER

22 AUGUST 2010, ST LOUIS, MISSOURI

I WAS THERE: BILL DROEGE

They opened for somebody at the Kiel Auditorium. I think it was Kiss. That's when I fell in love with them. They became my favourite band from that point on. My first Rush album was *A Farewell to Kings*. I got to see again in 2010. I was really blessed because I won the Rush tickets on a radio station. Their concert was just full of energy.

Nate's bass playing has been inspired by Geddy

NEW YORK STATE FAIR

2 SEPTEMBER 2010, SYRACUSE, NEW YORK

I WAS THERE: NATE KALNITZ

I was 10 years old. A few weeks before their Syracuse, New York show on the *Time Machine* tour, my Dad caught wind that some pit seats were available and insisted we went as it was only a couple of hours by car from our home in Buffalo. In the car he said it would be a once in a lifetime, life-changing experience. However, I don't think he knew just how literally that statement would come to fruition.

The first half of the show absolutely enamoured me. At the time I had just started taking bass lessons, and watching Geddy at work from about six or seven rows back was one of my earliest memories of being truly amazed by a master musician at work. I was ecstatic from the downbeat of the first song. The energy of this show was unlike anything I had ever been a part of before.

When the guys were about to play 'YYZ', a very friendly fan recognised me as one of the few young people at the show. He had a spot staked out right at the front of the stage and offered to my parents for him to take me up there with him. I stood right at the corner of stage left with the man, and as we assumed the position the guys went into 'YYZ'. When the bass/drum solo section of the song began, Geddy walked right up to the corner of the stage and started playing literally five feet away from my face. I was absolutely beaming. This was by far the coolest thing I had ever witnessed. Geddy must have noticed, because right before starting the third bass solo fill he looked me directly in the eyes, ripped the fill and gave me a hip little head shake before walking back towards Alex for the guitar solo.

I had just started taking bass lessons. I don't think any experience could've inspired me more at that point in time. I still get goosebumps because that was the exact moment I fell in love with the bass. Geddy Lee became my hero, my idol, my inspiration and I could feel my passion for this instrument ignited like a roaring flame, a passion that burns strong to this day!

QUICKEN LOANS ARENA

15 APRIL 2011, CLEVELAND, OHIO

I WAS THERE: CHRIS GRZYBOWSKI

I saw them many times, once on the *Time Machine* tour in Cleveland, Ohio, which show they recorded for the DVD. It was almost like a religious experience seeing those magical three on stage. As a fan it was great to see how tight they always were live. That's what attracted me to their music. Their musicianship is undeniable. Actually learning their songs on bass as a teenager in the early 80s made me a better player. Their music is never easy to play.

I WAS THERE: CHRIS LUNDQUIST

I played guitar in a band in high school around 1976 and one of the guys had *2112*. It blew me away. Then I got *All the World's a Stage* for Christmas and they were my favourite band from then on. *Hemispheres* is when I really fell in love with them. I heard it first at a pool party and couldn't get enough of it. I played it over and over, learning every song on guitar. I went to college at Washington State University in 1981. I passed by a guy in a dorm room air drumming to 'Xanadu' and I immediately said, 'You want to be in a band?' I was in a cover band for two years.

I saw the *Moving Pictures* tour in Spokane and drove 200 miles for *Roll the Bones* in Seattle. I watched them come off the bus into the arena at show time and yelled down to them from the second floor ramp. They ignored me!

The last time I saw them was when they recorded *Live in Cleveland* on the *Time Machine* tour. The hot air balloons were buzzing around the arena taking video. I was with my 22 year old son, his first time of seeing them. A girl got into a fight in front of us during 'The Camera Eye' and was dragged out, which was uncomfortable and distracting on one of my favourite songs. The *Time Machine* tour was brilliant, with the set list in reverse chronological order and the stage progressively simplified, ending with the stripped down stage and their first songs. It almost brought a tear to my eye.

BELL CENTRE

20 APRIL 2011, MONTREAL, CANADA

I WAS THERE: KAREN L PARKER

Karen Parker and her family got to see Rush

40 years ago when I met my husband, he came into my bedroom, saw my Bay City Rollers posters plastered all over my walls and ripped them all down. That was the end of that and the beginning of Rush. We lived in a small northern community 500 miles north of Winnipeg, so as a young kid there were many school dances dancing to 'In the Mood' (yes, Rush has dance songs). Later I had a young family with two kids. We couldn't afford to go to concerts but many albums were listened to.

When we could afford to travel the miles, we went to the *Snakes& Arrows* tour. We were in the nosebleed section but all the same we were there. In 2010 we got tickets to the *Time Machine* tour in Toronto. I was so excited to be going to their home city. Arriving at the airport to get the rental car we discovered we were victims of credit card fraud so it was a cab to the hotel. We were not letting anything ruin the fact that we were going to see Rush so walked to the venue from our hotel, met up with other fans doing the same and stopped at a beer vendor and hot dog vendor along the way to enjoy the parks and scenery.

We arrived at the concert venue and went to our seats, I had no idea we were second row centre. Needless to say that concert was amazing and I didn't want it to end. If you were not a fan before, you would be after seeing them live like that! They start off with South Park skits and some Monty Python-like humour. It was so entertaining.

I went to school to become a denturist so could now afford to travel and saw Rush another five times. We went to Montreal in April 2011. The Montreal Canadians had to postpone their play off games for Rush. Again, the concert was just incredible. They started off with 'The Spirit of Radio' and their comedy skits. After that concert we wanted to go again.

This time we took our three-year-old grandson. You're thinking 'who in their right mind would take a three-year-old to a concert?' but on the plane ride to Vancouver, out for dinner and at the concert he was a gem. And he was mesmerised by the amazing trio on stage. We were second row on Alex's side. Alex spotted my grandson in the audience and was making faces at him. A picture of my husband and grandson was posted on the Rush website for a while. After the concert a few fans shook my grandson's hand and praised him for being a good kid. They thought we'd be leaving with a crying baby in the middle of the show.

We got to meet Brad Maddox, Rush's sound man (my husband is a sound engineer) and got a picture of my grandson with Brad! So needless to say we now have a new generation of Rush fan in the family. We also went to the *Clockwork Angels* concert in Winnipeg in September 2012. They had violinists at this concert playing all the intricate violin parts. It's unusual for Rush to have an opening band, never mind a string ensemble to accompany them.

For the *R40* tour we went to Calgary. I really regretting we didn't go to the Toronto or Inglewood shows but just couldn't quite afford it at the time without going bankrupt. I was in denial that that was the last we would see of our immortal three. Leaving the venue I had such a feeling of disbelief that this was the end.

We went to Winnipeg to watch the theatre production of *Time Stand Still*. There wasn't a dry eye leaving the theatre that night and I cry as I think about it now. And we got to go see Geddy in Winnipeg for his *Big Beautiful Book of Bass* tour. Me, my husband and two grandkids stood in line for eight hours to be nearly first in line to get his autograph. Never did we think he had such a burden of a secret knowing the condition Neil was in. The day we received the devastating news of Neil will forever play on repeat in my memory.

MOTORPOINT ARENA

16 MAY 2011, SHEFFIELD, UK

I WAS THERE: ROBERT PARKINSON

I travel to this show in the company of two long-time fellow followers of the holy trio, Lynda and Martin. We arrive at the venue around 5pm, open the car doors to stretch our legs and hear the rumble of the heavy keyboard intro to 'Subdivisions' as the sound check is carried out. The song stops midway through but – hurrah! The omens are good.

The concert hall is about 9,000 capacity and set out virtually the same as the MEN in Manchester but on a smaller scale. My seat is in the nearest block to the stage on Alex's side, one row from the top of the block. I have an uninterrupted view of the stage. But the guy on my right is easily the size of a Zeppelin and crowding me to the extreme left of my seat. And the female half of the 60s-ish couple in front of me is so voluminously proportioned she spills backwards over the top of her chair. Moving my knees will disturb her semi-beehive hair-do. I make my way to the empty first row and am twice as close to the stage as my ticketed seat.

At 7.40pm the house lights go out and the three-year-plus wait for the return of Rush is over. The intro video is clever and witty, featuring genuinely comedic turns from Alex, Geddy and Neil appearing in *The Real History of Rash*. The video gives way to the true start of the gig as 'Spirit of Radio' starts a night of what becomes the tightest, most brilliantly delivered musical performance I have seen Rush give.

Songs like 'Spirit of Radio', 'Marathon', 'Leave That Thing Alone', 'Caravan', 'Working Them Angels', 'Presto', the whole of *Moving Pictures* and (most especially) 'Freewill' were absolutely nailed. The instrumental breaks in 'Freewill' and 'Marathon' are ridiculously hard to play and they really did hammer them perfectly. The show climaxes with the hardest-hitting rendition of 'Working Man' you're likely to see. It's a truly breath-taking aural and visual experience.

Neil's solo must get a special mention. How he constructs all that playing, remembers where to hit everything with both hands and feet in odd-time patterns, and then play it night after night is totally beyond me. The atmosphere was good, the band was in fine humour and it was a great performance but the crowd seemed reserved and static and not as into it as I thought they might be. Boring almost, and unusual for a Rush audience.

A few days later I was in Manchester with my friend Alan. When the chorus of 'Spirit of Radio' starts, it sounds like everybody is singing it. You can hear the crowd match the band's volume and the seated side blocks are on their feet much more than at Sheffield. And this is from the get-go, no messing about. There just seems to be more craziness. Manchester are really giving the band back everything that they are giving, and as a result the band play harder. This is now a very special night.

During the second set performance of the instrumental 'YYZ', the whole evening just goes nuclear. I've been to a lot of Manchester gigs and never seen insanity at any venue from an audience as was evinced during that second set. At the climax of the pre-encore song, 'Far Cry', Geddy proclaims we have been an 'awesome' audience, a far more enthusiastic proclamation than he gave at the close of the Sheffield show. When they return for an encore of 'La Villa Strangiato' and 'Working Man', the band repay our enthusiasm by going even more hammer-and-tongs at those songs. It was a fittingly high-octane performance end to a stellar evening's entertainment.

02 ARENA

25 MAY 2011, LONDON, UK

I WAS THERE: BRENDAN FRASER

I kind of got sick of waiting for Rush to tour Australia, which was never going to happen, so I flew from Melbourne to the UK for the *Time*

Photos - Brendan Fraser

Machine tour in 2011 and then again in 2013 for the *Clockwork Angels* tour, both at the 02 Arena. Quite an expensive exercise, but well worth the trips.

I WAS THERE: IAN NICHOLSON

I feel a bit of a fraud. I spent 30 years hating their music apart from the odd song such as 'Xanadu' and 'Closer to the Heart'. Back in the mid-70s, mates of mine were raving over Rush's first album but I hated it, thinking it a poor imitation of what my favourite band, Led Zeppelin, was doing.

Fast forward to 2008, when I started working from home. I'd have the DAB station Planet Rock on while I worked. My ears pricked up when I heard the song 'Time Stand Still' and I really liked it. Other Rush songs followed and I began my collection of Rush albums and DVDs until I had them all. At the time, I thought that I would never get a chance to see them live, but then the 2011 *Time Machine* tour was announced, and I got tickets for the O2 show. Wow, Rush were really great live! That tour included the whole of my favourite Rush album, *Moving Pictures*. Highlights were seeing 'The Camera Eye' performed live and Neil Peart's drum solo.

I got to see them again at the O2, on the 2013 *Clockwork Angels* tour. I loved the fact that the band not only showed their great musical prowess but also their great sense of humour, and the warmth between the three of them shone through. How refreshing to see musicians who truly cared about each other. I regret not seeing them in the early days, but at least I finally got to appreciate why Rush is such a loved band by its loyal legion of fans.

Alex in action at The Gorge in George, Washington – photos Melinda Myra

The *Clockwork Angels* tour consisted of 73 dates across North America and Europe, starting in September 2012 after a couple of warm up Scandinavian gigs in June 2012. It wrapped in Kansas City, Missouri in August 2013.

Skip Daly with Geddy's basses at Bristow

Skip Daly's backstage pass for the Bristow show

JIFFY LUBE LIVE

9 SEPTEMBER, 2012, BRISTOW, VIRGINIA

I WAS THERE: SKIP DALY

Eric Hansen and I were a couple years into our work on *Wandering the Face of the Earth*, the official Rush tour history. At this phase in the process, we were knee-deep in conducting interviews with crew members, both past and present. About a month prior to this concert, I had interviewed Tony Geranios (aka 'Jack Secret') and just three days earlier had interviewed monitor engineer Brent Carpenter. The crew had arrived in town the previous day, so we made arrangements to meet up for drinks at their hotel. I couldn't resist asking Brent and Tony if it would be possible to catch soundcheck the next day, a bucket list experience for me.

On the afternoon of the show, my friend Andy and I arrived at the venue. I called Tony, as had been arranged, and met him in the backstage area, where he gave us passes and we were able to stand off to the side and observe the load-in. When Brent arrived, we hung out at his sidestage position and he showed us the monitor console. The band's in-ear monitor battery packs rested there on a table, clearly labelled 'Geddy', 'Alex' and 'Neil'. It was fascinating to observe the professional crew, scampering around with single-minded purpose, like worker bees, putting up the show. The scale and magnitude of how much stuff had to not only go up, but also come down again – on a daily basis – really hit home.

Then the band started walking in. Geddy and Alex arrived on stage first, chatting with some of the crew. Andy and I just tried to blend into the background – it was clear that this was 'all business' and there was no way we were going to engage any of the band members with even a quick 'hi'. It was enough of an experience just to be a fly on the wall. A few minutes later, Andy tugs on my sleeve and whispers 'Neil'. I look over, and there's The Professor himself, Neil Peart, standing about six feet away, chatting with a friend - who I recognised to be none other than Richard Foster, author of *A Nice Morning Drive*. (Fans of 'Red Barchetta' will recognise the name.) I've never worked so hard to avoid eye contact, and we tried our best to be invisible.

Rush took the stage for soundcheck and, before I knew it, the introduction to 'Clockwork Angels' rumbled through the arena. You could feel the air moving, and it was an honest-to-god goosebumps moment as the band launched into the song, mere feet away. Soundcheck progressed with parts of various songs being performed before concluding with the opening number from the set list, 'Subdivisions'. I don't know that I've ever had a wider grin on my face. After the band departed the stage, we thanked Brent, said our farewell, and left the backstage area to head back out front.

The show itself was stellar – the first of four gigs that I would go on to attend on this tour. *Clockwork Angels* remains a masterpiece of an album, and I can't think of another band that ever put out a record that strong that late in their career. In retrospect, it was the perfect swan song, and that tour sits right up there with *Roll the Bones* and *Vapor Trails* as being my favourites of all the outings I was fortunate enough to experience.

SCOTTRADE CENTER

22 SEPTEMBER 2012, ST LOUIS, MISSOURI

I WAS THERE: JASON HARTSFIELD

I only saw Rush once, in St Louis on the *Clockwork Angels* tour. I had a third row seat and it was amazing!

I was 16 in the summer of 1991 and driving with my friend, Mike. We were drummers in our high school marching band. 'Tom Sawyer' came on the radio and Mike said, 'You have to listen to this.' I went out and bought the *Moving Pictures* cassette that day. It was then that I saw this band had a lot of albums. I listened to the world premiere of *Roll the Bones* on the radio and heard their voices for the first time. My parents wouldn't allow me to go to a concert where 'everyone would be smoking pot', so I missed that tour and Rush's last stop in Memphis. But my love for the band grew and grew.

I bought *Roll the Bones* as I was filling in the other holes in my Rush cassette collection. I tried to buy them in order. I drove a pickup and had the cassettes in an index on the floor between the seats. The van scene in the movie *Fanboys* - 'in my van it's all Rush, all the time' - is literally how it was in my truck. I continued to buy all the music I could find, and switched to buying CDs. *Counterparts* and *Test for Echo* were released and I added those to my collection, along with Neil Peart's first drum instructional video. I still have that VHS.

Once Rush began moving forward again after Neil's tragedies, I was either getting married, getting a divorce, getting married again, having a child, or getting divorced. I continued to buy all their music, but until the *Clockwork Angels* tour, I only knew my favourite band through their recordings. My second divorce was in 2012, and when Rush announced the *Clockwork Angels* tour, I told myself that I had just gone through the worst year of my life fighting for, and gaining custody of, my son, and I was going to do one thing for myself, and that was go see 'my' band.

I bought my VIP ticket. I only knew I was in the first 15 rows. I arrived at the venue very early. I heard the band soundchecking a few sections of songs through the closed arena doors. When the box office opened, I finally got my ticket and saw I was on the third row in the centre. When the doors opened, I made my way down near the stage. I had about an hour's wait until seeing the greatest band of all time perform. *Power Windows* is one of my favourite Rush albums and I loved the set list, which had several songs from that album. I will always cherish that one show with an excellent seat. Of course, I wasn't sat down. I was on my feet for the whole show.

I was at the Nashville stop on Geddy's book signing tour in 2019, along with the Q&A with Nick and Peter Collins. I can now say that I have fist-bumped Geddy Lee! And my autographed copy of the *Big Beautiful Book of Bass* will be a treasured possession, along with the signed Neil Peart *R30* picture that hangs above my mantle in my living room.

WELLS FARGO CENTER

12 OCTOBER 2012, PHILADELPHIA, PENNSYLVANIA

I WAS THERE: TROY PRETKO

Me and a buddy purchased nosebleed seats. We were sat high up listening to the opener of 'Subdivisions' when my buddy's friend texted him and said he just got his tickets upgraded to stage right seating. If we met him in the lobby he would swap out one of his tickets with ours to get us in. The next thing I know I am two to three rows away from Alex Lifeson, his Hughs and Kettner amplifiers glowing a lightning bolt electric colour, Neil's drums covered in a juxtaposition of gears meshed together in a mechanical array and Geddy's keyboard stand also vibrant with all kinds of metal gears and components. A backdrop of all kinds of videos and short films were being played between songs and from time to time Geddy and Alex would wander from side to side to the fans on either end of the stage. You could almost touch them.

PRUDENTIAL CENTER

21 OCTOBER 2012, NEWARK NEW JERSEY

I WAS THERE: ROMAN DOLINSKY

I had been bringing in my physical license plate off my truck into Rush concerts since 2007 when I was lucky

Roman Dolinsky with Rush's lighting director Howard Ungerleider

enough to get FLYBYNT in New Jersey. Alex and Geddy had both given me nods of approval throughout various shows. Unfortunately, Neil's toms were arranged such that he really could not make eye contact with me, even if he tried. As I was exiting the arena following the concert, I noticed Howard Ungerleider still behind the lighting board. I shook his hand, congratulated him on the brilliant colours he used and the various chase scenes and washes that he employed to create an amazing spectacle. At one point in our conversation, I commented, 'With the advances you made in lighting, and the incredible palette of textures, who is going to miss those green, boring lasers from 1984? Seriously, what lasers?' He grinned from ear to ear, tapped me on the shoulder and said, 'Thank you.'

TD GARDEN

24 OCTOBER 2012, BOSTON, MASSACHUSETTS

I WAS THERE: PHIL J DENONCOURT

They played a three hour set, the first half playing stuff from the new album and the second half their usual set list. In my early teens. I'd heard 'Tom Sawyer', 'Limelight' and all their big hits on the radio every now and then, but it wasn't until my friend let me borrow his copy of *2112* that I was hooked. I've listened to *A Farewell to Kings*, *2112*, *Fly by Night*, *Moving Pictures* and *Hemispheres* front to back more times than I can count.

KEY ARENA

13 NOVEMBER 2012, SEATTLE, WASHINGTON

I WAS THERE: JOHN RIVERA

My son, his best friend and I had good seats. I watched 'Far Cry' with its pyrotechnics from up close and it was awesome. The *Clockwork Angels* String Ensemble played the *Clockwork Angels* songs and several other Rush hits. It was a nice touch, and hearing 'YYZ' with strings was awesome. Is there really a bad Rush show?

I was outside my house with my youngest daughter on a rare sunny day in the Puget Sound area when the radio announced a second leg of the *Clockwork Angels* would stop in the Portland, Oregon area. I stammered, freaked out and flipped out while my youngest daughter laughed out loud at the way her dad was acting like a teenager over a rock band. I got tickets for me and my son. Of course, we had seen it before but it was just as entertaining. It was kind of cool knowing what songs were going to be performed and watching it all play out again.

ROCK 'N' ROLL HALL OF FAME INDUCTION

18 APRIL 2013, LOS ANGELES, CALIFORNIA

I WAS THERE: JOHN HILL

I travelled to LA for their induction into the Rock 'n' Roll Hall of Fame. I was a little disappointed the way they shut the fans out of it and they were very stand offish while in LA. I saw Geddy at the Four Seasons Hotel in Austin a few months after the induction and told him so. He said they didn't have much control over that.

The last photo I took with Geddy was in Austin on his book tour in 2019. I jokingly told him, 'I'm available to drum if Neil can't do it,' not knowing Neil was dying at the time. I feel awful now when I think of that. I was very surprised that Neil passed away like he did and so suddenly. I felt like a piece of me was gone also. It's hard to wrap my head around the fact that I will never see Rush again. A part of me will always be missing. They were not just a band, they were like a part of my family that I got to see every year. And then reality sets in. So long my childhood friends, and so long to my childhood.

BB&T CENTER

26 APRIL 2013, SUNRISE, FLORIDA

I WAS THERE: TONY FERRARI

I saw them in Florida in November 2012 and again in April 2013, two weeks before my birthday. I was able to get a Club Red Package which included VIP parking, unlimited food and drinks and very good seating. Since it was my 'birthday', one of the bar girls personally brought beers to me at my seat courtesy of my friend who also ended up paying for the tickets, refusing my money. Nicko McBrain from Iron Maiden was sitting a few seats away.

I regrettably never attended the farewell tour. I only missed that one and *R30,* which was because I'd had major back surgery three weeks before their Long Island show and my friends wouldn't let me go. Only missing two shows in 40 years? Not bad.

The day before Neil passed I was in my car and had noticed the license plate on the car in front of me. I live in Florida and the plate was from Quebec (Canada) and the numbers and letters were 998 NEP. Neil was from Canada and his initials were NEP for Neil Ellwood Peart. A sign? I was at home, the radio playing from another room, when Neil's passing was announced to the world. At first I thought I hadn't heard the DJ correctly. When I started getting calls, texts and Facebook messages from friends old and new asking me if I was OK, that was when it hit home.

Each and every one of the 50 shows I saw stand out, especially the very early ones. The band and the progressiveness of their songs and talents on their instruments were unrivalled and it was amazing to see, and be a part of, live at their concerts.

MANCHESTER ARENA

22 MAY 2013, MANCHESTER, UK

I WAS THERE: ROBERT PARKINSON

I was originally only going to Manchester but my dear friend Lynda had a Geddy-side fifth row Sheffield ticket so how could I refuse? In Manchester my eldest daughter Katie was along for her first Rush experience. The Arena was healthily populated but not sold out thanks to hard economic times plus the admittedly high ticket prices. But there were enough people to make a good racket and at lights out the noise swelled encouragingly. I was about two thirds of the way back in the arena, on Alex's side. The sound is really excellent for the first few songs but then Alex's guitar starts to periodically disappear from the mix. It's not for every song, but it is disappointing; thankfully during the second set this issue is rectified. The creeping despair comes when I notice that nobody in the blocks is standing. How can this be at a rock gig? Two years ago Manchester had an astonishing crowd which fairly blew the roof off. Why do they now think they're at a Beethoven recital?

I grit my teeth and content myself with 'chair-drumming', vigorous leg-work with furious finger-tapping on the thighs, and glory in the set list. It's hard for Rush to come up with unpredictable set lists but for this tour they have brought out some not-played-for-decades classics like 'Where's My Thing', 'The Pass', 'The Body Electric', 'The Analog Kid', 'Territories' and 'Bravado'. Throw in a healthy slab of *Clockwork Angels* material and it's a transcendent list. In Manchester they even played the one Rush song I would retain if someone held a gun to my head and made me burn my whole catalogue; 'Middletown Dreams'.

So, overall the evening is a success despite the pancake-flat audience. The string ensemble works really well in the second half with the *Clockwork Angels* songs. They even enhance stuff like 'YYZ'.

Skip six days forward to Sheffield's Motorpoint Arena. My seat is on the left aisle, immediately in front of Geddy. Bloody hell! Both Lynda and I confessed to being quite nervous prior to kick off. After all when - if ever - would we be this close to the masters again? The house lights dim, and then go out, and we're off! It's very evident even during the opening few songs that the feel of the gig is different. It's more up-and-at-it in the audience; there's a feeling of electricity that's not just feeding the band. That magic connection has been made between the audience and the stage.

We get a slightly different set list from Manchester and the excitement becomes palpable, aided by a much better, clearer sound. Things are getting volcanic even before half time. The conclusion of 'Far Cry' brings us some breathing space and a chance for a reflective chat about the first set. In honour of Alex's now-famous 'blah, blah, blah' acceptance speech at the Rock and Roll Hall of Fame ceremony, a slew of A4 sheets have been printed up with BLAH in large bold black font.

The second set is a continuation of the brilliance of the first. The band almost takes the arena down with an apocalyptic firework and flame conclusion to 'Carnies'; there's a grossly insane version of the maddest song on *Clockwork Angels*, 'Headlong Flight', before the classics keep on coming; 'Manhattan Project', 'Red Sector A' and what must be the song of the night, 'YYZ'. Its concert status rose to legendary levels when the Brazilian fans in Rio de Janeiro tried to 'sing' this instrumental in 2002. This started to be imitated by fans at all subsequent shows and we give it a go. Alex is so enamoured with our enthusiasm that he points to the crowd, looks at Geddy and mouths 'what the fuck?' and then proceeds to grin like the Cheshire cat. After 'Spirit of Radio', Neil fires t-shirts into the crowd with his pneumatic gun and Geddy and Alex throw stuff liberally among the audience. We are then treated to a blistering version of 'Tom Sawyer' followed by the evening's finale, '2112'.

Those A4 sheets with BLAH typed in bold black? I had been holding mine up periodically throughout the evening, joining in the spirit of spoofing Alex. During the 'Temples of Syrinx' section of '2112', Alex started to wander over to Geddy's side of the stage. The lighting was such that the crowd was well lit so, as Alex sauntered across, I shot the sign up and he looked straight at it, then looked directly at me and as he strummed a chord he mouthed 'blah' right at me. I started laughing and punching the air in delight whilst Alex nodded, smiled and continued playing. What a quality moment!

'2112' proves to be a suitably deafening and beautifully chaotic finale. Geddy proclaims most enthusiastically that we have been an awesome audience and the band departs the stage for the final time.

02 ARENA

24 MAY 2013, LONDON, UK

I WAS THERE: RUSSELL BUTCHER

A mate introduced me to them back in the 90s. My favourite ended up being *Test for Echo*. Their lyrics were complex and their music incredible considering there were only three of them! I only saw them live once, at Wembley Arena, and it was a fantastic concert. I was very saddened at Neil's passing. I read his book *Ghost Rider* and it's strange as I'm a biker and learned the drums some years ago. Neil was an incredible character. The guitar skills of Alex are phenomenal and I love watching Rush live on YouTube.

SHEFFIELD ARENA

28 MAY 2013, SHEFFIELD, UK

I WAS THERE: MARK WINTER

In 2004 came news of the *R30* world tour. I purchased tickets for me and my son Ivan at Birmingham NEC. It was worth the ticket fee just to witness the opening medley. Ivan was converted to the church of Rush and 'Subdivisions' is his particular favourite. We also saw them at Sheffield Arena on the *Snakes & Arrows* tour.

My final time was the *Clockwork Angels* tour. My wife Debra decided to tag along, although she does not get the Rush 'thing'. I will be honest and say this was not the most enjoyable Rush concert I have been to. Possibly it was the venue but it did not feel or sound right. Geddy's voice felt a bit strained at points. Or maybe it was just me. We changed seats and positions during the show to no avail. But you can't take away what great musicians they are.

I attended the *Cinema Strangiato* showing in Sheffield in 2019 and what a brilliant show that was. They did the right thing calling it a day when they did, and knowing the extent of Neil Peart's illness they were exactly right in their thinking. They always kept their integrity and moved in their own direction. To go on for that long and be that consistent gives them rock legends status. Their music will never die.

SECC

30 MAY 2013, GLASGOW, UK

I WAS THERE: RICHARD MILLER

The last time I saw them, on the last UK date of the *Clockwork Angels* tour, will always stick with me. I'd already seen them in Manchester and Sheffield but when my friend Martin offered to get us tickets for Glasgow as well I couldn't refuse! It was a three and a half hour drive we could have a road trip which involved listening to Rush the whole way there and back.

Richard Miller met Geddy on Geddy's book signing tour

I recall the usual buzz outside the arena before the show started, and Martin and I both commented on the vast array of Rush apparel being worn. I went to the merchandise stall and bought a grey tour t-shirt as well as black hoodie. We were a little late entering the arena, and there was an issue with staff not letting people get through to their seats as the show had already started. We started to get anxious and a little annoyed as the opening video was playing, thinking we were going to miss the start of the show that we'd paid good money for. Suddenly the opening keyboard riff to 'Subdivisions' started playing out, sending the crowd into raptures. We took our opportunity to storm the security line and charge towards our seats a few rows from the front on stage right.

The first half set list included a variety of songs primarily from the band's synth era, including 'The Big Money' and 'Territories'. After the interval the band returned to the stage supported by a string ensemble, and performed the *Clockwork Angels* album in full. The highlights for me were 'Clockwork Angels', complete with the crowd swaying and copying Geddy's actions for the chorus, 'The Wreckers' and 'The Garden', which felt particularly emotional. The set was rounded off with the classics – 'The Spirit of Radio', 'Tom Sawyer' and '2112'. All too soon it was over, and we left on a high wondering when the next tour would be. Little did we know at the time that this would be the last time we'd get to see the band live.

I've seen hundreds of live bands over the last 20 years, but very few come anywhere near the levels of Rush in terms of musicianship and stage show. Since the band's retirement in 2015, my interest hasn't wavered. I'm the proud owner of one of Alex's signature ES Les Paul guitars, and was lucky enough to meet Geddy at a book signing in Manchester in 2019. I was devastated by the death of Neil, and have to taken to reading his books and listening to Rush as a comfort. It is my strong hope that one day I may get to see Alex and Geddy perform again, but if not I'll just be thankful that I got to see them as much as I did.

SARATOGA PERFORMING ARTS CENTER

25 JUNE 2013, SARATOGA SPRINGS, NEW YORK

I WAS THERE: ED MOTTSEY

I've seen them many times, starting with the *Power Windows* tour. I've been a huge Rush fan since high school, and have so many good memories, including seeing them at Madison Square Garden on the *Hold Your Fire* tour, to seeing them at RPI Field House in Troy, New York, where it was open seating and we ran into the hall and up to stage right, right in front of Geddy Lee. I remember taking my toddler son Andrew to see them in Albany on the *Test for Echo* tour and, many years later, going to see them on the *Snakes & Arrows* tour with him as a grown up. And I remember my wife getting me tickets to my last show in Saratoga Springs. It was a wild ride. I miss them so much. No other band will ever take their place.

COPPS COLISEUM

6 JULY 2013, HAMILTON, CANADA

I WAS THERE: BRAD WINDECKER

I am a fan, if not an overly huge one, and respect their abilities to perform and connect with the fans. I only saw them once. I purchased my ticket on the day of the show and wound up in the lower bowl of Copps, two rows away from the stage, seeing Geddy, Neil and Alex up close. They played my favourite song, 'Subdivisions', right away and it was outstanding live. We'll never see them again, but I will have that memory to cherish.

HALIFAX METRO CENTRE

14 JULY 2013, HALIFAX, NOVA SCOTIA, CANADA

I WAS THERE: JEAN-LUC ROBERT AMIRAULT

I saw them with my dad and some of his friends at the Metro Centre. The show was over three hours long and Neil did two solos. They even had the Trailer Park Boys on stage while they were playing 'YYZ'! Sadly, they didn't do 'Closer to the Heart'. I would have loved to see them do that song.

The *R40 Live* tour was the final tour, commemorating the 40th anniversary of Neil joining the band in July 1974. The tour grossed over $37 million, with 442,337 tickets sold at 35 concerts.

BOK CENTER

8 MAY 2015, TULSA, OKLAHOMA

I WAS THERE: BOB KALKA

Believing the *R40* tour would be the last, I finally made plans to attend a Rush tour's opening night for the first time, in Tulsa, Oklahoma. I had a sales rep in Tulsa who'd been trying to get me to visit his clients in that area for years, and let's just say I became really interested that particular week! I started hanging out behind the BOK Center after work to see if I could meet the band during rehearsals leading up to opening night. During that time, I met some of the coolest Rush fans – now my friends – of my life.

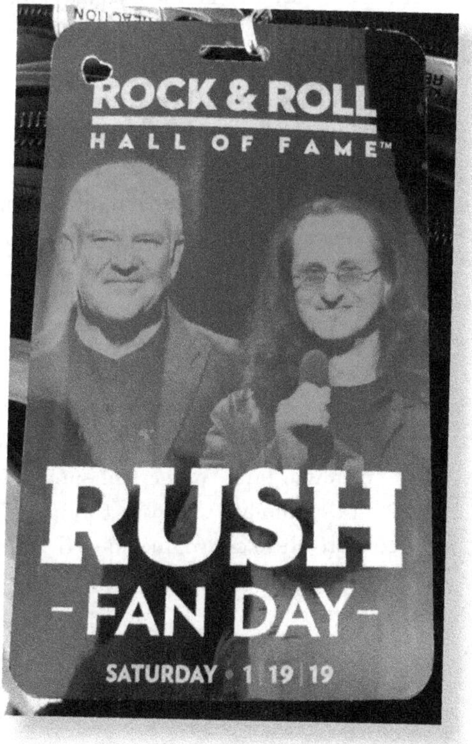

Bob Kalka with Howard Ungerleider (left) and Geddy's mom (below)

Being part of opening night, knowing this was probably the last one they'd ever have, was beyond belief. I had 13th row centre floor. Finally, after seeing the *R40* tour a few more times, it became clear that this was the end of the road for the guys. As a result, when Eddy Maxwell and the other amazing women who run RushCon later announced an event in Toronto for the world premiere of the tour DVD I was there. It was incredible and meeting Geddy's mom and lighting director Howard Ungerleider made the event timeless for me.

Yet, there was one more unfulfilled dream for me. After all these years, I finally had a chance to meet Alex and Geddy. When the Rock and Roll Hall of Fame announced the Rush fan day in January of 2019, to celebrate the release of *Geddy's Big Beautiful Book of Bass*, I was Cleveland bound. The RushCon ladies had arranged for a meet and greet with Alex, but as the 30 to 40 of us sat in the room waiting for him, we were crushed when they announced that he had gotten sick and wouldn't be able to meet with us. And then, equally worse, for the three to five seconds I stood in front of Geddy to get his book signed, I was more distracted trying to get someone to take a photo of us and really didn't have any exchange with him.

But all was made well. A few months later, the RushCon ladies sent us a personalised, hand signed photo of Geddy and Alex, and I was able to have a meaningful chat with Geddy at another book signing in my current hometown of Austin, Texas.

My connection to the band is beyond the deep identification of the experiences detailed in their iconic track 'Subdivisions.' They never let the trappings of the rock star life take over. They were premier musicians, each unique, each loyal to their bandmates and families and fans, and writing about things that matter, not the typical sex, drugs and rock and roll topics - 'A Passage to Bangkok' aside.

I think that vibe permeates across the world's collection of Rush fans, which is why myself and every fellow Rush fan I know still tears up every time we re-watch the moment that Jann Wenner announced at the 2013 Rock and Roll Hall of Fame Induction Ceremony, 'And from Toronto…', followed by a jet-engine roar from the decidedly pro-Rush crowd, including Tom Morello, Chad Smith, Dave Grohl, Taylor Hawkins and thousands of others. There will never be another band with the technical skill, consistency and creativity.

SMOOTHIE KING CENTER

22 MAY 2015, NEW ORLEANS, LOUISIANA

Alex in action - photo Austin Stockstill

I WAS THERE: AUSTIN STOCKSTILL, AGE 17

We bought tickets from a man standing away from law enforcement outside of the venue. Everything was very up to par for a Rush concert. I have been to many old and new shows and it was one of the best I've been to. Rush has some of the ballsiest fans. As soon as you walk in, the only thing you can smell is marijuana in a venue and city which prohibits exactly that. The fans were crazy and knew all the words, which I found astonishing due to the diction, lyrical structure and meaning behind all of Rush's songs. Alex came out with his alpine white Gibson EDS-1275 double-neck guitar and that moment seemed very surreal. Anyone that had a chance to see Rush live, but did not, missed out.

I WAS THERE: AMY DAVID VALENTINE

I was seeing Rush again in New Orleans, but at a different venue. This time many were sad and drinking and there was a collective feeling in the air of excitement at witnessing a rock concert yet a subdued energy as if many knew they were witnessing living legends for the last time. I had a feeling, especially after witnessing the breakdown of the sets and props as the years went backward in time, that this would be their final show.

One woman in the crowd was so drunk and unruly her husband had to remove her. She almost fell on us! And just before the show began my husband, who is not nearly as much of a fan as me, asked me for the ear plugs I usually bring with me to concerts. In my haste to leave the hotel room and get to the show I had forgotten them.

I can still remember Neil, head down, waving and bowing behind his kit. I stood up from my nosebleed balcony and clapped and yelled my heart out. This was right after the encore. For one brief nanosecond, it looked as if Geddy and Neil were looking up at the crowd up there with me. I had misting tears in my eyes. Now it is certain this is the last time I would see Neil on a stage. It was an amazing experience, but it definitely had an air of finality to it. The musicianship was stellar and perfect. Truly, I wish that I could live it all again.

VERIZON WIRELESS AMPHITHEATER

26 MAY 2015, ATLANTA, GEORGIA

I WAS THERE: KEVIN BATCHELDER

My dad planted the Rush seed in my brain at a young age. By the time I got to see my first show at The Omni in Atlanta, on the *Presto* tour, I was an angsty teenager, so I went with friends. I attended many shows after, from sneaking down to the lower levels of Madison Square Garden on the *Roll the Bones* tour trying to elude security, to convincing my friend his girlfriend didn't have to join us so we could afford better seats to the *Counterparts* tour at the Kickerbocker Arena in Albany, New York, to finally getting floor seats on the *Vapor Trails* tour. When I mentioned to my recently retired father that the *R40* tour was coming through Atlanta and having him remind me, 'I've always wanted to see them.'

It was a gloomy, rainy day in North Georgia but my dad drove down from Chattanooga to my house in Marietta, Georgia and we packed up a cooler and some chairs and headed for the Verizon Wireless Amphitheater. We waited patiently in a long line of cars for the parking lots to open, blasting a mix of Rush from every era. Once we reached the security guard allowing cars to enter, we asked if handicapped parking was

Kevin Batchelder took his dad Bob to the Rush R40 show because he 'always wanted to see them'

available. My dad had a failed ankle surgery years prior that left him walking with a cane. The guard gave us rough directions on where to go, which only led us to asking another security guard, and then another.... until we end up parking right next to the gate!

The rain was coming down pretty heavily at this point so we opened up the back of his van as a sort of umbrella, put our chairs underneath and cracked open a couple of beers just as the soundcheck started. I'd never been able to hear Rush do a soundcheck so I was pumped! I was explaining my excitement to my dad when they went into 'Losing It'. I gave my dad a hug and explained that they never played that song live, trying to impart what a big deal it was. Turns out they didn't play it during the show that night - so it was an even bigger deal!

Our seats were under the cover in the amphitheatre that night so we stayed mostly dry. My dad was blown away. We saw several of my friends that he knew. We especially rocked out to 'Jacob's Ladder', which was very appropriate given the weather, but my mind always goes back to sitting under cover in the parking lot, listening to the boys perform 'Losing It' with the man who had given me so much.

GREENSBORO COLISEUM

28 MAY 2015, GREENSBORO, NORTH CAROLINA

I WAS THERE: DEVIN BRENT HEDGE

Neil's book *Ghost Rider* was published at a time I was contemplating suicide from the loss of everything during the dot-com bubble burst. Neil's words of how he struggled with the loss of his child and wife, and his road to 'living' again, got me through the darkest days of my own life and kept me from doing the unthinkable. From those days onward, both as a drummer from my youth and a motorcycle rider, my deep emotional connection to Neil and his new family couldn't have been more profound. My daughter was born not long before his. My life's renewal started around the same time as his relationship with Carrie started. My life's twists and turns sometimes mirrored his through different stages of life, separated by more than a decade in age, and certainly by fame and fortune, watching his career continue to bloom even after such tragedy helped me fuel the drive for me to continue to grow my own career.

Like Neil's quiet and humble voice penning the lyrics to a song that would unleash a million memories, I now advise some of the world's top executives from the shadows, in shyness understanding how profoundly I'm touching the lives of hundreds of millions of people. All this, I owe to my wife, my children, my God, and Neil and the band called Rush.

I saw them live every two but two from 1984 until the last tour. I missed the *R30* and *Counterparts* tours. My first show was in Birmingham, Alabama on the *Grace Under Pressure* tour in the fall of 1984. I had been playing as a jazz, marching and concert drummer in secondary school for five years. Buddy Rich and John Bonham were my heroes but both were dead. The senior drummers in marching band, me being a freshman (ninth grade), were coping with a new band director who was young and vibrant and who was willing to let us innovate and compete against other bands and indoor drumlines. We picked 'Red Lenses' and arranged a drum cadence.

Every Friday night I got to watch as an entire stadium danced and frolicked to this rhythm Neil had created. So when the concert came around, I got tickets to see this new heir to the top drummer throne. Never had I experienced anything like it. Three men. Just three, with lights, lasers and music that resonated, and lyrics that I could connect with. And then came hearing 'Red Lenses' live. I was hooked, awestruck at the musicality, masters nearing the top of their craft. But they kept sharpening and evolving their craft, year over year, just amazing.

My last concert was the first concert for my eldest daughter, just a year older than Neil's. And the torch was passed from me to my 16 year old, the circle being completed and the next generation learning to understand how special this band was. And then, 'Suddenly you were gone from all the lives you left your mark upon.'

JIFFY LUBE LIVE

30 MAY 2015, BRISTOW, VIRGINIA

I WAS THERE: BRITTNEY BRINKLEY

My son was due in a few months so we wanted to see Rush before he arrived. We drove to Virginia and grabbed some food before the show. We headed to Jiffy Lube Live about an hour before the concert to make sure we had a good spot in line. The line was long, and for very good reason! We grabbed some merch before going in - cups, bracelets and a bandana.

I have listened to Rush my whole life. I remember jamming to 'Tom Sawyer' with my dad as a kid so this was very surreal for me, the idea that I was actually going to be singing the songs I knew so well. We chatted with some awesome folks in line about how excited we all were. When we finally got inside we got a nice spot to sit down.

The lights went dark and the crowd went crazy. As the lights flashed back on I could see Neil take his drum set and I got tears in my eyes. It was finally happening, I was seeing Rush! The show seemed to last forever yet not long enough at the

Brittney Brinkley saw the R40 tour in Virginia

same time. We sang as a crowd, we cried, laughed and shared a moment together that we will all remember. That was the final year that Neil was touring. It means so much to me to have these special memories. This band is a once in a lifetime band, and I feel truly honoured to be among the many to see them!

I WAS THERE: SKIP DALY

This was my second-to-last Rush show and man, was this tour ever bittersweet. I think most fans knew in our heart-of-hearts that it would be the final tour, though many of us clung to hopes of more studio releases, or possibly short live residencies somewhere.

I had long dreamed of bringing my kids to a Rush show, once they were old enough, so that they could experience 'Dad's favourite band', but the clock was now seriously ticking! My oldest child, my eleven-year old daughter, Ciara, was game - so off we went to run the typical gauntlet of traffic that came part-and-parcel with any concert at this questionably designed venue. (The venue itself is actually fine, but the six-mile, two-lane road that one must navigate to get in and out – along with 20,000 other people - definitely tries the patience).

The traffic issue was side-stepped by getting there early and setting up camp in the parking lot. Ciara and I met up with my old friends David Arnold and Andy Yarrish – I attended almost all of my 26 Rush concerts with some combination of these guys, so it was appropriate for us all to finish this journey out together. We were able to hear some of the soundcheck from the parking lot, including 'Losing It', which the band was polishing up for its soon-to-come live debut a couple weeks later.

Skip Daly with daughter Ciara at the 2015 Bristow show

The gates opened and we filed into the venue. I had gotten to know a couple of the crew guys in a casual way, and I'd been talking with Dave Burnette, Neil's bus driver, about saying 'hello' before the gig. I called him and he took Ciara and I on a brief backstage tour, showing us Neil's bus and bike. We chatted for a few minutes, thanked him, and then made our way to our excellent seats. It was fun to see Ciara's excitement over just how close we were sitting – six rows back, on Geddy's side.

My daughter was blown away by the lights, the lasers, and all of that wondrous sound coming off of the stage – not 30 feet away from us. As things progressed, the 'devolution' of the stage, and the set list's relentless march backwards in time, was quite moving. Unless you catch the opening night of a tour, in this day and age it's almost impossible not to be 'spoiled' prior to a show, so none of this shocked me… but I was surprised at how powerful it was to actually experience it.

The second set came and suddenly we were back in the 70s, with *Hemispheres* transitioning back into *A Farewell to Kings* ('Xanadu!') and beyond. It truly felt like a wrap-up. With the conclusion of the second set, I could tell that my 11 year old was crashing hard. She'd been a trooper and had enjoyed the show, but it was time to call it a night, so we headed out. I knew I would be seeing the band one final time in Philadelphia about three weeks later, so I'd still have a chance to see that encore.

As we were leaving the pavilion, I could hear the strains of 'Lakeside Park' ringing out, and the phrase that came to mind was perhaps the most appropriate summary of all: 'Though it's just a memory, some memories last forever….'

PALACE OF AUBURN HILLS

14 JUNE 2015, AUBURN HILLS, MICHIGAN

I WAS THERE: DEB HUSTON

I made a music video to 'Subdivisions' when I was in high school. But I was only a casual fan back in those days. It wasn't until much later in life that I got married to a huge Rush fan who introduced me to their earlier music and took me to a concert on the *Vapor Trails* tour, in Buffalo. I was very impressed with their musicianship. I grew up the daughter of a classical concert pianist so I was never allowed to listen to crap!

It was the combination of watching the documentary, *Beyond the Lighted Stage*, and playing the video game, *Rock Band*, that what pushed me right over the edge. And then I just dove right into reading all of Neil's books and joined Bubba's Bar and Grill forum and met all these people through the forum. I started a Facebook group through Bubba's Bar and Grill and we ended up meeting in different cities for the next couple of tours. U2 was one of my favourite bands and I never connected with the fan base for U2 in the same way. The Rush fan base are kind of the misfits, the kids who were overlooked and not really a part of the popular crowd. Being a part of something that not everybody else is into gives you that sense of 'yeah, we're in this together. We're going to be the uncool kids group.'

But people also bonded over the lyrics. You don't go to a Foo Fighters concert and bond with people over the lyrics. It's not the same as getting together with a group of people who are so emotionally connected to the lyrics for all the songs, for whatever reason. After watching the documentary, you'd say to other Rush fans, 'Can you believe that Geddy did this or Alex said that?' I just don't get that sense from any other band.

Female Rush fans just love the fact that these are genuinely good guys still married to the same women all this time. They're not sleaze bags, they're not all sex, drugs

and rock 'n' roll and I think that really speaks to women in a different way. You just don't find that in the rest of rock 'n' roll. There were definitely more female fans between *Vapor Trails* and *Time Machine*. But you could still walk right into the ladies rest room at
a Rush concert without a line, and walk by the line to the guys' rest room, wave and go 'woo-hoo!'

I took my son Alex to his first concert when he was 11. That was the *R40* tour at the Palace of Auburn Hills. It inspired him to pick up the guitar. He's become quite the enthusiastic musician in lots of different instruments. He was definitely inspired initially by Rush.

Neil's passing was a shock. We were all hoping that somehow, some way, they would come back together in some way, shape or form. None of us had met Neil, but we still felt so emotionally connected to the man because of his lyrics. Once we get through Covid, I think the audiences for tribute bands are going to multiply like crazy. People are going to be aching for that live Rush thrill that you just can't get listening to their music over headphones or in the car.

AIR CANADA CENTER

17 JUNE 2015, TORONTO, CANADA

I WAS THERE: MARC BROUGHTON

In the late 1980s, I saw a Rush tribute band called YYZ. The keyboard player was taking money on the door and we got chatting about our mutual love for Rush. Gary and I would become close friends. YYZ played at my wedding. The announcement of Rush's *R40* tour came with the rumour it would be their last. If there was one thing on my bucket list, it was to see Rush play live in their home town. Every tour I'd think 'this time I'll do it' but for various reasons I never did. There were two shows in Toronto on the tour itinerary. It was now or never!

I called Gary. He didn't hesitate - he was in! Tickets, flights and hotel were booked and the itinerary sorted. We decided to have commemorative t-shirts made, with a tour-type back print listing each of the shows we'd attended over the years – 'From BHX to YYZ' we called it. Gary said he'd still got the ticket from his first ever Rush show and suggested it would make a good print for the front of the shirt. That was when I discovered that his first show was the same Birmingham Odeon show I'd been at.

We'd got our plans for the day of the show. Firstly, a trip to the offices of SRO, Rush's management, where we were allowed to peruse the plethora of gold and platinum discs plastering the walls. After SRO there was a pilgrimage to Massey Hall, and to Victoria Park to visit the Ontario Legislature, the background for the cover of *Moving Pictures*. Every Rush fan who's ever visited Toronto must have had their picture taken in front of that building, as the security guard attested.

After a few afternoon 'refreshments', it was time for the show. Our hotel was a two-minute walk from the ACC so it was just a casual stroll to the gig. We were there an hour before show time, taking in the atmosphere and chatting to other Rush fans, who were amazed that we'd travelled from England for the show. But as we found out in the foyer, there were people from all over the world who'd travelled to be there, and plenty from the UK.

Finally, curtain up and the place was rocking. I was lost in the moment for the first half hour or so. This amazing band, this amazing venue, it seemed surreal. Then came the moment I almost lost it (no pun intended) emotionally. There had been chatter on the internet about Rush playing 'Losing It' during their sound checks, but they had never played it at a show. I saw Ben Mink's gear being moved onstage (though at that point I didn't know what it was) and then Geddy's announcement that they were about to play a song they'd 'never played live before'. I was transfixed, the first time this song was being played live, at my 'bucket list' show on what was likely to be their last tour. I admit I welled up, both happy and sad emotions battling for attention.

I composed myself for the second half of the show, letting it all sink in. I wanted to remember every second of this. There was the most amazing performance, both musically and visually, of 'Jacob's Ladder', a song I'd seen them play four or five times previously. Each time was great but this was another level and I still get goosebumps now when watching the *R40* DVD.

And then all too soon it was over: the roll back through history, from new to old; 40 plus ears of Rush songs, each and every one memorable in its own way and for different reasons. There were mixed emotions leaving the venue, sadness that this was, as it transpired, our last ever Rush show but happiness that we'd been there to see it. A dream fulfilled. As Gary said, 'The music will always be there, and we'll always have Toronto.'

I WAS THERE: RICHARD STAINFORTH

It was September 2004 when I saw Rush again. My wife Wendy was curious to see the band which I fussed over more than any other. Rush were back and here for the long term. I saw more than one show on each of the UK legs of the *Snakes & Arrows*, *Time Machine* and *Clockwork Angels* tours. Then word got out that they were going to do one more tour and then that would be it.

Years ago I'd been given a 1,000 piece jigsaw puzzle of Vancouver, Canada. When I was completing this puzzle I started thinking what a great place Vancouver would be to visit, better than the place I was in at the time. Then I thought, 'Wouldn't it be great to see my favourite band play

Richard Stainforth marked his 50th birthday by seeing Rush in Toronto, and got a tattoo to remember the occasion

in their home country?' Then that became 'wouldn't it be great to see Rush play in their home town of Toronto?' and that eventually became a bucket list item.

The *R40* tour was announced and I was debating whether I wait for them to release the UK dates or go to Canada. It took my wife Wendy to point out to me the two nights they were playing in Toronto in June included my birthday. It wasn't just any birthday, it was my 50th. It's as though Rush themselves grabbed me and were shaking me, telling me, 'For God's sake, you always wanted to see us in our home town. Now's your chance!'

I started looking up tickets on the internet and found a ticket in the VIP section in row 11 on Alex's side, just like the first time when I saw them from row 14 on Alex's side. So now I've got my ticket and I'm going to see Rush play in Toronto on my 50th birthday. But without Wendy, who could not get the time off. I was staying in the Fairmont Royal York Hotel because I wanted to stay as close to the Air Canada Center as possible. When I looked it up on the net I thought, 'Bloody hell, it's where the Queen stayed when visiting Canada.' My mates kept winding me up, saying 'You'll have go in by the service entrance.'

So I'm flying from Glasgow Airport, it's the 15th of June and I'm feeling very anxious as I'm going as far I've ever been in the world. There were a lot of other Rush fans too. I can remember acknowledging a guy with a Rush t-shirt. I would end up getting to know Jim Scott, who was with his son David. Our paths would cross again queuing to get in the CN Tower and we've since become good friends.

Settled in the hotel, my only thought is getting my ticket. I head down to the ACC and I'm put at ease when I have my ticket. I've had some good birthday presents - one of my best ones was getting a Chopper bike as a kid - but now I hold the best birthday present I've ever had and probably will ever have, thanks to my wife Wendy.

On 17th June 2015 I've got my cards up in the hotel. The day before I'd visited Niagara Falls, been to the CN Tower and visited Queen's Park, the scene of the front cover of *Moving Pictures*. I get something to eat and then meet up with Rush fans in Casey's Bar. Before the gig I'll have no more than three pints. I want a clear head, thinking this could be the last time I see Rush. Around half an hour before the start, into the arena I go to take up my seat. I just want to take everything in. I take out a Union Jack flag and the guy next to me sees it. He turns out to be from London.

The show gets started. During 'Headlong Flight', Geddy's bass packs up. It's the first show I see where something went wrong. That's if you don't include the delayed *Clockwork Angels* O2 show where a fox got into the venue!

Just like my first Rush concert I was taking everything in. In the second half it was fitting that 'Spirit of Radio' and 'Red Barchetta' were played, the first two songs that got me hooked from *Exit... Stage Left*. The second half rolled on and then the encore and this was the end for me of seeing Rush live.

I knew once I walked out of the arena that was it. In the back of my mind, I was thinking, 'No, they'll come to the UK or do the odd gig,' but we knew they weren't going to tour any more. Eventually, like most of the fans, I had to leave. I went to a bar, had a couple of birthday beers and rang Wendy. It was 5am at home and I knew she'd be up for work.

Looking back at the concert I got my flag on 'Distant Early Warning' and a close up on the footage from someone filming from the audience in the 'Spirit of Radio' crowd scene. The next day I was back on the plane home with some other Rush fans. *R40* gave me something I missed in the 80s and the *Hold Your Fire* tour. I got my dream with a few extras, being in the audience on the DVD.

I don't know why this band means so much more than any other band. Maybe I was just rocking too hard to Iron Maiden or Motörhead after being a punk rocker and Rush came along and said, 'You need to calm yourself, take a chill pill. There's plenty of time for rocking hard. Learn to appreciate the music again just like the *1812 Overture*.' Whatever the answer is, there's one thing you may be sure about and that is that I think Rush chose me rather me choosing them.

I WAS THERE: NICK BASILICO

Roll the Bones had just come out and I was working for a retail store called Athlete's World, not that far from where Geddy and Alex live. I was playing the *Roll the Bones* CD over the store's sound system just after we'd opened up that morning, right about 10am, when this guy walked in. I said to myself, 'Holy shit it's Alex Lifeson.' I said to him, 'Wait, I know you. Are you Alex?' He said, 'Yes I am. Be very quiet.' I said, 'Oh man, what are you doing here?' He said, 'I'm buying shoes for Geddy.' In concert, Geddy wears Converse All Stars and Alex was buying shoes for Geddy! I said, 'Why can't Geddy come and get them?' He didn't answer that. He signed his autograph for me. I lost it since, but it's the memories that count.

Nick Basilico's plectrum collection

I also 'met' Alex at Yorkdale. He was eating lunch with his wife and looked up and I just waved at him. He gave me a thumbs up. I knew who he was right away. But I wasn't going to go up to him – no selfies, no trouble, no this and that. I left him alone.

Vapor Trails was released the day after my mom passed away. Some of the songs on there bring back memories of good things.

Rush have been a part of my life since I first saw them on the *Hold Your Fire* tour. I didn't miss a tour after that. I saw them 13 times. But I knew *R40* was the end. Their very last concert in Toronto was the most special for me. I couldn't get a ticket because it was sold out but my buddy rang me up and said, 'I have a spare ticket – wanna come?' At the end of the show I couldn't believe it was all over.

It was all about 'YYZ' for Alison F

I WAS THERE: ALISON FARRINGTON

In 1981 I was 16, still at school and had met my first boyfriend. His older sister had been to see the *Moving Pictures* tour at Newcastle and talked of how brilliant they were. With my pocket money I bought the album from a record shop in Leeds. I was fascinated with the lyrics, guitar riffs and drum solos. I listened to that album over and over until I knew every word off by heart. It was a treasure I still have today.

For the *Signals* tour at Birmingham NEC in May 1983. We got tickets and travelled by coach. Donning my denim jacket and smelling of patchouli oil, I couldn't wait to see them and listen to my favourite song, 'YYZ'. The seats were centre floor about 20 rows back, the lights went out and they appeared. The euphoria and emotion was unbelievable. I felt nauseous and praying I wouldn't faint and miss it. Alex stood out with his guitar, in a white t-shirt with a red sun on it like a Japanese flag, Geddy doing his spectacular bass with his long hair and Neil – oh, Neil - his drumming was sublime. All my favourites were played, including 'Broon's Bane' leading into 'The Trees'. 'Please play 'YYZ',' I thought. They did, as the finale. I was so overwhelmed I nearly cried. I looked at my boyfriend and said, 'I shall them again on their home turf - it's my dream.'

The next time I saw Rush was at Sheffield Arena in 1992 on the *Roll the Bones* tour. Our tickets had us seated right of the stage on the tier section, so we had a brilliant view of Geddy. They had a blow up rabbit on stage to represent *Presto*. That was another fantastic concert.

I was turning 50 in 2015. Looking on the computer I saw news of the forthcoming *R40* tour, but not in England, just the States and Canada. I felt old now so they must be feeling it too. I wondered, 'Could it be their last?' I had to go. I asked my partner and my grown up kids to come with me but no one was willing to go just for three days. I couldn't afford to go for longer. I researched all the venues and then the set lists. I had to hear 'YYZ' live once last time.

Starting with the Tulsa show on May 8th, I looked at the set list and no 'YYZ'. In Lincoln on May 10th they changed the 12th song to 'The Camera Eye' and then in St Paul on May 12th – jackpot! I checked another six shows and could see a pattern emerging. The twelfth song at every third show was changed to 'YYZ'. I worked out that for the upcoming shows they'd play 'YYZ' in Toronto on June 19th. I'd never travelled abroad alone before but, armed with my credit card, I sorted flight and hotel details. I was just about to pay when my daughter appeared over my shoulder and said, 'Mum, you can't go to Canada alone.' Finally she agreed to come with me.

We flew into Pearson airport. That was exciting enough. All those times Rush have landed there. At that moment, 'YYZ' was ringing in my head. Toronto was beautiful and so was Niagara. We arrived on Thursday, Friday night was the concert and then we were going home Saturday. My daughter wouldn't go to the concert so I went alone. I didn't care. I was so excited. I felt I was the only English person in the crowd. They came on stage and I felt weak at the knees. What a concert. At half time it was 'No Country for Old Hens', and then my favourite. I cried. I cried at the end too. I didn't want it to be the last time but I felt it was somehow.

In 2019 Geddy had a book signing in Manchester for the *Big Book of Bass*. I got a ticket and was prepared to drive over to meet him. But I was ill and couldn't make it. I imagined out of all the people that attended there must have been one copy of his book on the table and Geddy beside it thinking, 'Oh, someone didn't show.' Yeah, it was me. I was devastated. It was my one and only chance to meet one of my childhood heroes.

Their music will never leave me. And as for Neil, it was utter shock to hear of his death. I cried along with thousand of others no doubt. For me he was the best drummer in the world and a beautiful, talented man. 'YYZ', over and out, Neil.

I WAS THERE: PETER DA COSTA

In the mid 70s we had a rock and roll TV show in Canada called *The NewMusic* and '2112' was the theme song. It was such a great tune. Sometime later I saw the video to '2112' and I was blown away. Soon after, A Farewell to Kings came out and that really

Geddy and Alex in action – phot Peter Da Costa

blew me away. I was just a kid thinking, 'How can three guys produce amazing music?' I saw them on the *R40 Live* tour in my - and their - hometown of Toronto. I saw both shows. For the Saturday show I was on the floor, fourth row.

Steve Potter and wife Emma saw the two Toronto shows on the R40 tour

I WAS THERE: STEVE POTTER

There were rumours it might be the last tour. A lot of British fans thought they'd play the UK. But I was just turning 50 and I'd always wanted to see them play their home town so we decided to go for it. We booked the holiday and managed to get tickets for both the Toronto shows and Montreal. There were a few little glitches on the first night in Toronto. It was a good show but Geddy broke a string on the bass at the start of 'Headlong Flight'. Everything fell into place on the Friday night. On the Friday they also played 'Losing It' for the first time ever, featuring Ben Mink on electric violin. There were rumours they'd been doing it in soundcheck and that it might happen. Every time I hear that song now it takes me straight back to that night.

Between the two Toronto shows, a guy had organised a get together at a bar called the Orbit Room which Alex Lifeson co-owned. We met up with a few people from the US, Canada and the UK. There was another get together on the anniversary of the Toronto shows the following year. We went over in 2018 to what is now called the Rush Family Reunion with the best part of 100 fans. It was three or four great days with like-minded Rush fans. We should have been over there in 2020 but COVID put paid to that.

I WAS THERE: PETER SHIPMAN

In the summer of 1977, I was 11. My older brother brought home a seven inch single and played it on our dad's record player. 'What on earth is that?' It was high-pitched vocals, a sublime intro and mesmerising lyrics. 'Closer to the Heart' was my first ever taste of Rush. I bought the *All the World's a Stage* trifold second hand off of my brother's friend (who was way too funk to appreciate it) as my first album, and started collecting from there. I was too young to go and see them, but my brother bunked off school in 1979 to go to Stafford's Bingley Hall and his friend came home with a drum stick. I was very jealous – git!

Peter Shipman was introduced to Rush by 'Closer to the Heart' – photo Richard Houghton

I went to see them as much as I could. Wembley Arena was my favourite venue and I could get there easily on the train if I left straight after school. The *Exit... Stage Left* and *Signals* tours were the first milestones in my live gig repertoire. I always tried for two or three nights whenever they came to Wembley, funds permitting. And every summer when they brought out a new album, I'd pre-order it from the local record shop, Slip-a-Disk.

I took time out to have a family. Live gigs became expensive and difficult and my fellow Rush-admiring friends had drifted away, until… *R30*. My daughter expressed a very slight interest in Rush and I bought tickets and off we went to the NEC in Birmingham in late 2004. I was blown away (again) and my erstwhile admiration came flooding back. 'La Villa', 'Xanadu' and 'Red Barchetta' all sounded as good as ever.

My daughter's interest came and went, but unbeknown to me my son had been listening to my digital collection of Rush whilst playing computer games on our PC. The first track that hooked him was 'Cinderella Man', from *A Farewell to Kings*, the very same album as 'Closer to the Heart' was taken from and hooked me all those years before. We went to the *Snakes & Arrows* tour several times in 2007 and have been to every tour since. The culmination was *R40*… in Toronto!

We always said we would see them in their natural environment one day. We spent a few days there and went to both gigs. I even made a pilgrimage to Massey Hall where 'my' first album was recorded. I wore my faded *R30* shirt to the *R40* gigs and I was in very good company. It seems to be a tradition to see who has the oldest tour shirt. I even saw a guy with very small Bingley Hall shirt from '79! Legend.

I feel extremely lucky to have had Rush in my life and even more so now my son is as fanatical about them. Rush is always on my playlist and always will be. RIP, and thank you, Neil Peart.

I WAS THERE: DAN SHIPMAN-TOON

I remember years back when digital music was just becoming a thing, back when you ripped CDs rather than downloading. I was browsing our home PC when I was 13 or 14 years old and found a music track called 'Rush – AFTK - Cinderella Man.mp3'. I remember playing it on the PC speakers and the feel of the music, how the song built and progressed just made me want to listen to more. It later transpired that *A Farewell to Kings* was the album that got my dad hooked years earlier.

Skip forward to 2007 and the *Snakes & Arrows* tour with my dad. I'll never forget when the intro to 'Limelight' played out, with that first chord left ringing. It's made my hair stand on end remembering that whilst writing this. The concert was unlike anything I'd ever seen before – a level of perfection and power that no other band that I've seen before or since has matched; add in to that they played for an insane three hour set with a killer drum solo and it's not hard to understand why, at the dinner table the night after, my dad booked tickets for the next UK gig in another day's time.

This sparked off a great 'father-son' activity of going to every tour since, and more than once. I remember when *R40* was announced saying to my dad, 'I'm going to buy tickets for Toronto, then we'll just have to find a way of getting there!' Easy to say, but once you've bought them, right…? I even asked my boss if I could have a short break at 10am to get the tickets when they were released. With the tickets bought for the Wednesday evening, I went back to work. Less than an hour later I'd bought two more tickets for the Friday.

June 2015 came along. We'd bought the cheapest flights to Toronto we could and were booked in

Dan and his father Peter made it to Toronto for the R40 Live tour

to a hotel not very far from Toronto Pearson International Airport (Y-Y-freaking-Z!). People on the flight were talking about Rush – this was the pilgrimage for us 'lonely travellers as grey traces of dawn tinge the eastern sky'. One of my fondest memories of the trip is sitting outside a bar just a stone's throw from the Air Canada Centre with a Molson lager in sheer awe of the number of Rush fans milling about. It was unreal, until we were inside the Air Canada Centre in Rush's home town, about to embark on the most amazing *Rush* retrospective imaginable.

The *R40* gigs were spectacular, although that seems an understatement. The fans were just phenomenal, the band magnificent and the atmosphere just so much more electric than ever before. The music seemed to have more meaning in Toronto, which makes literally no sense at all, but it genuinely did feel that way. We knew that the Toronto gigs were being recorded so in between the Wednesday and the Friday gigs we went hunting for a flag to wave. After a drive down to Niagara Falls, we managed to secure a small Canadian flag. We had to get spotted on that Blu-Ray, and we did!

As the Friday gig drew to a close it was bitter sweet. Obviously we'd heard the rumours that this would be their last tour, but as we left the Air Canada Center we both said to each other, I think that'll be the last time…' with a sad smile on our faces. But we thought, 'If you're going to go out, what a way to end it.'

And I truly can't explain how lucky I feel to have been there, for that final foray into Ayn Rand, the final bite of Honeydew and the final walk down the Garden Road with the greatest band around.

BELL CENTRE

21 JUNE 2015, MONTREAL, CANADA

I WAS THERE: BRIAN DICKINSON

My first tour was *Hemispheres* back in 78. I've seen every tour since, 23 shows in total. The last tour I saw was their final tour, *R40*. I always wanted to see them in Canada, so when I heard they were going to retire I knew I had to make it happen. I drove the six hours from Connecticut to Montreal by myself.

I WAS THERE: STEVE POTTER

Montreal was my last Rush show. We'd got gold tickets which meant we got early admission. Neil had a drum kit set up at all the Canadian *R40* shows that you could sit behind in return for a donation to charity. We saw the signs and scooted over there.

Steve Potter got his photograph taken behind Neil's kit

There were only about half a dozen people in front of us so I paid my $5 or $10 or whatever and got my photo taken sat behind this kit. I was lucky the queue was so short. It got so popular that one guy I talked to ended up missing the first half of a show because the drum kit queue was so huge.

If I could go back and see of those 25 shows again, it would be the first time I saw them in '81. I didn't know all the material really well. I probably only knew three or four of the eight studio albums they had out at that time. I'd love to experience New Bingley Hall all over again.

I'd just bought a Rush album and was about to play it when my wife saw the news about Neil on Facebook. She just said, 'Neil's dead.' There had been nothing in the news about him being ill. It was such a cruel blow for someone who had had so much tragedy in his life.

PRUDENTIAL CENTER

27 JUNE 2015, NEWARK, NEW JERSEY

I WAS THERE: ED TREMBICKI-GUY

It might have been *Roll the Bones* when I came back. I liked the song. I got the CD. My wife got tickets for the *R30* anniversary tour at the Garden State Arts Center in New Jersey. It was like rediscovering them all over again.

For the *R40* tour we left it to the wrong guy to get tickets. He forgot. Then it was all sold out and tickets were on the scalper sites for ridiculous amounts of money. But the

Ed Trembicki-Guy and wife Christine saw the R40 tour in New Jersey

local radio station was having a contest every morning in which you had to guess the song the female DJ was humming. One morning I managed to guess and they said, 'You've won a pair of tickets. We'll call you when the tickets come in.' I called my wife and said, 'I've won a pair of tickets.' She said, 'That's nice. Take one of your friends.' Once was enough for her.

Two days later the radio station called and said, 'The tickets are in. Come in and pick them up -' A slight pause. 'Oh, and by the way, yours are the pair we upgraded to front row.' I called my wife and she had a change of heart about going. In the run up to the show we went to dinner with friends. One of them offered to buy my wife's ticket. He got up to 600 dollars and she kept saying 'no'.

We were right there, not 20 feet from Geddy Lee. He used to wear a t-shirt that said 'Disco sucks'. That night I was wearing a t-shirt that said 'Disco still sucks' and a copy of Neil's Kufi cap with the symbols from *Snakes & Arrows* on it. When the lights were hitting the audience I caught Geddy doing a double take when he saw me.

Seeing Rush in New Jersey again after first seeing them at the Capitol Theatre in Passaic all those years ago meant it came full circle.

MADISON SQUARE GARDEN

29 JUNE 2015, NEW YORK, NEW YORK

I WAS THERE: PREM CHOPPALA

As a life-long, broken-hearted fan, I've seen Rush a number of times. I was lucky enough to catch their final tour, not knowing at the time that it was, in fact their final tour. I saw them then at Madison Square Garden in New York. I caught their *Clockwork Angels* tour in LA, their *Snakes & Arrows* tour in San Diego and a number of tours in the DC area. They are an amazing band. What I loved about their concerts is that they do their best to give the audience what they know (meaning, they don't change up their songs live, to the point of being almost a different song), and they give an amazing show - lights, effects, video and laser. And, of course, the complete sound. Their ability to play multiple instruments in a live setting gave them the opportunity to make their sound so familiar and so full and just amazing. Clearly, they enjoyed what they did, with whatever fun and goofiness they brought, but they also were consummate professionals and musicians, who knew their craft.

I love this band. And my heart broke twice, once when they announced the end and then when word got out at the passing Neil Peart. I hope to hear something from Geddy and Alex soon. Until then, I will have my memories of their shows deeply ingrained in my psyche.

PEPSI CENTER

11 JULY 2015, DENVER, COLORADO

I WAS THERE: TONY JACKSON

I worked as management at the Pepsi Center and got to see Rush perform there as well as see their music equipment up close back stage. I even saw the washing machines up close!

I WAS THERE: JON QUIST

I started listening to Rush in 1979. I was a freshman in high school and a friend had *2112*. I just loved hearing Geddy on his bass guitar and let's not forget Neil on drums. My first Rush concert wasn't until I was in the army, stationed at Fort Sill, Oklahoma. When *Signals* came out I saw Rush for the first time in Oklahoma City.

I saw their last concert in Denver, Colorado at the Pepsi Center. I have seen Rush a couple of different times at Red Rocks. There was a storm over Denver and as they started to play 'Spirit of Radio' you could see the lightning in the background over the city. The music and the lightning seemed to be in sync which made it even better and more exciting! When the stage

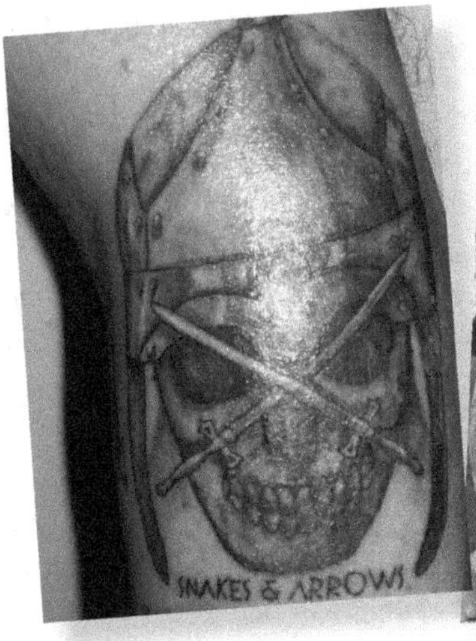

Jon Quist is a Rush fan and has the tattoos to prove it

hands started to take down the speakers after the show is when reality hit and I knew that would be the last time I ever see them in concert.

KEY ARENA

19 JULY 2015, SEATTLE, WASHINGTON

I WAS THERE: I WAS THERE: JOHN RIVERA

Rumour was that this was it for the boys and they were going all out. I got tickets on the floor for my son and myself. My anticipation was beyond words. The place was literally buzzing. The concert started with the customary video showing different cities and stopping at Seattle. The crowd went nuts. The boys started with their steam punk stage theme from the last two tours. But the roadies walked on stage and began to move stage props off to reveal a different stage. It dawned on me that they were playing songs from the most recent album and going chronologically backwards in their music archive. Only Rush could pull that off.

'How It Is', a favourite from *Vapor Trails* was played. They played 'Animate', 'Roll the Bones' and 'Jacob's Ladder'. Then excerpts from 'Cygnus X-1: Book I' and 'Book II'. I thought I was going to flip. Then I saw the double-necks come out and I about fainted: 'Xanadu', my favourite Rush tune which I haven't heard live since 1980.

They continued with four parts of '2112' and ended by repeating, 'Attention all planets of the solar federation. We have assumed control,' three times to complete the '2112' suite. We thought we were done, but no. The stage was stripped again to a high school gym so they could finish with songs from their first three albums.

Rush is the only band where the fans don't go to the bathroom during the drum solo. Anytime during the show, you would catch many fans air drumming to the music. I must be a fan because I found myself air drumming in front a bunch of people I didn't know and *I did not care*.

The post concert video played and it truly felt like goodbye. My favourite part of the video is when the boys try to enter the green room. The marionette from the cover of *A Farewell to Kings* opened the door and you see props from all the Rush album covers having a party. The marionette tells them they can't go inside and Alex says 'fuck you, puppet'. The last thing we see is the band walking off into a hallway muttering to each other, a goodbye of sorts.

I got the news about Neil on my phone while waiting for an appointment and thought it was of those internet jokes. I called the local rock station but the phone was busy. I tuned into the station and heard '2112' playing and knew it was true.

I am still in disbelief at the news. I joined two Rush Facebook fan sites and have found the same disbelief. But I have also found a family of sorts. They have been supportive in every aspect of the life one shares on the site. There are rock fans and then there are Rush fans. I have learned to really listen to the words I only heard when I was younger. I now have noticed how wise Neil really was when he penned his lyrics. I'm grateful to have seen Rush the times I did, and to have shared those five Rush experiences with my son, who is now a diehard fan.

SAP CENTER AT SAN JOSE

23 JULY 2015, SAN JOSE, CALIFORNIA

I WAS THERE: MATT MARIN

My last time seeing Rush was the last time 25,000 Northern California die-hard Rush fans saw the band as well, on *R40 Live*. Me and my best friend Si drove the four hours from the foothills of Northern California to San Jose. We enjoyed it and the excitement and adrenaline rocked us well into the first hour. As the band started the hypnotic 'Jacob's Ladder', the entire crowd hushed for the iconic part, and the lasers and smoke entranced the crowd. I looked over to Si. I noticed a tear was running down his face. I asked him what was up and he said, 'That's the last time we will see this... This is the last time.' My eyes filled with tears too. It was the end of something that meant everything to us as fans... their live performances.

FORUM

1 AUGUST 2015, LOS ANGELES, CALIFORNIA

I WAS THERE: DAN BELL

Dan Bell was at the final show

I had just finished my sophomore year of high school. I'd had my driver's license for about two months and was going to the Ingham County Fair in Lansing, Michigan. Several area high school youth groups were going to be there for a fun outing sponsored by Youth for Christ. My group consisted of a couple of my buddies and about three or four girls, a group date.

As we were roaming the fairgrounds we came across the local rock radio station, WILS, broadcasting from their little trailer. They were playing 'Dream On' by Aerosmith. It was something the girls liked. Then the DJ introduced a song by a new band out of Canada called Rush and put the needle down on 'In the Mood'. The guitar intro started, the cowbell came in keeping time and things took off from there. I stood listening intently to the song while the rest of my group were urging me to move along.

A couple of the girls started whining, asking how could I like this song and saying something to the effect of 'I can't stand his voice! It sounds terrible!' I just told them to be quiet. The song finished and we went about doing our thing for the remainder of the time we spent at the fairgrounds, but I couldn't get that song out of my mind. I intently listened to the radio for the next several days hoping to hear that song again. If I happened to be home and had the opportunity to phone in a request, that was the song I kept requesting. A couple of times I got lucky and they played it.

Later that summer, I stopped by a friend's house to hang out and he mentioned that he bought this new album by Rush and showed it to me. He put the needle down on the first song, 'Finding My Way'. When it came to 'In the Mood', I told my friend this was the song I'd heard at Ingham County Fair. When it came to the last song, 'Working Man', that was a whole other story at a whole new level. These guys were Led Zeppelin recreated - and it was only three of them!

2015. I took the red eye into LAX the night before the show at The Forum. I didn't get into my hotel until 3am. The next afternoon I met up with some new Facebook friends at a bar and grill half a mile from the venue and enjoyed a couple of beers with a great jalapeno burger. We made our way to the venue and I met a couple of friends from Australia.

As everyone made their way to their seats, you could sense the atmosphere was a little different from most other Rush shows. My feeling was that this was possibly the end. It had been 41 years. Both Neil and Alex had some health issues and Geddy's voice wasn't what it once was. Although he still sounded a thousand times better than anyone else that's out there today.

The show started as usual with 'The Anarchist'. As they got towards the end of the first set, Geddy introduced Jonathan Dinklage and they played what we all had hoped for, 'Losing It'. It was my first cry of the evening. The second set brought on a few more tears, first with 'The Spirit of Radio' and again with 'Closer to the Heart' and then at the end of the 'Grand Finale' of '2112'. I really lost it after their final encore, 'Working Man', when Neil came out front for probably the first and only time.

I had a few more cries that night. Talking to some people when we were all waiting for taxis, one thing led to another and all of us were wiping away a tear or two. When I got back to my hotel and saw the many posts about the show on Facebook, the tears started flowing once again, tears of joy at having been part of this great ride for all these years.

The next day, I made my way to Hollywood Boulevard to find their star on the Walk of Fame. It's kind of a frumpy area, but clean. It took me the longest time to find their star, but was able to locate it with the help of a couple of young chaps from the UK. A couple of nice young men from Arizona took my picture in front of it.

I got back to LAX quite early, so there was plenty of time to rest before my flight. And then it was delayed about two hours. As they called the initial boarding, who did I see out of the corner of my eye but none other than Jonathan Dinklage himself. I told him how much I enjoyed the concert and especially his performance. I was too awestruck to remember to get my picture taken with him.

I WAS THERE: STEPHEN SALAZAR

One of my cousins introduced me to their music when I was a preteen. I was fascinated by their album cover artwork; *Moving Pictures* says so many things by looking at it, and the music is as dark-sounding and heavy as the photos evoke. I was blown away by the rhythmic and melodic complexity of *Hemispheres*. It's hard to pick a favourite album or song, because each offers something different. *Moving Pictures* is a perfect album. 'The Garden', the final song on *Clockwork Angels'*, can move me to tears. These weren't the typical three minute songs I heard on radio stations. Rush's music is defined by substance.

When *Exit... Stage Left* aired on MTV I could not believe how three people could execute that kind of performance. The fact that Geddy Lee could sing and play bass with such authority, on top of playing keyboards and bass pedals, left a huge impression on me while Neil Peart's gigantic drum set and larger-than-life playing left me in a state of awe and wonder. Mesmerised by Alex Lifeson's guitar playing and stage presence, I was motivated to take up guitar playing and develop writing skills. He has remained my favourite guitarist, and they have remained my favourite band.

I saw them live for the first time on the *Grace Under Pressure* tour and was overwhelmed by what I witnessed. The performance, presentation and production kept me coming back for any tour I could get tickets to. On the *Counterparts* tour at Reunion Arena in Dallas, Texas, part of the PA system was down for almost half the night. That didn't stop Rush from giving a good performance, and that was one of the few times I got to hear sections of *Hemispheres* played live. I was fortunate enough to see their final show at The Forum. When Neil took that bow with his bandmates, I knew it was coming to an end. It will always serve as a cherished memory.

I have long respected Neil Peart as a lyricist, songwriter, author and person. His books will always hold a special place in my heart, giving a rare glance into the life of a very private man. Having dealt with loss in a very painful way, I can relate to how heavy his experience was as shared through *Ghost Rider*. I was shocked by the nature of his untimely and unexpected death. It's quite ironic that someone with such a gifted mind could pass away from brain cancer. I have lost one of my biggest heroes, but now that he is gone, I will celebrate the influence his work will have for future generations of musicians and listeners. I'll be a Rush fan forever.

I WAS THERE: VICTOR JOHNSON

I was 14 or 15 and hanging out in the garage at a friend's house. His brother had given him a copy of *A Farewell to Kings*. We put it on the turntable. I was entranced. I had no idea anyone could create music this phenomenal. I obtained my own copy, along with *Archives*, *2112*, *Hemispheres* and *Signals*. *Grace Under Pressure* was their most recent release. The more albums I bought, the more devoted I became.

Seeing them on their *Power Windows* warm up tour in Lakeland, Florida brought me back down to earth. I had viewed them as demigods. Seeing them on stage, they were apparently human just like me. But whatever disappointment I experienced was short-lived. I knew that Rush was my favourite band of all time.

Much of my high school years was spent in my room reading Tolkien and Del Rey fantasy books and listening to Rush and other bands. I loved *The Lord of the Rings*, so hearing 'Rivendell' and 'Xanadu' just endeared them to me even more. That such incredible music could be inspired by great literature made a huge impression.

Come 2015, I had moved to Oregon from Atlanta and, come hell or high water, I could not miss seeing Rush on their *R40* tour. Since that *Power Windows* warm up show, I had never missed a tour and sometimes saw them twice. But the closest *R40* show was going to be Portland, three hours away and on a weeknight. A friend in Idaho suggested a road trip to Seattle but I decided to fly to LA, stay with a friend, and see their final performance ever at the Forum.

By the time the end of July rolled around, I was ready. It was probably the most sublime, beautiful, and surreal concert I have ever been to. They began with a song from *Clockwork Angels* and worked their way backwards. 'Losing It' was one of the last songs in the first set. Seeing it performed live, with guest violinist Jonathan Dinklage, remains one of my favourite moments ever.

They closed the set with 'Subdivisions' and took a short intermission. They would come back and play 'Tom Sawyer' and the infrequently performed 'Jacob's Ladder'. 'Red Barchetta', 'Xanadu' and 'Closer to the Heart', during which people held up Starmen lit up with little lights, were played. It all seems like a blur now. They were progressively going back further and further, ending up with 'Working Man' and the 'Garden Road' outro. An evening that had been so surreal felt even more surreal when they finally arrived at the end of the show.

Neil came out from behind the drum riser and took a bow with Geddy and Alex, something he had never done. I felt immense gratitude and wonder to be there for that moment, as they thanked the fans for 40 great years. Then Geddy said, 'And I do hope we meet again sometime. Bye bye.'

Those words continued to reverberate in my head even as I made my way out of The Forum in a daze. I knew what had taken place, but I was still trying to wrap my mind around it. I was literally stunned, even though I had known this moment would come. I left the parking lot, got on the expressway and drove to downtown Topanga. I parked and wandered around, looking for some place to go, somewhere to process everything I had seen, heard and felt.

In an art gallery, there was a gathering of sorts, people talking and milling about. A couple of musicians with hand drums and a fiddle player or two were setting up and began to play some gypsy music. There was a table with food and a few craft brews. I took one and drank it slowly as I listened to the music and watched a few people dance to the rhythm.

I continued to feel very much in a daze. Although I was there in body, my mind seemed very far away. I finished the beer I was drinking and left to make that drive back up the mountain. Around and around the roads seemed to go, much like my mind. I fell asleep, lost in dreams of Rush.

I WAS THERE: RICK ZACCARO

For my 14th birthday I received a bass guitar. I played along with Led Zeppelin and Aerosmith records. One fateful day, while hanging out in my friend's room, an album in his collection immediately caught my eye. The spacey, science fiction-looking cover and title was intriguing. Rush *2112*. I asked my friend to put it on. I was blown away by the wall of sound coming out of the speakers. The musicianship, the songwriting, the vocals… all done by these three guys dressed in kimonos.

I immediately purchased the back catalogue, learned every bass note and followed the rest of their career as a dedicated and lifelong fan. To this day, Geddy Lee has been my biggest inspiration and has had the most influence over my bass playing. I was lucky enough to live through 16 new studio albums and experience 60 live shows. I was blessed to be able to share my love of Rush with my wife who went from sceptic to avid fan. We attended multiple shows together and had the good fortune to meet Geddy and Alex. We were also privileged to witness their final bow at the Los Angeles Forum.

To quote the lyrics to 'Headlong Flight', 'I wish that I could live it all again.'

Rick and his wife were at the final Rush show in LA

NEIL PEART DIES

7 JANUARY 2020, SANTA MONICA, CALIFORNIA

Neil Peart passed away after a three year battle with glioblastoma, an aggressive form of brain cancer. The statement from Geddy and Alex called Neil their 'friend, soul brother and bandmate over 45 years.'

I WAS THERE: SUSAN SISTARE

The morning after Neil died Susan Sistare's eyes were still puffy

I was tempted to start this story with the joke, 'You know you're a Rush fan if….' We can all come up with a few. Like, you know you're a Rush fan when you eat a piece of honeydew melon and you can't stop yourself from thinking that you're dining on it and drinking the milk of paradise. Corny, I know, but every true Rush fan can probably think of a few.

Here's a twist: You know you're a *female* Rush fan if.... But I won't make this story about being a Rush fanatic chick. Something else came to mind about Rush when beginning this story. I have never *not* known them.

Their first album was released the year I was born. My older brother Kevin came home one sunny day in the late 70s and played this weird music on his record player. The only music I'd really known up to that point was Kiss and Alvin and the Chipmunks, and I was immediately enthralled with the song about 'living on the Fish Islands'. I wanted to live there too!

All of my earliest memories are of being in my brother's room, begging him to let me hang out in there while he put *Moving Pictures* or *Permanent Waves* on the record player. My first sexual awareness was looking at the back cover of *2112* and seeing Alex wearing that tight, white robe, and thinking that that bulge down there was something I'd like to investigate further.

Their faces and voices are as familiar to me as my own family. I'm quite sure Geddy and Alex don't feel the same way about me because a) they have never met me; and b) Neil once wrote, 'I can't pretend a stranger is a long-awaited friend.' They may not regard me as family, but in a way, they are mine. I have never not known them.

If you saw the *R40* show, you know it was unlike any other. They began with their most recent music first and played songs in reverse chronological order, so that by the end, they were playing songs from their first album, the one released just after I was born. It was like listening to the soundtrack of my life, going back in time. With each song, a memory surfaced, and I am not ashamed to say that listening to certain songs during that show brought tears to my eyes. If it was released during a particularly tumultuous year of my life, it was most certainly their music that gave me solace. They may have been in their sixties, but they still rocked that auditorium as much as they did the first time I saw them on the *Hold Your Fire* tour in 1988, when I was finally old enough for my parents to let me go to a concert.

We all know where we were when we heard of Neil's passing. My husband, also a Rush fan (whose first words to me were 'nice shirt', owing to the *Roll the Bones* t-shirt I was wearing) came home early from work and told me. 'I didn't want you to be alone when you heard it,' he had said. That night, we cried together on the couch listening to our favourites. 'Losing It' was played more than once. Some are born to move the world and live their fantasies, and that's just what Neil did. They all have.

So eternal thanks to that holy triumvirate, those poets who taught me to ignore the critics, whose words, 'It's a far cry from the world we thought we'd inherit' got me through some seriously fucking dark times. This is for the guys whose music is the soundtrack of my entire life.

Thanks from all the chick fans. Our bras are off to you.

ENCORES

Some Rush memories are timeless.

I WASN'T THERE: DAVE KITCHING

One of my ex-wife's co-workers claimed she once convinced the members of Rush to come to her apartment to wish her husband well on his birthday. When he showed up who should be sitting on the couch but the members of Rush? I can't imagine a better birthday present.

I WAS THERE: ALICE CSUKA

They didn't follow the rules and didn't march in tune with those that attempted to and succeeded in ruining original rock ('Video Killed the Radio Star' was all too true). Their prose and poetry and mix of instruments told their own stories. I am one helluva lucky woman to have been born when I was.

I do not remember when it was the first time I heard Rush as back then they were basically blacklisted from radio. However, I was a very young kid when I became a mega fan. I was bought albums and then cassettes - ha ha! I even had the *Permanent Waves* bubble gum album cover and kept that for many years.

My friend Carol Beaudry and I had a wicked and thriving babysitting business. We went on a super long bus ride to as close to the Max Bell Arena as we could get and then walked forever to get to the grounds at the edge of the city. We snuck in the back by some roadie trucks and almost got to the main floor, but a security guard found these two giggling school girls hiding. We were so determined and cute as hell, and we talked our way into the general admission arena, made our way to the stage, rocked out and danced in a large crowd of boys. Out in the parking lot after the concert we were looking for other girls, saying, 'Where are the other chicks?'

I WAS THERE: DEREK DAVID Z

I saw them six times in total. My first show was in 1997 on the *Test for Echo* tour. I also saw them on the *Vapor Trails*, 30th anniversary, *Snakes & Arrows*, *Time Machine* and 40th anniversary tours. All great shows! The only tour I missed since 1997 was the *Clockwork Angels* tour. I wasn't able to get tickets that year.

I WAS THERE: WILLIAM SHEPLEY

I was 14 in 1985 and although rock music was all around me, nothing was sticking. That was also the end of the breakdancing era that infected my generation. High school started and I drifted more to the hippy crowd, which led to smoking, etc. One day I bought a $1 joint at school to smoke afterwards. I ended up at a friend's house and he put on MTV while we blazed up. I remember that A-ha video catching my attention and, as soon as it ended, they played the world premiere of 'Big Money'. It was like a big fish hook went right in my brain.

The Cinderella story verse is what stuck. My friend was like, 'You like this band?' I was like, 'Yeah.' He went in his older brother's room and got me a blank cassette. It just said 'Rush' on it. All I had was that chorus stuck in my head and a cassette of an album with no clue what it was. I was on a mission to find the Cinderella story album. I went to a local department store with my mom and the Rush section was a mile long. It was also in a locked case. No luck that day! I started mowing lawns and was making $22 a week. I'd get a ride to a local music trader store and there were all those Rush albums waiting at $5 a piece. I think my actual first album purchases were *Signals* and *Permanent Waves*. I got two albums every week. I was in heaven! But still no Cinderella song, other than 'Cinderella Man' on *A Farewell to Kings*, and I was disappointed to find out that wasn't the one I was chasing. Anyway lo and behold one day somehow I finally bought *Power Windows* on cassette and from that point on it hardly ever left my Walkman. That entire album was like magic to me. Life is most exciting when there's a chase involved, whether it's a car a woman or a song. It drove me.

I WAS THERE: ANNE HOOD

It was my first concert and it was the 70s, with lots of hippie children and long hair everywhere. There was lots of Tolkien and *Lord of the Rings* stuff. Geddy had really, really long hair. I hung out with an older crowd and I'll never forget what I was told by my friend Dana while we were waiting to get in, which was that this band was really unique. He said they pulled off great shows and music with just three people compared to the norm of four or five players. I was stoked. They definitely had a unique sound and Geddy's voice was unforgettable. The only thing I didn't like was the flash pots at the end of the show. We were in the crowd on the floor right up front. I had no idea they were going to do that, so it scared me and then it blinded me for a few seconds!

Anne Hood remembers the flash pots at the end of the show – photo Anne Hood

I WAS THERE: DENNIS RUGGS

I was stationed at RAF Mildenhall in Britain. TDY began in September. We were moved to Rhein Main air force base in Frankfurt where we saw a concert poster advertising Gentle Giant, the Mahavishnu Orchestra, Genesis and Rush in Stuttgart and Heidelberg Castle. We decided to go to

Heidelberg. It was an all-day show outdoors near the castle. I had a great time.

(Genesis played the Rhein-Neckar-Halle in Heildelberg on 4 July 1976. Gentle Giant played in Heidelberg on 5 October 1977. Rush played the Rhein-Neckar-Halle on 11 May 1983, with Nazareth in support. I have been unable to confirm that the three bands ever shared a bill).

I WAS THERE: DON GEE

I first heard Rush at about 2am on a college radio station in the summer of 1975. The DJ played 'Working Man' but I missed the name of the band and didn't really seek them out. Maybe a month later I tuned in and heard 'By-Tor and the Snow Dog', starting from the battle section, and I was blown away. I was about two years into playing guitar and the solo section really caught my attention. I knew it was the same band I'd heard before because of Geddy's voice but I remember thinking the drums sounded so much better than on 'Working Man'. The DJ then played 'Beneath, Between and Behind', which I thought was really complex sounding because there were these lush chords I'd never really heard before. Then the DJ took a break for some station ID and local commercials without saying the name of the band again so I was calling the station to ask who it was when the DJ came back on air and said, 'Here's another number from Rush' and played 'Anthem'. That song hit me hard. At last I knew who it was.

I went to the local record stores to find their albums (I had no idea how many they had out at the time) but none of them carried Rush. I think I ended up buying *Physical Graffiti* instead. I continued to hear songs on the college station but never heard them played on the commercial stations. The only song from *Caress of Steel* I heard was 'Bastille Day'. Record stores still didn't have Rush albums and I stopped searching. In late '76 my buddy Pat and I ditched school and ended up at a record store. I picked up a copy of UFO's *Lights Out*. Pat walked over with *2112*. We went to his house and threw on *2112* and - it was magical. A utopian society in the future that banned guitars? What a crazy concept! We listened to the entire album four times. *Lights Out* remained in the shrink wrap.

I WAS THERE: GARY ROCK

I didn't pick up on them until their second or third album, which made me want to go back to their first album with John Rutsey. I really started to like them after *2112*. I got through three copies of that album. In my opinion they're one of the best two or three bands in the world.

We did a couple of tech rehearsals for them in upstate New York. One was for *Moving Pictures*, and they were there for a whole week. They were having problems with the video screen. The video crew was having a hard time getting everything to sync and to work out. I bumped into Geddy Lee and he wasn't the amiable guy that everybody thinks he is. I remember him saying to one of the guys in the video crew, 'I'll be back tomorrow at 8am. I want this thing cleared up, or you guys and your stuff can be on the truck headed back to Toronto.' It was really interesting how Geddy was willing to take on the whole business thing.

There was a baby there and I remember Neil Peart coming down off his kit and doing all kinds of things for this baby. As a drummer you hardly ever saw him smile. I thought the way he interacted with that baby was incredibly interesting.

I'm a guitar player. Alex's guitar tech Jimmy Johnson was in the guitar pit. I walked in and looked at all the stuff and Jimmy actually let me take Alex's guitar out the stand and hold it and play it a little bit. That blew my mind. I said, 'I don't want to get you fired for this shit.' It was just so cool. But I don't have one because it weighed a ton!

I WAS THERE: JULIAN BERTSCH

I am a Rush fan and have been since the release of *2112* on April Fool's Day, 1976. I was a mere 13 years old at the time. I've seen them seven times. As a musician, I truly believe that the music of the *Three Stooges* was my inspiration to teach myself how to play the piano. I always wanted to learn a Rush song. Neil had an amazing blog covering his quirky travels as he motorcycled from gig to gig whilst on tour. The way it reads lets you into the mind of a legendary lyricist and gives an insight into the band's lyrical brain.

I lived in Toronto for a couple of years for school before moving to Florida in '83. As I was a sound tech during those days, living in Florida, I managed to use my pull to get an All Access Pass to one of their shows at the Orlando Arena. I was able to say a quick star-struck hello to Geddy but unfortunately that's about as far as the conversation went. I did, however, manage to sit on my own in an empty arena – empty apart from the techs and staff - and witness both visually and through amazing sound a one hour remix of 'Spirit of Radio' during their sound check. This was a very magical moment in my life as a Rush fan. If only we would have had portable recording abilities back then. I was so enthralled by it all I had to call my brother from a pay phone in the corridor so he could listen in too.

I WAS THERE: MARC BARDINI

I saw them at Madison Square Garden or it could have been in Connecticut. But I remember my first time. I was simply overwhelmed. I remember anticipating the next tour or album, going back to their first one and to *A Farewell to Kings*. They were way ahead of their time.

I WAS THERE: RICK WEEKS

I was working as a bartender in Colorado Springs, Colorado at a bar called Kelker Junction and another bar called Superstar Night Club when Rush was just starting out as a club band. I used to bring them their bottle of Jack Daniels back stage and whatever else they wanted. I also rounded up all the best looking girls to take back stage. They were good times.

I WAS THERE: ROB BLACKMORE

I got my first drum set at age 15 in 1977. My first Rush album was *2112*.Peart became a god to me, but his style was 'inapplicable' for lack of a better word when I got in the business because no one was doing stuff that called for Peart's fills and what not.

But what I did borrow was the way he phrased every fill. Most drummers were just jamming, kinda like the 15 minute Allman brothers stuff, and throwing in as many Peart fills as they could muster. I figured out early on that there's only one Neil Peart and I had to be a team player for what a particular groove a song called for, not be a 'dig me' show off. Peart convinced me of phrasing where I did the same licks in the same spot every gig. I saw Rush twice in concert, once in 1978 and then in 1979, when I had fourth fucking row seats and they opened up with '2112'! I purposely didn't get high or drink so I could absorb and comprehend the whole orgasmic experience. All other concerts were just a big party.

I WAS THERE: TOM DUSELL

I saw them at the Laylor Convention Center in Reno, Nevada between 1974 and 1977. UFO opened, Judas Priest was next and then Rush headlined.

(I was unable to substantiate this concert from my research. They played the Centennial Coliseum in Reno on 11 November 1978. Pat Travers Bnad supported).

I WAS THERE: TOMAS PADRON

They were supported by Uriah Heep. It was a great concert in 1982 at the now extinct Market Square Arena in Indianapolis, Indiana. Actually, it was the first concert I went to in the USA while I was an English student from Venezuela.

(Other records suggest that April Wine (5 January) or UFO (30 November) supported Rush on the only two occasions they played the Market Square Arena, both in 1978).

I WAS THERE: SHANE THACKERAY

I took my little brother to a Concert in Lowell, Massachusetts in 1976. It was Uriah Heep, Foghat and Rush. The boys wore their Japanese attire on stage. They blew the other bands away for stage presence and sound. It was an incredible light show also. The last song was 'Working Man' and it rocked the house down.

(There is no record of a Rush show in Lowell, Massachusetts).

I WAS THERE: STEVEN VICKERY

It was at Dane County Veterans Memorial Coliseum in November 1975. They were third on the bill behind Kansas and Aerosmith. Of course we had never heard of them. They came out cold and played the *2112* album starting with side one. They were pretty good but the sound was not. At the mixing board they were still making adjustments. As they got further into their set they got tighter. And then - '2112'! It was awesome! I had never heard anything like it. From the power intro to the part where he finds the guitar and then the priests of Syrinx, it was like a rock science fiction novel. (I have to admit that at the time I was reading the chronicles of *Gor* by John Norman).

And then the finale: power, power, power. And the end. 'We have assumed control.'

Echo, echo, echo. It was awesome! Of course after that the crowd went wild and called for an encore but it didn't happen because they were third on the bill. There wasn't much time to digest the show, because next up was Kansas. Their show was super freaking awesome. Again, the crowd called for encore but alas they only gave one.

And then the headliners came out. Aerosmith were on the *Toys in the Attic* tour. They played great and they were who most came to see. Steven Tyler strutted and Joe Perry jammed but at the end of the night they were in third place.

The next day I bought the *2112* album. Many years later I heard that Steven Tyler was so mad that the other two bands stole the show that he had Rush kicked off the tour immediately, and Kansas was let go soon thereafter. Kansas was headlining within weeks of the show. And Rush headlining within a year. My friends and I went out and bought all of the Rush albums prior to *2112* and we're happy that we did.

(Other sources suggest Ted Nugent was on the bill and not Kansas. This date may not be correct).

I WAS THERE: TONY PETTIJOHN

I'm in Price, Utah in about late '81. I'm in eighth grade. Kiss was my first concert, then Boston. I was into Van Halen, April Wine, Black Sabbath, and Ozzy and Randy. Walking home from the local strip mall, I kicked a cassette that was lying on the ground. The cover had a naked guy on a brain. I thought, 'WTF?' I took this cassette home and – mind blown! What is this? That voice! Those drums? Guitar from heaven! The next day I went to the same strip mall record store and bought *Caress of Steel* and then *Exit... Stage Left* and… holy shit!

At high school I caught the *Grace under Pressure* and *Power Windows* tours in Salt Lake City. I had kids after that and had less time to give to the endless hours you needed to devote to Rush. I got Roll the Bones and Counterparts later, which I loved, but I do not know it inside and out like *2112*, where I know every note. I have an iPod full of Rush. I have been listening this year more than for a long time. RIP Neil.

I WAS THERE: WILLIAM BOBBITT

It was in Denver. I was in the USAF serving in Cheyenne, Wyoming. We drove down for the show. What I clearly remember thinking was how on earth could three men could make such beautiful and clever music?

I WAS THERE: EDDIE GRESELY

Neil is pretty much responsible for my being a singer. While it's very common for Neil to be a huge influence on a drummer, when I found out that he was the lyricist, I decided to take on that task in the band I was in at the time. I had a three piece band in high school with a truly remarkable guitar player and bass player. But we had no singer. I decided to take on lyrics just like my hero, Neil. Somewhere along the line, we began recording the songs we wrote instrumentally. I decided that, since I had written the lyrics, I would record how the lyrics would go in the song. I decided to overdub my lyrical ideas with the music so that a singer would know what to do when we found one. Well, the more I did this, the better I got at singing. It wasn't long before I was a full on singer and started studying singing at the performing arts school I was going to. I have been a lead singer, voice teacher and lyricist to this day.

I WAS THERE: RAYMOND OULLETTE

I love that they had the funds to live like kings and remained Canadian, never giving up their citizenship. I've been a Rush fan since 1976 and the age of 16. My best memory of private school is first hearing *2112* in a high school dorm room and thinking it was Mahogany Rush!

I WAS THERE: TODD GARBARINI

My memories of Rush begin in May of 1981 when I was in the sixth grade at my town's local middle school. I saw several students walking through the hallways wearing the *Moving Pictures* tour shirt. I envisioned Rush to be some type of heavy metal band, purveyors of hard-driving loud music. I was heavily into Billy Joel's music at the time. In December 1982, now in eighth grade, several fellow students who were in a band came into school wearing the *Signals* tour shirt, jeans and sneakers. Rush had just played at Madison Square Garden in New York. Something about the image of the dalmatian sniffing a fire hydrant affected me in a way that no other image did before or since. It filled me with a curiosity, and it made me wonder what the music sounded like.

Todd Garbarini says that every new Rush album punctuated a new time in his life

I collected my allowance and bought *Signals* on cassette. It was the first time that I ventured out on my own like that, a motif enunciated in the lyrics of 'The Analog Kid'. There were no photos or lyrics to accompany the cassette, and I had no idea who comprised the band, but the sound coming from my single-speaker cassette player was unlike anything I ever heard. A trip to another record store soon afterwards led me to purchase *Moving Pictures*, and I originally thought there were two drummers in the band. It sounded like five or six people playing. I was hooked.

Rush has written, recorded and released 167 songs and with the exception of the 'Didacts and Narpets' section of *The Fountain of Lamneth* (the drumming is amazing, but the lyrics are ridiculous), I love everything they've released to varying degrees. I haven't been the same since. Every new album punctuated a new time in my life.

I WAS THERE: KEITH KAUFMAN

I remember being 9 years old and sitting on a bench getting ready for a baseball game. I was listening to 'Tom Sawyer' and thinking, 'Fuck baseball'.

I WAS THERE: PATRICK WOODS

One afternoon, during the fall of 1993, my musical life would be altered forever when a friend of mine let me borrow a certain album. It was Rush's *Moving Pictures.* I had seen their album covers in stores and heir guitar tabs in music shops. I knew enough to be aware that they were a famous band, but I had never heard their music, which added to the mystery. I also knew that the band consisted of only three guys, but beyond that I was absolutely in the dark. On first listen, I thought 'Tom Sawyer' was a pretty good rock song and I found Geddy's voice unique.

But it was 'Red Barchetta' that totally blew me away. The visual imagery was intoxicating, like I was actually sitting behind the wheel, accelerating at top speed. To this day, the song can still fire on all those emotional burners while driving that imaginary car with the adrenaline, the freedom and the rebellion. From then on, my journey with Rush would intertwine with my everyday life, and serve not only as an escape but an inspiration to build my own musical path.

I became an obsessed fan - a certified Rush geek. With the vast, overwhelming volume of endless bands that have dominated the 21st century via the internet, finding a 'favourite' is becoming next to impossible. But if someone held a gun to my head, I wouldn't have to think twice about saying that my number one choice is still Rush. I loved the fact that they hailed from Toronto, instead of New York or LA, like so many other acts. When I was still in my teens our family took a vacation to Toronto, and as you might imagine - it was constantly interrupted with Rush fanboy quirks at every turn. I was ecstatic the whole trip, begging my parents (or driving them nuts) to take me to Queen's Park to get my picture taken where the *Moving Pictures* album cover had been shot in '81. I also tried looking up Lee, Lifeson, and Peart in the Toronto phone book, not that I was going to call them. Of course I had no idea at the time that Alex's last name wasn't really Lifeson and Geddy's last name wasn't really Lee.

The brilliance of Rush is that each member is a band within a band; an individual force to be reckoned with. All three have a sound and style, that makes the picture complete. You couldn't randomly pick just anyone to play in Rush. They are a unit that developed a sound like no other band, and have a unique chemistry.

Alex Lifeson made playing simple suspended chords into an art form, building tension and sheer beauty. He often sounded like more than one guitar player. And then there are his searing solos, which can melting your face off in songs like 'La Villa Strangiato', or simply let one note echo for miles into the cosmos.

Neil Peart is the Einstein of rock drumming, influencing more drummers in a single generation than most guitarists - and also acted as the bands wordsmith, penning some of the most thoughtful and poetic lyrics, ever put to paper.

To top it all off, there is Geddy Lee's voice, and stage presence - one of the most iconic voices in rock. In addition to his stratospheric singing, he is also balancing playing bass, keyboards, and choreography, leaping around stage whenever he finds an instrumental break.

If ever a band should win a Grammy just for building their audience from endless touring, then Rush is a prime example on how it's done. Even if you can't stand their music, the one thing the harsh critic cannot accuse Rush of is laziness.

Rush earned the right to do whatever they pleased, and steadily evolved with each album. Some albums are stronger than others, but every release that they have ever put out is different from the one before it. And in my humble estimation, that goes for every song as well. No two songs in the Rush catalogue sound the same. I can't recall any moment where I was completely let down as a fan, or remember a time when I listened to a Rush album and went, 'What were they thinking?'

The guys in Rush were all-around down to earth human beings. The band was never known for any type of drama, controversy or exhibiting the negative behaviours that have taken so many other bands down. They were like a silent beacon of reason in the midst of so much chaos that surrounds the rock universe.

There was no infighting, alcoholism, drug abuse or custody battles. Their lack of egoism is simply unparalleled. How did they do it? They laughed a lot. Just watch the video on YouTube of the three of them having dinner at a hunting lodge. It basically sums up the essence of the band. Serious musicians but goofy men who love a good laugh. That's why they remained friends. It doesn't get any better than that.

There will be Rush fans a hundred years from now, discovering the band's live concert footage or reading about their history. They will always have the listeners, but I'm proud to say that I was lucky enough to have been in one of those audiences during my lifetime.

I WAS THERE: MARCO DIGIOSIA, AGE 13

It was spring 1978 and it was my first concert. For a year or so I'd get together with friends in Ross O'Neil's basement and listen to the first Rush album over and over. I remember my friend Barry saying that they were going to the concert and did I want to go with them? A year or so before, my parents had said no to me going to see Kiss so I didn't have much hope. But I asked, and then pleaded, until they said yes. The excitement building up to the day was magical because it was my first concert and I was scared. The crowds at the Metro Centre in Halifax were overwhelming. We pushed our way through the doors and found our seats which were side on to the stage but far enough forward that we could see the stage well. I was just excited to be in the same building with Rush, who had become my idols.

The concert started and they came out in robes, a very mystical look and feel. Their first song was '2112' and they were casting video on a massive screen depicting the flight through space. The ambience was amazing and the sound incredible and of course Neil Peart and his drums, chimes and bells were beating through my soul.

As we were sitting there listening, the guy next to me tapped me on the arm and offered me some pot. I looked at my friends and they nodded so I took my first drag of a joint, started coughing and the guy laughed at me. He said, 'Have another and pass it along to your friends.' I didn't know what to expect but I can say it was magical. It actually put me at ease and I wasn't nervous, which I was for most of my childhood. I don't even remember leaving, and nothing else has ever come close to matching that experience. Years later, I saw the Clockwork Angels tour and was expecting the same feeling as my first Rush experience, but I didn't know the new songs which left me a bit disappointed. For 40 plus years that concert has been cemented in my mind and heart as a beacon.

I WAS THERE: GARY STEWARD, AGE 16

Having been introduced to Rush at secondary school in Southampton, and going round to mates' houses to listen to Hemispheres, 2112 and the like, we wanted to see them live. Southampton Gaumont was the 'go to' theatre in the south of England at that time. Chris (Clubber) Carrett and I walked down to the Gaumont on the first date of the UK leg of the Permanent Waves tour and it was a belter; a three hour set and all of 2112 and Hemispheres, plus old material and the new Permanent Waves, the Professor's legendary drum solo and the encore, 'La Villa Strangiato'. Afterwards we went to the stage door and after a time were greeted by Neil, who duly signed our programmes, with the long hair and that moustache. But where were Geddy and Alex? We guessed they might be staying at the local Polygon Hotel, so legged it round there just in time to see Geddy and Alex emerge from a car at the front. We were the only ones there and, engaging in a short conversation and obtaining autographs, they asked us if we wanted to come in and have a beer. Being 16 and it being late, we declined. 40 years on, we both now think that was the biggest mistake and wish we could turn the clock back. We have grown up with Rush. RIP Neil.

I WAS THERE: ALEX LIFESON

'It wasn't until a year (after the final show) that I started to feel better about it all. I realised we'd gone out on a high note… I remember looking around the whole arena and trying to take it all in. The lighting. The crowd. The people around me. It was very emotional for us.'

ACKNOWLEDGEMENTS

In compiling this book I've really come to understand the sense of community that exists in the wider Rush family and it's been a real pleasure talking to and hearing from fans, so I'd like to say a big thank you to everyone I reached out to, or who reached out to me, whether or not they provided me with a story for the book. Many people were generous with their time and their memories and I had more offers of stories and photographs than I could possibly have included. Maybe in Book 2….

In identifying the venues for shows, I have largely followed the naming convention adopted by Rush.com. *Rush – Wandering The Face of the Earth*, by Skip Daly and Eric Hansen, was a useful reference both for dates and support acts. I also referenced www.cygnus-x1.net for information and various Facebook groups too numerous to list here.

I'd like to thank in particular: James Gibbon, for permission to quote from his blog jamesgibbon.com/35-years-ago-tonight/; David Egan; Abdul Wahid Khan, for introducing me to Rush; Stan Nelson; Neil Cossar and Liz Sanchez at This Day in Music Books; Gary Bishop for his design wizardry; Bill Houghton, who heard me playing *Moving Pictures* while I was working on the book and said, 'Is that Rush?' Good parenting on my part, or just a really smart lad? Who knows….; Sidney Sullivan Houghton for dragging me away from the keyboard; and Kate Sullivan, for her continual good patience, culinary skills, love and support.

ABOUT THE AUTHOR

Richard Houghton lives in Manchester, England with his girlfriend Kate and pomapoo Sid. He is the editor/compiler of *The Day I Was There* series, published by This Day In Music Books. Titles so far include Led Zeppelin, Jimi Hendrix, Pink Floyd, Black Sabbath, Bruce Springsteen, The Beatles and Rush. Future titles include Cream, Thin Lizzy, Neil Young and Queen.

Did you see Rush live? Send your classic gig memory (of Rush, or any other band) to iwasatthatgig@gmail.com.

CPSIA information can be obtained
at www.ICGtesting.com
Printed in the USA
LVHW081611201120
672263LV00001B/1

9 781916 258204